Education for Peace Curriculum Manual

A Conceptual and Practical Guide

H.B. Dᴀɴᴇsʜ
Sᴀʀᴀ Cʟᴀʀᴋᴇ-Hᴀʙɪʙɪ

International Education for Peace Institute
Vancouver, Canada

Education for Peace Integrative Curriculum Series: Volume 1
Education for Peace Curriculum Manual

ISBN 978-0-9782845-1-0
Copyright 2007 International Education for Peace Institute

Printed simultaneously in the United States and the United Kingdom.

H.B. Danesh, *Series Editor;* Christine Zerbinis, *Copy Editor;* Amelia Epp, *Cover Designer;* Arman Danesh, *Graphic Designer and Typesetter;* Sara Clarke-Habibi, *Production Manager.*

Previously published in Bosnian, Croatian, and Serbian translations
Copyright 2006 International Education for Peace Institute

Cover art copyright 2005 *Skeena River* by Edward Epp

All Web links in this book are correct as of the publication date but may have since become inactive or otherwise modified.

Also available as an e-book through the International Education for Peace Institute website and online booksellers.

Available from:
EFP Press
International Education for Peace Institute (Canada)
101-1001 West Broadway, Suite 900
Vancouver, B.C., V6H 4E4 Canada
Phone: 604-733-9242
Website: www.efpinternational.org
Email: info@efpinternational.org

Library of Congress Cataloguing-in-Publication Data

Danesh, Hossain B., 1938–
    Education for Peace Curriculum Manual / H.B. Danesh and Sara Clarke-Habibi
        p. cm.
    Includes bibliographical references.
    ISBN-978-0-9782845-1-0

Contents

Acknowledgements v

Introduction vii

Unit 1: The Concept of Unity 1

Unit 2: The Concept of Worldview 29

Unit 3: The Concept of Human Nature 61

Unit 4: The Nature and Dynamics of Violence 89

Unit 5: The Developmental Model of Civilization 119

Unit 6: Humanity's Transition to a Civilization of Peace 155

Unit 7: Power, Authority, and Leadership for Peace....193

Unit 8: Conflict-Free Conflict Resolution 231

Unit 9: Creating a Culture of Healing 275

Unit 10: Educational Methodology Guide 301

Bibliography 379

About the Authors 385

About the Contributors 386

Acknowledgements

This book is based on seven years of research and lessons learned from the implementation of the Education for Peace (EFP) Program in 100 schools in Bosnia and Herzegovina. The manual integrates concepts, principles, and methodologies of the multivolume *Education for Peace Integrative Curriculum* Series. Publication of the book in English, its translation into the three major Bosnia and Herzegovina languages, and its multimedia online version were all made possible by a four-year grant to the International Education for Peace Institute from the Swiss Development and Cooperation Agency (SDC). For their generous support we are most thankful.

The authors wish also to gratefully acknowledge the contributions of: Dr. Roshan Danesh, co-author of the CFCR conceptual framework and training materials; the original EFP Pilot Project Team, who planted the seed of Education for Peace in Bosnia-Herzegovina; Naghmeh Sobhani, Nermana Sukalić, Arijana Balić, Dina Afkhampour, Sanna Heikkinen, Alma Alma Sabanović-Alikadić and the other EFP-Balkans staff, whose personal dedication and sacrifice have caused that seed to blossom; John and Barbara Rager, who provided valuable pedagogical direction to the EFP Program; Dr. Elaine McCreary and Dr. Ruth Yates, who carefully reviewed earlier drafts of these materials; Stacey Makortoff, who provided elementary school activity samples; Christine Zerbinis, who edited the final copy; the many readers, family members, and friends who encouraged and helped fine-tune this publication.

INTRODUCTION

The *Education for Peace Curriculum Manual* is Volume One of the *Education for Peace Integrative Curriculum Series* produced by the International Education for Peace Institute. This unique model of peace education is based on the view that peace represents an inherent longing and capacity within all human beings and that it is humanity's foremost need and ultimate destiny to achieve peace in all dimensions of life: intrapersonal, interpersonal, intergroup, international, and global. Within the framework of Education for Peace, every student is trained to use his or her capacities to actively contribute to the creation of peace, justice, and prosperity for all humanity.

Rather than studying peace as a separate subject, the Education for Peace (EFP) Curriculum proposes that peace should constitute the very framework within which *all* subjects of primary and secondary education are studied. Peace results from wholesome application of a "peace-based worldview" to all aspects of life: survival and security, identity formation, establishing relationships, learning processes, professional pursuits, society-building, and leadership and governance.

The principles of a peace-based worldview include:

- Recognition that humanity is one;
- Recognition that the oneness of humanity is expressed in diversity;
- Recognition that the fundamental challenge before humanity is to maintain its oneness while celebrating and fostering its diversity; and
- Recognition that this task cannot be accomplished through violence, but rather through open, creative, peaceful, just, and unifying decision-making and problem-solving practices.

At the core of the EFP implementation process is the integration of these principles of peace into the daily lessons and experiences of every subject and every classroom. The universal character of these principles of peace makes them relevant to every aspect of human learning and activity. In each subject area it is possible to (1) discern truths about the characteristics and prerequisites of peace, and (2) apply the perspective of a peace-oriented worldview to the direction, development, and application of that field of knowledge.

The Education for Peace Curriculum Manual, co-authored by H.B. Danesh and Sara Clarke-Habibi, is composed of 10 units, each focusing on a conceptual theme related to the foundations of a culture of peace. Each unit provides, in a concise and accessible manner, conceptual materials, methodological guides, sample lesson-plans and activities for teachers and students to engage in the exploration of Education for Peace in creative and meaningful ways. The conceptual framework of the EFP Program is based on research findings and practical insights learned in the course of seven years (2000–2007) of implementing the EFP Program in 112 public primary and secondary schools in post-war Bosnia and Herzegovina (BiH), as well as input provided by an international group of educators who reviewed the curriculum and offered valuable recommendations. A 10-unit multimedia e-Learning program, entitled "EFP-WORLD" has also been produced as a companion to the EFP Curriculum Manual and is available through the International Education for Peace Institute.

Recognizing that each classroom and community has unique characteristics, we invite the educators using this manual to experiment with the materials presented here and to find creative and original ways of integrating them into the discourse of your respective classrooms and wider school communities. We wish you success in your efforts to do so, and invite you to share with us your experiences, questions and feedback along the way.

H.B. Danesh
Sara Clarke-Habibi
June 2007

Unit 1

THE CONCEPT OF UNITY

This unit introduces three "Laws of Life": Unity, Growth, and Creativity, which are evident in all life processes. These Laws of Life apply universally to all living entities—from plants, to animals, to human beings. These laws operate in organic life processes, as well as in social systems. When we are aware of these laws, life processes can be helped to flourish. When we ignore them, the forces that hold life together break down, causing illness, decay, and ultimately destruction.

Context

The aim of this unit is to provide an opportunity for participants to think critically about the concepts of unity, growth, and creativity and to discover how these concepts relate to their lives.

Unity is the foundation upon which all life processes depend and on which the fundamental concepts of Education for Peace are built. Unity is the process of diverse entities coming together through the forces of cohesion and love. Unity always connotes diversity. An understanding and appreciation of how unity in the context of diversity is intrinsic to life on earth are critical to creating a culture of peace. It can be argued that the absence or breakdown of unity is the most significant factor at the centre of many problems facing the world today. If the absence of unity is the cause of problems, the recognition and cultivation of unity forms the basis for any effective and lasting solutions.

Learning Process

In this unit, participants should be assisted to:

1. Describe, through biological, ecological, and social examples, how the condition of unity is a prerequisite for all healthy life processes and is inseparable from the condition of diversity;
2. Compare and contrast historical events to demonstrate how the concept of unity has been used and misused by societies;
3. Reflect on the condition of unity in themselves, their social relationships, and their environment;
4. Demonstrate their ability to use a unity-based perspective to diagnose the root causes found in conflict scenarios and to brainstorm creative strategies for their resolution.

Points for Understanding

Teachers can guide their students to understand and remember these main points:

- Unity is the key prerequisite for life, growth, and creativity;
- Unity is not the same concept as uniformity, but rather unity exists only in conditions of diversity;
- Unity is present wherever healthy life processes can be observed, be they physical, psychological, social, or spiritual;
- Underlying all conflict, dissension, illness, and lack of progress is the absence of unity;
- Growth—whether physical, mental, emotional, ethical, or spiritual—is a necessary indicator of life and vitality; where growth is observed, life exists. Where no growth takes place—or where decline or decay is observed—life is in danger or has already ceased to exist;
- Growth is necessary for health, maturation, progress, and peace;
- The natural and necessary outcome of growth is creativity—the creation of something new that fosters life processes further. Conversely, that which is destructive, is not creative;
- The prerequisite for both growth and creativity is unity in the context of diversity.

Key Vocabulary

Consciousness: the unique and distinguishing human faculty that encompasses not only rational thought but also emotional and spiritual awareness; the foundation of all human development, activity, and civilization.

Creativity: the process of conceiving of, expressing, or bringing forth something new that is unique and fosters the continuation and enhancement of life processes.

Development: refers to positive, qualitative, and/or quantitative change.

Diversity: different, distinctive, or unique qualities or elements; richness, variety.

Growth: a process of increase or expansion, usually associated with positive change that is quantitative ("He grew in height") or qualitative ("She grew to be more insightful and sensitive").

Law: a statement that describes regular or patterned relationships among observable phenomena;[1] a general rule that states what always happens when the same conditions exist;[2] a binding principle of conduct or enforced by a controlling authority.[3]

Life: a force or condition resulting from the unity of matter and consciousness, and characterized by processes of growth, development, and creativity.

Love: a dynamic force of attraction that draws and binds together two or more elements in a condition of unity, bringing life to the collective whole.

Maturation: simple, biological reference to the life cycle ("maturing to the stage of reproductive readiness"), but also used to refer to psychological or character development, and in some cases to cultural development of a society.

Principle: a standard one adheres to, generally associated with the notion of "right" or "good"; a comprehensive and fundamental law, doctrine, or assumption; a rule or code of conduct; a value that guides one's actions.

Spirituality: a conscious, dynamic, progressive, and integrative process in which human individuals and/or societies achieve their fullest potential in a condition of unity. This developmental process produces ever higher levels of consciousness and understanding, and results from influences that have their roots in both science and religion.

Transcendence: the quality or state of going beyond or rising above the limits of ordinary experience.

Uniformity: the quality or state of being uniform, same, without diversity (for example, in conduct, opinion, form, manner, or appearance).

Unity: the purposeful integration of two or more unique entities in a state of harmony and cooperation, resulting in the creation of a new, evolving entity, usually of a higher order.

Universal: a concept, condition or thing that exists everywhere or under all conditions; that includes everyone and/or everything and is comprehensively broad and versatile.

---

1. Wikipedia.
2. *Cambridge Advanced Learner's Dictionary.*
3. *Merriam-Webster Online Dictionary.*

The Fundamental Laws of Life

In all healthy living organisms and systems—whether plant, animal, or human—three conditions are present: Unity, Growth, and Creativity. If any of these three conditions are lacking, then life is threatened and may become feeble or dysfunctional. We can actually identify certain Laws of Life derived from our observations of the effects that the presence or absence of these three basic conditions have on the quality of life processes. Let's now look at the Laws of Life more closely.

1. The Law of Unity

Unity is Life, Life is Unity

Unity is the precondition for all healthy life processes, whether biochemical, physiological, ecological, psychological, social, political, moral, or spiritual. Without unity, life cannot exist. Life is an extraordinary condition emerging from the coming together of two or more entities in a condition of unity. In this view, life is the outcome of unity, and it will be sustained as long as the condition of unity is maintained.[4] Expressed differently, the relationship between unity and

life is reciprocal—unity enables life, and healthy life processes foster unity. This phenomenon is observed at all levels of existence and in all forms of life.

The following are some examples of the principle of **unity is life, life is unity**:

- On the biological level, the sperm and ovum come together in the womb of a mother and, although very different, create a new life of much higher order once the single cells unite.
- On the physical level, electrons and neutrons come together and create an atom, the basic unit of all material existence.
- In the human body, atoms, cells, organs, and systems function together in a unified whole in order for the body to live, grow, and remain healthy.
- In the social realm, individuals and groups unite to form families, communities, and societies.

Definition

Unity is the purposeful integration of two or more unique entities in a state of harmony and cooperation, resulting in the creation of a new, evolving entity, usually of a higher order.

Whenever diverse components are brought together in a condition of unity, a new and higher state of life can emerge. When the parts of our body function in a harmonized and unified manner, the body is alive and healthy. When our relationships are characterized by unity, our social systems (families, organizations, cities) thrive. When our thoughts, feelings, and actions are unified with each other and are in harmony with universal ethical principles, two outcomes occur: our psychological condition is peaceful, and our

---

4. In biological life processes, unity can also be understood as "homeostasis." "Homeostasis is the maintenance of a stable internal environment, be it in a cell or an organism as a whole." This is a necessary condition for life and must be maintained throughout the entire life cycle. "The human body constantly adjusts to changes in order to maintain biological equilibrium. Unity is shared by all living species in that they have certain biological, chemical, and physiological characteristics in common. All organisms adapt to their specific environments in order to survive. Organisms must somehow live in harmony with other organisms and the physical limitations that might be set by the surrounding environment." <http://www.msnucleus.org/membership/html/k-6/lc/lcoverview.html>.

---

spiritual condition progresses. As long as unity is maintained, life continues. In contrast, whenever unity breaks down, so does life: conflicts appear, resulting in disorder and ultimately destruction.

Consider what happens to the human body when the unity and homeostasis maintaining the health of all the body's systems are undermined. The body becomes sick; the individual is no longer healthy and cannot perform functions at work or at home. Psychologically, the person may become disconcerted; and if the illness remains untreated, the physical disunity may even threaten that person's life. Indeed, when we understand the importance of unity in maintaining life and health, we can readily recognize that the absence of unity is a common factor underlying all conflicts, illnesses, and general lack of progress. This is a fundamental law of existence.

Unity in Diversity

Many people find the concept of unity to be surprising in both its simplicity and complexity. It is especially this latter quality, 'complexity', which makes unity such an enigma. While unity refers to a state of oneness, it also requires diversity and differences in order to exist.

The human body, with its various organs and systems, demonstrates the truth that unity only works if there is also diversity. We would be very limited in what we could accomplish if we were each just one organ, such as a set of lungs. Indeed, it is the presence of many different types of cells, organs, and systems that allows a human body to thrive. The more diverse the elements, the more advanced life becomes. Compare your body and that of an amoeba. The difference between the two is the degree of diversity and complexity of its component parts. Environmental sciences show us how important diversity is to maintaining life. Likewise, the more diverse a society, the greater its challenges, but also the greater its resources and sophistication.

Let's now review some examples together.

Example: The Human Body

Our bodies are living proof of how the condition of "unity in diversity" works to maintain the life and health of a complex living being. Among other things, we each have a heart, lungs, and brain. The only way these extremely important organs are able to function is for them to work together. The brain signals the lungs to take in oxygen; the oxygen is circulated in blood by the heart, which also receives its cue from the brain. The oxygenated blood feeds the brain. It is a cooperative relationship in which a series of different organs with diverse functions work together to sustain life. **If,** even for a brief moment, this relationship were to break down, the life of the whole organism would be endangered.

Organs of the body working together, provide an example of a healthy living process or system. Imagine if the brain decided not to send out signals. All the organs and tissues would starve from lack of oxygen—even the brain itself. If the organs were to be in competition with each other, the result would not be a healthy system. All organs would be adversely affected, the system would break down, and death would be the ultimate result.

As in the body, we can see that human social systems—like our families, communities, and societies—are also composed in a similar way. Human social systems are composed of many different peoples. Each person is unique, and when our unique thoughts, feelings, talents, and capabilities are brought together, we can accomplish great things. It is through the processes of cooperation and unity that science develops; new technologies are invented; equal, just, free, and prosperous societies are formed; and a civilization of peace is created.

Example: The Art of Cooking

Certain dietary substances such as vitamins, proteins, carbohydrates, fatty acids, and minerals are essential foodstuffs necessary for the continuation of life. All people need them: on the biological level, humanity is one. In order to meet our biological needs, these nutritional components must be combined to produce a balanced diet. Therefore, it is not surprising that all peoples have developed elaborate approaches to preparing and consuming food so as to achieve common nutritional objectives. At the same time, each cultural group has developed its culinary arts in a unique way, adding social and cultural meaning to the basic task of physical nourishment. If we could travel around the world, sampling the culinary arts of different nations and peoples, we would find numerous recipes that draw on a common set of ingredients. This remarkable diversity of approach to both the preparation and consumption of food adds an immeasurable degree of pleasure and meaning to the common act of eating, and makes this human activity one of the most potent examples of creating unity while celebrating diversity.

The concept of "unity in diversity" points to the fact that, at the core of our humanness, we share a common nature; as such, we are in reality "one." It is also accurate to refer to our "diversity in unity." The concept of "diversity in unity" refers to the process of sharing different views, characteristics, needs, and aspirations together as we pursue legitimate objectives within a united and just framework. These two definitions combined—*"unity in diversity"* and *"diversity*

in unity"—encompass important aspects of the concept of unity.

True unity cannot be established through force, power, authoritarianism, or control. Some societies have attempted to establish unity by sacrificing diversity and enforcing uniformity by trying to make everyone the same.[5] Other societies have sacrificed unity in order to pursue the perceived benefits of individualism and group diversity. Ample evidence demonstrates that both of these approaches inevitably result in either oppression or chaos—conditions that ultimately result in disunity, conflict, and social breakdown. Greater than the mere tolerance of differences, true unity refers to a conscious desire for the type of richness in life that can only be provided by the unification of diversity into a single greater expression. Unity such as this promotes growth; secures individual and social well-being; and fosters creativity. Through the power of unity, the quality of human life becomes a deliberate, intentional, purposeful phenomenon, a matter of choice, rather than merely the outcome of biological forces alone or social processes beyond our control.

When we fully understand the principle of *Unity is Life, Life is Unity,* we then eliminate one of the most difficult obstacles to the achievement of peace. We began to realize that creating unity, while safeguarding and nurturing the diversity is

---

5. There is ample evidence from the 20th century alone of the failure of "forced unities," which established seemingly harmonious societies through the coerced suppression of diversity among its member populations. Thus these experiments at establishing social order have invariably failed, often causing extreme suffering and loss in the process. The observed pattern in such situations is that almost as soon as the authoritarian power enforcing this condition of uniformity is dissolved, the natural diversity within the society resurfaces, often accompanied by competition for power among groups thus leading to confrontation, conflict, and violence.

an essential and undeniable condition for all that exists. The concept of unity in diversity requires a full comprehension and acceptance of the fact that, at the very core of our humanity, we are one and the same, sharing a common nature. We are all noble beings with the capacities to love, to understand, and to create. However, the manner in which we develop and express these capacities will be unique to each individual and group. This uniqueness is at the core of the issue of diversity. In other words, diversity is neither sameness nor preference, but uniqueness in the context of equal opportunities and variations of interest and accomplishment.

Humanity's Development Towards Unity

The story of humanity's disunity is also that of its unity. In its march toward maturity, humanity has achieved many remarkable acts of unity, such as the successive creation of family, clan, tribe, state, and nation. These are ever-widening circles of unity. Humanity has also achieved limited, but significant, unities in respect to issues of religion, race, and culture. In recent decades, we also have achieved considerable unity of thought about the undeniable, but grievously ignored, fact that women are equal to men, and that peace and tranquility could not be achieved if women continue to be denied their rightful, equal place in the administration of human affairs. There are other examples of unity in human history, but they are all limited unities and, as such, have limited results. They even may cause serious disunity. The primary requisite, which assures a permanent and stable unity, is consciousness of the oneness of humanity. Humanity has always been one. However, our consciousness of this oneness has been greatly limited due to the self-centered and identity-based preoccupations of earlier stages of our development. It is only after childhood and adolescence that we gradually begin to see humanity as one and ourselves as an integral part of this oneness.

The developmental perspective of unity removes one of the most difficult obstacles for its achievement: creating unity while safeguarding and nurturing the diversity that is an essential and undeniable fact of all that exists. In fact, various governments and societies are increasingly embracing the concept of unity in diversity. We will discuss the developmental concept of unity further in Unit 5.

The Force of Love

This significant and direct relationship between life and unity, on the one hand, and conflict and disunity, on the other hand, is due to another fundamental force that operates in the context of life, namely, love. Love is the essential force of unity. In human relationships, love occupies a central position, and its absence is quite often, if not always, the underlying reason for the presence of conflict.

Love is not merely an emotion. It is commonly perceived as such, but in fact, love is a much broader phenomenon with many different modes of expression. Love is that powerful force of attraction which brings people together and creates friendships, marriages, families, communities, and civilizations. Love is also the motivating force behind those joyous, cooperative, and creative initiatives that render life meaningful and productive.

Furthermore, love is more than just a human experience. The primary attractive force of love also operates in the physical universe. We call this force by different names—such as cohesion, bonding, magnetism, and gravity—but in its various expressions we can see that its properties and effects are alike. Described simply, love establishes relationships between things and holds them together—whether they are particles, components of living organisms, planets, peoples, or societies.

Example: The Force of Gravity

Adapted from "From Apples to Orbits: The Gravity Story" (<http://library.thinkquest.org/27585/frameset_intro.htm>)

Gravity is the attractive force between all objects in the universe. It is the weakest known force in nature, but it still manages to hold galaxies and solar systems together. Every piece of matter is surrounded by an invisible gravitational field that pulls any other matter inside that field towards it. The more massive the matter is and the closer it is to another piece of matter, the stronger its gravitational field will be.

One of the unique characteristics of gravity is that it is always attractive. This gives it an advantage over other forces like electromagnetism, which can be attractive or repulsive and therefore tends to cancel itself out. Second, gravity can act over very large distances. Whereas the strong nuclear force cannot even reach from atom to atom, gravity's attractive powers can stretch across almost infinite amounts of space.

The force of love in human life is very similar to the force of gravity in physical life. It cannot be seen, but its effects are felt throughout the world. Love is the powerful force of attraction that brings people together—even over great distances—to create friendships, marriages, families, communities, and civilizations.

What other correlations can you draw between the force of gravity and the force of love?

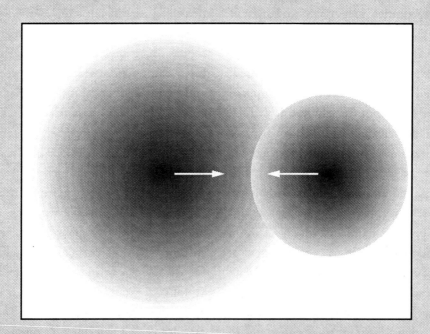

Figure 1: Gravitational fields, such as the ones shown here, are not actually visible, but we know they exist due to the effects they have on the movement of matter.

Definition

Love is a dynamic force of attraction that draws and binds together two or more elements in a condition of unity, bringing life to the collective whole.

In human life, the art of loving does not come automatically. We need education, guidance, and examples on how to love in a healthy and mature manner. It is true that the natural tendency of children is to have love for their parents, family members, and others they encounter in their small universe. However, this love is a limited and dependent love, and it is also self-focused. From these beginning seeds of love, we need to learn to love others in a universal, unconditional, autonomous, and authentic way. Such a mature expression of love is only possible within the parameters of the oneness of humanity and the inherent nobility of human nature.

2. The Law of Growth

Growth as a Sign of Life

Growth is an inherent quality of every living entity and a sign that healthy life processes are present. Both individuals and societies are subject to the laws of growth, as are all biological and social organisms. No living entity is exempt from the law of growth. Where growth is observed, life exists. Where no growth takes place—or where the opposite of growth, i.e., decline or decay, is observed—life itself is in danger or has already ceased to exist. Growth and life are mutually interdependent: life creates growth and growth maintains life.

While the principles of life and growth are clearly observed and understood in the biological sciences, their operation in sociological entities (such as the family; economic, educational, religious, and political institutions; and society as a whole) is not fully appreciated or understood.

In plants and animals, the course and limits of growth are predetermined, whereas in human beings, growth is determined in great part by our choices. Human beings are not only subject to biological growth but also experience intellectual, emotional, social, and spiritual growth. As human growth is as much qualitative as it is quantitative, we may also refer to it by the term "development."

Definitions

Growth describes positive quantitative change, increase, or expansion.

Development describes positive qualitative change resulting from a process of evolution or specialization towards a more advanced state of being and/or consciousness.

Unique Dimensions of Human Development

Here let us now briefly review the various aspects of human development and their relevance to peace.

When we observe the general patterns of individual growth—within the womb and in all the stages of this life—we can find parallels with the general evolution of the human species on earth. Within these parallel processes, three distinctive yet interrelated dimensions of human growth can be identified: biological growth, psychosocial growth, and spiritual growth. We know a lot about the biological, psychological, and social aspects of human development but less about the spiritual dimension.

Biological Development

Biological development in its broadest sense is called evolution and dates back to the appearance of life some four billion years ago. According to

Discussion: Universal Laws Governing Human Life

What is a "law"?
What universal laws govern human life?
What happens if we ignore a law?

There are many laws that apply to human life: some of these have been created by cultural or legal systems and differ from place to place, from society to society; others are universal laws, independent from any given culture, political system, or group, and applicable to all of humankind. A "law" can be defined as follows:

Law: (a) a statement that describes regular or patterned relationships among observable phenomena; (b) a general rule that states what always happens when the same conditions exist; (c) a principle of conduct binding or enforced by a controlling authority.

When in operation, laws are not subject to personal opinions. In other words, laws operate whether or not someone likes, believes in, or accepts the law. If we disregard laws, we must face the consequences that automatically follow.

There are two types of universal laws that govern human life: scientific laws and spiritual laws. One of the scientific laws is the law of gravity. Imagine yourself with someone on a seven-story building, and someone says, "I don't believe in the law of gravity. I am a big person and intelligent and free. I am not going to let a superstitious law that I have not seen dictate what I can do." Yet, we all know that if this individual steps off the roof of that building out into the air, we might imagine the law of gravity immediately replying: "Hello sir, please come down and let me introduce myself!" It doesn't matter whether one believes in the law of gravity or not: if it is disregarded, one will suffer the consequences. The only way to be free in regard to the law of gravity is to understand it and to use it properly. As humanity improved its understanding of the law of gravity, we learned to dive, to ski, and to fly! This was possible not because we tried to violate the law of gravity, but because we figured out its properties, obeyed it, and worked with it to our benefit.

There is also the category of spiritual laws. One of the most important of these laws is the counterpart to the law of gravity: that is, the law of love. The law of love operates in human life. If we go against it, we suffer its consequences. It does not matter who we are or how powerful we are, we are subject to it. When a person violates the law of love, what arises instead is rejection, hatred, destruction, violence, and war. Just as with the law of gravity, the only way that we can be free in respect to the law of love is to learn how to love. And the more universal our love is, the more outstanding its outcome; whereas, the more limited our observance of the law of love, the more dangerous its outcome. An example of a limited love is when someone says, "I'm willing to kill others for the love of my family, group, religion, and country." These are limited kinds of love. Therefore, the more limited that love is, the more destructive the outcome; and the more universal love is, the more creative the outcome will be.

the generally accepted theory of evolution, the earliest known human species, *Homo habilis*, appeared in Kenya some two million years ago. About one million years ago *Homo erectus* evolved into *Homo sapiens*. It is postulated that, in response to environmental forces and the imperatives of survival in a wild and dangerous world, the basic features of the human physique as we find it today emerged. An upright posture, the unique human hands with opposable thumbs for dexterity and flexibility, and keen human eyesight, are noteworthy examples of the evolution of the human species.

Since life, as we experience it, takes place not only at the biological but also psychosocial and spiritual levels, it is necessary that we understand the dynamics of these aspects of human development as well.

Psychosocial Development

When higher levels of consciousness, due to further development of the brain, appeared during evolution of the human species, a new era of human life began. The survival of the species was no longer solely dependent on the interface of biological and environmental forces. Human consciousness, albeit still primitive in its development, had entered into the arena of human development. Human beings now not only experienced a host of feelings and emotions such as hunger, sexual arousal, pain, fear, anger and anxiety but also were *conscious* of these emotions and were able to respond to them with a certain degree of *choice*. The era of conscious decision-making had begun. It is this consciousness and choice that shape the character of the psychosocial phase of human evolution. Thus, *natural selection* now was accompanied by *conscious choice* as mechanisms of human evolution.

During this phase of our development, agriculture, domestication of animals, and community-building skills were invented. We also have evidence that as early as 100,000 years ago,

human beings had amulets and had developed ritual burials. Our ancestors had begun to ask such fundamental questions as, Who are we? What is the purpose of our lives? What is the source of life? And, what is the mystery of death? These are existential and spiritual questions.

Some 45,000 years ago, human beings began to communicate more clearly and coherently. Language was invented. The means of communication between people improved dramatically. Both ideas and experiences were shared more easily and clearly. With this development, the human species traversed its age of infancy and entered its active, inquisitive period of childhood. During this phase, make-believe, superstitions, and fear of the unknown and strangers were mixed with experimentation, trial and error, and cooperative living in small settlements.

Central to all aspects human life during this phase were the twin powerful forces of survival and gratification. Human beings were gradually learning that survival need not take place only in poor and difficult circumstances. They now understood that life was indeed more than survival and that they had the capacity to create a less painful and even pleasant life. For each of us individually, the forces of survival and gratification play significant roles in shaping our lives, especially during our childhood and adolescent stages. Likewise, these same dynamics can be found to affect our collective societal development as well.

From one perspective, we could state that the stages of biological and psychosocial development of humanity correspond with stages of our collective childhood and adolescence. However, spiritual development is directly related to the process of humanity's emergence into adulthood.

Spiritual Development

Whereas biological development results from the environmental demands and imperatives of *survival*; and psychosocial development takes place in response to drives for *gratification* and *self-fulfillment*; human spiritual development occurs in response to our innate needs for *transcendence* and *universality*. Through the process of spiritual growth, we human beings begin to demonstrate qualities and capacities that we most admire, both in ourselves and in each other. Among these qualities are love, truth, justice, service, and attraction to beauty. In order to develop these qualities, both as individuals and societies, we need to achieve true transcendence—the process that takes us beyond a life bound to the dictates of our instinctual forces and self-centered objectives.

We could give other names to this third phase of human development, and some commentators have done so. The fact remains that the entire drama of human history is moving away from the limited confines of matter to the unlimited, equally real yet abstract, domains of consciousness and spirit. Spirituality, however, remains an enigma for most people. This is so because the concept of spirituality has been poorly defined and researched.

In the EFP curriculum we offer the following definition of spirituality:

Definition

Spirituality is a conscious, dynamic, progressive, and integrative process in which human individuals and/or societies achieve their fullest potential in a condition of unity. This developmental process produces ever-higher levels of consciousness and understanding, and results from influences which have their roots in both science and religion.

Whereas the central objectives of biological and psychosocial phases of human development are survival, security, domination, pleasure, and accomplishment; spiritual growth is characterized by the consciousness of the oneness of the human race and the interdependence of *all* forms of life. In this domain, individuals and societies together embark upon a coordinated process of making life safer and more comfortable, equitable, peaceful beautiful, joyful, creative, fruitful, and meaningful.

Thus, while we as humans experience physical growth for a limited time only, our ways of thinking and understanding continue to develop throughout our lives. Evidence of intellectual development is witnessed in increased knowledge and wisdom in meeting life challenges and opportunities, and applying acquired proficiency in appropriate ways to various contexts and challenges. Spiritual growth can be seen in a deepened understanding of the complexity of life, and in an increasing appreciation of those universal principles that unite our thoughts, feelings, and actions in service to humanity.

A mature individual recognizes the potential for growth in all areas of life, cultivates this growth, and strives to build a life that fosters creativity and creates unity. The growth process is universal. We need to respect the growing process in ourselves and to inspire a cooperative atmosphere that encourages those around us to grow. Humans learn and grow through study and deep reflection, experience and experimentation, and relationships and interaction. Meeting the challenges of life together builds our capacities for the strength of character, visionary determination, perseverance, and flexibility so necessary for mature relationships.

Individuals and societies need to grow physically in order to remain healthy; to grow intellectually in order to become knowledgeable and informed; and to grow spiritually in order to make life meaningful, creative, and enlightened. Such a growth process is demanding and painful, and requires a fundamental shift in our thinking. This shift of consciousness is already upon us, but we are responding to it by doing everything in our powers to ignore, discredit, and downgrade its revolutionary and far-reaching implications. We are resisting this new paradigm of reality because it goes squarely against the views and experiences that characterized individual and collective lives during the biological and psychosocial phases of the evolution of our species. This shift in our thinking is the gradual, but definite, realization of our fundamental human *unity*. Unity is the watchword and the main characteristic of the next phase of human development.

Our changing ideas and the resulting actions shape the communities we live in and the societies we build. If a living organism stops growing, it becomes sick. If it stops growing for a long time, it dies. The same is true for individuals and societies that do not grow to meet the changing needs of the times.

3. The Law of Creativity

The natural and necessary outcome of growth is creativity. When life evolves, when we grow, we create something new—something that further fosters life processes. Creativity means the constructive outcome or positive effect resulting from healthy life processes, such as buds emerging on a tree branch. That which is destructive of life, like a windstorm uprooting a tree, is not creative.

A tree brings forth fruit that both feeds other living beings and also continues its own life by producing seeds and yielding new trees. A couple brings forth a new child who will grow and enrich their lives and contribute to the world around them. An institution of learning brings forth ideas, inventions, or programs that will foster the development of various segments of society. Certain philosophers have reflected creatively on fundamental questions of life and yielded as their fruit, new ideas and models for a better society. All major religions through their teachings have shaped new ways of life, modes of relationships, social institutions, laws, ethics, and patterns of belief, thereby giving birth to whole new civilizations.

Definition

Creativity is the process of bringing forth something new and unique that fosters the continuation and enhancement of life processes.

Creativity is commonly and crudely believed to be unrestrained or unconventional expression of whatever the person "creating" wishes to convey, regardless of the positive or negative impact of that expression on anyone else. However, when a human mind creates an atomic bomb, for example, or other new ways to kill, this is invention but not true creativity. In order for a living being to have creative fruits in life, rather than destructive ones, he/she needs to be in a condition of unity with all humanity, as well as in a state of continuous growth and development in his/her individual mindset. Such an individual becomes a catalyst for inventions and creativity that leads to building new, better, and more peaceful societies.

Creativity takes many forms and is always the result of growth in the context of unity-in-diversity. Unity, growth, and creativity are in continuous relationship with one another.

In the life of an individual human being, growth and creativity take place in their physical, intellectual, social, and spiritual aspects. The fruits of human creativity can be expressed through literature, science, social organization, and any other way that contributes to the further development of humanity and the enrichment of our daily lives. Creativity inspires growth; and reciprocally, we grow through creative endeavors. Creativity thrives in a state of diversity since different stimuli and experiences inspire new conditions of human togetherness and unity.

We create on two levels: we create our own unique being (that is to say, who we are as individuals), and we contribute to the creation of our society. The beauty of the world is due largely to the fact that each of us contributes something different to the whole picture. Every society and every individual within that society is unique. Every person brings with him or her unique thoughts, feelings, and experiences. In a peaceful society, the uniqueness of smaller groups and individuals is valued and celebrated, while maintaining an overall sense of solidarity and unity with the larger group. A civilization in its truest sense is a civilization that is capable of creating unity while actively nurturing and celebrating diversity.

Summary

In this unit, we have learned that:

Unity Is the Main Prerequisite for Life, Growth, and Creativity

- Unity is not uniformity;
- Unity necessitates diversity;
- Absence of unity is the main cause of all conflicts, dissensions, disorders, and lack of progress.

When Unity Is Present, Creative Growth and Development Take Place

- Growth and development—physical, mental, emotional, moral, and spiritual—are indicators of healthy life processes, which are possible only in the condition of unity;
- Where no growth takes place—or where the opposite of growth, in other words, decline or decay, is observed—life itself is in danger, indicating that unity has been compromised.

True Creativity Does Not Cause Destruction

- Creativity is the creation of something new that fosters the continuation of healthy life processes;
- Anything that is destructive cannot, by definition, be understood as creative.

Evidence Shows That Humanity Is Progressing Towards Unity

- There are many developments in our world today indicating that humanity is progressing towards unity in political (for example, the United Nations, European Union, and African Union), economic (globally interconnected), environmental, communication (for example, the Internet, television), and other spheres of human life.

Key Questions for the Classroom

The following questions can be used to review and explore further the concepts of Unit 1 with your students:

1. Why is unity the primary law of existence?

2. If unity is a law of life, why do we see so much conflict and turmoil in the world?

3. Why do people often consider unity and uniformity to be same? What is the relationship between unity and diversity?

4. Analyze this statement: "Life is unity, unity is life."

5. What simple examples might you give to explain the idea of "life is unity, unity is life"?

6. How can we know that a principle is "universal"?

7. What makes a principle a "law"?

8. What happens if we ignore the laws of life and act contrary to them?

9. What examples can you think of that demonstrate the oneness of humanity?

10. How can we increase unity in our daily lives, our families, communities, and societies, while maintaining and celebrating our diversity?

11. What is growth? How do we promote growth in ourselves and in our relationships?

12. How do we measure growth? What is the outcome of growth?

13. Are creativity and free experimentation the same?

14. What is the proper balance between freedom and discipline in processes of growth and creativity?

15. What if a person's "creativity" is considered constructive by some and destructive by others? How can one judge?

16. What causes conflict?

Personal Reflection

Reflection is a very powerful learning tool. It helps us to make sense of the things we are studying and the experiences we are going through. The more we reflect on ourselves, our relationships, and the world around us, the better prepared we are to discern, prioritize, and act upon issues of importance.

Becoming a peacemaker is a very important and challenging task. By reflecting on the principles of peace, we are better able to make decisions about our own development, which will help us undertake the goal of peace confidently.

As we go through each of the EFP Curriculum units, try to set aside some time for the process of reflection.

The following questions are provided to help you begin this process.

Questions for Personal Reflection

1. Reflections on Self

1. What makes me unique?
2. How can I increase the unity in my relationships with others?
3. Do I feel unity within myself? Explain why or why not.
4. What do I love, and how do I show that love?

Focus Questions

Inner peace comes when physical, intellectual, emotional, and spiritual dimensions of one's personality are developed and are in harmony with one another.

    a. Am I developing in every area of my personality?
    b. Are these developments in harmony with one another?
    c. What do I need to do to increase my inner peace?

2. Reflections on Family, Workplace, and Friendships

1. Is my family an example of unity-in-diversity? Explain why or why not.
2. Is my family or workplace a growing and creative environment? Why or why not?
3. Are diverse ideas and talents welcome and shared openly in my family? In my workplace?
4. Is the principle of gender equality fully observed in my family? In my workplace?
5. What can I do to contribute to unity in my family? In my workplace? In my circle of friends? Think of three examples of things I can do for each.

Focus Questions

Consider the following statement: "Family is the workshop of civilization."
- a. What do you think this statement means?
- b. If we want a civilization of peace to emerge, what kind of families do we need?
- c. What would their characteristics be?
- d. How is the issue of unity best expressed in the contexts of families and civilization?

3. Reflections on Society

1. What is my society's attitude towards diversity?
2. How does my society understand the concept of unity?
3. In which areas is my society progressing?
4. In which areas is my society experiencing conflict?
5. What can we do together, collectively, to strengthen unity and peace in our communities?
6. Whom should we involve and how?

Focus Question

Reflect on the following statement: "The more diverse a society, the greater its challenges and the stronger and greater its resources." *What do you think this means? Discuss.*

4. Reflections on the World at Large

1. When I look at the world, how do I see the *oneness* of human nature being expressed?
2. In what ways do I see human *diversity* being expressed?
3. What will the world be like when humanity accepts both its rich diversity and its fundamental oneness?

Focus Questions

Consider the world and all its peoples as a single body:
- a. What is the condition of this body?
- b. Is it healthy? Is it ill? What signs do we see and where?
- c. How can the health of "the body of humankind" be increased?
- d. What is the relevance of unity to the health of humanity?

Classroom Tools

As a teacher in the Education for Peace Program, it is now your task to introduce the discussion of Unity into your classroom, and to assist your students to explore the meaning of Unity and its application in their own lives, the world at large, and the specific subject they are studying with you.

The more our young generation understands what unity-in-diversity is and how to create it, the more capable they will become to build an authentic and lasting culture of peace. Your role as their teacher and mentor in this process is tremendously important.

To help you get started, a number of tools are included in this section that you may find useful. These tools are only guides, and you are encouraged to develop your own ideas on how best to explore these topics with your students.

In addition to the examples here, please also refer to the Educational Methodology Unit where you will find practical guidelines on how to make your classroom a creative and effective learning environment, as well as other great ideas from fellow teachers who are integrating Education for Peace into their various subject areas.

As you work with the Education for Peace concepts, you will surely develop new ideas for lessons, activities, and assessment approaches. We encourage you to pass along your thoughts, ideas, or resource links to Education for Peace so they can be added to our EFP Resource Bank for other teachers to use. Please send us an email at <info@efpinternational.org>, or mail your ideas to our address:

International Education for Peace Institute (Canada)
101, 1001 W. Broadway, Suite 900
Vancouver, BC V6H 4E4
Canada

We look forward to hearing from you!

Activity Ideas for Secondary Schools

Biology

You are a member of the international Human Genome research team that has discovered that gene sequences are almost 99.9% the same in all human beings. You've been invited to speak at a conference on peace and development. What do you feel is important for the conference participants to understand about both human oneness and the great disparity of living conditions that we currently see in the world?

Music

Explore the concept and principles of harmony in musical composition. What distinguishes musical sounds from non-musical sounds? How would you define harmony? Why does harmony create a sense of beauty in music?

Computer Science

The emergence of communications technologies, and particularly of the Internet, has revolutionized individual and collective life worldwide. What are 10 ways in which the Internet has acted as a unifying force among the peoples of the world? If the Internet did not exist, what would it take for these same 10 things to be achieved?

Home Economics

You are a nutritional specialist who has been invited to explain the importance of a balanced diet for maintaining unity in the body and in other aspects of daily life such as learning and creativity. Explain the basics of good nutrition and its effects on human health. What effect does diet have on energy, academic performance, sleep patterns, moods, relationships, etc. What parallels can you draw between individual nutrition and health, and the necessities for societal health and progress?

History

Historically, wars have been waged for the purpose of gaining political, and particularly economic, advantages despite the enormous material and human losses that war invariably brings. After WWII, however, western European countries decided to use the principle of economic interdependency to prevent the possibility of war. What did these nations agree to do? Provide a brief historical account and, using a modern automobile or computer as an example, demonstrate this new system in action.

Activity Ideas for Primary Schools

Sciences

In learning the growth process of a tree or a plant, compare the different structures of the tree/plant to the human body. Describe how all of the parts of the tree/plant function within the laws of unity, just as the body does. Have the students draw all parts of the tree/plant beside their drawing of themselves and compare the various parts that make them whole. Discuss what would happen if different parts were missing or not working. What would happen to the tree/plant? What would happen to the child?

Plants have a cycle of life that goes through different stages. Do humans go through similar stages? As you explore the plant life cycle, compare it to the growth of people.

Just as a tree/plant grows, so do humans. In what ways do trees/plants grow? In what ways does a person grow? Do all people grow this way?

Social Studies

Discuss how a family is unified through the diversity of each member. Have students draw their families and describe how they are a unified family with all of their diverse members and share the drawings with the class. How is this similar to their class? Their school?

Sometimes family members might not get along. How can we create unity in our families? With our friends?

What are the similarities among families? In what ways are families different? Keeping in mind that all humans are one, in what ways are all families the same? What keeps families together? Create a mural in the classroom of families demonstrating their unity and diversity. How is this similar to the school? To the world?

Who are the different people that make up a community? Where are the areas of unity? Where is the diversity? Are all communities the same? Take the class on a field trip through their community and discuss how everyone works together to make the community work in cooperation.

Unit 1, Sample Lesson 1: UNITY

Focus: Unity is Life, Life is Unity

Context

Unity is the first fundamental law of life and a prerequisite for peace. Understanding unity will equip participants to understand and work on building peace more effectively.

Points for Understanding

- Unity is present wherever healthy life processes can be observed, whether physical, psychological, social, or spiritual;
- Unity is the key prerequisite for life, growth, and creativity;
- Underlying all conflict, dissension, illness, and lack of progress is a lack of unity.

Key Questions

1. How can we differentiate "unity" from "uniformity"?
2. What evidence is there that the laws of life are universal?

Activities and Assignments

Teachers can choose from among the following sample assignments, or create their own:

1. **Assignment:** write a short paper (250 words) on the following statement: "Around the world, in every sphere of life, from psychology to physics, from farming to the family kitchen, there is a growing awareness of the interconnectedness of all life…a rediscovery of values that have existed for thousands of years—values that recognize our place in the natural order, our indissoluble connection to one another and to the earth" (Helena Norberg-Hodge, *Ancient Futures: Learning from Ladakh*).

2. It can be argued that a breakdown in unity is at the centre of many issues facing the world today. Discuss current challenges facing global management of the environment from a unity-centered perspective. Students should consider the following questions in writing the paper:
   - How can environmental degradation be seen both as a result of disunity in the earth's natural systems and disunity in the world's political systems?
   - How can a unity-centered approach be employed to bring a solution to the problem?

3. **Journal:** Reflect on relationships in your life that could be improved through an increase in unity. What steps would you take to increase unity in these relationships? What other difficulties can you think of that would benefit from implementing the principle of unity-in-diversity? Why?

4. **Journal:** Reflect on the unit reading and class discussions. Using examples from your own life, describe what you feel is meant by "Unity in Diversity." How can this principle be cultivated more in your relationships and your community?

Unit 1, Sample Lesson 2: UNITY

Focus: The Law of Growth and the Law of Creativity

Context

Growth and creativity are two fundamental aspects of all life processes. Understanding what the prerequisites for growth and the indicators of creativity are provides a foundation for fostering thriving environments and relationships.

Points for Understanding

- Growth—whether physical, mental, emotional, ethical, or spiritual—is a necessary indicator of life and vitality; where growth is observed, life exists; where no growth is observed—or where the opposite of growth, i.e., decline or decay, is occurring—life processes are diminishing, and the inevitable end is death, unless the process is reversed.
- Growth is necessary for health, maturation, progress, and peace.
- The natural and necessary outcome of growth is creativity—the creation of something new that further fosters life processes; it is illogical that the term "creative" could be applied to technologies, agencies, or actions that are destructive.
- The prerequisite for growth and creativity is unity in the context of diversity.

Key Questions

1. Are creativity and free experimentation the same?
2. What is the proper balance between freedom and discipline in the processes of growth and creativity?
3. When individuals or groups are having difficulty or experiencing conflict in relations with one another, is this a characteristic and necessary sign of diversity? Or a symptom of the breakdown of unity?
4. What if a person's "creativity" is considered constructive by some and destructive by others? How could one choose between these two judgments?

Learning Process

1. Have students provide a review of the concept of Unity-in-Diversity as one of the fundamental laws of life.
2. Brainstorm other examples of how unity-in-diversity, growth, and creativity bring great results.
3. Use the Key Questions to facilitate a classroom discussion on the concepts of unity-in-diversity, growth, and creativity.
4. Review assignment instructions with students.

Activities/Exercises

Teachers can choose from among the following sample assignments, or create their own:

1. **Project:** An organic garden requires a high level of biodiversity and creative techniques to protect plants from insects and other infestations. Have the students form small groups and have them research the principles of organic gardening, paying attention to the aspects of time, discipline, technique, flexibility, and moderation required to yield a successful organic crop. Have students create a panel with illustrations/pictures and explanations of the processes involved. Ask them to draw conclusions about "Unity," "Growth," and "Creativity" based on their findings and to correlate their understanding to their own life and relationships.

2. **Written Assignment:** Refer to the set of quotations included at the end of this unit. Write a 1–2 page discussion of one of these quotations in light of the concepts introduced in Unit 1.

3. **Journal:**
   a. Are there distinct times in your life when you felt a change in the way you saw things? Describe how these might be seen as periods of growth for you. What did you learn about yourself or those around you during this period?
   b. Creativity is commonly equated with artistic ability. What other types of creativity are there? In what areas of your life do you feel yourself being creative? Where are you growing? In what other areas would you like to increase your creativity, your productivity or your constructiveness?

Unit 1 – Activity Reading

Choose one of the following quotations and discuss:

"The reason why the world lacks unity and lies broken and in heaps, is because man is disunited with himself."

—Ralph Waldo Emerson (1803–1882), U.S. essayist, poet, philosopher
Nature, ch. 8 (1836, revised and repr. 1849)

"Let us build altars to the Blessed Unity which holds nature and souls in perfect solution, and compels every atom to serve a universal end."

—Ralph Waldo Emerson (1803–1882), U.S. essayist, poet, philosopher
"Fate," *The Conduct of Life* (1860)

"From cradle to grave this problem of running order through chaos, direction through space, discipline through freedom, unity through multiplicity, has always been, and must always be, the task of education, as it is the moral of religion, philosophy, science, art, politics and economy...."

—Henry Brooks Adams (1838–1918), U.S. historian
The Education of Henry B. Adams, p. 731, The Library of America (1983)

"Perhaps, the highest pleasure in art is identical with the highest pleasure in scientific theory. The emotion which accompanies the clear recognition of unity in a complex seems so similar in art and in science that it is difficult not to suppose that they are psychologically the same. It is, as it were, the final stage of both processes. This unity-emotion in science supervenes upon a process of pure mechanical reasoning; in art it supervenes upon a process of which emotion has all along been an essential concomitant."

—Roger Fry (1866–1934), British painter, art critic
"Art and Science," *Vision and Design,* Brentano's (1920)

"Behold, how good and how pleasant it is for brethren to dwell together in unity!"

—Hebrew Bible, Psalms 133:1

"Egotism erects its center in itself; love places it out of itself in the axis of the universal whole. Love aims at unity, egotism at solitude. Love is the citizen ruler of a flourishing republic, egotism is a despot in a devastated creation."

—Wilhelm Schlegel (1767–1845), German poet
Philosophical Letters, no. 4

"The cause of existence is unity and cohesion, and the cause of nonexistence is separation and dissension."

—'Abdu'l-Bahá Abbas (1844–1921), Persian philosopher, humanitarian
The Promulgation of Universal Peace, p. 207 (1912)

"So it is safe, in working toward the political unity of mankind to build on the affirmation that every human being is born into a unity from which he cannot escape, in which he has rights, and to which he owes service—a unity which comprehends all diversity of human types, a unity which will triumph over all divisive tendencies, and a unity that will attain its ideal only when it has organs through which it can act when, in the might and enthusiasm of world consciousness, world purpose, and world will, it reaches the sublime heights of its own being, recognizes its own dignity and capacity, and essays to do what is befitting its lofty nature in order to promote its own peace and prosperity."

—Raymond Landon Bridgman, Legal philosopher
World Organization, pp. 114–15 (1905)

"Whereunto shall we liken the kingdom of God? or with what comparison shall we compare it? It is like a grain of mustard seed, which, when it is sown in the earth, is less than all the seeds that be in the earth: But when it is sown, it groweth up, and becometh greater than all herbs, and shooteth out great branches; so that the fowls of the air may lodge under the shadow of it."

—King James Bible, Mark (4:30–32)

"The well-being of mankind, its peace and security, are unattainable unless and until its unity is firmly established."

—Bahá'u'lláh (1817–1892), Persian nobleman, prophet
Gleanings from the Writings of Bahá'u'lláh, p. 286

"Blessed is the arising of the awakened;
Blessed is the teaching of the truth;
Blessed is the harmony of the community;
Blessed is the devotion of those who live in peace."

—*Dhammapada: Sayings of the Buddha* 2 (translation by J. Richards)

Extended Exploration

Publications

Danesh, H.B. (1995). *The Violence-Free Family: Building Block of a Peaceful Civilization.* Ottawa: Bahá'í Studies Publications.

————. (1986). *Unity: The Creative Foundation of Peace.* Fitzhenry-Whiteside, Toronto and Ottawa: Bahá'í Studies Publications.

Bortoft, Henri. (1996). *The Wholeness of Nature: Goethe's Way toward a Science of Conscious Participation in Nature.* Herndon: Lindisfarne Press.

Laszlo, Ervin. (1996). *The Systems View of the World: A Holistic Vision for Our Time (Advances in Systems Theory, Complexity and the Human Sciences).* Cresskill: Hampton Press.

Norberg-Hodge, Helena. (1992). *Ancient Futures: Learning from Ladakh.* Oxford: Oxford University Press.

Web Links

"Stanford Encyclopedia of Philosophy." *Aristotle's Metaphysics – Revisiting Unity.* <http://plato.stanford.edu/entries/aristotle-metaphysics/#UR>.

"Stanford Encyclopedia of Philosophy." *Friedrich Wilhelm Joseph von Schelling – Identity Philosophy.* <http://plato.stanford.edu/entries/schelling/#3>.

"The Columbia Encyclopedia Online." *Life.* <http://www.bartleby.com/65/li/life.html>.

"Unity in Diversity" Website and Online Professional Development Video. <http://www.learner.org/channel/workshops/socialstudies/session3/index.html>.

"Public Broadcasting Service (PBS) TeacherSource – for K-12 lesson samples and resources for all subjects." <http://www.pbs.org/teachersource/>.

General Online Resources

The Columbia Encyclopedia Online. <http://www.bartleby.com/65>.

The Columbia World of Quotations. <http://www.bartleby.com/quotations>.

The Merriam-Webster Online Dictionary. <http://www.merriam-webster.com>.

The Stanford Encyclopedia of Philosophy. <http://plato.stanford.edu>.

Wikipedia: The Free Encyclopedia. <http://www.wikipedia.org>.

Art History Timeline: The Metropolitan Museum of Art. <http://www.metmuseum.org/toah/splash.htm>.

Unit 2

THE CONCEPT OF WORLDVIEW

The term "worldview" refers to a mental framework within which individuals and groups interpret the nature of reality, the nature and purpose of human life, and the laws governing human relationships. Worldviews are shaped by our life experiences, and at the same time they reshape our approach to life. This unit discusses the development and transformation of worldview and explains why a systematic and conscious effort to cultivate a peace-based worldview among the peoples and nations of the world is needed. The Worldview Unit provides an opportunity for students and teachers to think critically about their own worldviews at both the individual and collective levels.

Context

Everyone has a worldview, whether or not they are aware of it. Our worldviews shape how we perceive, interpret, understand, and respond to the realities around us. Worldviews shape all that we think, do, or consider to be normal or abnormal and acceptable or unacceptable. For example, a "conflict-oriented worldview" considers conflict to be normal and acceptable. Within a conflict-oriented worldview, our thoughts, feelings, and actions become characterized by conflict. We measure and express everything in terms of its degrees of conflict. If our goal is to create a culture of peace, then it is very important that we come to understand how worldviews are formed and changed. This knowledge helps us to better understand ourselves and others and to consciously foster a "peace-oriented worldview" in our individual lives, families, communities, and the world.

Learning Process

In this unit, participants should be assisted to:

1. Understand the concept of worldview; how worldviews are formed and changed; and how societies become conflicted and violent, or united and peaceful, depending upon their worldview.
2. Identify the three types of worldview, as formulated in the EFP curriculum; illustrate these types with examples from everyday life; and compare and contrast the impact of these worldviews on the vision and character of a society.
3. Reflect, through critical questioning, upon their own worldview: where it comes from, and whether it is oriented towards conflict or towards peace.
4. Search, in conflict situations, for ways to shift worldview assumptions in order to bring peaceful resolutions to the problem.

Points for Understanding

Teachers can guide their students to understand and remember these main points:

- Each person, community, and group has a worldview shaped by such things as life experiences, cultural norms, education, family dynamics, belief systems;
- Worldviews influence how people consider themselves, what kind of relationships they have with others, what they consider to be the main purpose of life, and how a person is supposed to think and act;
- Worldviews shape the types of communities we create;
- Throughout human history, the Survival- and Identity-based worldviews have been the most prevalent, causing societies to rely on conflict and violence in order to achieve their objectives;
- Today, the inability of the world community to create a civilization of peace is due to the persistence of these conflict-oriented worldviews among people, groups, organizations, and leaders;
- The beginning of a civilization of peace rests on the conscious development of a peace-oriented worldview;
- Each person can benefit from becoming conscious of and reflecting on his or her own worldviews;
- Through questioning those assumptions or attitudes in our worldviews that take conflict for granted, we can decide to consciously develop our understanding of the prerequisites of peace and begin to implement them in our lives, our relationships, our studies, and our work.

Worldview: What Is It, and Where Does It Come From?

Definition

*A **worldview** is a mental framework through which individuals and groups view the nature of reality, the nature and purpose of human life, and the laws governing human relationships.*

On both a personal and societal level, worldview represents the way we view ourselves, others, and the world at large; and most importantly, how we turn that vision into reality.

Every human being has a worldview. Worldviews develop over the course of a lifetime and are transmitted from generation to generation through such means as education, family tradition, religious belief, political orientation, and the mass media. Worldviews evolve in direct response to the development of our **consciousness,** which in turn is shaped by the sum of our unique individual life experiences and collective cultural histories. Usually, we are only partially conscious of the worldviews we hold. For the most part, worldviews are taken for granted and remain just below the surface of our conscious awareness:

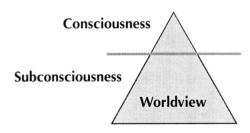

Diagram 1: Worldview Awareness

Yet, through the powerful medium of our worldview, we define our understanding of the nature of reality, the purpose of acquiring knowledge, and the purpose of human life both individually and collectively. Depending on which view of the world we eventually adopt, the way we live our lives will be dramatically different. Our worldviews do not just affect our perception of the world around us; our worldviews also determine the nature of our relationships, the type of societies we create, the ways we approach science and religion, and the manner in which we deal with opportunities and challenges that we encounter in our lives. Our worldviews affect every aspect of our lives and everything we do.

Conflict-Based Worldviews

In the contemporary world, life is experienced and understood by most of us from a conflict-centered perspective. This is so because the predominant worldviews in societies today are informed by philosophies, concepts, and scientific/pseudoscientific theories that consider conflict to be an inherent, even necessary, aspect of human nature and the life process itself. Conflict-based worldviews are characteristic of earlier stages of our individual and collective maturation process.

The following are a few prominent examples of scientific and philosophical theories that have contributed to the wide acceptance of conflict-centered worldviews.

Charles Darwin and the Theory of Natural Selection[1]

According to this theory, all life takes place in the arena of struggle, competition, and conflict; and evolution results from a process of "survival-of-the-fittest." Social Darwinism, a theory that relied on Darwin's findings to legitimize colonialism,

1. "Darwin observed… that although all organisms tend to reproduce in a geometrically increasing ratio, the numbers of a given species remain more or less constant.

Key Vocabulary

Development: a process of growing, evolving, unfolding, or differentiating in a specialized manner towards a more advanced state of being; positive, qualitative change signifying—in human life and culture particularly—advancement toward maturity. Development refers to positive, qualitative, and/or quantitative changes on the axis of consciousness.

Dichotomous: opposing or contradictory concepts, qualities, or groups; divided into two mutually exclusive entities.

Identity: the distinguishing character or personality of an individual,[2] equated with individuality, as in the total character peculiar to and distinguishing an individual from others.[3] The sense of uniqueness, individuality, or distinguishing characteristics that a person or group regards as definitive about themselves and the basis on which differentiation from other individuals or groups is made.

Individualism: a doctrine that the interests of the individual are or ought to be ethically paramount, and that all values, rights, and duties originate in individuals.

Inherent: belonging to the constitution or essential character of a thing.

Objectivity: the capacity of judgment based on observable phenomena and uninfluenced by emotions or personal prejudices.

Pseudoscientific: a system of theories, assumptions, and methods erroneously regarded as scientific. A pseudoscientific concept is not based on either the evidential or rational methods required to qualify as "scientific."

Relativism: a theory that all points of view are equally valid; the view that the value of any one thing is relative to the particular framework or standpoint from which its assessment is being made; the view that there are no universal values.

Subjectivity: a perceived reality that may be modified or affected by personal views, experience, or background.

Transformation: a process of profound or significant change that leads to a new and higher level of consciousness, resulting in greater insight and integrity in one's character, choices, and behavior.

Worldview: A mental framework through which individuals and groups view the nature of reality, the nature and purpose of human life, and the laws governing human relationships—the overall perspective from which one sees and interprets the world;[4] a collection of beliefs about life and the universe held by an individual or a group;[5] a dynamic, reflexive lens through which human beings construct, interpret, and interact with all aspects of their reality.[6]

From this he deduced that there is a continuing struggle for existence, for survival. He pointed out the existence of variations—differences among members of the same species—and suggested that the variations that prove helpful to a plant or an animal in its struggle for existence better enable it to survive and reproduce. These favorable variations are thus transmitted to the offspring of the survivors and spread to the entire species over successive generations. This process he called the principle of natural selection (the expression "survival of the fittest" was later coined by Herbert Spencer)" (*The Columbia Encyclopedia,* 6th ed.). For

more on evolution, see http://www.bartleby.com/65/ev/evolutio.html. For more on Social Darwinism, see Wikipedia: The Free Encyclopaedia http://www.wikipedia.org/wiki/Social_Darwinism.

2. *Merriam-Webster Online Dictionary.*

3. *Merriam-Webster Online Dictionary.*

4. H.B. Danesh, "Towards an Integrative Theory of Peace Education," *Journal of Peace Education* 3.1(2006): 55–78.

5. *The American Heritage Dictionary of the English Language,* 4th ed., 2000.

6. H.B. Danesh and R. Danesh, "Has Conflict

laissez-faire capitalism, and even Fascism,[7] views human interaction as a struggle for each human to live and thrive, often at the expense of others.

Karl Marx and the Theory of Class Struggle[8]

According to this theory, history is driven by the continuous and inevitable struggle of two rigid classes: the owners of the means of production and those who work for the owners. The cycle of conflict that continuously propels history can only end when, through legislated peace, the capital-owning class is eradicated

Sigmund Freud and the Tri-Partite Psyche[9]

According to this theory, life is ruled by two (mostly unconscious) instincts: sexuality (eros)

and aggression (thanatos or death-instinct). Individuals always experience conflict due to these two instincts and the inner conflict that occurs between the psyche's "id," "ego," and "superego." Freud's writings have influenced Western society for close to a century, as generation after generation has used his theories of personality development to extrapolate the meaning of life.[10]

Adam Smith and the Free-Market System[11]

According to Adam Smith's theory, competition is the basis of a healthy economic life, as it motivates individuals to strive for success. A robust economy will be characterized by competition and survival-of-the-fittest. Increasingly, the principle of competition has been used to manage all types of relationships ranging from interpersonal to international.

Grown Up? Toward a New Model of Decision Making and Conflict Resolution," *International Journal of Peace Studies* 7(1) (2002): 59–76.

7. "The doctrine of survival of the fittest and the necessity of struggle for life is applied by fascists to the life of a nation-state. Peaceful, complacent nations are seen as doomed to fall before more dynamic ones, making struggle and aggressive militarism a leading characteristic of the fascist state" (The Columbia Encyclopedia, 6th ed). For a discussion on this point, see http://www.bartleby.com/65/fa/fascism.html.

8. Marx's theory of "dialectical materialism presumes the primacy of economic determinants in history. Through dialectical materialism, the fundamental Marxist premise that the history of society is the inexorable "history of class struggle" was developed. According to this premise, a specific class could rule only so long as it best represented the economically productive forces of society; when it became outmoded it would be destroyed and replaced. From this continuing dynamic process a classless society would eventually emerge....Once the bourgeoisie had been defeated, there would be no more class divisions, since the means of production would not be owned by any group. The coercive state, formerly a weapon of class oppression, would be replaced by a rational structure of economic and social cooperation and integration" (*The Columbia Encyclopedia,* 6th ed.).

9. "Sigmund Freud asserted that the human mind could

be divided into three significant components—the id, the ego, and the superego—which work together (or come into conflict) to shape personality. Psychoanalysis emphasizes unconscious motivations and the conflicts between primal urges and learned social mores, stressing the importance of early childhood experiences in determining mature personality" (The Columbia Encyclopedia, 6th ed.) Recent trends in developmental psychology continue to place a high degree of emphasis on conflict, as I.B. Dusek and W.J. Meyer state: "Development will occur only when a conflict is present" ("A Dialectical Analysis of Learning Theory: Contributions to Understanding Human Development," *Human Development* 23(1980): 382–88). See also Hans Thomae and Ursula Lehr, "Stages, Crises, Conflicts and Life Span Development," *Human Development and the Life Course: Multidisciplinary Perspectives,* ed. Social Science Research Council (US). et al. Hillsdale, NJ: Lawrence Erlbaum Associates, 1986.429–43.

10. For a concise comparative review of the theories of Plato, Marx, Freud, Sartre, Skinner, and Lorenz, as well as Christianity, see Leslie Stevenson, *Seven Theories of Human Nature* (Oxford: Oxford University Press, 1974).

11. Within the philosophy of laissez-faire economy, Adam Smith, father of classical economics, "believed that individual welfare rather than national power was

---

Historically, these theories provided powerful impetuses for social and political change. In contrast to the arguments of creationism, the theory of evolution provided a substantive explanation for the development of life on earth that could be further explored and tested. The free-market model opened earning profit to ordinary merchants, formerly impossible under the feudal and colonial economic structures. The theory of class struggle contributed to public consciousness about the need for greater equality and justice in economic, social, and political affairs. And Freud's theories demystified human psychological characteristics that, until then, were categorized as demonic and subject to harsh superstitious treatment.

In can be seen that, although focusing on rather different subjects, these and similar theories share certain assumptions that:

- Human life, society, psychology, and economy are all based on conflict;
- The purpose of life is to gain maximum power, to ensure one's survival, and to obtain pleasure;
- It is necessary to be competitive and to look out for one's own interests;
- Life is the arena of the survival of the fittest, resulting in winners and losers.

Due in part to the broad influence of these theories, two distinct categories of conflict-centered worldviews continue to predominate in the world today. These worldviews are present, to varying degrees, in all human societies. They reflect the characteristics of two distinct phases in the development of every individual and society, known respectively as the "survival" phase and the "identity" phase. In the following section, the "Survival-Based" worldview and "Identity-Based" worldview are discussed as discrete categories, though it should be noted that very few individuals or societies are strictly one or the other worldview; more often, a blend of the two worldviews can be observed.

The Survival-Based Worldview

The survival-based worldview is most common in conditions of power imbalance and where perceptions of vulnerability and danger are present.[12] The survival-based worldview usually corresponds to the first decade and a half of individual life and to the agrarian or pre-industrial periods of collective organization. It can also develop under conditions of poverty, injustice, anarchy, physical threat, or war at any time and in any cultural setting.

During the survival phase, human beings, both individually and collectively, fear for their survival and thus seek power in order to achieve security. In a world full of dangers, order and protection are highly valued. Thus, in conditions of survival, it is typical for one or a small number of people to gain power through demonstrations of might and force, and for others to follow them in order to ensure their own safety and protection. Thus, human relationships during this phase are characterized by the unequal distribution of power and rely primarily upon the use of force to achieve desired objectives. In the survival-based worldview, the

the correct goal; he thus advocated that trade should be free of government restrictions. When individuals were free to pursue self-interest, the "invisible hand" of rivalry or competition would become more effective than the state as a regulator of economic life....In the hands of Jeremy Bentham the doctrine of laissez-faire became a philosophy of individualism and of utilitarian ethics, and John Stuart Mill brought it to what was probably its highest point" (*The Columbia Encyclopedia*, 6th ed.).

12. Vulnerability and danger are at once objective and subjective conditions. A live poisonous snake, for example, represents an objective danger if we find ourselves close to one; whereas, a photograph of a snake represents a subjective danger if the mere depiction itself causes us to feel fear. Not everyone experiences danger and vulnerability in the same way. Furthermore, people also respond to dangers differently, based on their subjective experience of the situation.

use of force is justified by belief in the notion that "might is right."

Essentially, the survival phase of thinking is prone to a considerable degree of violence because people in such a stage (individually or collectively) view the world as dangerous, operate on principles of force and control, and assume that the ultimate purpose of life is to secure safety for oneself and one's group.

Societies that operate according to the survival-based worldview tend to be authoritarian in their power orientation, and as such are not conducive to the creation of lasting peace in the context of unity in diversity. Though the survival-based worldview has enabled human groups and societies to use their powers and resources to meet basic survival needs, the authoritarian use of power demands conformity, blind obedience, and passive resignation by the powerless. Authoritarian institutions and societies systematically place women, children, minorities, foreigners, and those devoid of power and wealth in conditions of disadvantage, neglect, and abuse. Under these conditions, individuals cannot fully develop their inherent talents and capabilities; consequently, the society itself cannot advance since it has deprived itself of the creative contributions of the majority of its people. As such, the peace and order that

an authoritarian system creates are illusory. The system lasts only as long as the imbalance of power precariously enables the rulers and the ruling class to impose order on the people who have been subjected to the will of those authoritarian rulers.

The Identity-Based Worldview

The identity-based worldview emerges out of the survival phase and corresponds to the gradual coming-of-age of human individuals and societies. Identity development, although a life-long process, attains its highest level of expression in adolescence and early adulthood. Once we have gained sufficient power and capacity to safeguard our basic survival, our attention is directed at the strengthening of our individual and group identities.

Definition

Identity refers to the sense of uniqueness, individuality, or distinguishing characteristics that a person or group regards as definitive about themselves and the basis on which differentiation from other individuals or groups is made.

Important Terms to Know for Discussing Worldview

Perspective: The point of view one takes on the nature or character of the world at large—how it is and how it ought to be.

Operating Principle: The general philosophy or values to which one adheres regarding how to function successfully in the world.

Ultimate Purpose: The end-result that one believes to be best, or the goal toward which one strives in varied life activities.

Mode of Decision-Making: The decision-making process used by an individual or group.

Mode of Relationship: The characteristics and patterns of relationship that one establishes.

On an individual level, when we reach adolescence, we become interested in exploring our emerging powers and establishing our unique identities. It is very common for adolescents to test the limits of (and even discard) established authorities in order to experiment with and develop a stronger sense of selfhood, as they redefine for themselves the "limits" they will adopt. In pursuing selfhood, this phase is characterized by the development of new ideas and practices on the one hand, and extremes of competition and rivalry on the other.[13]

On a societal level, the identity phase corresponds with the period of scientific and technological advancement and to the democratization of government processes within a "competitive power structure." When the personal aspect of identity-formation is emphasized, the society takes on a highly individualistic character. Likewise, when the group aspect of identity-formation is emphasized, it leads to the development of a "collectivistic" approach to the organization of the society. The intense competition and power-struggle that often characterize the identity phase of human development promotes the "law of the jungle," with each person and/or group focusing on differentiating and advancing their own way of life. Competition and "survival of the fittest" become the main operating principles in the identity phase.

The ultimate purpose of life for people or societies in this phase of development is to get ahead of others and to win. In its most extreme form, this phase results in anarchy; but most often, groups and societies establish certain parameters around the exercise of personal freedom in order to prevent extremes of individualistic behavior.

Table 1 on the following page summarizes the main characteristics of the survival- and identity-based worldviews.

The historical importance of humanity moving into the Identity Phase is best recognized when compared with the limitations of the Survival Phase. Under the authoritarian mode of the survival phase, opportunities for individuals and societies to develop creatively and to employ their various capabilities were greatly limited. As societies emerge from the shackles of blind obedience, the identity phase of their development begins fostering a vigorous increase in intellectual inquiry, human and material development, and experimentation with new modes of governance. In the final stages of the identity phase, which the majority of nations are now experiencing, two issues are taking central stage in global public discourse: (1) the need for balance between unique national identities in the context of peaceful, cooperative international relations; and (2) the need for pursuit of personal and group excellence—instead of extreme and destructive competition—within the parameters of ethical principles.

The Character of Our Times

While the survival-based worldview has dominated world political and socioeconomic trends throughout most recorded history, the identity-based worldview has been dominant for the past two centuries. In the contemporary world, both these worldviews are still present and shape the political, social, religious, and economic conditions of our times. In psychological terms, the survival-based worldview corresponds to

---

13. During adolescence, physical, emotional, and mental powers begin to blossom and bring both a new level of dynamism and extremism to the life of the individual and society alike (see E.H. Erikson, *Identity: Youth and Crisis,* New York: Norton, 1968; M. Hogg, D. Terry, and K. White, "A Tale of Two Theories: A Critical Comparison of Identity Theory with Social Identity Theory," *Social Psychology Quarterly* 58(1995): 255–69; and Jay Rothman, *Resolving Identity-Based Conflict in Nations, Organizations, and Communities,* San Francisco: Jossey-Bass, 1997).

	Survival-Based Worldview	Identity-Based Worldview	
Perception	World is Dangerous	World is a Jungle	
Operating Principle	Might is Right	Survival of the Fittest	
Mode of Relationships	Dichotomous	Individualistic	
Ultimate Purpose	To Survive and Control	To Win	
Mode of Decision-Making	Authoritarian/ Absolutist	Adversarial/Relativistic	

Table 1: Worldview Types and Characteristics

the period of childhood, and the identity-based worldview corresponds to the period of adolescence.[14]

Despite certain benefits these worldviews have historically brought, it has become apparent that they are no longer adequate to advance humanity's condition further, inasmuch as progress today depends upon overcoming the conflicts and injustice that persistently divide human individuals, communities, and institutions. The survival-based and identity-based worldviews are demonstrably ineffective in solving environmental problems, economic disparities, and widespread preventable diseases—all of which transcend limited boundaries and require a global perspective. Thus, while recognizing that the basic elements of security and individual expression are indispensable to a healthy society, neither the survival- nor the identity-based worldview can create peace because both lead to limited perspectives, separation of peoples from each other, and extremes of power-struggle and competition.

14. Though sequential in theory, the development experience reflects a gradual movement between these stages, and it is thus not unusual to witness a blend of worldview traits in different aspects of a person's or institution's character.

As humanity moves beyond the phases of childhood and adolescence, a new level of consciousness, characterized by a new worldview, is gradually emerging that will be uniquely capable of meeting the challenges and opportunities of collective maturity.

Peace-Centered Worldviews

Having fully explored the potential and limits of the survival- and identity-based worldviews, humanity is now searching for an alternative approach to life and society that can better enable global peace and prosperity. We are at last beginning to recognize that it *is* within human capabilities to undertake such a new approach. A process—only partially conscious—has begun, in which all peoples and nations are thoughtfully examining the foundation of their worldviews and reorienting their basic principles towards a more inclusive concept of peace. The emergence of a third metacategory of worldview, representative of human maturity, is gradually gaining momentum.

A civilization of peace has unique political, social, ethical, and spiritual dimensions—all founded on the principle of unity. Political and social dimensions of peace have always received considerable attention, and in recent decades, moral and ethical aspects of peace have also been acknowledged and incorporated into the agenda of humanity. The ethical aspects of peace that constitute the main components of such important documents as the *Universal Declaration of Human Rights,* adopted by the United Nations in 1948, are increasingly exerting influence and contributing considerably to the slow, painful, and costly move of humanity towards creation of a civilization of peace.[15] However, even the combined political, social, legal, and ethical efforts of leaders and peoples cannot by themselves alone yield the ultimate desired result, namely, an enduring, worldwide condition of peace. Peace is a *spiritual* state with political, social, and ethical expressions. The

human spirit itself must be civilized before we can create a progressive material, social, and political civilization. Peace must first take place in human consciousness—in our thoughts, sentiments, and personal objectives. The process of spiritualization is akin to the dynamics of acculturation and takes place within the framework of formulation of our worldviews. Peace is an expression of a certain kind of worldview.

The Unity-Based Worldview

The unity-based worldview characterizes the age of maturity of humanity and is based on the fundamental issue of the consciousness of the oneness of humanity. Within the parameters of this worldview, society operates according to the principle of unity in diversity and holds as its ultimate objective the creation of a civilization of peace—equal, just, progressive, moral, diverse, and united.

The unity-based worldview entails the equal participation of women with men in the administration of human society. It rejects all forms of prejudice and segregation. It requires the application of universal ethical principles at all levels of government. It ensures that the fundamental human needs for safety, freedom, prosperity, and peace are met within the framework of the rule of law and that fundamental human rights, at both the individual and collective levels, are fully safeguarded. Finally, it is organized around a consultative and cooperative power structure that enables the legitimate exercise of

---

15. Among the most notable of these declarations are: The adoption of The Universal Declaration of Human Rights by the General Assembly of the United Nations in 1948, The Convention on the Elimination of All Forms of Discrimination against Women (Adopted by UN General Assembly 1985, Optional Protocol adopted in 1993), The Declaration and Integrated Framework on Education for Peace, Human Rights, and Democracy (Adopted by the General Conference of UNESCO in 1994), The UNESCO Manifesto 2000 for a Culture of Peace and Non-violence (1999) and United Nations Declaration and Programme of Action on a Culture of Peace (Ref. A/RES/53/243), The Dakar Framework for Action – Education for All: Meeting Our Collective Commitments (World Education Forum, Dakar, Senegal, 26–28 April 2000), and Declaration on the Elimination of Violence Against Women (UN General Assembly, 1993).

Childhood	Adolescence	Maturity	
Early Human History	18th–20th Centuries	21st Century +	**?**
Survival-Based Worldview	Identity-Based Worldview	?	

Diagram 2: Humanity's Transition Towards Maturity

---

power within a framework of unified and caring interpersonal and group relationships.

The benefits of a unity-based worldview cannot be overestimated. Simply stated, conflict always requires an enormous expenditure of energy and resources. Because both the survival- and identity-based worldviews are conflict prone, enormous waste takes place in all aspects of human life. In addition to energy and resource waste, the conflict-based worldviews also waste inestimable potential assets as citizens, institutions, and industries are deprived of opportunities to develop. Unity enables human resources to be nurtured and used more fully, creatively, and effectively. Even a unity-based society faces challenges, but these can be met in the spirit of collective cooperation and pursuit of excellence, rather than in the spirit of extreme competition and survival.

The unity-based worldview is directly related to the concept of unity that we studied previously in Unit 1. Within a unity-based worldview or paradigm, certain key principles may be derived that become the framework for our relationships and modes of organization. These include the recognition that:

- The world is one;
- Humanity is one;
- Humanity's oneness is expressed through infinite diversity (of talents, thoughts, tastes, physical characteristics, and life experiences);
- The central challenge of life is to create unity in the context of diversity;
- To successfully meet this challenge, we need to learn how to resolve conflicts in a peaceful and just manner.

We already know these principles to be true, based on scientific facts and human experience. As we become peacemakers, recognition and celebration of the oneness of humanity becomes part of our daily thoughts, feelings, and actions.

In a unity-based worldview, we recognize that the greatest challenge facing humanity is to establish its unity worldwide, while maintaining its diversity. Many societies have attempted and failed to meet this challenge. To be successful, new modes of social organization and conflict resolution are needed.

In the unity-based worldview:

- Institutions aim to achieve justice through participatory, consultative processes;
- Individuals and groups seek opportunities for growth and development;
- Human relationships are based on truthfulness, equality, and service;
- The essential oneness and wholeness of the human race is recognized, and all forms of prejudice and segregation are rejected;
- Women and men participate equally in the administration of human affairs;
- Human development and prosperity are achieved through application of universal ethical principles and processes of consultative decision-making and governance.

Table 2 summarizes the main points of each type of worldview.

Consciousness and the Process of Worldview Change

Human beings are conscious beings. This consciousness gives us the capacity to make choices and to act with freedom. This freedom is our greatest challenge, and also our greatest opportunity. The opportunity for choice comes when we begin to question our worldviews in order to evaluate our assumptions about reality, human nature, and the dynamics and purpose of life. Many people begin the process of reflection on worldview as a result of crisis and turmoil, conscious soul-searching, or intellectual curiosity.

Once we have begun to question our worldviews, we have excellent opportunities to discover, understand, and choose modes of thinking and action that are conducive to the creation of unity and to a lasting civilization of peace—a process that has considerable potential to impact the course of our personal and collective history positively.

In these early years of the 21st century, it is clear that the process of unity is accelerating. We observe expressions of ever widening circles of unity in all areas of human life. The economic and financial integration of the world economy is increasingly visible. Nations are increasingly uniting their political agendas and practices. The European Union and the more recent African Unity movements are two significant examples of movement towards creation of international unities. Environmental and health crises are constant reminders that national boundaries and racial/ethnic prejudices are arbitrary distinctions. The international efforts of the World Health Organization and other international and national agencies to deal with the HIV/AIDS epidemic and Severe Acute Respiratory Syndrome (SARS) provide good examples of unity of effort in dealing with these serious diseases. Other examples of humanity's movement toward unity are found in information technologies that have obliterated national boundaries, and in transportation systems that have reduced distances and brought people from all parts of the world face-to-face. Everything points to the fact that humanity is one and all countries are inseparable parts of one planet.[16] The gradual emergence of the unity-based worldview demonstrates that human life, society, modes of governance, ethics, and economy all flourish in the context of unity-in-diversity. The unity-based worldview maintains that the ultimate purpose of life is to establish a peaceful and prosperous world civilization based on justice and equality for all, and that this aspiration is indeed within our reach.

This vision carries forward positive elements from the survival- and identity-based worldviews, while adding new dimensions to how we view

	Survival-Based Worldview	Identity-Based Worldview	Unity-Based Worldview
Perception	World is Dangerous	World is a Jungle	World is One
Operating Principle	Might is Right	Survival of the Fittest	Unity in Diversity
Mode of Relationships	Dichotomous	Individualistic	Just and Truthful
Ultimate Purpose	To Survive and Control	To Win	To Create Unity and Peace
Mode of Decision-Making	Authoritarian/ Absolutist	Libertarian/Relativistic	Consultative/ Integrative

Table 2: Worldview Types and Characteristics [17]

16. These concepts are further discussed by H.B. Danesh in "Education for Peace: The Pedagogy of Civilization," a chapter in a book, *Sustained Peace Education for Social Cohesion in International Conflict and Post-Conflict Societies,* edited by Professors Zvi Beckerman and Claire McGlynn, scheduled for publication in 2007.

17. H.B. Danesh and R.P. Danesh, "Has Conflict Resolution Grown Up? Toward a New Model of Decision Making and Conflict Resolution," *International Journal of Peace Studies* 7.1 (2002): 59–76.

our relationships, our societies, and ourselves. Specifically, the safeguards necessary for ensuring basic human security and survival are maintained, and the boundaries needed for guiding the healthy development of individual and collective identity are protected; but the authoritarianism of the survival phase and the competitive practices of the identity phase are replaced by more mature, cooperative, and just processes of social organization and governance.

The primary challenge before individuals and communities now is to dedicate their resources, talents, and energies to the creation of ever wider circles of unity within the family, community, and society at large.

Summary

In this unit, we have learned that:

Everyone Has a Worldview

- Each person, community, and group has a worldview shaped by culture, education, family, life experiences, beliefs, media, etc.;

Worldviews Influence All Our Decisions and Actions

- Worldviews influence how people view themselves, the kind of relationships they have with others, what they consider the purpose of life to be, and what types of communities they create;

Conflict-Based Worldviews Have Predominated Throughout History

- A civilization of peace has been beyond the grasp of the global community because of the persistence of these **conflict-oriented** worldviews among individuals, groups, organizations, and leaders;
- To date, the **Survival-** and **Identity-based** worldviews have been the most prevalent, causing our societies to rely on excessive competition, conflict, and violence in order to achieve their objectives;

Peace Will Be Possible When the World Adopts a Unity-Based Worldview

- A civilization of peace is only possible when a **peace-oriented** worldview is consciously adopted and implemented;
- By developing a **Unity-Based Worldview**, we can dedicate our resources, talents, and energies to the creation of peace.

Key Questions for the Classroom

The following questions can be used to review and explore the concepts of Unit 2 with your students:

1. What is worldview?

2. Do we have control over our worldview?

3. How do we know a worldview of peace is possible?

4. Looking at the three categories of worldview, some individuals and societies appear to have a blend of worldviews. Why does this happen? What causes it?

5. Are all worldviews based on reality? How do we know? Is there a way to test the objectivity of a worldview?

6. How can we be sure that "universal" principles are truly universal? What is a measure for universality?

7. How can young people develop a unity-based worldview when adults and community leaders do not hold that worldview?

8. The media are supposed to convey news and information in a "neutral" way. We know that this is often not the case. Is it possible to have "neutral" media? Would "neutral" media constitute "peace" media? Why, or why not?

Personal Reflection

Reflection is a very powerful learning tool. It helps us to make sense of the things we are studying and the experiences we are going through. The more we reflect on ourselves, our relationships, and the world around us, the better prepared we are to discern, prioritize, and act upon issues of importance.

Becoming a peacemaker is a very important and challenging task. By reflecting on the principles of peace, we are better equipped to make decisions about our own development that will help us to confidently undertake the goal of peace building.

As we go through each of the EFP curriculum units, try to set aside some time for the process of reflection.

The following questions are provided to help you begin this process.

Questions for Personal Reflection

1. Reflections on Self

1. What is my worldview?
2. Has my worldview ever changed?
3. Where did my worldview come from?
4. Could I change my worldview if I wanted to?
5. What would I need to do?

Focus Questions

Think of something about yourself that you feel brings people together.

1. In what ways do you think you can develop this part of yourself and use it more often?
2. What other aspects of yourself would you like to develop? How could you do this?

2. Reflections on Family, Workplace, and Friendships

1. What do my mother and father tell me is the purpose of life?
2. What have been the strongest influences on my family's identity and values? (e.g., history, culture, education, religion)
3. What do I learn at school about different peoples and cultures?
4. Is my classroom a place of peace and unity? Why, or why not?

Focus Questions

Think of a disagreement that you were involved in or observed. Reflect on the different perspectives and behaviors of each person involved, and try to identify which worldview(s) shaped and influenced the disagreement most.

1. What was the result of the disagreement?
2. If the individuals involved had held a unity-based worldview, how could the situation have gone differently?
3. What solution to the disagreement do you think would have created the most unity?

3. Reflections on Society

1. What is the worldview held by the majority of my society?
2. To what extent do I agree with it?
3. Is my society oriented towards building peace?
4. Who are the individuals who hold alternative worldviews?
5. To what extent do I agree with those alternatives?

Focus Questions

The world is currently in a phase of rapid development and change. Every society is undergoing crisis or change of some kind.

1. Are there signs that my society is experiencing a change in worldview?
2. What important events have occurred in my country before, during, and/or after this period of transition?
3. Has this transition led my society closer to peace? Describe your observations.

4. Reflections on the World at Large

1. What type of worldviews do I see to be dominant in international politics, economy, culture, and media?
2. What do I see as the essential causes of conflict that are currently taking place around the world?
3. If the principles of truth and justice were to be applied to international issues, what would have to change?

Focus Question

Reflect on an aspect of an international situation you have read about, seen on TV, or heard on the radio that you think could be better dealt with using a peace-worldview.

1. What ideas could you come up with using a peace-oriented worldview to help resolve the situation?

Classroom Tools

As a teacher in the Education for Peace Program, it is now your task to introduce the discussion of worldview to your class and to assist your students in exploring the meaning of worldview and its application in their own lives and the world at large.

The more our students understand the meaning of worldview and how our worldviews can develop and transform, the more capable they will be in building an authentic and lasting culture of peace. Your role as their teacher and mentor in this process is tremendously important.

To help you get started, a number of tools that you may find useful are included in this section. These tools are only guides, and you are encouraged to develop your own ideas on how to best explore these topics with your students.

In addition to the examples here, please also refer to the Educational Methodology Unit, where you will find practical guidelines on how to make your classroom a creative and effective learning environment, as well as other great ideas from fellow teachers who are integrating Education for Peace into their various subject areas.

As you work with the Education for Peace concepts, you will surely develop new ideas for lessons, activities, and assessment approaches. We encourage you to pass along your thoughts, ideas, or resource links to Education for Peace so they can be added to our EFP Resource Bank for other teachers to use. Please send us an email at <info@efpinternational.org>, or mail your ideas to our address:

International Education for Peace Institute (Canada)
101, 1001 W. Broadway, Suite 900
Vancouver, BC V6H 4E4
Canada

We look forward to hearing from you!

Activity Ideas for Secondary Schools

Social Studies

You are a delegate to a Global Forum on the Role of Youth in Creating a Culture of Peace. There are 2,000 other delegates from every country of the world. You attend working sessions, strategy consultations, and cultural celebrations. Write a journal entry describing your impressions of the gathering, what you gained from it, and what actions you plan to take when you return home.

Art

Have students make a pair of colored glasses using construction paper and colored cellophane. Ask students to discuss how looking through colored glasses makes them feel, and how different the world looks. Students can then try on glasses made by others with different colors to compare experiences. Initiate a discussion about how we all see the world in slightly different ways, depending upon culture, beliefs and life experiences. Older students can write a story explaining how two people, who shared the same experience, actually took away different impressions from it. Younger students can draw a story or create a drama about "Magic Glasses" which change the way people interact depending upon whether or not the glasses are being worn. This could be particularly good for problem-solving scenarios in which students must find ways to create justice and unity.

Political Science

Many attribute the political motivation behind the Cold War to a clash in worldviews. Research the Reagan/Gorbachev Cold War negotiations. What worldview(s) were the two sides representing in their talks? What interests did each consider most important? Take one side and rewrite the negotiations using a unity-based worldview. Ask your teacher if you can perform this as a class skit.

Economics

A variety of approaches to economic development in poorer countries have been experimented with in the past few decades. The recent success of micro-credit schemes has begun to revolutionize what giant funding agencies like the International Monetary Fund consider "good development practice." Investigate a project in micro-credit financing and describe how this approach contributes to a shift in economic worldview.

Language Arts/ Literature

Find a short story or novel that is concerned with international or interpersonal conflict. Analyze the motivations of the main characters and compare them with the principles introduced in this unit. Suggest solutions that characters might employ to reach a different, more positive outcome.

Activity Ideas for Primary Schools

Arts

Have students make a pair of colored glasses using construction paper and colored cellophane. Ask students to discuss how looking through colored glasses makes them feel, and how different the world looks. Students can then try on glasses made by others with different colors to compare experiences. Initiate a discussion about how we all see the world in slightly different ways, depending upon culture, beliefs and life experiences. Older students can write a story explaining how two people, who shared the same experience, actually took away different impressions from it. Younger students can draw a story or create a drama about "Magic Glasses" which change the way people interact depending upon whether or not the glasses are being worn. This could be particularly good for problem-solving scenarios in which students must find ways to create justice and unity.

Drama

Using a 3-part skit format, help students to re-interpret a popular story or nursery rhyme through the perspectives of the three types of worldview described in this unit. After viewing the 3-part presentation, open a discussion with the students on the effect that worldview played in each segment.

Unit 2, Sample Lesson 1: WORLDVIEW

Focus: My Personal Worldview

Context

Every person's worldview shapes his or her thoughts, behavior, and interaction with others. Understanding the tenets of your own worldview is key to understanding where you can begin to strengthen your role as a peacemaker.

Points for Understanding

- Each person has a worldview shaped by culture, education, family, experiences, beliefs, etc. While mostly subconscious, our worldviews influence how we view both the world and ourselves, how we think and act, what kind of relationships we make with different people, and what we consider to be the purpose of our life and other people's lives.
- Many people believe that conflict is a natural, inevitable and even beneficial part of life. They do not question whether this is really a fact or simply an outcome of their choices based on their worldviews. It is not surprising then that, quite often, the information we receive or the opinions that we hear reflect a conflict-based perspective or worldview.
- If we want to foster a culture of peace in ourselves, our families, our classroom, our community and our world, we need to become conscious of our own worldviews and question any assumptions that take conflict for granted. We also need to understand and consciously practice the peace principles in our lives, relationships, studies and work.

Key Questions

1. Do we have control over our worldviews?
2. How do we know a worldview of peace is possible?
3. Looking at the three categories of worldview, some individuals and societies appear to be a blend. Why does this happen? What causes it?
4. Are all worldviews based on reality? How can we know that? Is there a way to test the objectivity of a worldview?

Learning Process

1. Write the term "Worldview" on the board and ask your students to provide words they associate with the term "worldview." Then initiate a discussion by asking students such questions as: Where do you get your worldview? Are worldviews different from person to person and at different times in your life? What comprises your worldview today?

2. Shift the conversation to the nature of worldview, first in developmental terms. Review with students some of the main types of worldview, and ask them to cite examples that they have seen in society, family, movies, etc.

3. Divide the class into small groups, ask them to identify what components they think comprise a unity-based worldview; present the components to the whole class; and foster discussion among students about peace principles in relation to examples from their daily lives and from international affairs.

Activities and Assignments

Teachers can choose from among the following sample assignments or create their own:

1. **Classwork:** Write down some of your thoughts using the following questions as a guide:
    *   What is my worldview?
    *   Where did it come from?
    *   Has my worldview ever changed?
    *   Could I change it if I wanted to?
    *   What is my purpose in life?

2. **Written Assignment:** Refer to the set of quotations included at the end of this unit. Write a 1–2 page discussion of one of these quotations, in light of the concepts introduced in Units 1 and 2.

3. **Drama:** Break students into groups of 4 or 5, and ask them to create a short play that depicts the three types of worldview. Have the students perform their plays in front of the class. Use the attitudes and scenarios in the performances to hold a classroom discussion on the concept of worldview and worldview change.

4. **Journal:** Think of something about yourself that you feel brings people together. In what ways do you think you can develop this part of yourself to bring it out more often? What other aspects of yourself would you like to develop?

Additional Resources

Activity Reading 1 – Quotations

Unit 2, Sample Lesson 2: WORLDVIEW

Focus: Worldviews Around Me

Context

Cultivating in participants an understanding of their own worldviews, combined with an appreciation for other worldviews, provides a framework for the participants to better understand themselves and the messages they receive daily from leaders and the media. It also helps them to interact with family and peers and the surrounding world with a greater degree of understanding and insight.

Points for Understanding

- Each person, community, and group has a worldview;
- The inability of the world community to create a civilization of peace now is, in part, due to the persistence of conflict-oriented worldviews among people, groups, organizations, and leaders;
- The beginning of a civilization of peace is the conscious development of a peace-based worldview.

Key questions

1. How can young people develop a unity-based worldview when adults and community leaders do not hold one?
2. Why should we strive for a common "worldview of peace" at all? Why not leave people to think and act as they choose?
3. The media is supposed to convey news and information in a "neutral" way. We know that this is often not the case. Is it possible to have "neutral" media? What would this look like? Would "neutral" media constitute "peace" media?

Learning Process

1. Building on Lesson 1, encourage students to start considering worldviews expressed in sources around them.
2. Stimulate class discussion by distributing preselected newspaper or magazine articles and having students discuss them in terms of the worldviews these materials express. Samples may include:
   - A piece of literature
   - Lyrics of a popular song
   - An article on social or political affairs

- An excerpt of historical theory
- An editorial on economic or biomedical ethics, etc.

Activities and Assignments

Teachers can choose from among the following sample assignments, or create their own:

1. **Class activity:** Write down or discuss some of your thoughts using the following questions as a guide:
   a. Generally speaking, what type of worldviews do I see demonstrated in our classrooms, communities, families, international politics, economy, culture, and/or media?
   b. What do I see as the essential causes of conflicts that are currently taking place around the world?
   c. If the principles of truth and justice were to be applied to personal, interpersonal, community, and international issues, what would have to change?

2. **Written Assignment:** Read "John Rawls and the Politics of Social Justice" for homework. At the next class, discuss the nature of John Rawls's worldview. What are the tenets of his worldview? What are the implications of such a worldview? How does this compare with the views of the students in the class?

3. **Group Project:** Have a group of students develop a proposal for a "peace media" news agency. What would be its guiding principles? What would be its professional mandate? How could it cover both "good" and "bad" news in ways that foster peace instead of conflict? In a follow-up assignment, students could be asked to investigate and report on a piece of news through the perspective of a peace-worldview.

4. **Journal:** Reflect on a personal, interpersonal, or international situation you have read about, seen on TV, or heard on the radio that you think could be better dealt with using a peace-worldview. What ideas could you come up with using a unity-based worldview to effect a change in the situation?

Additional Resources

Activity Reading 2 – "Reflections on a Mote of Dust"
Activity Reading 3 – "Wealth of Nations"

Unit 2, Activity Reading 1

Choose one of the following quotations and discuss:

"Humankind has understood history as a series of battles because, to this day, it regards conflict as the central facet of life."
—Anton Pavlovich Chekhov (1860–1904), Russian author, playwright
Complete Works and Letters in Thirty Volumes, Works, Notebook I, vol. 17, p. 7, "Nauka" (1980)

"Every man is in a state of conflict, owing to his attempt to reconcile himself and his relationship with life to his conception of harmony. This conflict makes his soul a battlefield, where the forces that wish this reconciliation fight those that do not and reject the alternative solutions they offer."
—Rebecca West (1892–1983), British author
The Strange Necessity, ch. 6 (1928)

"I am in politics because of the conflict between good and evil, and I believe that in the end good will triumph."
—Margaret Thatcher (b. 1925), British Conservative politician, former prime minister
Quoted in the *Guardian* (London, October 23, 1990)

"Struggle is the father of all things…. It is not by the principles of humanity that man lives or is able to preserve himself above the animal world, but solely by means of the most brutal struggle."
—Adolf Hitler (1889–1945), German dictator
speech, Feb. 5, 1928, Kulmbach, Germany
Quoted in Alan Bullock, *Hitler, A Study in Tyranny,* ch. 1, sec. 3 (1962)

"America is a country that seems forever to be toddler or teenager, at those two stages of human development characterized by conflict between autonomy and security."
—Anna Quindlen (b. 1952), U.S. journalist, columnist, author
Thinking Out Loud, p. 55, Random House (1993)

"Our attitude toward our own culture has recently been characterized by two qualities, braggadocio and petulance. Braggadocio—empty boasting of American power, American virtue, American know-how—has dominated our foreign relations now for some decades….Here at home—within the family, so to speak—our attitude to our culture expresses a superficially different spirit, the spirit of petulance. Never before, perhaps, has a culture been so fragmented into groups, each full of its own virtue, each annoyed and irritated at the others."
—Daniel J. Boorstin (b. 1914), U.S. historian
America and the Image of Europe, foreword (1960)

"A private should preserve a respectful attitude toward his superiors, and should seldom or never proceed so far as to offer suggestions to his general in the field."
—Mark Twain [Samuel Langhorne Clemens] (1835–1910), U.S. author. 1881
"The Benefit of Judicious Training," p. 774, *Mark Twain: Collected Tales, Sketches, Speeches, & Essays, 1852–1890,* Library of America (1992)

"From the point of view of their sameness, all things are One. He who regards things in this light does not even trouble about what reaches him through the senses of hearing and sight, but lets his mind wander in the moral harmony of things. He beholds the unity in things, and does not notice the loss of particular objects."
—Chuangtse (275 BC), Chinese mystic and humourist
Tao, p. 23

Unit 2, Activity Reading 2

"Reflections on a Mote of Dust"

by Carl Sagan

We succeeded in taking that picture [from deep space], and, if you look at it, you see a dot. That's here. That's home. That's us. On it, everyone you ever heard of, every human being who ever lived, lived out their lives. The aggregate of all our joys and sufferings, thousands of confident religions, ideologies and economic doctrines, every hunter and forager, every hero and coward, every creator and destroyer of civilizations, every king and peasant, every young couple in love, every hopeful child, every mother and father, every inventor and explorer, every teacher of morals, every corrupt politician, every superstar, every supreme leader, every saint and sinner in the history of our species, lived there on a mote of dust, suspended in a sunbeam.

The earth is a very small stage in a vast cosmic arena. Think of the rivers of blood spilled by all those generals and emperors so that in glory and in triumph they could become the momentary masters of a fraction of a dot. Think of the endless cruelties visited by the inhabitants of one corner of the dot on scarcely distinguishable inhabitants of some other corner of the dot. How frequent their misunderstandings, how eager they are to kill one another, how fervent their hatreds. Our posturing, our imagined self-importance, the delusion that we have some privileged position in the universe, are challenged by this point of pale light.

Our planet is a lonely speck in the great enveloping cosmic dark. In our obscurity in all this vastness—there is no hint that help will come from elsewhere to save us from ourselves. It is up to us. It's been said that astronomy is a humbling, and I might add, a character-building experience. To my mind, there is perhaps no better demonstration of the folly of human conceits than this distant image of our tiny world. To me, it underscores our responsibility to deal more kindly and compassionately with one another and to preserve and cherish that pale blue dot, the only home we've ever known.

—Excerpted from a commencement address delivered May 11, 1996

Unit 2, Activity Reading 3

D.C. Dispatch, *The Atlantic* (magazine) | December 10, 2002

Wealth of Nations
John Rawls and the Politics of Social Justice

Social reformers such as Rawls are in a tradition that emphasizes the best over the possible

by Clive Crook

Rawls was a radical egalitarian—more radical than he seemed to realize. In *A Theory of Justice,* his most celebrated book, he famously proposes a way to crystallize our underlying ideas about justice. Imagine that you are asked to choose the basic rules by which society will be run, but without knowing anything about your personal circumstances—how intelligent you are, what talents you have, how rich your parents are, and so on. Rawls argues that from behind this "veil of ignorance" you would choose two key principles.

   First is the liberty principle: You would insist on certain basic political and civil liberties to protect your autonomy as a person. Second is the so-called difference principle: You would want to live in a society that made improving the lot of the poor its highest priority. Why? Because the person at the bottom might turn out to be you. More precisely, Rawls argues that people stripped of self-knowledge would choose a system that, so long as it did not infringe basic political liberties, would strive to reduce inequality until cutting it any further would do such harm to the economy that the position of the poorest person would actually be worsened.

Unit 2 – Further Reading

Talking Peace but Thinking Conflict
The Challenge of Worldview in Peace Education

by Sara Clarke

Worldview shapes the way an individual or group perceives itself, others, and the world around them, and how s/he defines the principles by which relationships between the self and the world are to be conducted. As Danesh and Danesh (2002) state, "the foundation of every culture is its collective worldview." The perspectives that constitute a worldview are usually learned in the context of the family, school, culture, religious community, and the historical and political views prevalent in a given society—what Moscovici (1993) calls "social representations," and Hägglund (1999) describes as "cultural fabric":

> Normative rules for human relationships, such as trust and social concern, and qualities in societal structures, such as distribution of power and social justice, constitute elements of the cultural fabric into which a child is born. Any child in any society learns what is socially expected and accepted when interacting with others. Children also reach insights about social, political, and economic hierarchies and their meaning in relation to their own and the group's position.

Worldviews "constitute discursive complexes of norms, values, beliefs, and knowledge, adhered to various phenomena in human beings' lives" (Häggland, 1999). For the most part, we are only partially conscious of the worldviews we hold. Zanna and Rempel (1988) note, "for some attitudes, the initiation may be early in development and may therefore be unknown (unconscious) to the individual" (Van Slyck, Stern, Elbedour, 1999; see also Guerra et al., 1997).

Yet, through this powerful medium, we define our understanding of the nature of reality, the purpose of acquiring knowledge, and the purpose of human experience both individually and collectively. As Häggland (1999) explains, "…social representations are constructed, transmitted, confirmed, and reconstructed in social interactions, and they mediate social action." For example, within a conflict-oriented worldview one will be inclined to interpret reality as an arena of endless conflicts, and the purpose of knowledge as a means for gaining advantage over others, and the purpose of life as competing for survival. Bjorkqvist and Fry (1997) recognize this phenomenon and explain that in examining the causes of conflict "awareness of the impact of culture is clearly important because it allows for consideration of how individuals may be limited in their approach to conflict by culture-based beliefs and norms. Indeed, it has been argued that societies may in fact establish 'cultures of conflict', consisting of a network of scripts or schemata which provide models for dealing with conflict situations."

According to Van Slyck, Stern, and Elbedour (1999), most of the peoples of the world live with conflict-oriented worldviews, whether ethnically, religiously, or environmentally based. Tragically, as long as conflict-oriented worldviews persist, the individuals and communities that constitute our global society will continue to be burdened by conflicts resulting from choices and behaviours that stem from these worldviews. Though seeming tautological, the argument is nonetheless true, inasmuch as worldviews shape our attitudes and behaviours. Worldview, like vision, determines where we see ourselves going, what we understand to be the processes taking place around us, and how we view what our role in these processes can and should be. If our vision condemns humanity to endless cycles of violence and injustice, what opportunity do we have to act otherwise?

Creating a culture of peace is essentially the process of transforming worldviews. Transformation of worldview is a lengthy process, primarily because change requires a heightened motivation to alter one's mode of operation in life. At minimum, this process requires the following elements: (1) new knowledge—i.e., familiarization with a conceptual framework that is capable of re-ordering knowledge and experience within a unity-centered paradigm; (2) self-reflection—i.e., critical examination of one's attitudes about one's self, others, and the world—including a willingness to keep, modify, or discard accepted attitudes according to their value in relation to the standard of peace; (3) new experience—i.e., testing the reality of the principles of peace by putting them into practice.

Worldview signifies a society's understanding of the nature of civilization and the manner in which that understanding is both translated into reality and transmitted to the next generation. It is thus of critical importance that programs of peace education center, first and foremost, upon an examination of prevailing conflict-inducing worldviews and on the development of a new worldview that is capable of creating and sustaining inner, interpersonal, intergroup, and international peace. As Danesh and Danesh state: "At the core of a *culture* of peace, therefore, is the education of every succeeding generation in the nature, principles, and practices of peace."

References

Bjorkqvist, K., and D.P. Fry. (1997). "Conclusions: Alternatives to Violence." In D.P. Fry and K. Bjorkqvist, eds. *Cultural Variation in Conflict Resolution: Alternatives to Violence.* Hillsdale, NJ: Erlbaum. 243–54.

Danesh H.B., and R. Danesh. (2002). "Has Conflict Resolution Grown Up? Toward a New Model of Decision Making and Conflict Resolution." *International Journal of Peace Studies* 7(1): 59–76.

Guerra, N.G., L. Eron, L.R. Huesmann, P. Tolan, and R. Van Acker. (1997). "A Cognitive-Ecological Approach to the Prevention and Mitigation of Violence and Aggression in Inner-City Youth." In D. P. Fry and K. Bjorkqvist, eds. *Cultural Variation in Conflict Resolution:*

Alternatives to Violence. Hillsdale, NJ: Erlbaum. 199–213.

Hägglund, Solveig. (1999). "Peer Relationships and Children's Understanding of Peace and War: A Sociocultural Perspective." In Amiram Raviv, Louis Oppenheimer, and Daniel Bar-Tal, eds. *How Children Understand War and Peace*. San Francisco: Jossey-Bass. 190–207.

Moscovici, S. (1993). Introductory address given at the First International Conference on Social Representations. Ravello, Italy, 1992. *Papers on Social Representations: Threads of Discussion*, 2. 160–70.

Van Slyck, Michael R., Marilyn Stern, and Salman Elbedour. (1999). "Adolescents' Beliefs about their Conflict Behaviour." In Amiram Raviv, Louis Oppenheimer, and Daniel Bar-Tal, eds. *How Children Understand War and Peace*. San Francisco: Jossey-Bass. 208–30.

Zanna, M. P., and J.K. Rempel. (1988). "Attitudes: A New Look at an Old Concept. In D. Bar-Tal and A.W. Kruglanski, eds. *The Social Psychology of Knowledge*. Cambridge: Cambridge University Press. 315–34.

Extended Exploration

Publications

Danesh, H.B. (2006). "Towards an Integrative Theory of Peace Education." *Journal of Peace Education* 3(1): 55–78.

———. (Forthcoming)."Education for Peace: The Pedagogy of Civilization," a chapter in a book *Sustained Peace Education for Social Cohesion in International Conflict and Post-Conflict Societies.* Edited by Professors Zvi Beckerman and Claire McGlynn. Scheduled for publication in 2007.

Danesh, H.B., and R. Danesh. (2002). "Has Conflict Resolution Grown Up? Toward a New Model of Decision Making and Conflict Resolution." *International Journal of Peace Studies* 7(1): 59–76.

Erikson, E.H. (1968). *Identity: Youth and Crisis.* NewYork: Norton.

Hogg, D., and K. White. (1995). "A Tale of Two Theories: A Critical Comparison of Identity Theory with Social Identity Theory." *Social Psychology Quarterly* (58): 255–69.

Rothman, Jay. (1997). *Resolving Identity-Based Conflict in Nations, Organizations, and Communities.* San Francisco: Jossey-Bass.

Literature Reviews

Clarke, Sara. (2002). "Talking Peace, Thinking Conflict: The Challenge of Worldview in Peace Education." Landegg International University.

Web Links

"Public Broadcasting Service (PBS) TeacherSource—for K–12 lesson samples and resources for all subjects." <http://www.pbs.org/teachersource/>.

General Online Resources

The Columbia Encyclopedia Online. <http://www.bartleby.com/65>.

The Columbia World of Quotations. <http://www.bartleby.com/quotations>.

The Internet Encyclopedia of Philosophy. <http://www.utm.edu/research/iep/>.

The Merriam-Webster Online Dictionary. <http://www.merriam-webster.com>.

The Stanford Encyclopedia of Philosophy. <http://plato.stanford.edu>.

Wikipedia: The Free Encyclopedia. <http://www.wikipedia.org>

Art History Timeline: The Metropolitan Museum of Art. <http://www.metmuseum.org/toah/splash.htm>.

Unit 3

THE CONCEPT OF HUMAN NATURE

This unit surveys scientific, religious, and ideological notions of human nature; analyzes the worldviews that underlie these concepts; puts forward an integrative formulation of human nature based on current scientific, spiritual, and empirical data; and explores the relationship between human nature and peace. Finally, correlations between how human nature is viewed and how human societies function will be discussed.

Context

There are different views on the true human nature. Our view of our own nature influences our expectations of ourselves and others, and affects how we understand historical facts, use scientific data, approach the phenomenon of religion, and adopt our moral values.

There exists a strong link between our view of human nature, what we *expect* of human beings, and what human beings ultimately *become*.

This unit explores how human nature evolves and can transform from a selfish, conflict-prone state to a more universal and unity-creating condition through a comprehensive program of peace education.

Learning Process

In this unit, participants should be assisted to:

1. Understand how our common acceptance of conflict-based worldviews are related to various theories that portray human nature as essentially conflict-ridden;
2. Describe the developmental dynamics of human nature;
3. Express their own sense of self, through critical self-questioning and life-experience review;
4. Identify ways to apply their capacities to know, love, and choose to adopt unity-based and peace-oriented approaches to life and relationships.

Points for Understanding

Teachers can guide their students to understand and remember these main points:

- There is a direct relationship between our conceptual understanding of human nature and our ability to create peace;
- Many current views on human nature consider conflict, violence, and war to be natural, even necessary expressions of human life;
- These theories emerge out of various cultural, religious, and scientific traditions and are shaped by specific worldviews that are predominant at a given time and place in history;
- Human nature is an enigmatic phenomenon capable of growth, change, and transformation into a peace-creating power or instead decay, stagnation, and descent into a destructive force;
- Evidence of human creative and noble qualities can be seen in the arts, sciences, inventions, and relationships that we humans create through exploring the universe in which we live and the one we contain within ourselves;
- Human beings are at once biological, psychological, and ethical/spiritual beings, but what distinguishes us most is our main capacities to know, to love, and to choose;
- These three main capacities are subject to processes of maturation and when fully developed, yield relationships and behaviors that are reality-based, unity-creating, and peace-oriented;
- A peace-based education, in contrast to the common conflict-based approaches, is the most effective medium for development of the finest, noblest human capacities and potentialities.

Key Vocabulary

Animalistic: qualities associated with animals; a natural unrestrained, unreasoned response to physical drives or stimuli; the animal nature of human beings, chiefly referred to as physical and non-rational.[1]

Biological Determinism: the view that social or psychological phenomena, including acts of human will, are causally determined by biological factors, events, or laws.

Consciousness: the unique and distinguishing human faculty that encompasses not only rational thought but also emotional and spiritual awareness; the foundation of all human development, activity, and civilization.

Dichotomous: opposing or contradictory concepts, qualities or groups; divided into two seemingly mutually exclusive entities.

Environmental Determinism: the view that social or psychological phenomena, including acts of human will, are causally determined by environmental factors such as culture or education, political climate, and economic status.

Freedom: the self-disciplined exercise of choice.

Human Nature: that ever-present force behind universally shared human qualities—biological, psychological, social, moral, and spiritual—that shapes our basic humanness and effloresces in response to education and experience.

Love: a dynamic force of attraction that draws and binds together two or more individuals in a condition of unity and creates new entities such as marriage, family, friendship, and community.

Mechanistic: related to the doctrine that holds natural processes to be mechanically determined and capable of complete explanation by the laws of physics and chemistry; the fundamental physical or chemical processes involved in or responsible for an action, reaction, or other natural phenomenon (such as organic evolution); mechanically determined (as in a *mechanistic* universe); or relating to the doctrine of mechanism, i.e., done as if by machine; seemingly uninfluenced by the mind or emotions; automatic.[2]

Nobility: dignity, refinement, decency, goodness, righteousness.

Noble: dignified, refined, decent, good, righteous.

---

1. *Merriam-Webster Online Dictionary.*

2. *Merriam-Webster Online Dictionary.*

Prevalent Conceptions of Human Nature

For human beings, thinking precedes doing: what we **think** is the beginning of what we **do**. Nothing can happen in this world, without our first thinking about it. In other words, ideas have causal power. The more deeply held the thought, the more causal power it has to shape behavior.

Definition

Human Nature is a term used to describe the inherent set of forces that animate human biological, psychological, social, moral, and spiritual capacities. Human nature is dynamic, efflorescing in response to education and experience.

Something that we all think about at one point or another, but often take for granted, is the concept of human nature. What do we mean by "human nature"? Where do our views on human nature come from?

We first develop our views about human nature within the family. This is where we begin to observe human nature expressed through the words, deeds, and ideas of people around us. As we grow up, we learn more about human nature in the context of our culture, religion, science, ideology, and history. Gradually, we develop an understanding of human nature that reflects, primarily, the views of our own individual and community perspectives.

There is a direct relationship between our understanding of our own nature and the kind of life, society, and politics we create. As Paul Tillich observes, "Without having a picture of man, of his powers and tensions, it is impossible to make any statement about the bases of political existence and thought. Without a theory of man there can be no theory of political tendencies that

is more than the presentation of their external appearance."[3]

In searching for a universal and definitive understanding of human nature, we find that over the course of history, philosophers, leaders, writers, and scientists have presented different and often conflicting theories on the concept of human nature.

Science, for example, often rejects the validity of religion and spirituality when examining the dynamics of human nature. Consequently, scientific definitions of human nature frequently ignore many important aspects of human experience—particularly the spiritual experience—or else explain them through the lens of a materialistic framework.

Similarly, religious views on human nature often present superstitious and pessimistic theories of human nature that are devoid of scientific or rational coherence.

In this unit we will briefly review some of these approaches to human nature. As well, an integrative approach to the understanding of human nature will be considered and its significance with regard to peace discussed.

Humans as Sinful/Evil

This concept of human nature states that human beings are inherently inclined towards evil. It posits that humans are created imperfect, having been born in a condition of sin and shame with an innate tendency towards sin and error. Such a perspective maintains that human nature is relatively unchanging with only a certain limited degree of ability of human beings to better themselves by developing praiseworthy attributes and committing good deeds.[4]

3. Paul Tillich, (1936) "The Two Roots of Political Thinking" in *The Interpretation of History*, trans. Rasetzki and Talmey, New York: Charles Scribner's Sons.
4. For example, see Prof. A.I. Osipov of Moscow Theological Academy, "Why Orthodoxy is the True Faith" (2000), Meeting of the Lord School in Moscow:

Interestingly, though individuals may feel strongly that this definition accurately describes other people, they seldom feel that it describes them. This is because the notion that humans are intrinsically evil contradicts each person's sense of their own goodness, dignity, and worth. The idea that humans are intrinsically *bad,* quite frequently, undermines their motivation to develop and leads to an internal battle against a negative self-image.

A variation of the view that all humans are sinful, is the view that humanity is in fact divided into two categories: the "good" people and "bad" people. This dichotomous concept of human nature divides humanity into two camps that are often in battle with each other. "Life is a battle between good and evil," we say, "and we are the good." Again, this is a concept that stems from religious, cultural, and ideological conflict-centered worldviews. From this perspective, violent behavior can be justified if the violence is directed at a person or thing that is considered "bad." In some instances, being "bad" has been equated with being not fully human. For example, the moral endorsement of slavery was based on the argument that people of certain skin colors are less than human, are prone to evil behavior, and therefore may legitimately be forced from their homes into bondage to "civilized" or "good" people. Also in the 1930s and '40s, Hitler's regime used a similar dichotomous ideology to put millions of Jews and other "non-Aryans" into concentration camps and to conduct a program of genocide.

Indeed, throughout history, virtually all wars are legitimized using some claim of "good versus evil" or "us versus them." When humanity is divided into "us versus them" categories, unity collapses and so, consequently, do all other processes that foster life and prosperity. Conflict and violence are the most common results of this perspective.

Humans as Animals

In this view of humans as animals, it is argued that human nature is like animal nature and that life rests on following biological instincts of survival. An instinct-based view of human nature denies any claim that a higher purpose or moral reality applies to human life. Rather, everything that human beings do is argued to be the result of the biological need to survive and the urge to seek pleasure. Furthermore, some proponents of this view argue that given the power of our instinctive nature, humans either *cannot* or *need not* learn new patterns of behavior of a higher and transcendent quality.

Some variations of this view emphasize the power of biological forces in shaping our thoughts, feelings, and actions. Modern psychology was founded on the instinct-based view of human nature and continues, in great part, to explain human psychological conditions in terms of the

---

"Christianity believes that human nature in its current state is ill. Christianity affirms that the condition in which we people are born, exist, grow, are educated, take courage, mature, the state in which we find enjoyment, amusement, learning, make discoveries, etc., is a state of serious illness, bringing us profound harm. We are ill, but not with flu, bronchitis, or psychiatric illness. We are physically and psychologically well, we are capable of solving problems, and can fly into space. Nonetheless, we are gravely ill. In the beginning, unified human nature sustained a strange and tragic fracture, dividing into apparently autonomously existing and frequently warring, mind, heart, and body....If Christianity is correct, this is the root problem, the reason human life, life of the individual and of all mankind, goes from one tragedy to another. If man is seriously ill but does not try to heal the sickness because he is unaware of it, it will do him harm. Only Christianity affirms that our current state is a deeply damaged one, so damaged that no one can by himself repair it. This is the fundamental truth on which the great Christian dogma of Christ as Savior is built. This idea is the principal watershed between Christianity and the other religions."

---

conflict between primal urges for enjoyment and self-preservation, on the one hand, and learned modes of social interaction and fulfillment on the other.[5] Current considerable interest in Evolution Psychology applies the concept of "human as animal" to all aspects of human nature: biological, psychological, moral, and spiritual.

Likewise, a great proportion of anthropological and sociological studies base their conclusions (about such things as human relationships, beliefs, arts, and sciences) on principles of biological need or on comparison of human behavioral patterns with animal behavioral patterns. In this perspective, even human cultural artifacts do not indicate the presence of higher consciousness or knowledge of an authentic reality beyond material life. Rather, they represent merely functional tools for coping with the environment (survival), and maintaining social order (regulating human urges). Frans B. M. de Waal puts forward the notion that aggression is not an antisocial instinct in primates; rather, it is "a tool of competition and negotiation." His main conclusion is that human "aggressive conflict is subject to the same constraints known of cooperative animal societies" (586).[6] German ethologist Konrad Lorenz made a case in the 1960s that, extrapolating from his studies of birds and fish, humans are innately aggressive with a fondness for violence that leads to clan and tribal warfare, that free will and virtue

are illusions, that human behavior is the same as animal behavior and that humans differ from animals only in degree and with respect to certain functions.[7]

Lorenz's perspectives on human violence, like those of many other scientists, were based on an underlying assumption that humans and animals are subject to the same processes. While, on the one hand, this assumption is true in regard to the biological processes and needs, on the other hand, it is not true about human consciousness and its powers of knowledge (cognition), love (emotions), and will (choice). Nonetheless, the view that humans are fundamentally the same as animals is probably one of the most universally accepted perspectives on human nature. This perspective is at the core of Darwin's theory of evolution, which is broadly used by most scientists as the framework for understanding of almost all human behavior, including violence.

Fundamentally, this view emphasizes the overriding importance of survival as the primary objective of human life. The survival mentality argues that in an environment with limited resources, living creatures must compete with each other for access to goods in order to survive.[8] In a survival competition, the result is that some win, and some lose; if violence is necessary to ensure survival, then it is justified. This view propels most of our modern sports, our various forms of entertainment and media, as well as economic and political activities worldwide. It is a dogma that claims it is not only natural and inevitable but also right and even beneficial for humans to compete with one another and to be occupied with self-preservation and self-gratification. It treats human indulgence, conflict, and even

---

5. In Freudian psychology, it is maintained that human thoughts, feelings, and actions are determined by two powerful instincts: Eros, sexuality, and Thanatos, aggression. According to this perspective, there is no such thing as free will, and all our actions can be explained (and justified) through analysis of the conscious and primarily unconscious dynamics of our psyche. For a concise comparative review of the theories of Plato, Marx, Freud, Sartre, Skinner, and Lorenz, as well as Christianity, see Leslie Stevenson, *Seven Theories of Human Nature,* Oxford: Oxford University Press, 1974.
6. F. B. M. de Waal, *Science* 289 (2000): 586–90.

7. Konrad Lorenz, (1966) *On Aggression.* Reprinted by London: Routledge.
8. See Thomas Hobbes, *Leviathan, or the Matter, Forme, & Power of a Common-Wealth, Ecclesiasticall and Civill,* London: Andrew Crooke, 1651.

violence at best as praiseworthy, at worst as unfortunate, but almost always as inevitable. We say things like "Human nature always places people in conflict with themselves and with others. People are animals, and the name of the game is to survive."

Humans as Machines

The mechanistic view of human nature has its roots in Cartesian philosophy and Newtonian physics, as well as empiricism.[9] The perspective states that the "world is like a machine composed of parts that operate in time in space."[10] This view places great importance on factors outside of human choice that determine human behavior. These determinants may be biological (such as genetic make-up) or environmental (such as place or culture of birth).

A mechanistic view of human nature maintains that human beings are like computers: "What you put in, is what you get out." Thus, if one inherits certain genetic attributes or is born in a certain socioeconomic environment, he or she will be more likely to become aggressive or successful than another person with different genetic traits or environmental conditions. Much of modern medicine views genetic and biochemical factors as the primary determinant of *both* physical and psychological illness. Some scientists argue that human actions are controlled by a series of chemical processes triggered by electrical impulses in the brain and that all human behavioral patterns can be modified and controlled chemically.[11] For example, Richard J. Davidson and colleagues posit that "impulsive aggression and violence arise as a consequence of faulty emotion

regulation…. Individuals vulnerable to faulty regulation of negative emotion are at risk for violence and aggression." The authors then suggest that research on the neural circuitry of "emotion regulation" may show the way for prevention of human violence.[12] Thus, for example, in the fields of medicine and psychology an ever greater and all-inclusive emphasis has been placed on the development of chemical agents that will calm our anxieties, counter our sorrows, and decrease our confusion. We have also seen this view expressed in the search for genes that "cause" not only birth defects and diseases but also such conditions as

---

9. Patricia H. Miller, *Theories of Developmental Psychology*, 4th ed., New York: Worth, 2002. A.C. Crombie, *The History of Science from Augustine to Galileo*, New York: Dover, 1995.

10. Patricia H. Miller, *Theories of Developmental Psychology*, 4th ed., New York: Worth, 2002, 14–15.

11. Determinism—The belief, implicit in certain schools of psychology, that there is no free will—that is, that human and/or animal behavior is predictable to a greater or lesser degree. While the basis of the prediction (in the case of behaviorism it might be conditioned reflexes; in the case of psychodynamics it might be early psychosexual experiences) may differ, the fact of predictability remains intact. Perhaps the most common argument for determinism has its roots in a reductionist, neuroscientific view of the brain. The argument might run that each neuron in the brain is analogous to a switch in an electrical circuit, with an *on* and an *off* state. Thus the brain might be analogous to some vast project of electrical engineering. Such a project would operate in strict accordance with *physical* laws: in other words, its "behavior" (if we could still call it that) would be physically *determined*. However, this argument does not prove that the behavior of the brain is not equally "determined" by individual decisions, and by individual thought: in other words, it fails to prove that it is not the result of "free will". After all, "decisions" may be incorporated ("hard-wired" as the expression has it) *into* the functioning of the brain. To enter into this argument then is to become enmeshed in an exceedingly complex network of supposition and argument. Indeed, the arguments are so tenuous and subtle that the student is more often than not left wondering whether anything meaningful has been said at all in the debate.<http://www.psybox.com/web_dictionary/determinism1.htm>.

12. Richard J. Davidson, Katherine M. Putnam, Christine L. Larson, "Dysfunction in the Neural Circuitry of Emotion Regulation—A Possible Prelude to Violence," *Science* 289 (2000): 591.

---

loneliness, hot-temperedness, sexual frigidity, humor, and even proclivity to religion.

A biologically/environmentally deterministic approach explains negative human characteristics without appeal to moral reasoning and responsibility. It allows us to argue that some people "just can't help" but be violent, self-destructive, or deviant because their "make-up" makes this inevitable. Deterministic arguments have been used to reduce the causes of violence among certain populations (such as among minorities in the United States) to biological or cultural factors, thus ignoring the legacy of social, economic, political, and psychological damage produced by generations of institutionalized racism. And in other parts of the world, such as in the former USSR, deterministic perspectives on human nature were used to support inhumane modes of utilitarian political and economic activities.

A mechanistic or deterministic perspective on human nature considers conflict and even violence as inevitable natural aspects of human life, and as such it takes responsibility for human actions out of the hands of those who act. Yet, to live a conflict- and violence-free life, human beings have to make conscious choices to think and act differently, to strive for different goals, and to assist those around them to do so as well. A mechanistic view discounts the power of human will to make such choices despite difficult biological or environmental conditions. It thus considers the cycle of violence inevitable.

While moral perspectives on human nature portray the psyche to be caught between positive and negative impulses, materialistic science depicts the human psyche to be a by-product of the body. Within the materialistic framework, all research on human psychological conditions focuses either on the biological conditions of the body or the evolutionary explanations that consider all human psychological and behavioral processes to be the automatic and thoughtless

outcome of the interface of the organism with its environment.

An Integrative Formulation of Human Nature

Each of the above theories—humans as sinful, as animals, as machines—describes different aspects of human nature, but they fail to address all its aspects with their multiple and rich qualities. To address this fundamental shortcoming an integrated and more comprehensive definition of human nature is needed. For this purpose, we will first review the three main dimensions of human nature, as they can be empirically observed:

- *Biological Dimension*
  All human beings have biological drives that are related to issues of survival and pleasure. We need food, shelter, safety, and medical attention in order to survive and be physically healthy. And we take pleasure in the colors, scents, tastes, sounds, and textures that make our physical environment pleasing and comfortable. With respect to our biological dimension, we are indeed similar to animals.

- *Psychological Dimension*
  All human beings are emotional and thoughtful beings. Our emotions include positive feelings such as happiness, calmness, assurance, intimacy, and closeness; and negative feelings such as sadness, anxiety, fear, shame, and anger. These are feelings that we all may experience, depending on certain circumstances. Animals also experience feelings, but they are not necessarily aware of them. In contrast, humans are aware of their emotional experiences and can choose whether or not to act in response to them.

- *Moral/Ethical/Spiritual Dimension*

    All human beings have a relationship with that which we perceive as *good*. Through our experiences and guidance from our parents, teachers, and mentors, we develop systems of values, ethics, and morals, which shape the nature and quality of our decisions and actions. It is this dimension of human nature that connects us with these principles of goodness and righteousness no matter what situation we encounter. Ultimately, it is our relationship with whatever is authentically good that can guide us towards the best course of action in a given situation. Moral and ethical issues are aspects of the spiritual dimension of human nature, that dimension that gives meaning to life and makes it possible for us to transcend the biological limitations and psychological constraints of our nature. It defines our humanity.

The Capacity for Choice

While it is true that human beings share similar biological and psychological drives with animals, the capacity to choose whether or not to follow these drives is a uniquely human quality.[13] It is this capacity for choice that allows us to evaluate different factors appearing in a given situation, and on the basis of this evaluation, to choose to override our biological urges and to contain or channel our psychological tendencies. Similarly, we can choose to stand by our principles in a given situation or ignore them. It is through choice that humans express their freedom.[14]

To argue that human beings are fundamentally like animals is to argue that we consistently choose to use our psychological and moral capacities solely for survival purposes. It is true that we have witnessed this process—self- or group-survival at all costs and by any means—repeatedly throughout the history of humanity. But there are also many examples of people making choices that put other considerations before their own survival and well-being. So the argument does not hold. The act of choice remains the key to all human behavior, both positive and negative, and originates in our consciousness.

What makes humans unique and distinct beings is the nature and quality of our consciousness: our ability to know and to know that we know, our capacity to love and to know that we love, and our freedom to choose and to know that we have a choice. These three cardinal human capacities—to know, love, and will—make it possible for human beings to transcend the limits imposed by nature on all other living beings. Thus we humans become creative and free agents in the arena of life. We create arts and sciences; we design various forms of government; we choose different approaches to express our individuality and uniqueness; and we innovate particular ways to love, worship, and relate. In short, we create civilizations.

---

13. "In nature, there is a wholly unified life-process which unfolds itself without question or demand, determined by what it finds in itself and its environment. In man there is a life-process which questions itself and its environment, which therefore is not at one with itself but is divided, at the same time being within itself and confronting itself from without, thinking about itself, knowing about itself. Man has a consciousness of himself; or, expressed in relation to nature: man is the being who is dualized so that he has himself at the same time as subject and object. Nature lacks this dualization. Nevertheless man

is not—this is implied in these statements—a creature compounded of two independent parts, for example of nature and mind, or of body and soul; he is one being, but doubled within himself, in his unity" Paul Tillich, "The Interpretation of History" (1933) Available online: <http://www.religion-online.org/cgi-bin/relsearchd.dll/showchapter?chapter_id=50>.

14. Many different and incompatible concepts of freedom exist. The most common understanding of freedom today is a notion of liberty, license, or absence of restraints, particularly on choice and behavior. The

---

Unique Capacities of Human Consciousness

Human consciousness is distinguished by three unique capacities or powers:[15]

- The capacity **to know** (i.e., to search for, recognize, understand, and communicate **truth**);
- The capacity **to love** (i.e., to create **unity** by giving to, receiving from, and including others universally);
- The capacity **to will/choose** (i.e., to make decisions that are **just** and to willingly be of **service** to others).

Knowledge

We acquire knowledge through life experience, intellectual pursuits, self-reflection, meditation, and prayer. Our reservoir of knowledge is made up of rational and logical, intuitive and creative, spiritual and divine forms of knowing. The rational and logical apply to the realm of science and are particularly important in our understanding of the laws governing the physical world as well as, for example, the purely medical, legal, and economic aspects of our personal and social lives. Intuitive and creative knowledge is especially suited to the development of the arts and the refinement of human relationships. Spiritual and divine forms of knowing give purpose and meaning to our lives and provide us with insight into good and evil. Both spiritual and scientific forms of knowing must have rational and logical as well as intuitive

and creative properties. Absence of rational and logical principles in science creates pseudosciences, and when religion is devoid of rational and logical explanations, it is mere superstition.

In general, as we mature, we understand more. Our self-knowledge, combined with our knowledge of the world, help us form our approach to life. If, however, for any reason our views about ourselves, our world and reality are inadequate or incorrect, then we are faced with a disorder of knowledge, and our life becomes burdened with misconceptions, fears, and anxieties. Another fundamental disorder of knowledge emerges when we think that we possess absolute and ultimate knowledge of reality. If this disorder of knowledge existed in science, scientific development would cease. There would be no new discoveries or breakthroughs in knowledge. And when absolutism is applied to religion, it creates fanaticism and its integrity is undermined.

Love

Love is an active force of attraction to beauty, unity, and growth. We human beings are continuously attracted to whatever we perceive to be beautiful; to cause closeness, intimacy, and unity; and to nurture our growth and development. Unfortunately, as our perceptions are not always accurate, we also become attracted to individuals, conditions, or ideas that are not beautiful, that cause disunity or inhibit growth. The *quality of our love* is closely related to the *quality of the **object*** of our love.

Merriam-Webster Online Dictionary states, "freedom has a broad range of application from total absence of restraint to merely a sense of not being unduly hampered or frustrated, e.g., "freedom of the press." Liberty suggests release from former restraint or compulsion, e.g., "the released prisoner had difficulty adjusting to his new liberty." License implies freedom specially granted or conceded and may connote an abuse of freedom, e.g., "freedom without responsibility may degenerate into

license" <http://www.merriam-webster.com>. Education for Peace looks at human freedom in a different light, defining it as "the self-disciplined exercise of choice." See this unit for more discussion.

15. For a full treatment on the human capacities of knowledge, love, and will, and their expression under both healthy and pathological conditions, see H.B. Danesh's *The Psychology of Spirituality*, Hong Kong: Juxta Publishing, 1997.

For example, some people fall in love with war. Whether out of a sense of righteousness or duty, some people choose war as an object of their love. They do so because they perceive war to have an intrinsic beauty, to be a cause of harmony, and to foster progress. These sentiments are usually expressed in glorification of war, portrayal of warriors as handsome figures, admiration of beautifully crafted uniforms and military instruments, and fascination with military strategies. Much of the literature of bygone ages glorifies war and describes its beauty. There is also much rhetoric about the value of war, how it safeguards cultures and civilizations, brings people together, and causes a higher level of harmonious and unified patriotism. Lovers of war also claim that war is the cause of growth and development because it adds to scientific knowledge and technology, helps sluggish economies, and allows for the victory of good over evil.

It is a demonstrable fact, however, that wars are anything but beautiful, unifying, or life-enhancing. While there are some limited and just wars, even those, however necessary they may have been, nevertheless brought with them much ugliness, disunity, and destruction, and left legacies of damage for decades even centuries. Yet despite these facts, much of humanity continues to be enamored with war. To the thoughtful person, however, war and love are totally irreconcilable.

Will

Human will refers to our freedom to choose between good and evil and between action and inaction. Through our capacity of will, we also determine the direction and quality of our lives. Our will gives us motivation and the courage to act, and the means to be creative. The signs of human will are present from the earliest days of life. As with our capacities of knowledge and love, the human will can be either abused or used creatively to improve the quality of life. Many people are afraid to use their will and may abuse

or abdicate it altogether. When we are afraid to make a choice, we tend to blame someone else for our experiences, such as our neighbors, our enemies, or God. We abuse our will by committing destructive acts, and we abdicate our will by refusing to act when action is needed.

Most of our difficulties in life are related to the abuse of or discordance among our capacities of knowledge, love, and will. The secret for avoiding anxiety and stress is to achieve inner peace, which can only be achieved when we use these three capacities in a united, creative, life-endowing, growth-inducing, and universal manner. [16]

The human capacities of knowledge, love, and will develop over the course of our lifetimes, gaining strength and breadth. A closer look at the processes of human development both individually and collectively will be taken in the next unit, entitled "The Developmental Model of Human Civilization." Essentially, however, all living beings develop: development is an inherent and inevitable aspect of being alive. In human life, the capacities to know, to love, and to choose develop over time, as we gain greater experience and reflect on our experience consciously. When these capacities remain undeveloped or develop in an unhealthy way, life becomes characterized by ignorance, dishonesty, conflict, self-centeredness, prejudice, and injustice. In contrast, when we mature in a healthy manner, our capacity to know and understand truth becomes farther-reaching and more insightful; our capacity to love becomes more universal and unifying; and our capacity to choose becomes a powerful instrument to serve the cause of justice and to be of service to others. When incomplete, our powers become the tools of conflict, violence, and injustice. When complete, these same abilities are used in the service of unity and truth. These capacities represent the hallmark of our consciousness and

16. The above descriptions of knowledge, love, and will are extracted from H.B. Danesh, *The Psychology of Spirituality*, beginning p. 67.

are inseparable aspects of our human nature.[17] The healthy development of these human capacities lays the natural foundation for relationships and choices that are reality based, peace oriented, and unity creating.

Humans as Noble Beings

Due consideration of the biological, psychological, and spiritual dimensions of human nature opens the door to an integrated and comprehensive formulation of our nature. This new formulation recognizes that:

1. **Human nature is developmental**, meaning that over the course of our lifetimes, our capacities to know, to love, and to choose grow and mature, and we become ever more capable of building relationships and communities characterized by unity, peace, and justice.

2. **Human nature is noble**, meaning that all human beings are born with the natural potential and desire to live a positive and fruitful life, and that there are attributes within each person that inherently merit dignity and respect.

Evidence of human nobility can be seen in all the arts, sciences, inventions, and relationships that humans create through exploring the universe and themselves. And since humanity is one, all people have the potential to develop their inherent nobility—regardless of nation, race, culture, lifestyle, political or economic situation.

The integrative formulation of human nature has two significant implications: first, it suggests that peace is not only possible but also in fact inevitable. Second, it helps us understand that our histories of conflict, violence, and war are the expressions of earlier stages of development in human collective life. We will discuss the concept of collective human development in the next unit.

---

17. For more on this subject, refer to *The Psychology of Spirituality* by H. Danesh. See also *Fever in the World of the Mind* by H. Danesh for an examination of both healthy and unhealthy formation of these capacities.

Summary

In this unit, we have learned that:

Many Views on Human Nature are Conflict-Based

- Shaped by certain religious, cultural, and scientific worldviews, some views on human nature consider conflict, competition, and violence to be natural and even necessary expressions of human life.

In Reality, Humans are Biological, Psychological, and Spiritual Beings

- An integrative perspective on human nature recognizes that humans are simultaneously biological, psychological, ethical, and spiritual beings.

Human Capacities are Continually Developing

- Our unique capacities—to know, to love, and to choose—distinguish us from other creatures and develop over the course of our lifetimes. The more developed and advanced our capacities are, the more our attitudes and behaviors are characterized by truth, justice, and unity.

Humans Have the Capacity to Create a Civilization of Peace

- Human nature is essentially a noble reality subject to the processes of growth and creativity. The noblest creative impulse of humanity is the creation of a civilization of peace.

Key Questions for the Classroom

The following questions can be used to review and explore further the concepts of Unit 3 on Human Nature with your students:

1. If human nature is inherently noble, why do we have so many wars and so much corruption and violence?

2. What kind of worldview and education is conducive to the healthy and integrated development of human nature?

3. Is it possible to harmonize the biological, psychological, and spiritual dimensions of human nature without neglecting or rejecting any one of them?

4. What is "nobility" in the context of human development? How can nobility be recognized?

5. How can noble aspects of human nature effloresce in spite of conditions of untruth, disunity, and injustice?

6. Many societies are primarily concerned with issues of safety and economy. What notion of human nature does this reflect?

7. If life is *not* a battle between good and evil, why do we have to struggle against so much hatred, negativity, selfishness, and violence? Where do these things come from?

Personal Reflection

Reflection is a very powerful learning tool. It helps us to make sense of the things we are studying, and the experiences we are going through. The more we reflect on ourselves, our relationships and the world around us, the better prepared we are to discern, prioritize, and act upon issues of importance.

Becoming a peacemaker is a very important and challenging task. By reflecting on the principles of peace, we are better equipped to make decisions about our own development, which will help us to confidently undertake the goal of peace building.

As we go through each of the EFP Curriculum units, try to set aside some time for the process of reflection.

The following questions are provided to help you begin this process.

Questions for Personal Reflection

1. Reflections on Self

1. What is my concept of human nature? What influences have shaped it?
2. What do I believe is the purpose of life?
3. Have I ever felt violent? What factors contributed to this feeling? How did I deal with it?

Focus Task

Think of an important endeavour you have undertaken in your life. Describe your thought process and feelings before, during, and after this action.

2. Reflections on Family, Workplace, and Friendships

1. What assumptions do my parents and/or siblings make about human nature? How do my own beliefs differ from these? In what ways are they similar?
2. In my family, which of the three human capacities (knowledge, love, and will) have been emphasized and fostered?
3. How has my formal education nurtured these capacities in me?
4. What morals and ethics have been taught in my family?

Focus Task

Think of a disagreement in which you were involved or which you observed. Reflect on the different perspectives and behaviors of each person involved and try to identify which views of human nature were being displayed.

3. Reflections on Society

1. Is it possible for society to increase its capacity for love? What would this require in my society?
2. How does my society treat those deemed as "different" or "bad"? What does being "bad" mean in this case, and is this considered natural?
3. How can my society change its views on human nature? Can religion play a role?

Focus Question

It has been said that people perform up to standards expected of them. Do you think this is true on the societal level, and, if so, what would be the highest accomplishment of a loving and considerate society?

4. Reflections on the World at Large

1. How has our understanding of human nature evolved over the course of history?
2. Is there such a thing as universal ethics and moral values that are applicable to all the peoples of the world?
3. What level of maturity is required for adoption and implementation of ethics of truthfulness, unity in diversity, justice and service in a given society? Can you identify one or more examples of such a society in our world today? In the course of history?

Focus Task

Identify one event in the recent decade that required and received successful collective action on the part of societies around the world and that depicted some elements of the Integrative Model of Human Nature. Describe the thoughts, feelings, and actions that took place.

Classroom Tools

As a teacher in the Education for Peace Program, it is now your task to introduce discussion about human nature to your class and assist your students in exploring the meaning of human nature and its application in their own lives and in the world at large.

The more our students understand that, by their very nature, humans are developing and are inherently noble, the more capable they will be in building an authentic and lasting culture of peace. Your role as their teacher and mentor in this process is tremendously important.

To help you get started, a number of tools are included in this section that you may find useful. These tools are only guides, and you are encouraged to develop your own ideas about how to best explore these topics with your students.

In addition to the examples here, please also refer to the Educational Methodology Unit, where you will find practical guidelines on how to make your classroom a creative and effective learning environment, as well as other great ideas from fellow teachers who are integrating Education for Peace into their various subject areas.

As you work with the Education for Peace concepts, you will surely develop new ideas for lessons, activities, and assessment approaches. We encourage you to pass along your thoughts, ideas, or resource links to Education for Peace so they can be added to our EFP Resource Bank for other teachers to use. Please send us an email at <info@efpinternational.org>, or mail your ideas to our address:

International Education for Peace Institute (Canada)
101, 1001 W. Broadway, Suite 900
Vancouver, BC V6H 4E4
Canada

We look forward to hearing from you!

Activity Ideas for Secondary Schools

Biology/ Philosophy	Imagine you could argue against Konrad Lorenz or Thomas Hobbes and their theories that humans are like animals or machines with a love for and natural inclination to violence. What would you say? Draw on your understandings from Unit 2 on Worldview and Unit 3 on Human Nature.
Philosophy/Art/ Social Studies	Divide the class into three groups and ask each group to discuss one of the following quotations. Ask each group to then present and share their findings with the rest of the class.

"Ethics is a code of values which guide our choices and actions and determine the purpose and course of our lives."

—Ayn Rand

"That which is beautiful is moral. That is all, nothing more."

— Gustave Flaubert

"Without civic morality communities perish; without personal morality their survival has no value."

— Bertrand Russell

History	Think of two people in your community who, in your estimation, have led noble lives. Offer a brief biography of their lives and describe what they have contributed to their community through the use of their capacities. One of these figures should be from your community, while the second figure should not.
Biology	In biological studies we observe both the phenomenon of "the survival of the fittest" and the dynamics of co-dependence/interdependence among all living organisms. In small groups, discuss how these two processes have been emphasized or de-emphasized in the Darwinian theory of evolution.
Art	Go online and research pre-Renaissance art. How is the concept of evil depicted in these works? In what context do sin and evil appear? Where does human will figure in? Compare and contrast two major works from two different artists.

Philosophy	Form discussion groups and explore the meaning of the word *natural*. What do people mean when they say, "That's just his/her nature"? In your society, what is deemed as 'natural'? What is 'unnatural,' and in what ways do we hinder our capacities from growing when we think in these dichotomous terms?
Literature/History	Create your own "Ring of Nobility" by making a collage of heroic figures you believe have demonstrated the qualities and characteristics of human nobility through their thoughts, sentiments, and actions, and have reflected in their life and work an integrative model of human nature.
Social Studies	My Epistemology Chart: Track your own history of knowledge. How do you know what you know? How does what you know change as you grow? Is there such a thing as "absolute truth"? Make sure you refer to your family, school, religious institution, society, and media. Use pictures.
Social Studies/ Psychology	The two following quotations place importance on one of three human capacities—will. Do you agree or disagree with these statements? Describe why?

"All that is necessary for evil to triumph is for good men to do nothing."

— Edmund Burke

"The sad truth is that most evil is done by people who never make up their minds to be good or evil."

— Hannah Arendt

Activity Ideas for Primary Schools

Language Arts   Read the book *Where the Wild Things Are* by Maurice Sendak. After reading the story, ask the students if they think that Max is a bad person. (Or find a suitable story in which the main character gets into trouble and is shown love and understanding by a family member or friend.) Then ask them to think of a time that they were naughty or got into trouble for something they did wrong. Did that make them a bad person? What makes a person a good person? Have the students break into pairs and write a story about all of the good things they see in their friend and why they are a good friend.

Social Studies   Draw a chart on the board divided into three columns with the words *love, know,* and *do* in each of the columns. Ask each child to write in each of the columns things/people that they love, what they know, and what they can do. Have the children share and compare each of the charts and identify areas that are similar. Students can then discuss if there are similarities throughout the school, their community, the world in each of these areas.

Drama   Ask the students to create a play about a person having a bad day describing how they treat either their friends or families when they were upset, angry, or frustrated. Ask the students to conclude with a way that the bad day was overcome in a positive way instead of through violent action.

Unit 3, Sample Lesson 1: HUMAN NATURE

Focus: Influential Perspectives on Human Nature

Context

There are many influential views on the true nature of the human being. Philosophers, leaders, writers, and scientists of all kinds have presented a variety of theories on human nature—some of which claim that conflict and violence are natural in humans, others of which say exactly the opposite. These theories raise certain questions: Why has humanity thought about itself in these ways? And, what impact have these different views had on human civilization?

Points for Understanding

- There is a direct relationship between our conceptual understanding of human nature and our ability to create peace;
- Many influential views on human nature consider conflict, violence, and war to be natural, even necessary expressions of human life;
- These views emerged out of various cultural, religious, and scientific traditions that were shaped by the then prevalent worldviews;
- When we understand human beings to be biological, psychological, and spiritual beings who undergo continuous processes of development, then we can see that human beings have much greater capacities to live peacefully than these theories acknowledge.

Key Questions

1. Where and how do views on human nature develop?
2. If life is not a battle between good and evil, why do we have to struggle against so much hatred, negativity, selfishness, and violence?

Learning Process

1. Introduce students to the concept of human nature by relating to them the English proverb "From little acorns mighty oaks grow." Ask students what conditions pre-existed, and what conditions were necessary in order for the tree to emerge from the acorn. Relate the analogy of the acorn to a newborn baby. Ask students to tell what potential they believe is in the baby, and what conditions are necessary in order for a "fully realized human" to emerge. Jot down projections, questions, and qualifications that students include in their answers. Set aside for later reference.
2. Define the term "human nature" and guide students through the following three notions of human nature found in this EFP Unit: sinful, animalistic, and mechanistic.

3. Ask students to share their thoughts on why these ideas emerged; whether they know of any other views on human nature; and what their own views on human nature are.

4. Have students write in their journals for 5 minutes each on the following two questions (prompt their thought process with one question at a time): (1) If I were *not* a human being, I couldn't…(identify at least 10 things); (2) Human nature is…(identify at least 5 things).

5. Have students volunteer to share some of their answers.

6. Close the class with a questions and discussion period, and follow-up with one of the homework assignments.

Activities and Assignments

Teachers can choose from among the following sample assignments or create their own:

1. **Group activity**: Have students divide into four groups, each representing one view on human nature: (A) sinful, (B) animalistic, (C) mechanistic, (D) integrative. Present the following scenario to all: You are part of a small community comprising four distinct subpopulations (the *A*'s, *B*'s, *C*'s and *D*'s). You live alongside each other in a region where the climate is difficult and the available necessities of life are minimal. Current food production cannot adequately feed all community members. What will the people in this community do? What can they do? Have each group discuss the issues from their assigned perspectives. Bring the groups back together to present their conclusions. Ask students to share their own feelings and thoughts about these projected outcomes.

2. **Essay:** Consider the following view: "Human beings are animals; animals live according to the instinct of survival. Everything that human beings do is to ensure their survival. Because we live in a world with limited resources, there is a constant competition for survival. Because of that, violence is going to be with us always. It is inevitable." Question: What does this concept reveal about the speaker's worldview and understanding of human nature? Discuss the limitations of this view in terms of what you know about other human capacities. What positive qualities of human nature does this view overlook?

Additional Resources

Activity Reading 1.

Unit 3, Sample Lesson 2: HUMAN NATURE

Focus: A Noble Human Nature

Context

When we take time to reflect on the nobility of human nature, we can gain confidence in our abilities to discover reality, to love universally, to celebrate the rich diversity of humanity, and to choose unity-based and peace-oriented approaches to life and relationships.

Points for Understanding

- Humans are physical, psychological, and spiritual beings;
- Human nature is both noble and developmental;
- Our nobility increases the more we draw upon universal ethical/spiritual principles to guide how we develop and how we use our physical and psychological capacities;
- The more we develop our inherent nobility, the more peaceful our friendships, families, communities, workplaces, and societies become.

Key Questions

1. What is "nobility" in the context of human development? How can nobility be recognized?
2. How can someone develop their "nobility" when conditions in the environment are materialistic, competitive, immoral, and violent?
3. Is it possible to harmonize the biological, psychological, and spiritual dimensions of human nature without neglecting or rejecting any one of them?

Learning Process

1. Review briefly with students the four views of human nature discussed in this unit, concluding with the integrative/developmental model.
2. Ask students to look up definitions for "nobility" or "noble" and share with the class. Select definition pertaining to actions of "high quality," "dignity," "excellence," and "exalted moral character."
3. Recognizing that humans are physical, psychological, and spiritual beings, ask students to consider what the noblest expressions of these various aspects of human nature could be. Try to evoke concrete ideas from which principles can be extracted—note ideas on the board.
4. Ask students if they can think of any individuals—historic or contemporary—who demonstrated noble principles in action, and have them explain their examples.

5. Drawing on these examples, summarize how the human capacities of knowledge, love, and will mature as we undergo development in accord with universal ethical principles.

6. Conclude the class with a journal-writing exercise in which students reflect on the concept of nobility in the context of their own lives.

Activities and Assignments

Teachers can choose from among the following sample assignments or create their own:

1. **Journal:** Some people say that if a person is left alone from birth, he or she will be no different from an animal; others say that if a person is left alone, he or she would be better than people today, as he or she would not be corrupted by the forces of society. Question: What are your views on this statement? How does the concept of human nobility respond to this debate?

2. **Class Discussion:** Divide the class in small groups. Have each group select one of the quotations included at the end of this unit. Discuss for 15 minutes in light of the concepts introduced in Unit 3 on Human Nature. Regroup and share conclusions.

3. **Reading:** Read the piece entitled "Yang Zhu and the Concept of Human Nature" included at the end of this unit, and answer the following questions:
   a. What was the worldview of Yang Zhu? What was the worldview of Mencius?
   b. In what ways did Yang Zhu's and Mencius's views on human nature differ?
   c. In your opinion, do ethical virtues develop by living life alone or with other people?

Additional Resources

Activity Reading 2.

Unit 3, Sample Lesson 2 – Activity Reading 1

Choose one of the following quotations and discuss:

"Human nature is a scoundrel's favorite explanation."
—Mason Cooley (b. 1927), U.S. aphorist
City Aphorisms, Seventh Selection, New York (1990)

"The only thing that one really knows about human nature is that it changes. Change is the one quality we can predicate of it. The systems that fail are those that rely on the permanency of human nature, and not on its growth and development."
—Oscar Wilde (1854–1900), Anglo-Irish playwright, author
"The Soul of Man Under Socialism," *Fortnightly Review* (London, February 1891, repr. 1895)

"There is a very remarkable inclination in human nature to bestow on external objects the same emotions which it observes in itself, and to find everywhere those ideas which are most present to it."
—David Hume (1711–1776), Scottish philosopher
A Treatise of Human Nature, bk. 1, part 4, sect. 3, p. 224, ed. P. Nidditch, 2nd edition
New York: Oxford University Press (1978)

"It is human nature to hate the man whom you have hurt."
—Tacitus (c. 55–c. 120), Roman historian
Agricola, sec. 42

"The principle that human nature, in its psychological aspects, is nothing more than a product of history and given social relation, removes all barriers to coercion and manipulation by the powerful."
—Noam Chomsky (b. 1928), U.S. linguist, political analyst
Reflections on Language, ch. 3 (1976)

"An indiscriminate distrust of human nature is the worst consequence of a miserable condition, whether brought about by innocence or guilt. And though want of suspicion more than want of sense, sometimes leads a man into harm; yet too much suspicion is as bad as too little sense."
—Herman Melville (1819–1891), U.S. author
in *Israel Potter* (1855), ch. 7, *The Writings of Herman Melville*, vol. 8
ed. Harrison Hayford, Hershel Parker, and G. Thomas Tanselle (1982)

"Regard man as a mine rich in gems of inestimable value. Education can, alone, cause it to reveal its treasures, and enable mankind to benefit therefrom."
—Bahá'u'lláh (1819–1892), Persian philosopher
Gleanings from the Writings of Bahá'u'lláh, p. 260

"To prefer evil to good is not in human nature; and when a man is compelled to choose one of two evils, no one will choose the greater when he might have the less."

—Plato (c. 427–347 BC), Greek philosopher
Protagoras, c.358

"The white man regards the universe as a gigantic machine hurtling through time and space to its final destruction: individuals in it are but tiny organisms with private lives that lead to private deaths: personal power, success and fame are the absolute measures of values, the things to live for. This outlook on life divides the universe into a host of individual little entities which cannot help being in constant conflict thereby hastening the approach of the hour of their final destruction."

—Policy statement, 1944, of the Youth League of the African National Congress
pt. 2, ch. 4, qtd. in Fatima Meer, *Higher than Hope* (1988)

"It is possible so to adjust oneself to the practice of nobility that its atmosphere surrounds and colors every act. When actions are habitually and conscientiously adjusted to noble standards, with no thought of the words that might herald them, then nobility becomes the accent of life."

— 'Abdu'l-Bahá Abbas (1844–1921), Persian philosopher, humanitarian
Bahá'í Scriptures, Selections from the Utterances of Bahá'u'lláh and 'Abdu'l-Bahá (1928)

Unit 3, Sample Lesson 2 – Activity Reading 2

Yang Zhu and the Concept of Human Nature

Yang Zhu was a fourth century B.C.E. contemporary of Mencius who engendered great antipathy in this Confucian thinker for suggesting that the basic tendencies of human nature were not what we might call 'other-regarding.' Mencius condemned Yang for being so egotistical as to be unwilling to sacrifice even a single hair in order to benefit the state (Mencius 7A26; Lau, p. 275). However if we are to base our understanding of Yang's doctrines on these two surviving sources, a much more complex and interesting picture of his philosophy emerges.

Yang Zhu may have been the first Chinese philosopher to speak of the concept of human nature (*xing*), and the parameters for all early Chinese discussions of this concept seem to have been established by Yang and Mencius. In brief, human nature is given to us by Heaven, the power responsible for everything in life beyond human control. The early Chinese conceived of two major aspects of our lives that fall into this category: *ming* (fate, destiny), the various things that occur as the result of agencies other than ourselves and *xing* (nature), the sum total of our genetic inheritance both as a species and as unique individual members of it. According to Graham and Ames, human nature in early China is conceived as totally dynamic, in contrast to the implicit static basis of human nature we find in the West (Graham 1967, Ames 1991). The Chinese concept of human nature can be best understood as referring to the spontaneous tendencies that an individual has from birth that govern its development as a particular individual within a species and which also act as forces in its daily life. Thus this concept implies both the potential to develop in a certain way and the spontaneous tendencies for this development and for certain characteristic types of activities. We might call the former tendencies 'genetic' and the latter tendencies 'instinctive.' Mencius argued that the essential goodness of human nature rested in the spontaneous tendencies to act selflessly and respectfully, tendencies that persist throughout the lifetime of an individual even if left undeveloped. In other words, it is a basic human instinct to act selflessly. For him the purpose of self-cultivation was to nurture these spontaneous instinctive tendencies until they blossomed into complete ethical virtues. The Yangist challenge to the social emphasis of the Confucians consisted in the primacy they placed on the maintenance of the individual life and the fact that they supported this mode of living with the theory that to act in this fashion was to nourish the nature that we receive from Heaven. Since Confucians placed a high value on the sanctions and approvals of Heaven, it was incumbent upon them to argue for a different vision of human nature.

—Excerpted from "Zhuangzi: The Yangist Chapters," *Stanford Encyclopedia of Philosophy*
<http://plato.stanford.edu/entries/zhuangzi/>

Extended Exploration

Publications

Crombie, A.C. (1995). *The History of Science from Augustine to Galileo.* New York: Dover.

Danesh, H.B. (2006). *Fever in the World of the Mind: Unique Dimensions of Human Conflict and Violence.* Vancouver: EFP-International Publications.

————. (1997). *The Psychology of Spirituality: From Divided Self to Integrated Self.* 2d ed. Hong Kong: Juxta Publishing.

Hobbes, Thomas. (1651). *Leviathan, or the Matter, Forme, & Power of a Common-Wealth, Ecclesiasticall and Civill.* London: Andrew Crooke.

Lorenz, Konrad. (1966). *On Aggression.* Originally published 1963. Reprint, London: Routledge.

Miller, Patricia H. (2002). *Theories of Developmental Psychology.* 4th ed. New York: Worth.

Tillich, Paul. (1936). "The Two Roots of Political Thinking." In *The Interpretation of History.* Trans. Rasetzki and Talmey. New York: Charles Scribner's Sons. Available online: <http://www.religion-online.org/cgi-bin/relsearchd.dll/showchapter?chapter_id=50>.

Web Links

"Public Broadcasting Service (PBS) TeacherSource – for K-12 lesson samples and resources for all subject." <http://www.pbs.org/teachersource/>.

General Online Resources

The Columbia Encyclopedia Online. <http://www.bartleby.com/65>.

The Columbia World of Quotations. <http://www.bartleby.com/quotations>.

The Merriam-Webster Online Dictionary. <http://www.merriam-webster.com>.

The Stanford Encyclopedia of Philosophy. <http://plato.stanford.edu>.

Wikipedia: The Free Encyclopedia. <http://www.wikipedia.org>.

Art History Timeline: The Metropolitan Museum of Art. <http://www.metmuseum.org/toah/splash.htm>.

Unit 4

The Nature and Dynamics of Violence

In order to become better at putting the principles of peace into action, it is necessary to understand the psychological dynamics of conflict and violence in the context of life challenges and opportunities. In life, we face many challenges, some of which are experienced either as threats or opportunities, depending on the magnitude of the challenge. Opportunities are presented to us as chances to grow and to be creative. Threats can cause us to enter the path of conflict, leading towards violence. Violence is a destructive process expressed in words, attitudes, and/or behaviors. It is the culminating act in a series of psychological stages beginning with a fundamental inner conflict or absence of unity. This unit explains what happens when people become conflicted and violent, and helps students understand that conflict and violence result from a series of choices that are influenced by our worldviews. As such, conflict and violence are not random events and can, in fact, be prevented.

Context

Before making peace our goal, we must answer a fundamental question: Are humans by nature violent? If our answer is affirmative and if we accept that violence is an inevitable and unavoidable aspect of being human, then we are doomed to a violent life, and the best we can do is to regulate that violence to the extent possible. However, if we maintain that humans are not fundamentally violent by nature, then there is hope for peace, and it is imperative that we make every effort to understand the causes of our past and present violence. Unfortunately, while there is considerable agreement about the existence of violence and its undesirability, there is far less consensus about what causes violence and even less on how to deal with violence.

Our objective in this unit is to demonstrate that creating societies and living lives that are considerably free from violence is indeed within our powers. However, to accomplish this task we need to alter our understanding of the nature, causes, and dynamics of violence. When these processes are better understood, we can transform our attitude toward issues of conflict and violence, and lay the foundations for conflict- and violence-free environments—in ourselves, in our homes, and in our communities.

Learning Objectives

In this unit, participants should be assisted to:

1. Understand the basic psychological processes that underlie human violence, including responses to life threats and opportunities.
2. Discuss the characteristics of violent environments and analyze the nature and dynamics of unhealthy responses to life challenges.
3. Reflect on their own psychological responses to life challenges, threats, and opportunities, and consider how they can strengthen their inner resources to deal with these experiences without resorting to thoughts, feelings, and acts of violence.
4. Identify and implement strategies for home, school, and community to become nonviolent, nonthreatening environments.

Points for Understanding

Teachers should help their students to understand and remember these main points:

- Violence is a process that begins in the mind and that expresses itself in our thoughts, feelings, and actions.
- There are five stages in the evolution of violence before an act of violence actually takes place.
- Effective violence prevention recognizes the earliest signs and causes of this violence-cycle, and concentrates efforts on creating safe, encouraging, and nonthreatening environments so that the cycle of violence is counteracted before reaching the point of manifest actions.
- Human tendencies to think, feel, and act in ways that produce violence greatly increase when we hold conflict-based worldviews.
- Central to effective resolution and prevention of conflict and violence is understanding our worldview, modifying our conflict-based attitudes, and learning about the psychological and social dynamics of building unity.

- A "conflict-free" approach to resolving conflict and violence means that we:
  1. examine the underlying causes of conflicted thoughts, feelings, and choices within ourselves;
  2. proactively work to transform those conflict-based internal processes; and
  3. establish safe and nonthreatening environmental conditions in order to establish unity and create peace.
- Such an approach is needed in our homes, schools, and communities, and must be practiced simultaneously by individuals, groups, institutions, and governments in order to establish a peace-oriented society.

Key Vocabulary

Challenge: a stimulating task or problem; an invigorating opportunity; a calling to account or calling into question.

Conflict: contention, discord, or direct clash resulting from disunity.

Opportunity: a good chance for advancement or progress.[1]

Threat: an expression of intention to inflict evil, injury, or damage.[2]

Violence: any act—physical, verbal, or emotional—that is intended to, or results in, harm to oneself or another person or group. Violence is by nature destructive and represents the final act in a series of conflicted developments within the individual or institution that commits it.

---

1. *Merriam-Webster Online Dictionary.*
2. *Merriam-Webster Online Dictionary.*

The Pervasiveness of Human Violence*

Human beings around the world and throughout history have committed violence. The faces of violence are many, among them self-mutilation and suicide, injury to others and homicide, conflicts and wars, cruelty to animals, and destruction of nature. In recent times, however, both the extent and intensity of human violence have increased dramatically. The 20th century has by far been the most violent period in human history. Two world wars, many extremely destructive regional wars, the Holocaust, the atomic bombs at Hiroshima and Nagasaki, the political purges of the Stalin era, the Cultural Revolution in China, and religious, racial, and ethnic conflicts witnessed around the world are among the most widely acknowledged examples of violence during this century. There are, as well, other virulent forms of violence: violence against women, children, the poor, the minorities, and the underprivileged.

Violence is found in every culture and stratum of human society. When we review even a small sample of the statistics on violence, or witness instances of "unusual" violence or cruelty through reports in the media, we may find ourselves shocked and horrified, and it may cause us to search for answers to profound questions about human nature. It is not unusual, however, that after feeling shock and horror, we soon recover our equilibrium, forget the statistics and the events, and return our attention to the so called real tasks of our everyday lives, such as our jobs, health, education, vacations, and recreational preoccupations. We do so because a very common response to violence is to avoid facing it and to try

---

* Adapted from *Fever in the World of the Mind: Unique Dimensions of Human Conflict and Violence* by H.B. Danesh. *Fever in the World of the Mind* is volume 3 in the *Education for Peace Integrative Curriculum* Series.

forgetting about it, if possible. Usually, we focus on violence only when we are forced to do so, such as when we ourselves are victims of violence or live in the midst of a very violent environment.

While there is considerable agreement about the existence of violence and its undesirability, there is far less consensus about what causes violence, and even dramatically less agreement about how to deal with violence. Schools of psychology prescribe psychotherapy; sociological theorists advocate social changes and improvements; biologists search for the magical drug and the defective gene; jurists call for bigger jails and stiffer penalties; and traditionalists appeal for a return to traditional values such as differentiation of gender roles. On the whole, there seems to be little support for the notion that we can create a violence-free society.

Why does violence occur? Where does it come from? And can we ever hope to live in a world where violence is a rarity and an anomaly?

What is Violence?

Violence, in whatever form, is an act of destruction. For our purposes, we define violence as follows:

Definition

Violence is any act—physical, psychological, verbal, or structural—that intentionally or accidentally results in harm to oneself, another living being, the environment, or one's own or another's property.

Violence is always destructive and represents the final act in a series of conflicted developments within the individual or institution that commits it.

While some scientists still argue that violence is part of human nature, the majority agrees that such a statement is scientifically false. More than two decades ago, the *Seville Statement on Violence*

(1986), adopted by UNESCO, made the following conclusions about human violence:

Human Violence Is Different from Animal Violence

"Although fighting occurs widely among animal species, only a few cases of destructive intra-species fighting between organized groups have ever been reported among naturally living species, and none of these involves the use of tools designed to be weapons. Normal predatory feeding upon other species cannot be equated with intra-species violence. Warfare is a peculiarly human phenomenon and does not occur in other animals."[3]

Violence Is Not Genetic

"[Neither] war [n]or any other violent behaviour is genetically programmed into our human nature….Except for rare pathologies, the genes do not produce individuals necessarily predisposed to violence. Neither do they determine the opposite. While genes are co-involved in establishing our behavioural capacities, they do not by themselves specify the outcome."

Evolution Has Not Selected More Aggressive Behavior

"In all well-studied species, status within the group is achieved by the ability to cooperate and to fulfill social functions relevant to the structure of that group. 'Dominance' involves social bindings and affiliations; it is not simply a matter of possession and use of superior physical power, although it does involve aggressive behaviours. Where genetic selection for aggressive behaviour has been artificially instituted in animals, it has rapidly succeeded in producing hyper-aggressive

3. All quotations in this section are from the Seville Statement on Violence. <http://www.unesco.org/cpp/uk/declarations/seville.pdf>.

individuals…who [when] present in a social group,…either disrupt its social structure or are driven out."

Humans Do Not Have a 'Violent Brain'

"While we do have the neural apparatus to act violently, it is not automatically activated by internal or external stimuli. Like higher primates and unlike other animals, our higher neural processes filter such stimuli before they can be acted upon. How we act is shaped by how we have been conditioned and socialized. There is nothing in our neurophysiology that compels us to react violently."

War Is Not Instinctual

"Modern war involves institutional use of personal characteristics such as obedience, suggestibility, and idealism, social skills such as language, and rational considerations such as cost-calculation, planning and information processing."

Scientists Around the World Agree

"[International scientists have concluded that] biology does not condemn humanity to war, and that humanity can be freed from the bondage of biological pessimism and empowered with confidence to undertake the transformative tasks needed [to establish peace]. Although these tasks are mainly institutional and collective, they also rest upon the consciousness of individual participants for whom pessimism and optimism are crucial factors. Just as 'wars begin in the minds of men', peace also begins in our minds. The same species who invented war is capable of inventing peace. The responsibility lies with each of us."

Worldview and Violence

So if violence is not biological, and yet is a pervasive reality in our world, where does it stem from? Violence, like most human behavior, begins in our thoughts, and if not stopped, it expresses itself either gradually or abruptly in our emotions, our words, and/or our actions. Since violence begins in our minds, its occurrence is strongly influenced by the worldviews we hold. There are certain widely held ideologies that by their very nature promote and sanction violence. Common to many people's ways of thinking, these ideological tenets usually have no scientific or empirically valid base. Here is a list of ideas that lead to violence:

- The idea that "might is right";
- The idea that men are superior to, or more important than, women;
- The idea that some people are created "evil";
- The idea that the purpose of justice is to punish;
- The idea that individual rights and freedoms take precedence over those of the society;
- The idea that the welfare of the society may be defended at the expense of individual rights and freedoms;
- The idea that human values, moral standards, and ethical principles are all relative and that there is no code of ethics which could be applied universally;
- The idea that human diversity begets violence;
- The idea that the best antidote to violence is violence;
- The idea that power and force create security and ensure survival;
- The idea that competition is essential for success;
- The idea that human reality is extinguished at death;
- The idea that God does not exist or is irrelevant to human actions.[4]

---

4. Adapted from *The Fever in the World of the Mind: Unique Dimensions of Human Conflict and Violence*, which is volume 3 of the *Education for Peace Integrative Curriculum* Series.

Indeed, each of these ideas has been and is regularly the originating cause and justification for violent acts.

There is always significant shock and grief when a society suffers a major crisis. This shock and grief is particularly acute and difficult when that crisis is violent, and more particularly when the violence was due to human actions rather than natural causes like earthquakes or floods. Human violence affects us more deeply because we recognize it to be the product of free will, rather than the result of climate or other forces over which we have no direct control.

Societies that have experienced human violence are often ready to reflect on their worldview and to evaluate its assumptions about reality, human nature, the purpose of life. Such a society has an excellent opportunity to map out a new and different future for itself, and its success depends to a large degree on the manner in which its parents and teachers assist the younger generation to develop worldviews that are conducive to the creation of a lasting civilization of peace. To the degree that a society is successful in this regard, it changes the course of its history from violence to peace.

Effects of Violence

Violence does damage to everyone involved in the conflict. The nature of the damage caused to each person is different. Nonetheless, when there is violence, everyone who is part of the violent act is adversely affected.

In general, violence causes three types of damage:

1. Physical damage;
2. Psychosocial damage;
3. Moral/spiritual damage.

Let us reflect on an example.

> Imagine that person *A* attacks person *B*, breaking the leg of person *B*. Clearly, person *B* has suffered damage, but of what type? And what, if any, damage has person *A* experienced?

In this scenario Person *B* has physical damages (his/her leg is broken), and to some extent, psychological damage resulting in feelings of fear, pain, probably anger, and possibly confusion over what has happened. Person *B* will also suffer socially, because his/her relationship with the person *A* is negatively affected. In moral and spiritual ways, person *B* may or may not have experienced damage, depending upon why person *A* had attacked person *B*. If person *A* attacked person *B* without any cause, then *B* doesn't have any moral or spiritual damage. If he or she was attacked because s/he had done something wrong, then s/he will also have some guilt about doing the wrong thing.

Person *A*, however, may not have experienced physical damage but definitely has profound psychosocial as well as moral/spiritual damage depending upon why s/he committed the violent act. This person will experience a lot of inner conflict over the violence s/he has committed and will, one hopes, begin to question, "Why did I do that? What kind of a person am I to do those things? I thought I was a loving, civilized person….How could I have behaved this way?" The inner moral conflict and possible loss of self-integrity—what some call "loss of one's humanity"—can lead to considerable psychological, moral, and spiritual inner conflict and even damage.

Physical damage can usually be healed, unless the violence has resulted in permanent injury or death. Psychological damages can also be healed. But spiritual damages cannot be healed easily, and they call for a fundamental transformation in the individual's worldview and view of self. In the current literature, when we talk about post-trauma recovery, attention is typically given to physical and psychological damages. Modern psychology generally does not deal with the spiritual aspect. The tendency is to focus on person *B* as the obvious "victim," but both parties need attention so that they can regain their "humanity" and their relationships.

Causes of Violence

Violence does not appear randomly or without cause. Rather, violence is the final act in a series of conflicted developments within the individual who commits it. These developments take place in the world of the mind and have emotional, intellectual, interpersonal, and behavioral dimensions. We can identify five stages in the chronology of violence and will describe them in reverse order, beginning with the stage in which violence has, in fact, taken place. This reverse order has been chosen because in our world today, both governments and individuals tend to pay serious attention to violence only after it has already taken place and caused destruction. By starting from the last stage in the process of the development of violence, we aim to demonstrate graphically the futility and insincerity inherent in this approach. Although the outcome is always far more easy to identify than the causes, it is the cause that we must find and root out.

Violence Prevention

Usually, there is a tendency to wait until violent behavior has occurred before taking action. For example, a student has become violent and we try to do something about it. However, it is too late at that point. It would be much easier and much better if we can recognize the precursors of violence before they are manifested in acts of violence. The simplest way to do this is effective and genuine communication with the troubled

Stages of Violence

Stage 5 of Violence occurs when an *act of violence* (with all its destructive consequences) has taken place; therefore, all we can do is to take care of the damage and learn from the experience to prevent its repetition. The decision to commit violence is dependent on a number of factors related both to the conditions of the violent person and the environment with which the person is interacting.

Stage 4 of Violence comprises the immediate moments before violence is committed. The main characteristic of this stage is the presence of a strong *urge for violence* and a desire to fight. However, this is not the only urge that the person has. Under these circumstances, the individual also has a very strong urge to escape from the situation (flight). It is this choice that separates those who commit violence from those who do not. As such, understanding how this choice is made and who is most likely to make one or the other choice is very important.

Stage 3 of Violence occurs when the *feelings of violence* are rising. This is a period of time in which the person is filled with a mix of strong feelings of anger, fear, and anxiety. These three feelings are always together, usually with one of them in the forefront. These feelings, when very strong, indicate a heightened sense of vulnerability. They focus the mind of the person on the perceived dangers and create a condition in which violence is both dreaded and contemplated. In this phase, some individuals share their feelings with others and ask for assistance and assurance so that they could adequately deal with their inner turmoil. Others become so angry, fearful, and anxious that people in their environment become alarmed and take measures to help the person defuse the situation. However, there is a third group that feeds on the feelings of anger, fear, and anxiety, and proceeds to the next stage. Usually, when the feelings of anger are predominant, there is a greater likelihood of violence than if fear and/or anxiety were more predominant. However, this is not always the case. In fact, some of the most destructive acts of violence take place in the context of extreme fear on the part of the violent person.

Stage 2 of Violence is the phase in which the person is feeling the agony of past violence and/or the threat of future violence—both of which increase awareness of one's vulnerability. Under these conditions, the world is perceived to be dangerous, and *thoughts of violence* begin to enter the consciousness of the person. At this early stage in the process of development of violence, these thoughts are not as much about committing violence, as they are about the fact that one's sense of security feels threatened. In the face of threats, people typically respond with a combination of the feelings of fear, anger, and anxiety. Depending on the nature of the threat, its intensity, and the level of maturity and capacity of the person, the individual may respond to these threats either constructively or destructively.

Stage 1 of Violence is the phase in which the *precursors of violence* are present both in the person and the environment in which the person lives. Research indicates that to the degree that we as individuals have not had the benefit of a secure, healthy, and enlightened upbringing, or are not yet endowed with adequate capacities to neutralize the origins of violence within ourselves and our environment, we tend to feel threatened and to think, speak, or act in ways that are violent. Also, it is a fact that the more unjust and violent a society is, the more likely it is that its citizens will also demonstrate violence. Therefore, in Stage 1, we encounter both individual and societal conditions that are conflict-ridden and act as precursors to violence.

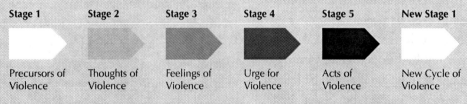

Stage 1	Stage 2	Stage 3	Stage 4	Stage 5	New Stage 1
Precursors of Violence	Thoughts of Violence	Feelings of Violence	Urge for Violence	Acts of Violence	New Cycle of Violence

Figure 1: The sequential stages of violence

person. In other words, it would be much better to talk with the person to discover why this person is feeling the way they are. It would be even better if we could create a nonthreatening environment that would prevent students from developing the intense feelings of anger, fear, anxiety, and often, depression that can lead to thoughts and acts of violence. One of the things that we ought to learn is how to create safe, unthreatening, and compassionate—i.e., unified—environments.

Life Processes: Challenges and Opportunities

Life constantly puts before us challenges and threats, which may be physical, intellectual, emotional, social, or spiritual in nature. We may get sick, make fools of ourselves, lose our social status, or find life meaningless and our inner connection with God (if we are so inclined) severed.

When challenges arise, it is natural for us to feel a certain degree of apprehensiveness or uncertainty about how to handle the situation, as well as a certain degree of tension over how the challenge will affect our life. Usually, these feelings motivate us to think about the situation, to try to understand it, to consider various options, and to choose a suitable solution.

However, life challenges are not always easy to face, and at times we may experience them as threats. Threats can be actual or imagined and can have varying degrees of severity.

Emotional Responses to Life Threats

When we feel threatened, we experience three feelings: anger, fear, and anxiety. Anger and fear are symptoms of perceived threat, whether physical, psychological, or spiritual. Anxiety accompanies both feelings of fear and feelings of anger. These three emotions are always in some relation with one another and can be pictured as a triangle, with one of the emotions situated at "the tip of the iceberg," meaning it is obvious, while the other two emotions are below the surface or hidden.

Someone who is angry is also likely to be anxious and afraid. When a person is afraid, she or he is also likely to be feeling anger and anxiety. If the person is anxious, then the other two feelings are also present. These three emotions are like triplets, they are always together. Depending upon the nature of the threat and upon which of the emotions is most pronounced, people will react to threat in different ways. When someone is primarily anxious or afraid, then he or she will usually want to run away, withdraw, or escape, and may become depressed. If the person is mainly angry and anxious, then that person will likely become aggressive and violent. However, in extreme cases of fear, a person may become very violent; or in extreme cases of anger, a person may respond by withdrawing.

Imagine the following scenario: You (the most important person in the universe) are walking in the beautiful downtown of your city (the center of the universe). You're the most important person in

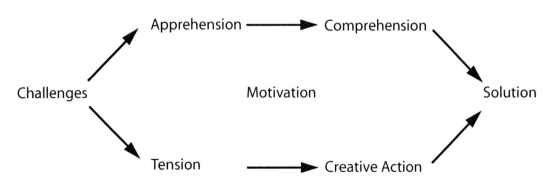

Figure 2: Healthy Response to Life Challenges

---

the center of the universe, and everybody is looking at you as you walk down the street. Suddenly, you see a little dog approaching, and it has sharp teeth, and you're sure it's going towards your calf, and you are wearing shorts, and this dog is going to bite your leg! When that thought happens, you have three feelings at the same time: you are anxious about whether or not it will happen, afraid that this dog is really going to bite you, and you are angry at this dog for making you look silly. This situation is perceived by you as a threat. It is a threat that you may be able to handle: you can run and hide, or you can kick the dog. However, if the dog is of a vicious variety, the situation may be much more threatening and precarious.

Under normal conditions, we think, "Okay, this is a threat, and I'm going to take care of it. I can handle it." However, if you are in the middle of a war or continuous violence, the threats become very great, and as a result, your levels of fear, anxiety, and anger become extremely high. In threatening situations, the typical response is either fight or flight: you face the threat with aggression, or you run away from it. Under the pressure of intense circumstances, people do irrational things. This is what happens to soldiers in a war. They feel so threatened and so afraid, that they kill and then become full of anger. You don't need to be a soldier to feel these things. You can be a victim of war or violence or abuse and feel similarly. In conditions of violence, everyone in the affected community has to deal with these issues.

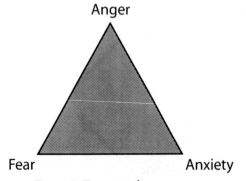

Figure 3: Emotional responses to threatening conditions

Furthermore, sometimes we may not be aware of what has caused the threat; or, even if aware, we may not wish to admit we have felt threatened. Because of this, it is important to note that people's responses to life threats are similar yet unique.

Consider the following scenario.

Scenario: A Family Faced with Divorce

The parents in a family with several children decide to separate. What happens? How does each member of the family respond to this situation?

It would not be unusual to notice many different responses to this threat of family breakdown. One child may feel very frightened, while another may feel very angry, and still another may begin to have nightmares. An older child may not be as seriously affected by the separation. In the same family we may also find a child who begins to have trouble at school and begins to fight with other children. Parents may also respond with different feelings. Father may develop health disorders, which may be due to repressed anger, and mother may become depressed because she feels rejected, hurt, angry, and sad. It could also be the other way around.

Therefore, several individuals may respond to the same threat in seemingly different ways. However, if we talk with them about what has happened, we will discover that all of them feel emotionally, physically (especially those with less power), socially, and spiritually threatened. Obviously, the best solution is to prevent separation, and if the separation has already occurred, to try to help the parents reconcile. Under all circumstances, however, it is necessary for the family members to learn about life threats and how to respond to them in a positive and healthy manner.

Types of Threats

The main types of threats include:

- Threats to Self-Integrity;
- Threats to Self-Identity;
- Threats of Injustice;
- Threats of Frustration;
- Threats of Violence.

Threats to Self-Integrity

These are the most serious types of threat. Some examples are serious illness (physical threat), the loss of someone we love (emotional threat), and the feeling that life no longer has any meaning (spiritual threat). This last category of threat is often found in suicidal or very violent people.

Threats to Self-Identity

These include threats such as self-doubt or failure, humiliation, manipulation, loss of autonomy and freedom (which are all psychosocial threats), or loss of self-respect if we participate in truly unethical conduct (spiritual threat).

Threats of Injustice

By nature, all human beings seek justice. When we experience injustice, or even become aware of injustice to those we do not know, we tend to feel threatened. In the face of injustice, we empathize with each other. We realize that *injustice to one is injustice to all.*

Threats of Frustration

By "frustration" is meant all those conditions in life that make us feel incapable and incompetent. Some examples are our sense of frustration when caught in a traffic jam, having to respond to the incessant questions of a three-year-old, and not being able to find a meaningful job. All of these situations have the potential to make us frustrated and then angry, and at times, violent, because they make us feel impotent and incompetent.

Threats of Violence

Violence itself is a mighty threat. That is why responding to violence with violence itself is not a solution. In reality, when we respond to violence with violence, we create a vicious cycle of violence. Such is the condition observable throughout human history with few exceptions. The only time that can violence be justified is when it conclusively ends the continuation and repetition of such a violence. One possible example of this type of response is the manner that World War Two was brought to an end and was followed by efforts to help all parties involved to recover from its monumentally destructive impact.

To summarize, when we are threatened, our thoughts, feelings, and actions are dramatically different from those when we are challenged. Our sense of apprehension intensifies to fear and even phobia; our tension escalates to anger, even rage; and our motivation is replaced by anxiety and panic. If a threatened individual is feeling primarily afraid or anxious, s/he will usually have the urge to run away, withdraw or escape, and may become depressed. If the individual is feeling mainly angry and anxious, then that person will likely become aggressive and violent. In extreme cases, these reactions can be reversed: an extremely fearful person may become violent, and an extremely angry person may withdraw. The following figure demonstrates the nature of transformation of a challenge to a threat.

Reasons for Varied Responses to Threat

Not all individuals perceive or respond to threats in the same way. Our response to threats is determined by the level of our maturity, the nature of our life experiences, our worldviews, and the source of the threat itself. Sometimes we may not be aware of what has caused the threat, or, even if we are aware, we may not wish to admit we have felt threatened.

Another reason why people respond differently to life threats may be related to the way they learn to take advantage of life's **opportunities**. There are basically two major opportunities in life—**to grow** and **to create.**

Opportunities to Grow

Growth is the fundamental aspect of life. All living beings have to grow; otherwise, they begin to decay and die. Physical growth takes place during childhood and adolescence then continues in the form of cellular repair for the maintenance of health. Emotional, intellectual, and spiritual growth also begins in childhood, but never stops. We always have the potential for growth with respect to such capacities as loving, learning, and becoming more world-minded and less self-centered.

Opportunities to Create

The other opportunity we have is to create—to create our personalities, identities, families, societies, and other meaningful expressions of our existence.

Individuals who develop and grow in a creative and meaningful manner become wholesome and universal beings: self-assured, loving, wise, and fulfilled. Individuals who fail to do so become frightened, immature, self-centered, and bored. They are less capable in the face of life threats and more prone to becoming violent and/or withdrawn.

In a healthy life process, loving relationships, and encouragement are essential for a healthy response to opportunities for growth and creativity that life offers. When these aspects are cultivated in the environment around us, we steadily mature and gain a deep sense of fulfillment in respect to our lives.

Children reared without the opportunities and encouragement necessary to develop a meaningful and evolving life purpose tend to live limited, boring lives and become easily threatened by the challenges of life.

That is why children who have been brought up in war-torn societies or in violent families and environments are more likely to respond to life threats with violence. Likewise, children and adults who are subject to prejudice, poverty, disease, anarchy, or repeated discouragement become anxiety-ridden, fearful, angry, conflicted and, if the situation persists, violent.

Ironically, this is also true for children reared in affluent, materialistic societies and families where all the physical needs are met but the psychological and spiritual needs neglected. These children grow up to have no purpose for their lives except for instant gratification and pain avoidance, and when their demands are not satisfied, they frequently become either withdrawn and apathetic or aggressive and violent.

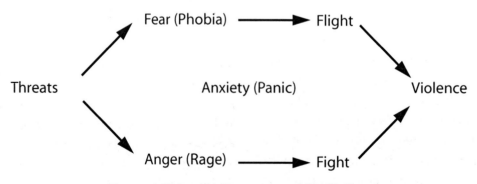

Figure 4: Unhealthy Response to Life Challenges

In short, any person may be prone to violence when living under conditions of deprivation or threat with few opportunities to develop, grow, mature, and be creative.

Responses to Violence

People respond to violence in several ways. The following are the various types of responses we may choose in facing violence.

Ignore the Violence

A very common response is to ignore violence, especially if we are not directly involved. In everyday life we hear or read about many acts of violence, but basically we ignore them and soon forget about them except, of course, for the direct victims of violence who can never forget what they have suffered.

Rationalize the Violence

The second common response to violence is to rationalize its occurrence. This response has become very common in our time. There are many biological, psychological, sociological, theories and even religious perspectives that legitimize human aggression and violence. Every violent act is seen to be understandable according to certain theoretical or ideological explanations and is therefore acceptable. This rationalization is probably one of the most dangerous responses to human violence, because it justifies violence and enables it to persist.

Scenario: Insecurities that Lead to Violence

Sometimes people feel insecure in their relationships. If these feelings of insecurity are not dealt with positively, fundamental questions about one's relationships with others can build up in the person's mind, gradually causing the mind to become feverish. Ideas begin to churn over in their mind, and they become more and more heated, bringing the person's thoughts to a boil, like a pot of water on the stove. Finally, emotions take control of the person and their actions, and soon their behaviors, are dictated entirely by these emotions. In extreme circumstances this process can end in physical violence against self or others.

A group or nation that feels threatened may have a range of responses. They may acquire more lethal weapons and further secure their borders. Likewise, the neighbouring group may feel insecure, may meet and raise the stakes, fortify their borders and acquire weaponry and heavy artillery. The mutually felt insecurity thus heightens rapidly, and before long, both sides are building armies and preparing military strategies. To feel more powerful and appease their insecurity, one of the groups may think it is better to strike first than to be vulnerable to an unexpected attack. Suddenly, these two neighbors are at war.

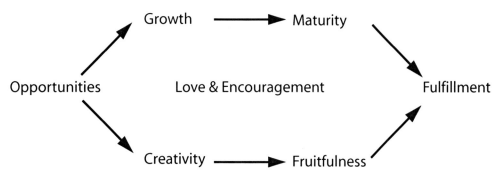

Figure 5: Healthy Response to Life Opportunities

React Violently Ourselves

The third common response to violence is violence itself. Our world situation today provides innumerable examples of this ever intensifying cycle of violence. Further elaboration is not needed on the consequences of violence as a reaction to violence. Such a descending spiral could, quite simply, bring us to the brink of self-destruction.

React Non-Violently

There is a fourth response, which has become well known through the activities of such individuals as Mahatma Gandhi and Martin Luther King, Jr. This is the nonviolent or "passive resistance" approach. This approach has proven very successful in curbing violence, decreasing its destructive consequences, and ultimately overcoming it. However, its effects usually have been short-term, primarily because in this approach no strategies for the prevention of violence itself are put into place. Consequently, violence tends to continue and nonviolent response to it gradually becomes exhausted and even deemed ineffective.

The goal, however, of a violence-free society is to prevent violence at its roots. An excellent resource for understanding the remarkable gains, but also some its limitations of the non-violence movement is the Public Broadcasting Service's "A Force More Powerful: A Century of Non-Violent Conflict" (http://www.pbs.org/weta/forcemorepowerful/background/whatis.html). The non-violence approach is definitely an effective approach for addressing violence, but it is not an effective approach for preventing it.

Preventing Violence

An effective way to prevent human violence is the most important item on the agenda of humanity. It is here that the concepts we studied in the previous units become extremely important. Fundamentally, the most effective approach to prevention of violence is creation of unity at interpersonal and intergroup levels within the framework of a unity-based worldview. This is the ultimate objective, which becomes ever more feasible, as we systematically and conscientiously dedicate ourselves to the training and education of every generation of children and youth within the framework of principles of peace rather than conflict, as currently done. Along with the education of a new generation of peace-makers, we need to bring to our methods of governance and social life those peace- and unity-based reforms that are conducive to equality, justice, unity and peace.

However, at the same time we need to deal with the day-to-day challenges that we face in our homes, schools, and communities. Here, we will focus our discussion on preventing violence in schools.[5]

Preventing Violence in the Classroom

Effective violence prevention among youth can begin by making the classroom a harmonious and nonthreatening environment. While there is no simple solution to violence, the following issues merit close attention by teachers and parents:

Tip #1   Create Nonthreatening Environments

Tip #2   Promote Unity-Based Worldview

Tip #3   Challenge the Students to set Noble and Far-reaching Goals for Themselves

Tip #4   Encourage Rather than Criticize

Tip #5   Stimulate Creativity and Growth

How do we reduce the experience of threats in the classroom? We begin by increasing

---

5. For more strategies on violence prevention in the home and community, see the *Best Practices in Youth Violence Prevention Sourcebook*.

opportunities for growth and creativity. Every human being has the potential and inner desire to grow, intellectually, emotionally, socially, and spiritually. What encourages growth?—love, in the form of encouragement.

Encouragement vs. Criticism

Giving encouragement is the attitude and act of giving another person courage, in general, and for the participants in the EFP Program, specifically, the courage to develop, mature, and be creative and the cause of unity and peace. To accomplish these monumental tasks, we all need considerable courage. There are several ways to give that necessary courage: First of all, knowledge is a source of courage. Second, a positive sense of self strengthens the courage of the young students as they come to recognize their own positive qualities. This is why criticism is so detrimental: it takes away a student's self-confidence. Focusing on positive qualities gives courage. Imagine you come to school in the morning after spending much time in front of the mirror and people say to you, "You look beautiful/handsome today." Every time you look in the mirror, you will say the same thing ("I look great today.") because somebody has said something positive to you. Alternatively, imagine if you come in feeling well and someone tells you that you look awful and you look sick. An hour later, you might discover you have a headache. Two hours later, you are sick. By halfway through the day, you go to the Director and say, "I think I'd better go home—I am sick." The principle is: Ideas have power to influence for better or worse.

If we criticize students, colleagues, and friends, we plant a negative idea in their minds. They may then think negatively of themselves, and their self-confidence will suffer. For students to grow and mature, they need guidance and assistance in the framework of love and encouragement. A growth-inducing love is different from the conditional love given, for example, by an authoritarian parent or teacher who puts the condition of conformity on love, e.g., "I love/value you if you do as I demand" or "Be 'good' and I will love/value you." With unconditional love and encouragement, people become mature individuals who are in a much better position to deal with the challenges and threats of life. If individuals receive mainly criticism rather than love, they do not mature fully and consequently cannot deal adequately with life's challenges.

Creativity vs. Boredom

The other key opportunity in life relates to the fact that although we all grow, we do not grow in the same way. Each individual and group grows in a unique way. Every human being becomes a unique human being. We are all shaping our own lives, and of all the things that we create in a lifetime, most important is the manner in which we approach our own life and its progress. In order to create the unique persons that we are, we need love and encouragement. If we grow fully, and in a creative way, then as an individual we feel fulfilled. However, many people don't grow in a creative way. In this situation, the opposite of fulfillment—boredom—happens. Boredom is expressed in many ways. In the absence of fulfilling activities, some people fill time with the pursuit of immediate gratification and numbing of their self-critical awareness through the use of alcohol or drugs. Some engage in vandalism or destroy the environment. Others find a semblance of intimacy in casual, transient relationships. To create a healthy environment, we have to create an environment where there is little threat and a great deal of positive, constructive challenges.

If a child doesn't have the opportunity to be creative, that child will become bored. If you have a student who hasn't grown and is immature, that student is likely to feel threatened. He or she doesn't know how to prove self worth and feel good about him/herself in that environment. This produces a vicious cycle characterized by less growth, less creativity, and ultimately more frustration, anxiety, and violence.

However, if we help students grow into mature and capable people, then instead of being bored, they can become fulfilled. Then you have a "universal person." This person has a much greater capacity to deal with life challenges and opportunities. In short, in order for children and youth to grow, they need courage. And for them to have courage, they need encouragement. And encouragement is only possible when we focus on the positive and authentic qualities of others. And for us to encourage others, we ourselves need the courage to be selfless, humble, generous, authentic, truthful, compassionate, and loving. It is a creative cycle.

Summary

In this unit, we have learned that:

Violence Is a Process that Begins in the Mind

- Violence is a process that begins in the mind and expresses itself in our thoughts, feelings, and actions. Human tendencies to think, feel, and act in ways that produce violence greatly increase when we hold conflict-based worldviews.

There Are 5 Stages in the Evolution of Violence

- There are five stages in the evolution of violence, beginning with **precursors** of violence, and followed by **thoughts, emotions, urges,** and finally **acts of violence.**

Effective Violence Prevention Requires Nonthreatening Environments

- Effective violence prevention concentrates efforts on creating safe, encouraging, and nonthreatening environments so that the cycle of violence is broken before reaching the point of manifest actions.

Key Questions for the Classroom

The following questions can be used to review and explore further the concepts of Unit 4 with your students:

1. What are the underlying causes of violence?

2. How many types of violence are there?

3. What are the various ways of responding to violence?

4. Violence is a major cause of human sufferings and problems. What are the main reasons for the prevalence of violence in our world?

5. Why do reactionary responses to violence usually not work to resolve the violence?

6. What measures can be taken to prevent future violence in the classroom, community, at home, and in the society at large?

7. How can promotion of a unity-based worldview assist in violence prevention?

8. What is encouragement, and how and why it is effective?

9. What is criticism, and what are its effects?

10. What is at the core of the process of human development?

11. Describe the nature of creativity and its relationship to one's sense of fulfillment.

12. What causes feelings of anger, fear, and anxiety?

13. Many international bodies are working at trying to reduce and eliminate poverty in order to reduce violence and terrorism. Do you think this is an effective approach? Why or why not?

14. Is there a relationship between poverty and violence, and if there is, what is the relationship? What steps do you think these agencies could take to promote and support violence-free environments in low-income families/schools/communities/or nations?

Personal Reflection

Reflection is a very powerful learning tool. It helps us to make sense of the things we are studying and the experiences we are going through. The more we reflect on ourselves, our relationships and the world around us, the better prepared we are to discern, prioritize, and act upon issues of importance.

Becoming a peacemaker is a very important and challenging task. By reflecting on the principles of peace, we are better equipped to make decisions about our own development that will help us to confidently undertake the goal of peace building.

As we go through each of the EFP Curriculum units, try to set aside some time for the process of reflection.

The following questions are provided to help you begin this process.

Questions for Personal Reflection

1. Reflections on Self

1. I feel angry when…
2. I feel afraid when…
3. I feel worried when…

Focus Question

How can I transform my life-threats into life-opportunities?

2. Reflections on Family/Group

- What was my most encouraging school experience?
- What is my preferred way of showing love and encouragement to others?
- How could my family environment be made safer and more nonthreatening?

Focus Questions

Criticism—whether directed at oneself or others—has a negative effect on one's confidence and enthusiasm to pursue opportunities for growth and creativity. In light of this, consider the following:

- What can I do to be more encouraging and less critical of others?
- What can I do to support my own positive development in the face of criticism?

3. Reflections on Society

- How can I contribute to making my community safe and nonthreatening?
- How can society become a source of encouragement to its children and youth?
- How can my school contribute to the betterment of my society?

Focus Question

Recognizing that

"Violence is a complex problem related to patterns of thought and behavior that are shaped by a multitude of forces within our families and communities...."

How should society deal with people who commit acts of violence so that future incidences can be prevented?

4. Reflections on the World at Large

- The world we live in is very threatening. How can individuals like me help make it less threatening?
- What encouraging developments in the world help me to feel optimistic about creating a peaceful, nonthreatening world?

Focus Questions

- Many world leaders respond to perceived threats and crises with threats, punishment, or violence. Why do you think this is so?
- If you were a leader of a nation, what steps would you take to prevent outbreaks of violence in your country in order to develop a model of peaceful leadership for the world?

Classroom Tools

As a teacher in the Education for Peace Program, it is now your task to create in your classroom a situation that helps students to transform the challenges they face every day of their lives into opportunities for further creative growth and transformation. Your role as their teacher and mentor in this process is tremendously important.

To help you get started, a number of tools are included in this section that you may find useful. These tools are only guides, and you are encouraged to develop your own ideas about how to best explore these topics with your students.

In addition to the examples here, please also refer to the Educational Methodology Unit where you will find practical guidelines on how to make your classroom a creative and effective learning environment, as well as other great ideas from fellow teachers who are integrating Education for Peace into their various subject areas.

As you work with the Education for Peace concepts, you will surely develop new ideas for lessons, activities, and assessment approaches. We encourage you to pass along your thoughts, ideas, or resource links to Education for Peace so they can be added to our EFP Resource Bank for other teachers to use. Please send us an email at <info@efpinternational.org>, or mail your ideas to our address:

International Education for Peace Institute (Canada)
101, 1001 W. Broadway, Suite 900
Vancouver, BC V6H 4E4
Canada

We look forward to hearing from you!

Activity Ideas for Secondary Schools

Social Studies
Have students design a healthy, violence-free environment of their choice (family, school, community, workplace, other). Outline the roles of each person/institution that influence the environment either directly or indirectly.

History
In groups of 4 or 5 persons, analyze a scenario of interpersonal or intergroup conflict. Retrace the steps of how a challenge became a threat and then deteriorated into violence, outlining areas that could have been addressed early on to prevent the conflict from occurring.

Art
Create a visual or dance interpretation of the statement: "Violence appears like a fever in the world of the mind." In preparation, familiarize yourself with the psychosomatic (mind and body) dynamics of fevers.

Home Economics
In groups of 4 or 5 persons, create 2 scenarios: one in which a family is encouraging and one in which the family is discouraging. Invite each group to role play their scenarios in front of the class. Then discuss together the impact of these two experiences on both the family and its members.

Creative Writing/ Contemporary Society
Assume the role of a "social analyst" covering a current world event or crisis situation on behalf of the United Nations. Report the story of this event, making sure to include an analysis of how the situation has built up over time and what preventative measures should have been taken. As well, include suggestions as to what could be done at this stage to de-escalate the violence and help bring about a violence-free resolution to the crisis.

Activity Ideas for Primary Schools

Language Arts

Students can create a reflective notebook about themselves in which they write about their emotions and feelings. For example, each page can have one sentence in which each student writes: I feel angry when…; When I feel angry I can…; I feel frustrated when…; When I feel frustrated I can…; I feel worried when…; When I feel worried I can…; etc. At the end of the book, there can be a page with the following sentence: My friends can encourage me by…. Another page can read: My family can encourage me by…. The last page can read: I feel most encouraged when…. Students can share these notebooks with their classmates and families.

Students can create a class story about the different ways that each of them can be an encouraging person in the classroom and their families.

Art

Host an "Encouraging Art Showing" for another class and/or the students' families featuring artistic pieces created by students during the semester. Each student chooses one piece of art that they are particularly proud of to be on display in the show. Have a comment sheet in which people who come to the show write one encouraging comment about each person's artwork.

Social Studies

Have students design a healthy, violence-free environment of their choice (family, school, community, workplace, other). This can be created on a mural and/or smaller piece of paper. Students can outline the roles of various persons in the environment, including their own role for being encouraging and creative beings in this environment.

Unit 4, Sample Lesson 1: LIFE CHALLENGES AND OPPORTUNITIES

Focus: Causes of and Responses to Threat

Context

Many things can make us feel threatened. Threats fill us with feelings of anxiety, fear, and anger. Sometimes the source of the threat is obvious to us, and sometimes we feel threatened without really knowing why. Reflecting on what is threatening to us helps us to understand and reduce our fears and to think clearly through what the healthiest, least harmful response to those threats can be.

Points for Understanding

- Acts of aggression and violence are the end results of unresolved, sustained, and considerable threats.
- To prevent violence, one of the first steps is to understand why thoughts and feelings of violence occur so as to reduce those factors.
- Threats cause three feelings in us: fear, anger, and anxiety. We often are aware of one or all these emotions without realizing that an underlying sense of threat has caused them.
- By learning to recognize and find the reasons for anger, fear, and anxiety in our personal life experiences, we become better at preventing ourselves from moving towards violence, instead using nonviolent ways of responding to the problems or challenges we face.

Key Questions

1. What kinds of threats have I experienced?
2. How do I respond to threats?
3. Do any of the nonphysical threats I feel provide me with opportunities for growth and self-development?
4. How can I help prevent conflict and violence in my family/school/community?

Learning Process

1. Begin the class by asking students to respond to the following questions privately on a piece of paper (10 minutes). Let students know that their answers will not have to be shared, but are just for personal reflection. A handout may be developed, or the questions can be written on the board:

    a. I feel angry when…
    b. I feel afraid when…
    c. I feel worried when…
    d. Things that threaten me include: 1)_____ 2)_____ 3)_____

    Ask students to set aside their responses.

2. Present to students a description of threats and common responses to them based on the sections in this Unit entitled, "Emotional Responses to Threats" and "Types of Threats." Summarize points on the board as you discuss. Be sure to draw the emotional triangle of anger, fear, and anxiety on the board, giving students an opportunity to discuss their views on it.

3. Next, have each student choose one of the threatening scenarios they described in their personal reflections above (d), and again in their notebook, use a diagram of the emotional triangle to identify what they felt at the time, especially why they felt those feelings. Students may not always recognize that, for example, if they were angry, they also felt afraid. It may be necessary to model a scenario for the whole class before giving them their individual assignment.

4. Remind students that any time they are feeling angry, afraid, or worried they can use the emotional triangle exercise to sort out the underlying reasons for their feelings.

5. Conclude the class with a discussion of the people whom students can approach for help when they have problems or negative feelings. Make sure they know that it is always better to discuss negative feelings and thoughts—either with their teacher, parents/guardians, school counselor, even siblings or friends—than to act out on them. Let students know that during their next class, you will discuss together what strategies can be used to make home, school, and community violence-free environments.

Additional Resources

Best Practices of Youth Violence Prevention: A Sourcebook for Community Action. Available online: <http://www.cdc.gov/ncipc/dvp/bestpractices.htm>.

H.B. Danesh, *Fever in the World of the Mind: Unique Dimensions of Human Conflict and Violence,* volume 3 in the *Integrative Education for Peace Curriculum* Series.

Worksheet: Triangle of Emotional Responses to Threat.

Unit 4, Sample Lesson 2: NATURE AND DYNAMICS OF CONFLICT AND VIOLENCE

Focus: Types of Violence and Responses to Violence

Context

There are many different types of violence and many common responses to violence. Responding to violence by ignoring it, rationalizing it, or responding to it with more violence only contributes to and intensifies the occurrence of violence in our relationships, families, schools and communities, and among the nations. Nonetheless, these responses are common because people are usually not trained in how respond to violence constructively and how to prevent violence. This lesson helps students become aware of various types of and responses to violence, as a basis for pursuing, in subsequent lessons, preventative approaches to creating violence-free communities.

Lasting Understandings

- Violence includes any act—physical, verbal, or emotional—that is intended to or results in harm to oneself or another person or group.
- Violence may be isolated or systemic. In either case, violence represents the final act in a series of conflicted developments within and among individuals and/or groups.
- Violence may also include economic, environmental, sexual, and/or spiritual harm.
- Violence is often preceded by a perception of threat, which is accompanied by feelings of anxiety, fear, and anger. Detecting these emotions and understanding their causes can assist in the violence-prevention process.

Key Questions

1. How many types of violence are there?
2. What are the various ways of responding to violence?
3. What measures can be taken to prevent future violence in the classroom, community, at home, and in the society at large?
4. How can promotion of a unity-based worldview assist in violence prevention?

Learning Process

1. Begin the class by asking students to identify as many types of violence as they can. Write their responses on the board. If necessary, prompt students to consider not only physical but also verbal, psychological, spiritual, economic, environmental, sexual, and domestic violence.

2. After brainstorming, ask students to identify what the common factors among these various types of violence are and to try to create a general but complete definition of violence.

3. Next have students identify all the ways that one may respond to violence. Write these in a list on the board. Beside each, discuss what the possible outcomes and consequences of such responses might be. Determine with students whether the building of a culture of peace delegitimizes any of these possible responses.

4. Focusing on interpersonal/intergroup violence, choose a real scenario from a region of the world or create a hypothetical situation that parallels the type of violence most common in our world. Prepare a number of students to role-play the scenario in front of the class.

5. After the role-play, ask the class to openly analyze the possible causes underlying the aggressive behaviors depicted in the scene. Be sure to use the "emotional triangle" diagram on the board to try to explain reasons for the anger, fear, or anxiety present in conditions of threat and violence.

6. Discuss what possible preventative step could have been taken to de-escalate the violence before it broke out.

Activities and Assignments

1. Written Assignment: Have students analyze another violence scenario for homework. Try to choose a scenario in which the precursors to the violence implicate both parties. If drawing from a real scenario in which background information is available, have students include in their analysis their observations on the worldviews of each of the main parties involved. How did the actors justify their violent behavior? What would be necessary to prevent the scenario from reaching the point of manifest violence?

Additional Resources

Best Practices of Youth Violence Prevention: A Sourcebook for Community Action. Available online: <http://www.cdc.gov/ncipc/dvp/bestpractices.htm>.

H.B. Danesh, *Fever in the World of the Mind: Unique Dimensions of Human Conflict and Violence* provides more detailed information on psychological responses to threat and violence, as well as strategies for violence prevention.

Worksheet: Triangle of Emotional Responses to Threat.

Unit 4, Lesson 1 – Activity Reading

Choose one of the following quotations and discuss:

"From the neighborhood bully berating a meek classmate to the rhesus macaque screaming at a rival, displays of aggression are the weapon of choice throughout the animal kingdom for asserting dominance, challenging a higher ranking individual, or laying claim to food, water, and other resources."

—*Science* 289. 5479 (2000): 569

"Violence can only be concealed by a lie, and the lie can only be maintained by violence. Any man who has once proclaimed violence as his method is inevitably forced to take the lie as his principle."
—Alexander Solzhenitsyn (b. 1918), Russian novelist
Nobel Prize lecture, 1973, quoted in *Solzhenitsyn: A Documentary Record,* ed. Leopold Labedz (1974)

"If family violence teaches children that might makes right at home, how will we hope to cure the futile impulse to solve worldly conflicts with force?"
—Letty Cottin Pogrebin (20th century), U.S. editor, writer
Family and Politics, ch. 1 (1983)

"Power acquired by violence is only usurpation, and lasts only as long as the force of him who commands prevails over that of those who obey."

—Denis Diderot (1713–1784)
French philosopher, encyclopedist, dramatist, novelist, art critic
s.v. "Political Authority," *Encyclopedia,* second paragraph (1751)

"The ultimate weakness of violence is that it is a descending spiral, begetting the very thing it seeks to destroy. Instead of diminishing evil, it multiplies it. Through violence you may murder the liar, but you cannot murder the lie, nor establish the truth. Through violence you may murder the hater, but you do not murder hate. In fact, violence merely increases hate. So it goes. Returning violence for violence multiplies violence, adding deeper darkness to a night already devoid of stars. Darkness cannot drive out darkness; only light can do that. Hate cannot drive out hate: only love can do that."

—Martin Luther King, Jr.
Where Do We Go from Here: Chaos or Community? pp. 62–63 (1967)

Extended Exploration

Related Readings

Adams, David, and Sarah Bosch. (1987). "The Myth that War is Intrinsic to Human Nature Discourages Action for Peace by Young People." In *Essays on Violence*. J. Martin Ramirez, Robert A. Hinde, and Jo Groebel, eds. Seville: University of Seville, 123–37. Available online: <http://www.culture-of-peace.info/myth/title-page.html>.

Adorno, Theodor et al. (1950). *The Authoritarian Personality*. New York: Harper.

Best Practices of Youth Violence Prevention: A Sourcebook for Community Action. Thornton, Timothy et al., eds. (1972). Georgia: Division of Violence Prevention, National Centre for Injury Prevention and Control. Available online: <http://www.cdc.gov/ncipc/dvp/bestpractices.htm>.

Brewer, John. (2003). *Post-Violence as a Sociological Issue*. School of Sociology and Social Policy. Belfast: Queen's University. Available online: <http://regnet.anu.edu.au/program/pastevents/link_documents/papers/2003/Postviolenceasasociologicalissueversion2JohnBrewer.pdf>.

Burton, John. (1997). *Violence Explained: The Sources of Conflict, Violence and Crime and Their Prevention*. Manchester: Manchester University Press.

Danesh, H.B. (2006). *Fever in the World of the Mind: Unique Dimensions of Human Conflict and Violence*. Volume 3. *Education for Peace Integrative Curriculum* Series. Vancouver: Education for Peace Publications.

———. (1980). "The Angry Group for Couples: A Model for Short-Term Group Psychotherapy." *The Psychiatric Journal of the University of Ottawa* 5.2: 118–24.

———. (1978a). "In Search of a Violence-Free Community." *Mental Health and Society* 5: 63–71.

———. (1978b). "The Authoritarian Family and Its Adolescents." *Canadian Psychiatric Association Journal* 23(7):479-85.

———. (1977). "Anger and Fear." *American Journal of Psychiatry* 134. 10 (October): 1109–12.

Dollard, John et al. (1980). *Frustration and Aggression*. Westport: Greenwood Press.

Erikson, Erik. (1963). *Childhood and Society*. 2d ed. New York: W.W. Norton.

Gregg, Richard B. (1966). *The Power of Nonviolence*. 2d ed. New York: Schocken Books.

Hamber, Brandon. (2003). "Healing." In *Reconciliation after Violent Conflict: A Handbook*. Stockholm, Sweden: International Institute for Democracy and Electoral Assistance. 77–96. Available online: <http://www.brandonhamber.com/publications/Chapter%20Healing.pdf>.

Lorenz, Konrad. (1966). *On Aggression*. Originally published 1963. Reprint, London: Routledge.

May, Rollo. (1972). *Power and Innocence: A Search for the Source of Violence*. New York: Delta Books.

The Seville Statement on Violence. David Adams et al. (1989). Adopted by UNESCO at the 25th Session of the General Conference, November 1989. Available online: <http://www.unesco.org/cpp/uk/declarations/seville.pdf>.

Wilson, James Q. (1998). *Crime and Human Nature.* New York: Free Press.

Educational Web Links

"Talking with Kids About War and Violence."
   <http://www.pbs.org/parents/talkingwithkids/war/>.
"Does TV Kill? A Teacher's Guide to Discussing Violence and the Media."
   <http://www.pbs.org/wgbh/pages/frontline/teach/tvkillguide.html>.
"A Force More Powerful: A Century of Non-Violent Conflict."
   <http://www.aforcemorepowerful.org/>.
"No Safe Place: The Crisis of Domestic Violence."
   <http://www.pbs.org/kued/nosafeplace/index.html>.
Lost Childhoods: Exploring the Consequences of Collective Violence."
   <http://www.pbs.org/pov/pov2003/discoveringdominga/pdf/study_guide.pdf>.

General Online Resources

Public Broadcasting Service TeacherSource for K-12 lesson samples and resources for all subjects. <http://www.pbs.org/teachersource/>.
The Columbia Encyclopedia Online. <http://www.bartleby.com/65>.
The Columbia World of Quotations. <http://www.bartleby.com/quotations>.
The Merriam-Webster Online Dictionary. <http://www.merriam-webster.com>.
Wikipedia: The Free Encyclopedia. <http://www.wikipedia.org>.

Unit 5

The Developmental Model of Civilization

This unit explains the developmental character of individual and collective human life. All human beings experience phases of development and maturation in their biological, intellectual, emotional, ethical, and spiritual capacities. Likewise, societies—as ordered systems of individuals and groups—experience phases of development.

The most significant development in human life takes place on the level of consciousness. As our consciousness evolves, the conflicts we experience and the manner in which we deal with these conflicts change. Indeed, once human consciousness becomes more universal, insightful, and mature, it positively influences all aspects of life, whether economic, social, political, or personal. Human development is an ongoing process from which no individual or society is exempt. Using examples, this unit explores the psychological and social processes that characterize human childhood, adolescence, and maturity; and draws on the model of these phases to understand the historical development of humanity as a collective.

Context

A developmental perspective on human history asserts that history does not simply "repeat itself," nor is it the outcome of purely random or arbitrary events; rather, history represents a dynamic progression of identifiable phases that correspond analogously to the psychosocial processes in individual life. A developmental perspective helps explain the causes and characteristics of many of the trends we see in the world.

When the developmental nature of human individuals and groups is understood, we are better able to appreciate where humanity as a whole has evolved from and where it is heading in the future. It helps us to see peace as the natural outcome of a healthy, evolving, and integrated human life. This notion has two significant implications: first, that our histories of conflict, violence, and war are the expressions of earlier stages of development in our human collective life. Second, that peace is not only possible but also in fact inevitable.

This unit lays the framework for a discussion of humanity's transition to a civilization of peace and also introduces patterns observed concerning the use of authority, power, and decision-making that will be discussed more thoroughly in Unit 6, "Humanity's Transition to a Civilization of Peace." Upon completion of this unit, participants will be able to assess their own current developmental state and that of their societies and the world, as well as identify ways to foster greater capacities for peace within themselves, their families, communities, and society at large.

Learning Process

In this unit, participants should be assisted to:

1. Understand the psychosocial characteristics of human development during childhood, adolescence, and maturity; and recognize similar patterns of development within groups and societies;

2. Consider their own physical, intellectual, emotional, ethical, and spiritual development and reflect on ways to actively foster this growth in themselves and their relationships;

3. Discuss key challenges and opportunities associated with the maturation process and analyze current world events through the framework of developmental processes;

4. Begin to plan local, national, and global activities designed to heighten their understanding of what a mature global society looks like and how to get there.

Points for Understanding

Teachers can guide their students to understand and remember these main points:

- Just as individuals develop through stages of childhood, adolescence, and maturity, so do groups, societies, and humankind as a whole develop through similar stages;

- History does not simply "repeat itself," nor is it a totally random or arbitrary process;

- Development is an inherent feature of human life, but its rate and quality of progress depend upon the opportunities that are available to us and the degree of conscious effort we put into our growth;

- The most important and defining aspect of human development is maturation of *consciousness*;

- The goal of development is to achieve ever greater levels of maturity, in which the unique powers of our mind—including the abilities to know, to love, and to will—attain full, integrated, and unified expression;

- The history of human discoveries, struggles, and achievements represents a coherent, gradual progress of development through the stages of collective childhood and adolescence towards the maturation of humanity's physical, psychological, social, and spiritual capacities;

- Humanity is now entering its phase of collective maturity, when its great capacity to establish a just and peaceful worldwide civilization will find ever fuller expression.

Key Vocabulary

Adolescence: (a) the period of physical, psychological, social, and moral/ethical growth following childhood and preceding maturity; a period characterized by intensified pre-occupation with issues of identity and autonomy; often associated with intensified interpersonal and intergroup competition, and a rejection of established authority. (b) a transitional period of development between youth and maturity: *the adolescence of a nation.*[1]

Childhood: (a) the first period of substantive intellectual, social, and emotional development in humans; a period characterized by dependency (for survival) on a greater power or authority; generally entailing an inability to comprehend issues and realities beyond immediate experience. (b) the early stage in the existence or development of something: *the childhood of Western civilization.*[2]

Competition: a contest between rivals.[3]

Cooperation: association of persons for common benefit.[4]

Development: a qualitative increase in capacity towards a more advanced state of being, resulting from a process of evolution or specialization. In human life particularly, development signifies the advancement of our consciousness towards higher levels of understanding, integration, and integrity.

Individualism: a doctrine in which the interests of the individual are or ought to be ethically paramount, and that all values, rights, and duties originate in individuals; a set of values that stress individual initiative, action, and interests.[5]

Infancy: (a) the stage of human development lasting from birth to approximately two years of age. A period characterized by physical growth, motor development, vocal development, and cognitive and social development.[6] (b) the earliest stage in the existence or development of something: *the infancy of modern science or a society in its infancy.*

Maturation: (in human life) a purposeful, conscientious, and integrated progression through stages of life towards ever greater levels of understanding and capacity. It is the condition in which one's capacities of knowledge, love, and will attain their fullest expression, refinement, and harmonization.

Maturity: (a) the state or quality of being fully grown or developed. (b) the state or quality of being mature.[7] The condition of being fully developed in all human capacities, particularly in one's moral and ethical consciousness.

1. *American Heritage Dictionary*, 4th ed., 2000.
2. *American Heritage Dictionary*, 4th ed., 2000.
3. *Merriam-Webster Online Dictionary.*
4. *Merriam-Webster Online Dictionary.*
5. *Merriam-Webster Online Dictionary.*
6. "Infancy," *The Columbia Encyclopedia*, 6th ed.
7. *American Heritage Dictionary*, 4th ed., 2000.

The Nature of Human Development

As discussed in the previous unit, the distinguishing characteristic of human beings is consciousness: the ability to know and understand, to love with full awareness and resolve, and to choose between right and wrong in the context of freedom.

This consciousness, in its primitive state, exists in each of us from the time we are born, but it develops gradually over a lifetime through the education we receive and the life experiences that we have. As our consciousness develops and we gradually formulate our worldviews, our lives change and our capacities increase; we develop new skills; and the nature of our relationships and modes of creativity in life evolve. Indeed, all development takes place on the axis of consciousness.[8] Matter does not develop; rather, it assumes ever more complex organization in accordance with the degree of consciousness applied to it. This distinction between physical growth and development of consciousness in the life of human beings is of particular importance if we are to understand what is happening in the world around us.

According to generally accepted anthropological findings, the anatomical evolution of human nature was virtually completed some fifty thousand years ago. Since then, the human body and brain have remained essentially the same in structure and size. On the other hand, the conditions of life have changed profoundly during this period and continue to change at a rapid pace. To adapt to these changes the human species used its faculties of consciousness, conceptual thought and symbolic language to shift from genetic evolution to social evolution, which takes place much faster and provides far more variety.

—Fritjof Capra, *The Turning Point: Science, Society and the Rising of Culture.* Toronto: Bantam Books, 1983, p. 298

Definition

Development describes a qualitative increase in capacity towards a more advanced state of being, resulting from a process of evolution or specialization. In human life particularly, development signifies the advancement of our consciousness towards higher levels of understanding, integration, and integrity.

The field of developmental psychology helps us to understand that the development of individual human consciousness passes through recognizable stages of maturation, beginning with infancy and childhood, followed by adolescence, adulthood, and maturity.[9]

8. "It is impossible to understand a system of political thought without uncovering the human reality in which it is rooted; that is, the interrelation of impulses and interests, of compulsions and strivings, that constitute human and social existence. It is just as impossible, however, to separate this reality from thought and, depriving thought of its independence and power, make it a merely accidental product of social and economic realities. Man's individual and social being is formed by consciousness in each of its elements down to the most primitive instincts. The attempt to dissolve this connection passes over the first and most important essential trait of man and therefore results in the distortion of the total picture of man" (Paul Tillich, *The Interpretation of History*, 1936).

9. This simplistic categorization of the stages of human development is certainly universal, but it may also be elaborated upon through adaptation of Erikson's eight stages or the application of any other such scheme.

Definition

Maturation in human life is a purposeful, conscientious, and integrated progression through stages of life towards ever greater levels of understanding and capacity. It is the condition in which one's capacities of knowledge, love, and will attain their fullest expression, refinement, and harmonization.

At every stage in the process of maturation, certain developmental challenges and types of behavior predominate. Development is an inherent feature of human life, but its rate and quality depend upon the degree of conscious effort we exert and the opportunities that are available to us. What this means is that the more conscious we are about our development, the greater is our capacity to evolve and mature as wholesome individual human beings. When maturation is a conscious process, our powers to know, love, and choose achieve ever higher levels of expression and integration. In maturity, we move from ignorance to enlightenment, from self-centeredness to universality, and from instinctual

"Social entities and the body politic have often been understood by analogy to the individual human organism. The ancient Chinese "thought the world came from the huge anthropos figure called Pan Ku" (Mindell, 1993: 18), and "Hindus believe we all live in the figure of Atman" (Mindell, 1993: 18). The body of Christ has endured as a metaphor for the world in many Christian traditions (Mindell, 1993: 18). In Muslim societies, philosophy employed similar metaphors. Ibn Khaldun, the great 14th-century thinker and father of sociology, fully developed a longstanding tradition of seeing the relative health and sickness of communities and houses in terms of the human body (Lewis, 1988: 127–28). Within the Ottoman context of the 17th century, the writer Katib Celebi saw society in organic terms going through stages of growth until death (Lewis, 1988: 24–25)" (Excerpt from Danesh and Danesh "Has Conflict Resolution Grown Up?"). See this article also for a treatment of the criticisms against developmental models.

obedience to conscious freedom. Maturity is at once a psychological, social, moral, and spiritual state. It is the process of becoming whole and complete human beings. However, the less developed our consciousness, the less capable we are of understanding the dynamics of our behavior, the more prone we are to behave selfishly and intolerantly, as well as impulsively and violently when our desires and expectations are not met. Many "adults" exhibit these behaviors; a sign that age and maturity are not synonymous. If we have not consciously nurtured our development, then our capacities may not have fully matured even though we have reached "adulthood" in years. To the degree that we are conscious about maturing healthfully and wholesomely, the more universal, peaceful, less self-centered, and less conflicted our lives become.

Online Video Quotation

Development is an awakening of consciousness, is participation in decision-making processes and improvement in living conditions. When someone lacks knowledge, s/he is not developed. When someone doesn't understand, s/he cannot be developed. When s/he doesn't participate, s/he is not developed. Development is expanding one's knowledge and improving oneself.

Development is not "Western" or "non-Western". It is not about having more, it is about being more: more of a man, more of a woman. It is about fulfilling your potential, feeling in harmony with yourself and your environment. If there is an imbalance between these, there is no development.

—Prosper Kompaore, 2002. Founder of the Atelier-Theatre Burkinabe (ATB) in Burkina Faso. To view this online video clip, visit <http://tv.oneworld.net/tapestry?link=866&window=full>.

Remarkably, a parallel process of maturation can be recognized in groups, institutions, and societies as well. Indeed, a developmental perspective on human individuals and groups helps us gain unique insights into the challenges currently facing humanity.

Characteristics of Individual Development

Maturation is a conscious, deliberate process based on accumulated life experiences and deepened insights. The maturation of our intellectual capacities results not only in understanding the laws of nature and discovering new facts but also in acquiring insight, wisdom, and moral rectitude. Likewise, the maturation of our emotional capacities (which at earlier stages of life focus primarily on our personal needs, desires, and interests) lays the foundations for a transcendent and universal love as we gradually gain greater understanding and wisdom. In the same manner, our power of will (which in its primitive state is demanding, self-serving, and inconsiderate of others) becomes, in the stage of maturity, a potent instrument of service and justice.

Consider the following two scenarios:

Scenario 1

Lena is a three-year-old girl. She is out shopping with her mother. In a store window display she sees a doll she would like to have. She asks her mother for it, but her mother says that they are not going to buy a new doll today. Lena throws a tantrum. She demands the doll. "I want it now!" she screams.

Scenario 2

Jack is a twenty-five-year-old man. He and his wife are out shopping when he sees a new large television he would like to buy. He asks his wife whether she thinks they could buy it. She says she thinks today is not the day to buy it. Jack becomes angry and accuses his wife of not respecting his ideas and needs.

Now answer the following questions:

- Is your reaction to the two scenarios the same?
- What are the primary points of concern for Lena and Jack?
- Why do we react to Lena's and Jack's behavior differently?

Human beings must grow physically in order to live healthy lives. We have little control over this form of growth.

Human beings must grow and mature intellectually, emotionally, and ethically in order to live healthy lives. We have a considerable degree of control over this form of growth.

Figure 1: Human growth

The above scenarios evoke different reactions from us because of our awareness of a universal human reality, namely, the processes of growth and development. Growth and maturation are natural aspects of human life. We expect individuals to mature as they grow up, and we sense that something is wrong when behaviors belonging to earlier phases in human development are displayed by adolescents and adults.

A growing child cannot will himself or herself to stop growing physically. Physical growth is mostly predetermined by a host of biological factors and does not rely on our conscious willingness to grow. However, how we think, feel, and make decisions and how our thoughts, feelings, and choices change and mature over the course of a lifetime are somewhat different. It is inevitable that how we think and the emotions which dominate our lives and the kind of decisions we make will change as we experience different conditions in life. It is normal and healthy to expect that we mature in every respect. But human beings can interfere with these processes of growth and choose to be resistant to change, development, and transformation, which are the hallmarks of maturation.

Our discomfort with Jack's behavior is that it appears he did not accomplish the normal healthy process of **maturation** which would lead him to act differently than the child Lena under similar circumstances.

This discussion of individual human development is very relevant to the larger discussion of society and peace. Our changing awareness of self and others alters our commitment to and comfort with less mature behaviors and processes. One's level of maturation determines whether a person is more likely to prefer peaceful modes of interaction and decision-making over conflict-based approaches. This is due to the developmental nature of our human capacities to know, to love, and to choose within the framework of ethical and spiritual awareness and sensitivity.

The healthy development of these capacities lays the natural foundation for reality-based, peace-oriented, and unity-creating social relationships and societal choices.

Childhood[10]

In childhood, we have three primary needs that require enormous attention from our parents/guardians, caregivers, school, and community. These three needs include:

1. Optimal physical care and nourishment for our rapidly developing physical and sensorimotor faculties;
2. Affection, attention, guidance, stimulation, and encouragement for the healthy development of our intellectual, emotional, and self-discipline capacities; and
3. Assurances, optimism, hope, and trust that the world is ordered and that the "unknown" can be gradually understood. This basic trust later leads us to discover the laws of nature and life (science) and to better comprehend the mysteries of the spirit (faith).

The period of childhood is characterized by the desire to reduce feelings of uncertainty and anxiety and to increase feelings of security and pleasure. Anger is common during childhood, appearing whenever a child's desires are frustrated.

Consciousness of moral principles first develops during this period and tends to be rigid; the categories of "right" and "wrong" are clearly defined, and authority figures—who in the child's mind represent the "right" way—are unquestioningly obeyed.

---

10. For a useful overview of the biological and social characteristics of infancy and childhood, see "Childhood Development," *Encyclopedia Britannica*; see this article also for a treatment of the criticisms against developmental models.

As discussed in Unit 2, childhood experiences form the foundations of our worldview along the three main human powers of knowledge, love, and will. Here, we briefly review development of each of these powers during the phase of childhood.

Knowledge

As children, we are constantly engaged in discovering both our environment and ourselves. We gradually distinguish the significant people in our lives—parents/guardians, siblings, family members, and friends—and better understand the nature of our relationships with them. During this period, we perceive reality in concrete, specific, and fixed terms. Later in adolescence and adulthood we gain more abstract, universal, and dynamic understanding.

Love

As infants and very young children, our love is centered on ourselves and our parents/guardians. Gradually, the circle of our love expands as we begin to realize that we are separate entities from our parents and the others in our environment. Over time, our circle of love expands, and we add our siblings, other family members, and an increasing number of friends to the world of our relationships.

Nonetheless, the distinction between self and others remains quite vague. A child's sense of self is enmeshed with the reality of significant family members and/or friends. We refer to this type of love relationship as the "**primary union**" phase of love. It can be mixed with feelings of anger, resentment, sadness, envy, and indifference if the family environment is not caring, positive, secure, happy, and healthy. A secure, caring, happy, and encouraging family environment helps us to develop a positive and strong capacity to both give and receive love. These processes are particularly powerful and consequential during childhood.

Will

As children, we have little patience or capacity to control our will. We want what we want, when and how we want it, and find it difficult to wait. Our **desires** have to be satisfied immediately. But this is neither always possible, nor even advisable. Therefore, one of the major tasks of childhood, and thus one of the main responsibilities of our parents/guardians and teachers, is to help us to develop **self-discipline** and **self-control**.

Adolescence[11]

The period of adolescence begins with puberty, during which time our physical development starts to peak and our intellectual curiosity becomes more intense. We experience extreme emotional highs and lows, and sometimes find ourselves engaged in intense battles of will with ourselves, our parents, and our society. Psychological, social, and spiritual powers start to accelerate.

During this period, we are at once confident and doubtful, happy and sad, smart and ignorant, humble and arrogant, obedient and rebellious, beautiful and ugly. We are trying to form our identity, to choose a path for our future, to establish new types of relationships, and to deal with an explosion of hormonal and physical changes.

During adolescence, the issues of sexuality, aggression, competition, love, success, and indepen-

---

11. According to the *Columbia Encyclopedia Online*, adolescence is the "time of life from onset of puberty to full adulthood. The exact period of adolescence, which varies from person to person, falls approximately between the ages 12 and 20 and encompasses both physiological and psychological changes....Psychological changes generally include questioning of identity and achievement of an appropriate sex role; movement toward personal independence; and social changes in which, for a time, the most important factor is peer group relations. Adolescence in Western societies tends to be a period of rebellion against adult authority figures, often parents or school officials, in the search for personal identity" (6th ed., p. 530).

dence preoccupy our thoughts and energies. It is a challenging age: we want to do everything by ourselves, but we also need guidance and support from our parents/guardians, teachers, and others with authority. This paradoxical state puts heavy demands on both adolescents and adults alike. A review of the dynamics of development of powers of knowledge, love, and will helps us to understand the sometime puzzling and paradoxical character of the adolescent stage of development.

Knowledge

When we enter the adolescent phase, our capacity and hunger to know and understand expands dramatically. Our quest for knowledge, however, takes different routes based on our life experiences, personal capacities, interests, and available opportunities. Some of us pursue the sciences, others focus on the arts, and still others specialize in various trades. This process is called **individuation** and **differentiation**.

During this period, we spend a lot of time and energy trying to understand ourselves, others, and the dynamics of relationships. The ultimate aim of our efforts is to develop a strong sense of identity that is acceptable to us. To do so requires not only our capacity to know but also our capacities to love and to choose.

Love

Adolescence is the age when our capacity for love blossoms. We gradually decrease our dependence on our parents/guardians and other significant adults, and instead start to explore the dynamics of love in new relationships. Childhood love relationships—usually centered on family members and friends—that were based on **sameness**, often enter a period of **otherness, separation,** and **competition** in adolescence. In the process of forming our identity, we feel that we are unique individuals and different from everyone else; yet, at the same time, we desperately need acceptance,

confirmation, and approval from others. These seemingly opposite processes of individuation and the need for acceptance by others, give adolescence its distinctive character. The primary challenge we face during this phase is to develop **self-confidence** and **self-acceptance**.

Will

Our ability to make important choices also begins to take special direction during this phase. Some adolescents become highly disciplined, self-assured, and productive. Others fall into an abyss of self-doubt and self-rejection, and instead of strengthening their abilities of creative decision-making, they abdicate their wills to the forces of drug and alcohol abuse and to other forms of escape from the day-to-day realities and challenges of life. A third group chooses to use their willpower to oppose authority and begin a period of overt or covert rebellion.

All of these developments in human consciousness and its powers of knowledge, love, and will, have a deep lasting effect on both the individual and the society. This is because the relationship between the individual and the society is **reciprocal** in nature: the quality of individual choices significantly determines the general condition of society, and the general condition of the society has a profound effect on the nature of development of its individual members.

When we enter the adolescent phase, we enter the period of individuation and differentiation. Adolescence revolves around discovering and solidifying one's **identity**.[12]

---

12. On the process of identity formation at the individual and collective level, see for example: Beswick (1990), Bindorffer (1997), Bjola (1999), Bringa (1993), Chae (2002), DePaul University (1993), Gavious and Mizrahi (1999), Lustick (2000), Lyles, Yancy, Grace, and Carter (1985), Mahoney (2001), Miguel (1978), Oka (1994), Steinberg (1999), Suutarinen (1998), Vorster and Sutcliffe (2001), Waever (1995), or Youniss, Mclehha, and Yates (1999).

Of particular importance, here, are the dynamics of adolescence in the authoritarian environments—families, schools, and communities. Authoritarianism demands absolute and blind obedience, two conditions that are contrary to the growing needs of adolescents. As children enter their phase of adolescence, they need freedom in the context of discipline and guidance. Adolescents need freedom to experiment, to express themselves, to make mistakes, and to assert their emerging personalities. And they need to go through these crucial processes in an environment that is at once free and disciplined, open-minded and principled, and personal and universal. Authoritarian environments, with their characteristic oppressive and controlling worldviews and practices, are incapable of providing such nurturing environments for their youth. Consequently, adolescents in authoritarian environments tend to remain psychologically, socially, and morally at the childhood level. These adolescents, usually, become highly conformist, obedient, and uncreative. And when the occasion arises for them to free themselves from the oppressive control of those in power, some of them become revolutionaries; others act as soldiers, fighting their revolutionary peers; and still others succumb to a life of apathy and isolation. Only a small number of adolescents in authoritarian environments escape their malignant impact and grow to become wholesome individuals—free, disciplined, creative, peaceful, and universal and unifying in outlook and approach.

If the phase of adolescence is experienced in a healthy manner, the young adult emerges with a comfortable sense of self that no longer requires continuous comparison with others. Throughout maturity, the young adult subsequently becomes more able to recognize and accept the uniqueness of others.

Maturity

Maturity is the longest and most dynamic phase of human life. In this phase, the limitations of childhood and adolescence are surpassed. The individual's capacities and skills, sense of self, and perception about the purpose of life, reach

	Focus of Knowledge	Focus of Love	Focus of Will
Childhood	Self-Experience	Primary Union	Primacy of Desires
	Gradual Recognition of the Other	Self-centered Love	Development of Self-Control
Adolescence	Self-Discovery	Self-Acceptance	Competition
	Focus on Differences	Exclusive Love Relationships	Development of Self-Confidence
Maturity	Self-Knowledge	Enlightened Union	Cooperation
	Recognition of Humanity's Oneness	Inclusive Love Relationships	Development of Selflessness

Table 1: Developmental expressions of knowledge, love, and will under healthy conditions.

a heightened level of development. Individuals in this stage of maturation exhibit an acceptance of both themselves and others, move from self-interest to universal-interest, and shift from the need "to have" to resolve "to become."

If the phase of adolescence is completed in a healthy manner, young adults emerge with a comfortable sense of self that no longer requires continuous comparison with others. Throughout maturity, they become more able to recognize and accept the uniqueness of both themselves and other people, therefore moving from self-interest to universal-interest, from self-service to serving others, from competition to cooperation, and from conflict to unity. These truly transformative qualities of the maturation process could best be understood along the three main powers of human consciousness; therefore, we briefly review them, as we did in the previous two phases.

Knowledge

In maturity, the quest for knowledge and understanding occupies a more prominent place in our lives. A mature person is not afraid of new ideas and in fact, welcomes them with interest and enthusiasm. Open-mindedness, which is seldom found in the earlier stages of development, is a necessary characteristic of adulthood if we wish to develop in a healthy and integrated manner.

A truly mature approach to knowledge is best found within the framework of the unity-based worldview. It is within this worldview that we resolve the dilemma of sameness and difference that troubled us in childhood and adolescence. We come to recognize that in the midst of great diversity, **humanity is one**: we are all heir to the same talents, capacities, dignity, needs, and rights that are developed and expressed in a rich variety of forms. Our capacity to know and understand truth becomes an established, indispensable aspect of our lives. In fact, pursuit of truth and truthfulness are the hallmarks of maturity. While individuals with authoritarian worldviews—characteristic of the childhood phase of development—are typically fearful of truth and while adolescents—with their competitive qualities—tend to manipulate the truth, mature individuals actively search for truth and make utmost effort to live accordingly.

Love

In the adulthood phase, a person's capacity for love becomes more universal and unifying. Mature love motivates us to consciously and purposefully undertake self-growth, while, at the same time contributing to the growth and progress of others. Mature love enables us to create unified and diverse relationships based on truth and justice. This type of love relationship can be called an "**enlightened union,**" as it is based on the mature recognition, acceptance, and appreciation of our uniqueness in the context of the oneness of humanity. In this phase, we are able to love ourselves without being selfish; love specially chosen others without being jealous and possessive; and love all of humanity without being either neglectful or possessive of ourselves, our families, and communities.

Will

A mature use of willpower is demonstrated through actions that enable us to put our evolving understanding, insight, and love at the service of all humanity. Through this process, competition gives way to the pursuit of excellence, cooperation becomes the norm in human undertakings, and concerns for survival and safety become less self-centred and more inclusive. Through **cooperation** and **selflessness,** our capacity to choose and to act becomes more just, effective, and service-oriented. Through the process of maturation, the **primary union** of childhood and **individuation/separation** phase of adolescence give way to the **enlightened union** of the period of maturity.[13]

Table 1 summarizes the preceding exposition.

13. For a more comprehensive discussion of the developmental characteristics of knowledge, love, and will, refer to *The Psychology of Spirituality* by H.B. Danesh.

Individual Stories and Collective History

What can an understanding of individual development tell us about the collective development of humanity? Can knowledge of development of psychosocial and spiritual dynamics in human life help us understand our collective histories? Before trying to answer these questions, let's review a few different theories about the nature of human history.

It is now generally accepted that the interpretation of historical events depends greatly on the worldview or perspective held by the historian who tells the story. Over the centuries, different philosophies regarding the nature of historical process have temporarily gained popularity among historians. In brief, four broad views on collective history have predominated:[14]

1. **Cyclical Views:** These views claim that history goes in cycles and that from age to age the same problems return in parallel forms. There is no direction to history and, indeed, no meaning or purpose in history except to live life for the moment, accepting that the future will look like the past due to the inevitable cycle of history. This view was held by the Greeks and is also reflected in the works of Nietzsche and Sprangler in more modern times.

2. **Providential Views:** These views claim that God guides or controls history completely. God's Will is the only active will in collective affairs; all great movements or changes in the order of things are God's doing, and human beings have no real choice or influence over the course of human history. The Bible represents one historical account that is framed within a providential view.

3. **Secular Teleological Views:** These views claim that history is propelled in a purposeful direction by non-human forces such as economic motives or the evolution of the state. Most views in this category, such as the theories of Hegel and Marx, center on the claim of some inherent conflict in nature that resolves itself in dialectical phases, thus propelling historical change.

4. **Unintelligible Views:** In recent decades, the view that history has no direction or pattern at all, that it is indeed "unintelligible," has emerged. In this view, history is interpreted as a purposeless collection of random events caused by environmental, economic, or political circumstances, and, due to extreme context-specificity and subjectivity of a given historical occurrence, it is impossible to make any comparisons between or across ages.[15]

In the first three views, the idea that human individuals are autonomous beings who can use their free will to choose and act—and are thus responsible for the impact of their choices on other people and events—disappears in the face of deterministic forces: either cyclical, providential, or materialistic. In the fourth view, whether or not humans have free will is ultimately unimportant because events have no objective significance or meaning and rather disappear in

---

14. Excerpted from the commentaries of historian Abdel Wahab El Messeri. Accessed at <http://www.muslimphilosophy.com/tvtk/ch30.htm>.

15. "The most profound thinkers of the twentieth century have directly attacked the idea that history is a coherent or intelligible process; indeed, they have denied the possibility that any aspect of human life is philosophically intelligible. We in the West have become thoroughly pessimistic with regard to the possibility of overall progress in democratic institutions. This profound pessimism is not accidental, but born of the truly terrible political events of the first half of

the mist of subjective human history as isolated occurrences.

We now come to a fifth view on the nature of collective history: the developmental view.

5. **Developmental Views:** These views share certain things in common with each of the views above, but differs in other respects. Human history is the reflection of human choices. While there may be trends that influence human history, such as economic or political movements, these too are the product of human thought and choices. Furthermore, human history (the tale of human collective life over time) has as a distinct direction, just as the unfolding of life in every individual has a predictable but highly fluid and not fully determined pattern. Basic parameters exist, which cannot be nullified by the human will. For example, a child cannot will itself to remain a child its whole life. Biologically, the child will grow into an adolescent and then an adult. Meanwhile, the quality of adulthood is influenced profoundly by the choices of and opportunities available to the growing individual.

---

the twentieth century—two destructive world wars, the rise of totalitarian ideologies, and the turning of science against man in the form of nuclear weapons and environmental damage. The life experiences of the victims of this past century's political violence—from the survivors of Hitlerism and Stalinism to the victims of Pol Pot—would deny that there has been such a thing as historical progress. Indeed, we have become so accustomed by now to expect that the future will contain bad news with respect to the health and security of decent, liberal, democratic political practices that we have problems recognising good news when it comes" (Francis Fukuyama [1992] "By Way of an Introduction," *The End of History and the Last Man.* New York: Avon Books. Available online: <http://www.marxists.org/reference/subject/philosophy/works/us/fukuyama.htm>).

Hegel also viewed the world as gradually progressing in somewhat predetermined degrees of complexity, such as the oak unfolding within the germinating acorn.

Characteristics of Societal Development

Like human individuals, human societies progress through developmental stages similar to those of childhood, adolescence, and maturity. We designate them respectively as the Formative, Assertive, and Integrative Stages of social development.

The Formative Stage

The Formative Stage corresponds to the collective childhood of humankind wherein the cumulative knowledge, understanding, and experience are still in their early stages of development. It is a stage in which scientific, social, and administrative aspects of the life of the community are just beginning to develop and the natural conditions of life are rudimentary and dangerous.

The predominant worldview during this stage is the survival-based worldview, and the most important commodity is power. Societies in their Formative Stage tend to be authoritarian in structure. Power is usually assumed by a few individuals, who force the majority population to conform to their wishes and dictates. Authoritarian rulers exercise absolute authority, strictly control every aspect of life, and require their subjects to obey without question. So long as the people are obedient, the leaders are pleased. Disobedience is rarely tolerated and is usually met with anger and punishment. Power always creates feelings of uncertainty and anxiety: the more power a person has, the more threatening the thought of losing it becomes. An authoritarian leader focuses on maintaining power through heightened security and control. For this reason, societies in their formative phase emphasize the importance of uniformity and conformity, and suppress any expression of autonomy and diversity.

Under these conditions, individuals cannot fully develop their inherent talents and capabilities, nor can the society as a whole advance. The peace and order created by an authoritarian system are illusory, lasting only as long as the balance of power allows the rulers to impose order on their subjects.

The Assertive Stage

The Assertive Stage of societal development corresponds to the collective adolescence of humanity and to the identity-based worldview. As in the Formative Stage, power is a very central issue during this phase as well. However, instead of the authoritarian control of power by a minority, decision-making power is now more widely distributed among the population. A representative example of the Assertive Stage is the adversarial mode of democratic governance, which is being established with some variations in an increasing number of countries.

In this type of government, through competitive and adversarial processes, the opinions of the society's majority dictate the patterns of leadership and governance, and various institutions such as the judiciary, executive, and legislative, as well as the media, use their power to assert influence on specific issues. This phase is highly competitive, and there are inevitably winners and losers.

In this phase, societies become excessively preoccupied with issues of personal freedom, independence, identity, and success, in brief, *individualism*. Not infrequently, citizens become actively involved in the political life of their society and express, debate, and compete to promote their views and objectives. Sometimes rapid change, akin to a state of anarchy, can take place in the nature of interpersonal and intergroup relationships, which dramatically impacts the structure and stability of the society and its institutions, such as the family, religion, education, the economy, and government.

Definition

Individualism refers to a doctrine in which the interests of the individual are or ought to be ethically paramount, and all values, rights, and duties originate in individuals.

Indeed, competition and individualism are two of the main reasons why many contemporary institutions, such as educational, economic, religious, and political institutions as well as marriage and the family are in a state of conflict and disharmony. The same dynamics also explain why in our world nations are in standoffs with one another, and why societies are internally disunited, or at war. This excessive power-struggle, competition, assertiveness, and conflict are the hallmarks of adolescence, and their prevalence today is one significant indicator that humanity is currently is still in its adolescent phase of collective development.

The Integrative Phase

From a psychological and social perspective, humanity is now gradually moving from its childhood and adolescence into adulthood and hesitatingly entering its Integrative Phase of societal development. This transition is most far-reaching and demanding, and requires a fundamental transformation in our individual and collective ways of thinking, relating, and acting. It calls for the adoption of the *unity-based worldview*, a process that may be considered variably as impossible, undesirable, demanding, or even frightening.

The Integrative Phase corresponds with the evolution of human consciousness and the maturation of worldview. During this phase the limitations of authoritarian control and adolescent competition are surpassed; the very nature of human society is altered; and the principles of equality, lawfulness, justice, unity-in-diversity, and peace become established norms and practices among individuals, groups, institutions, and nations. Above all, the Integrative Phase is characterized by the process of the spiritualization of human society, a process that makes the moral and ethical principles of truth, unity, justice, and service the framework for all human scientific, artistic, political, and economic endeavors. These are attributes of a civilization of peace, which has been and continues to be humanity's central quest.

Such a society is imbued with the spirit of compassion and generosity, both requisites to abolish the extremes of wealth and poverty, and to ensure that no individual is deprived of the essential necessities for survival—food, clean water, shelter, health care, education, dignity, and the opportunity to develop.

A mature society has both a universal and unique outlook: its overarching principles and aims are to establish the unity and ensure the well-being of the global community of humanity, while fostering the unique identities, capacities, and characteristics of its constituent peoples, cultures, and resources.

In the phase of maturity, human knowledge focuses on the cause of progress in civilization. Science is used to create peace, not war; and knowledge is transformed into wisdom instead of being used and exchanged as a commodity. Diversity within and across societies does not become a cause of competition or conflict, but is celebrated and respected. Decisions—whether in the family, at work, or in government—are based on truth; are made through consultative, non-adversarial processes; and are directed towards the creation of a truly just and united civilization.

Change and Resistance to Change

It is important to remember that change and development are not automatic, spontaneous processes. While development and change are inevitable aspects of life, the manner in which we focus on our personal and social development is crucial and highly influenced by choices we make.

Thus, an individual or society may function for an overly long period of time within an adolescent mindset and worldview, resisting the transition to the next phase. When peoples and societies resist responding to the imperatives of change and growth, they suffer the consequences of this resistance. High levels of anger and resentment, combined with feelings of hopelessness and helplessness appear, and these feelings in turn create aggression and violence, and dramatically increase the occurrence of destructive and violent forms of behavior.

The fundamental challenge before humanity today is to address the underlying causes of such problems as poverty, injustice, violence, social and environmental degradation, and inadequate and corrupt leadership that burden the world of humanity. These problems are symptoms of a fundamental underlying affliction—disunity—which saps human energies, distorts the standards of morality, misapplies scientific discoveries and technological developments, and abuses the vast reservoir of human talent and love, which are essential for the creation of an all-inclusive civilization of peace.

When we, as individuals and societies, choose to replace the competitive, aggressive, individualistic, and self-centered characteristics of the adolescent age with those of cooperation, tenderness, universality, and generosity of spirit, we accelerate the process of our growth towards maturity. As we do this, the conditions that create violence and allow conflict to take root in our societies decrease. The shift is most dramatic and demonstrates that history does not simply "repeat itself," nor is it the outcome of purely random or arbitrary events, but is instead the product of our consciousness, expressed in our worldviews, and reflected in our choices, decisions, and actions.

In this creative cycle, the development of the individual contributes to the advancement of the society, and an advanced society, in turn, fosters the development of the individual. Thus, change becomes a creative, continuous, and integrative process. Here, the true power of the individual and the capacity of the society to empower its members are expressed.

Humanity's Coming-of-Age

Humanity is moving into its collective stage of maturity, which is a stage of peace and unity. There is strong evidence of this shift, such as the growing united concern around the world regarding environmental issues; and the emerging commitment of world leaders to approach issues of global concern such as public health, the rights of women and children, and the eradication of poverty in a coordinated manner. The next generation of young leaders, who are committed to shaping the future of our society, has to be aware of this next stage in order to enter it. What should our world be like in its mature state? How do we reach maturity and peace? What is our role in advancing this process?

The establishment of peace—like the emergence of our personal maturity—is a process, which means that it takes time and effort. When we, as individuals and societies, begin to replace the competitive, aggressive, individualistic, and self-centered qualities of the adolescent age with those qualities of cooperation, tenderness, universality, and generosity of spirit, we accelerate the process of our growth toward maturity. And as we do this, the conditions that create violence and allow conflict to take root in our societies decrease. This transition is at once subtle and dramatic. It signifies the very important reality that history does not simply "repeat itself," nor is it the outcome of purely random or arbitrary events. Rather, it is the product of our free choice and collective creativity.

No human society has been able to move beyond its collective adolescence in the past. This is a new phenomenon in the history of humanity. It is the period of humanity's coming-of-age— that unique, dramatic, and unparalleled period of transition and change in human life. Our ideas and modes of behavior; social and political organizations; arts and sciences; and moral, ethical, and spiritual beliefs are all undergoing profound change. No individual or society is exempt; all are involved.

Such a fundamental change is characterized by the processes of integration as well as disintegration. Our old ways of thinking and behaving, as well as many of the institutions we created, are breaking down and being discarded. This disintegration is unavoidable. It is the chaos that inevitably comes before a new order is established. In the midst of this chaos, much insecurity develops. If we don't understand the process of transition that we are in, then this insecurity could mislead people into preparing for and committing an unimaginable degree of violence. One example of this was the arms race that the insecurity of the Cold War produced among many of the world's nations. Another example is the current wave of terrorism and the manner in which it is being addressed by the leaders and governments of the world. Terrorism is the most malignant expression of a misguided adolescent mindset. It, therefore, needs to be dealt with, not within the parameters of power-struggle, domination, force, and violence, but rather in a truly novel and creative manner. The central component of this strategy is the need for a unity of purpose and approach on the part of all the nations of the world, with the objective of simultaneously neutralizing the forces of terrorism and genuinely addressing its underlying causes.

As we pass beyond the insecurity of childhood and adolescent perspectives, a new level of consciousness emerges, and we gain greater confidence to conduct our affairs in the spirit of integration, collaboration, and cooperation— maturity.

Illustration: The Tree of Life

Think of development as we would the life cycle of a tree: In the tree of life, our roots are our ethical principles, our wisdom, and our self-knowledge. The more developed, universal, spiritual, and noble our roots, the stronger is the tree of our lives. Our trunks and branches are the preparations we make in this life to be people of capacity—our education, the development of our relationships, our experiences, and our skills. Our blossoms are the beginnings of the special things we can do—we each blossom uniquely; we show ourselves, we pride ourselves in our talents and capacities. Most people want to stay in the stage of blossoming forever. But the blossoming must give way to fruits—bearing fruit is a sign that the growth process has reached a point of maturity and fulfillment. Interestingly, the fruits of our lives, like the fruits of a tree, are not for ourselves—rather, they are for others, for the continuation of the lives of others. If we have not borne fruit, our process of self-development is incomplete, and we have not contributed to the lives of others.

We cannot wait to bear fruit on some other day—we may not have the chance. Our fruit-bearing must begin now and continue throughout each day of the remainder of our lives. What greater fruition can there be at this time than to become a peacemaker?

Summary

In this unit, we have learned that:

Human Consciousness Develops Throughout Life

- As human consciousness matures through the observable stages of childhood, adolescence, and maturity, our abilities to know, to love, and to choose gradually develop, becoming more universal and integrated.

Human Groups and Societies Develop As Well

- Similar to an individual's life experience, humanity collectively develops and is now beginning to enter the period of maturity, when its inherent capacity to establish a just and peaceful worldwide civilization will find ever fuller expression.

A Developmental Perspective Changes Our Understanding of History

- We discover that history does not simply "repeat itself," nor is it a totally random or arbitrary process; we recognize that conflict and war represent early phases in human development; and we see how a civilization of peace is the natural outcome of a healthy, mature, and integrated human life.

Key Questions for the Classroom

The following questions can be used to review and explore further the concepts of Unit 5 on the Developmental Model of Civilization with your students:

1. What is development?

2. What do you consider to be the qualities of a person who is "mature"?

3. Do all individuals and societies have the potential to mature?

4. Many adults act like teenagers, and sometimes worse. Why?

5. Historically, some theories of societal development have been used to create hierarchies among races and peoples. What did these theories claim, and how does the present model contrast with those perspectives?

6. Knowing that major events of the present and past are the result of a complex matrix of causes and circumstances, how can we say that history is following a demonstrably developmental path?

7. Why can't we let people and communities develop gradually as they are? What else can be done that we aren't already doing?

8. There is a common saying that "you can't change others." Is this true? If so, how can we possibly foster collective social transformation?

9. How will interpersonal relationships change when society has moved into collective maturity?

10. How long can we expect the adolescent period of human collective development to last?

11. Some individuals never reach maturity; is it the same with societies?

12. Does maturity require us to reduce existing differences like extremes of poverty and wealth?

13. Is the present chaos we see in the world, including the increase in violent responses to conflict, a necessary stepping stone to maturity?

14. To what degree are individuals actually responsible for peace or conflict in the world? Are we as individuals powerless to solve problems of global concern?

15. How much do our survival instincts override our learned social behaviors, and can we separate ourselves from these instincts?

16. Does collective development guarantee individual development and vice-versa?

17. How can we prevent deviant phenomena in the adolescent stage of human development?

Personal Reflection

Reflection is a very powerful learning tool. It helps us to make sense of the things we are studying and the experiences we are going through. The more we reflect on ourselves, our relationships, and the world around us, the better prepared we are to discern, prioritize, and act upon issues of importance.

Becoming a peacemaker is a very important and challenging task. By reflecting on the principles of peace, we are better equipped to make decisions about our own development that will help us to confidently undertake the goal of peace building.

As we go through each of the EFP Curriculum units, try to set aside some time for the process of reflection.

The following questions are provided to help you begin this process.

Questions for Personal Reflection

1. Reflections on Self

- How do I know what I know?
- How do I give and receive love?
- How do I make decisions?

Focus Question

Are my capacities for knowledge, love, and will mature? What can I do to develop them more?

2. Reflections on Family/Group

- What stage of development is my society in?
- Do my friends or family ever talk about the need for positive change in the world?
- How important are service, justice, and unity to the people around me?
- How does my family life challenge me to develop the positive aspects of my character?

Focus Question

Does a developmental perspective change my attitudes towards my relationships? How?

3. Reflections on Society

- Do women receive the same opportunities and treatment in my society as men do?
- Is diversity (of culture, religion, language, race, etc.) celebrated or protested in my society?
- Does my society value the oneness, equality, and unity of the entire human race?
- Is the dimension of "service" an important value in our society?

Focus Questions

At what developmental stage is my society? What are its main features and characteristics? How might my society be assisted to mature in its worldview?

4. Reflections on the World at large

- In your view, how mature are today's world leaders?
- Are attitudes towards poverty, terrorism, and environmental damage influenced by human development?
- What barriers to the advancement of consciousness exist worldwide? How might they be overcome?

Focus Questions

What kind of world leader would we need in order to make significant advances towards global peace? What would this leader's personal characteristics be, and what strategic plans would they have?

Classroom Tools

As a teacher in the Education for Peace Program, it is now your task to introduce the discussion of human development in your class and to assist your students in exploring the purpose of development in their own lives and throughout history. Your role as their teacher and mentor in this process is tremendously important.

To help you get started, a number of tools are included in this section that you may find useful. These tools are only guides, and you are encouraged to develop your own ideas about how to best explore these topics with your students.

In addition to the examples here, please also refer to the Educational Methodology Unit where you will find practical guidelines on how to make your classroom a creative and effective learning environment, as well as other great ideas from fellow teachers who are integrating Education for Peace into their various subject areas.

As you work with the Education for Peace concepts, you will surely develop new ideas for lessons, activities, and assessment approaches. We encourage you to pass along your thoughts, ideas, or resource links to Education for Peace so they can be added to our EFP Resource Bank for other teachers to use. Please send us an email at <info@efpinternational.org>, or mail your ideas to our address:

International Education for Peace Institute (Canada)
101, 1001 W. Broadway, Suite 900
Vancouver, BC V6H 4E4
Canada

We look forward to hearing from you!

Activity Ideas for Secondary Schools

Political Science   Security in the face of terrorism is an increasing concern for nations around the world. Imagine that you have been appointed to a Global Security Council. What antiterrorism strategies could you devise that identify and address the **root causes** of terrorism?

Computer Science   Imagine you are the inventor of artificially intelligent (AI) computers and you are striving to create a robot with near-human decision-making capabilities. What decision-making considerations would you need to incorporate into your programming so that your intelligent computer could make "wise" decisions? To learn more about AI, visit this site:

<http://www-formal.stanford.edu/jmc/whatisai/whatisai.html>

Sports   How has the concept of sport changed throughout history? Compare the sporting activities of the gladiators with those of the modern-day Olympics. What has changed, and what has stayed the same? In what respects do modern sports reflect a different consciousness towards human society and the goals of human life?

Biology   Find an online video of the early development of newborn animals: for example, lion cubs, a colt, or baby ape. What challenges does the animal face in the early phases of its development? How is a typical day spent? How do the adults of that species assist the young to learn and develop more?

Activity Ideas for Primary Schools

Science

Explore growth and the human life cycle, outlining the physical stages of growth. Students can represent the different stages of life in a chart format, beginning with birth and leading to old age. Initiate a discussion about other areas of growth, including emotional, cognitive, etc. Ask students to think about younger children in comparison to themselves, as well as adults in the various stages of development.

Social Studies

Over the course of a few months, identify a particular period in history and explore the differences in shelter, clothing, and beliefs compared to our current period in time. Ask the students to think about what the future would be like and to describe what kinds of beliefs they think would be important so that unity is created and everyone can live in peace. Create a mural in the class comparing the past, present, and future.

Language Arts

Read a story about growth, families, and the power of love. Robert Munsch's *Love You Forever* is one example of such a book, or choose another suitable story from your local curriculum. Create a discussion about the role love plays in the growth and development of children and families, asking students to think about their own experiences. Students can then create a story or play about how their family's love has helped them to grow.

Unit 5, Sample Lesson 1: DEVELOPMENTAL MODEL OF HUMAN CIVILIZATION

Focus: Individual Development

Context

All human beings undergo processes of development and maturation. We are most familiar with biological and intellectual development. But humans also develop emotionally, ethically, and spiritually throughout the course of their lifetimes. This lesson aims to assist students to explore the psychological and social processes that characterize human childhood, adolescence, and maturity, and to reflect on the processes of development within themselves.

Points for Understanding

- Human beings develop through stages of childhood, adolescence, and maturity.
- Full human development includes the physical, intellectual, emotional, social, and spiritual dimensions of life.
- Of all dimensions, the most important and defining aspect of human maturation is development of one's *consciousness,* characterized by our three main capacities: to know, to love, and to will.
- As we approach maturity, our powers to know, to love, and to will gradually attain full, integrated, and unified expression.
- Every human being has the capacity to develop; however, the rate and quality of this development depends upon the degree of conscious effort we put into our growth and the opportunities that are available to us.

Key Questions

1. What are some characteristics of childhood, adolescence, and maturity as stages of human development?
2. What makes a person "mature"?

Learning Process

1. Teacher asks: "What general life stages do all humans pass through?" (Infancy, Childhood, Adolescence, Adulthood/Maturity, Old-Age/Late Maturity).
2. Drawing on their personal life experiences, ask students to describe the features of these different stages. Draw a timeline from infancy to late maturity and write down student responses. Questions and discussion can be focused on students' own experiences, such as: When you were a child, what did you want to do with your time? What made

you happy? Afraid? Upset? Who made important decisions for you as a child? What did you learn or accomplish during that phase? In what ways were you developing? (Repeat the questions, inserting **adolescent** instead). Follow with questions such as: How will you be different when you are an **adult**? What **should** adults be like? Do all adults act maturely?

3. Teachers should then summarize the general characteristics of each developmental stage coherently, using Unit 5 as your guide.

4. Bridge the development of the individual with that of society by asking the students: If we were to say that societies go through similar stages, what stage do you think most societies are at currently? Why?

5. For homework, ask students to re-read Unit 3's description of the human capacities of knowledge, love, and will.

Activities and Assignments

Teachers can choose from among the following sample assignments, or create their own:

1. **Group Discussion**: What do you think it takes to be a mature person? What are the challenges of maturity, and what are the benefits of maturity? Use examples to discuss your views.

2. **Reflect on the following quotation:** *"When I was a child, I spoke like a child, I thought like a child, I reasoned like a child; when I became a man, I gave up childish ways. Then, we saw in a mirror dimly, but now face to face. Then I knew in part; now I shall understand fully, even as I have been fully understood"* (Bible, 1 Corinthians 13:11). Interpret what was meant by the sentence, *"Then we saw in the mirror dimly, but now face to face."*

3. **Journal:** Discuss the following questions: In which aspect(s) of myself do I feel the most development taking place? Physical? Intellectual? Emotional? Ethical? Spiritual?

Unit 5, Sample Lesson 2: DEVELOPMENTAL MODEL OF HUMAN CIVILIZATION

Focus: Societal Development

Context

Societies reflect the developmental level of their collective inhabitants. Understanding the human developmental model can help us to better understand the societies we live in and to chart strategies for raising the collective level of maturity in the community.

Points for Understanding

- Just as individuals develop through stages of childhood, adolescence, and maturity, so too groups, societies, and humanity as a whole develop on the collective level.
- The history of human discoveries, struggles, and achievements can be understood as the gradual progress of humanity through the stages of collective childhood and adolescence, towards the maturation of its physical, psychological, social, and spiritual capacities.
- Humanity is now entering its phase of collective maturity, when its great capacity to establish a just and peaceful worldwide civilization will find ever fuller expression.

Key Questions

1. What parts do 'unity-in-diversity' and 'worldview' play in a mature society?
2. Will humanity ever really reach the mature, integrative stage of development?
3. What will our society and the world look like in their mature state?
4. How do interpersonal relationships change in the stage of societal adulthood?

Learning Process

1. Drawing on the established connection between individual development and that of societies, ask students to imagine the characteristics of a mature society. Help focus discussion by asking students what they would like to see done differently and what are the steps to getting there.
2. Students are gathered into four groups and assigned one of four principles: (a) oneness and equality of the human race, (b) harmony of scientific and spiritual laws, (c) justice and service in human affairs, (d) non-adversarial, consultative decision-making.
3. Groups are given the task to first discuss the principle together and then to begin collecting samples that illustrate the principle they have been assigned. Samples may include imagery, news items, examples, and visuals of their own creation, speeches and commentaries, poems, etc. This process can be completed as homework.

4. During the following class, students consolidate within their group the examples they had researched. They should also decide on a way to present the material in a manner that involves all members of the group, and preferably, the other members of the class. A scrapbook, panel, or PowerPoint file of the presentation should be prepared for submission to the teacher. Included should be one paragraph from each member of the group on their thoughts about the principle under consideration.

5. At the next class, each group makes a presentation, followed by discussion.

Activities and Assignments

Teachers can choose from among the following sample assignments, or create their own:

1. **Investigate** one dramatic period of history—its rulers, its policies, the nature of its labor and family life, its ethical beliefs and practices, etc.—and analyze its characteristics on the basis of the developmental model.

2. **Group work**: The leaders in your country have come to the conclusion that, indeed, their society is in the adolescent stages of development. You and your classmates are called upon to form a council that will advise the country on steps to progress towards a mature state. Create a presentation to the leaders of your country that identifies the characteristics of a mature society and that makes recommendations for developing such characteristics, specifically through the areas of national education policy, media, and/or international relations.

3. **Written Assignment**: Refer to the set of quotations included at the end of this unit. Write a 1–2 page discussion of one of these quotations, in light of the concepts introduced in Unit 5.

Additional Resources

Lesson Reading 2.

Unit 5, Sample Lesson 2 – Activity Reading

Choose one of the following quotations and discuss:

"Our biological inheritance, the temperament with which we are born, the care we receive, our family relationships, the place where we grow up, the schools we attend, the culture in which we participate, and the historical period in which we live—all these affect the paths we take through childhood and condition the remainder of our lives."

—Robert H. Wozniak (20th century), U.S. developmental psychologist
Childhood, Thirteen WNET (1991)

"Adolescent development is characterized throughout by oscillating progressions, regressions, and standstills."

—Peter Blos (20th century), U.S. psychoanalyst
On Adolescence, ch. 5 (1962)

"Personal change, growth, development, identity formation—these tasks that once were thought to belong to childhood and adolescence alone now are recognized as part of adult life as well. Gone is the belief that adulthood is, or ought to be, a time of internal peace and comfort, that growing pains belong only to the young; gone the belief that these are marker events—a job, a mate, a child—through which we will pass into a life of relative ease."

—Lillian Breslow Rubin (20th century), U.S. psychologist
Intimate Strangers, ch. 1 (1983)

"Good schools are schools for the development of the whole child. They seek to help children develop to their maximum their social powers and their intellectual powers, their emotional capacities, their physical powers."

—James L. Hymes, Jr. (20th century), U.S. child development specialist, author
Teaching the Child Under Six, ch. 1 (1968)

"To be sure, we have inherited abilities, but our development we owe to thousands of influences coming from the world around us from which we appropriate what we can and what is suitable to us."

—Johann Wolfgang von Goethe (1749–1832), German poet, dramatist
Conversations with Eckermann (December 16, 1828)

"Competition has been shown to be useful up to a certain point and no further, but cooperation, which is the thing we must strive for today, begins where competition leaves off."

—Franklin D. Roosevelt (1882–1945), U.S. president
Nathan Miller, *F.D.R.: An Intimate History,* p. 89, Doubleday & Co. (1983)

"When I was a child, I spoke like a child, I thought like a child, I reasoned like a child; when I became a man, I gave up childish ways. Then, we saw in a mirror dimly, but now face to face. Then I knew in part; now I shall understand fully, even as I have been fully understood."
—Bible, 1 Corinthians (13:11–12)

"Until the reality of equality between man and woman is fully established and attained, the highest social development of mankind is not possible."
— 'Abdu'l-Bahá Abbas (1844–1921), Persian philosopher, humanitarian
The Promulgation of Universal Peace, p. 76

"The highest form of development is to govern one's self."
—Zerelda G. Wallace (1817–1901), U.S. suffragist
As quoted in *History of Woman Suffrage*, vol. 4, ch. 7
by Susan B. Anthony and Ida Husted Harper (1902)

"The proper aim of education is to promote significant learning. Significant learning entails development. Development means successively asking broader and deeper questions of the relationship between oneself and the world. This is as true for first graders as graduate students, for fledging artists as graying accountants."
—Laurent A. Daloz (20th century), U.S. educator
Effective Teaching and Mentoring, ch. 9 (1986)

"Fascism, the more it considers and observes the future and the development of humanity, quite apart from political considerations of the moment, believes neither in the possibility nor the utility of perpetual peace."
—Benito Mussolini (1883–1945), Italian dictator
The Political and Social Doctrine of Fascism (1932)

"[How] the young . . . can grow from the primitive to the civilized, from emotional anarchy to the disciplined freedom of maturity without losing the joy of spontaneity and the peace of self-honesty is a problem of education that no school and no culture have ever solved."
—Leontine Young (20th century), U.S. social worker and author
Life Among the Giants, ch. 1 (1965)

"That the world can be improved and yet must be celebrated as-it-is are contradictions. The beginning of maturity may be the recognition that both are true."
—William Stott (b. 1940), U.S. writer
Documentary Expression and Thirties America, Oxford University Press (1973)

"That mystic, all-pervasive, yet indefinable change, which we associate with the stage of maturity inevitable in the life of the individual and the development of the fruit must…have its counterpart in the evolution of the organization of human society. A similar stage must sooner or later be attained in the collective life of mankind, producing an even more striking phenomenon in world relations, and endowing the whole human race with such potentialities of well-being as shall provide, throughout the succeeding ages, the chief incentive required for the eventual fulfillment of its high destiny."

—Shoghi Effendi (1897–1957), Historian, global administrator
The World Order of Bahá'u'lláh, p. 163

"What, now, is the effort to Develop? There the disciple incites his will to arouse meritorious conditions that have not yet arisen; and he strives, puts forth his energy, strains his mind and struggles.

…What, now, is the effort to Maintain? There, the disciple incites his will to maintain the meritorious conditions that have already arisen, and not to let them disappear, but to bring them to growth, to maturity and to the full perfection of development; and he strives, puts forth his energy, strains his mind and struggles.

…Truly, the disciple who is possessed of faith and has penetrated the Teaching of the Master, is filled with the thought: 'May rather skin, sinews and bones wither away, may the flesh and blood of my body dry up: I shall not give up my efforts so long as I have not attained whatever is attainable by manly perseverance, energy and endeavor!'"

—Buddha
The Eightfold Path

Extended Exploration

Publications

Danesh, H.B. (2006). *Fever in the World of the Mind: Unique Dimensions of Human Conflict and Violence.* Education for Peace Integrative Curriculum Series. Volume 3. Vancouver: EFP Publications.

————. (1997). *The Psychology of Spirituality: From Divided Self to Integrated Self.* 2d ed. Hong Kong: Juxta Publishing.

Danesh, H.B., and R. Danesh (2002). "Has Conflict Resolution Grown Up? Toward a New Model of Decision Making and Conflict Resolution." *International Journal of Peace Studies* 7.2: 59–76.

Donaldson, Margaret. (1979). *Children's Minds.* London: Fontana/Collins.

Erikson, E. H. (1968). *Identity: Youth and Crisis.* New York: Norton.

————. (1959). *Identity and the Life Cycle.* New York: International Universities Press.

————. (1950). *Childhood and Society.* New York: Norton.

Featherman, David L., Richard M. Lerner, and Marion Perlmutter, eds. (1992). *Life-Span Development and Behavior.* Vol. 11. Hillsdale, NJ: Lawrence Erlbaum Associates.

Murray, Mary. *Moral Development and Moral Education: An Overview* (summarizing the main theories of Piaget, Kohlberg, Turiel, and Gilligan). Department of Studies in Moral Development and Education: University of Illinois. Available online: <http://tigger.uic.edu/~lnucci/MoralEd/overviewtext.html>.

Sørensen, Aage B., Franz E. Weinert, and Lonnie R. Sherrod, eds. (1986). *Human Development and the Life Course: Multidisciplinary Perspectives.* Hillsdale, NJ: Lawrence Erlbaum Associates.

Web Links

"Public Broadcasting Service (PBS) TeacherSource – for K-12 lesson samples and resources for all subjects." <http://www.pbs.org/teachersource/>.

"Erik Erikson's Life Stages summarized."
   <http://psychology.about.com/od/theoriesofpersonality/a/psychosocial.htm>.

"Erik Erikson's Life Stages and Virtues diagrams."
   <http://home.att.net/~revdak/spir243/erikson.htm>.

General Online Resources

The Columbia Encyclopedia Online. <http://www.bartleby.com/65>.

The Columbia World of Quotations. <http://www.bartleby.com/quotations>.

The Merriam-Webster Online Dictionary. <http://www.merriam-webster.com>.

The Stanford Encyclopedia of Philosophy. <http://plato.stanford.edu>.

Wikipedia: The Free Encyclopedia. <http://www.wikipedia.org>.

Art History Timeline: The Metropolitan Museum of Art. <http://www.metmuseum.org/toah/splash.htm>.

Unit 6

Humanity's Transition to a Civilization of Peace

This unit describes the opportunities and challenges presented by humanity's present transition from a history of conflict, division, and war, to a global civilization of cooperation, mutual development, and peace. In particular, the unit explores the twin processes of integration and disintegration that characterize the pattern of human affairs during this period of great change. Other topics of study include the specific roles that families, schools, leaders, and media can play in fostering humanity's transition to peace.

Context

The first five units of Education for Peace focused on the following essential concepts:

1. Identifying the law of **unity** as the prerequisite and characteristic of **healthy life processes**, their interdependency and their impact on us both as individuals and as a collective;

2. Understanding how **worldviews** are formed and how they affect the attitudes and behaviors of individuals and societies;

3. Discussing historical perceptions of **human nature** and the notion that human beings are **inherently noble**, developing, and capable of creating peace;

4. Understanding the **causes and effects of violence**, and looking for appropriate means to prevent its occurrence;

5. Analyzing the **dynamics of human development** and applying a developmental perspective to the interpretation of human interpersonal and societal divisiveness and inclusiveness.

This unit discusses the dynamics of humanity's transition from adolescence to collective maturity, highlighting the opportunities and challenges presented by this move towards global civilization.

Learning Process

In this unit, participants should be assisted to:

1. Understand that humanity's collective consciousness has evolved throughout history, enabling it to achieve ever greater levels of unity and ultimately establishing world peace;

2. Understand through examples that the nature of "transition" from one state of being to another entails the dual processes of "disintegration" and "integration";

3. Reflect on the dynamics of transitions in their societies and their own lives, and discuss how the experience of change involves relinquishing old modes of thought and behavior, and exercising new modes;

4. Think of strategies that various members of society such as families, leaders, and the media could pursue to assist humanity's transition to a culture of peace in their own communities.

Points for Understanding

Teachers can guide their students to understand and remember these main points:

- Successful transition towards a more advanced stage of human development—whether political, economic, social, moral, or ethical—requires a corresponding transformation in worldview.

- Worldview transformation can be a difficult and even painful process, as it demands the reformulation of fundamental assumptions about ourselves, our purpose in life, and the mode of our relationships.

- Today, humanity is in the midst of a transition from a divided world to a unified world. As governments, institutions, families, and individuals struggle to expand their worldviews in order to embrace the reality of human oneness, tensions and conflicts are clearly increasing between old and new ways of how we view ourselves and how we organize our societies.

- This transition—however demanding—is an inevitable and purposeful process, and is gradually leading the majority of humankind towards acceptance of the new and potential-laden phase of global peace.
- In this period of monumental change, one of our challenges is to stay focused on unity and peace-based developments taking place locally and internationally, and to continually exert ourselves to strengthen these developments, rather than become distracted and ineffective due to an overall focus on conflict and disunity.

- The ultimate objective of the transition that humanity is now making is the creation of a global civilization, which is safe and prosperous, equitable and just, united and diverse, ethical and progressive, scientific and spiritual, universal and peaceful.
- Every sector in society, indeed every individual, can play a creative and constructive role in the promotion of a civilization of peace. The more conscious and systematic our efforts are to creating unity, celebrating diversity, and

Key Vocabulary

Civilization: the totality of arts and sciences, values and philosophies, modes of societal organization and governance that emerge gradually over time and come to distinguish a large group or body of people.

Decay: to fall into ruin: *a civilization that had begun to decay;* to decline in health or vigor; waste away; to decline from a state of normality, excellence, or prosperity; deteriorate.[1]

Disintegration: the process of losing integrity, cohesion, and unity; and becoming reduced to components, fragments, or particles.[2]

Enlighten: to edify, illumine, improve, irradiate, uplift; direct, educate, guide, inform, instruct, school, teach, train; acquaint, advise, apprise, inform.

Integration: the process of making into a whole by bringing all parts together; of unifying or joining with something else; uniting.[3]

Integrity: 1: firm adherence to a code of especially moral or artistic values: incorruptibility; 2: an unimpaired condition: soundness; 3: the quality or state of being complete or undivided: completeness.[4]

Materialism: a doctrine that the only or the highest values and objectives lie in material well-being and progress, rather than in spiritual or intellectual well-being and progress.

Social or Cultural Change: a process in which the values, beliefs, modes of interaction or organization of a society and/or culture shift, often gradually but sometimes radically.

Transition: a movement, development, or evolution from one phase, form, stage, or condition to another.

Worldview Assumptions: beliefs or opinions about the nature of life and the world at large that are taken for granted and as true and in keeping with the facts.[5]

1. *American Heritage Dictionary,* 4th ed., 2000.
2. Composite definitions from those found in the *American Heritage Dictionary,* 4th ed., 2000, and the *Merriam-Webster Online Dictionary.*

3. *American Heritage Dictionary,* 4th ed., 2000.
4. *Merriam-Webster Online Dictionary.*
5. Adapted from definitions given in *Merriam-Webster Online Dictionary.*

preventing violence and war, the more effective they can be.

The Dynamics of Change

We are living in one of the most remarkable periods in human history. We live in a day when, as the philosopher Alfred North Whitehead says, "civilization is shifting its basic outlook: we are at a major turning point in history where the presuppositions on which society is structured are being analyzed, sharply challenged, and profoundly changed."[6] We live at that moment when it is possible to witness humanity's transition from our collective childhood and adolescent ways of thinking and behaving, to the phase of our collective adulthood. No other generation of humanity has had this opportunity: never in history have people found themselves at that period of change in which humanity comes of age.

Initial Responses to Change

All societies are subject to the dynamics of change. In the same way that every adolescent ultimately has to grow up, so every adolescent society has to grow up. This transition can feel turbulent at times and can bring feelings of uncertainty, anxiety, and fear. It can also bring great excitement, optimism, and determination.

When people face change, they often respond with fear, indifference, active anticipation, or hostile resistance. Some people become frightened of change: "The past was good enough," they say, "let's keep things the way they were." Often, such individuals have a profound fear of self-knowledge or fear of losing power, usually both, which leads them to resist the process of change

6. Alfred North Whitehead (1861–1947), British philosopher and mathematician, professor at the University of London and Harvard University. See the Stanford Encyclopedia of Philosophy: <http://plato.stanford.edu/entries/whitehead/>.

with hostility and violence. Others, by contrast, remain indifferent to the process of change: "I just want to live my life. Let others do the work, if they want change. I'll watch from here." And a third group of people are those who actively get involved because they are excited to undergo change and feel that they can play an active role in shaping the life of their society.

Identifying the Change Catalyst

Since the Industrial Revolution, the pace of change has dramatically accelerated, especially regarding the living conditions of people in many parts of the world. Along with these material changes, we have also experienced significant changes with respect to our interpersonal relationships and the structure of our families, communities, and nations. Some view these changes as the random outcome of various social, political, and economic events. Others view these changes as evidence of an orderly and purposeful process of transition gradually taking place in human affairs.

It is very common nowadays to hear about "societies in transition" on the news and in general discussion. How can we define this notion of "transition"?

Definition

Transition refers to a movement, development, or evolution from one phase, form, stage, or condition to another.

When we talk about "societies in transition," what exactly do we mean? Are we talking about economic transition, for example, from a centrally planned economy to a capitalist economy? Or political transition, for example, from a communist system to a democratic system? Or transition of a political economy from capitalist to social democratic organization? To some extent, these and many other examples are indeed indicators that a process of transition is taking place in a certain sector of a given society. But when a society as a whole is in transition, other aspects of its cultural life both contribute to and are affected by the processes of change taking place. These other aspects include the worldviews, sense of identity, and collective purpose held by the citizens of that society. Naturally, we hope that transition processes lead societies to become better, safer, more just, and more prosperous. Particularly as we emerge from the 20th century that has seen so much violence, injustice, and war, we also hope that societal transitions move the world community away from cultures of conflict towards cultures of peace. But is peace a guaranteed outcome of transition? If not, what factors might make humanity's transition to peace more successful and sustainable?

To better understand the processes of individual and social change, specialized fields of investigation in economics, political science, archaeology, anthropology, sociology, and psychology have been developed. In recent years, even a distinct scientific discipline devoted specifically to the study of change has emerged. These diverse disciplines now form the methodology by which we study the nature and causes of change in the past, evaluate our conditions at present, and try to predict and direct processes of change in the future. Much remains to be understood about the causes and dynamics of change, particularly with respect to change in human attitudes and behavior towards peace. This deficiency is not surprising. Material, psychological, social, and political progress are all necessary, but not sufficient, for the creation of a civilization of peace. Humanity's transition to a civilization of peace depends in great part on our understanding of the nature of peace. An integrated approach to peace requires consideration for psychological and spiritual, as well as social and political, aspects of peace.

Peace, in all its expressions—inner, interpersonal, intergroup, universal—ultimately **requires a transformation in human consciousness and worldview**, so that all the different but interrelated aspects of human experience— biological, intellectual, emotional, ethical, and spiritual—become integrated and infused within the framework of a peace-oriented worldview.

In this regard, we should note that the *spiritual dimension of human consciousness* is particularly important to the establishment of both interpersonal and structural peace.[7] Unfortunately, spirituality has become the subject of considerable misunderstanding, disagreement, and even conflict in the contemporary world and has been generally excluded from serious discourse on peace. However, spirituality is an indispensable aspect of both peace and development.

Consider the following definition:

Definition

Peace-based development is a conscious, dynamic, progressive, and integrative process in which individuals and societies achieve their fullest and finest potential in response to the continuous enlightenment of human consciousness. This development takes place in response to the progressive moral and ethical teachings of religion, and the corresponding insights and discoveries of science, both in the context of selfless, just, and compassionate deeds.

It is through the process of such an integrated and wholesome perspective on human

---

7. "Structural peace" is a term used in conflict resolution and peace education discourse that refers to peace-conducing policies and practices in the formal structures or institutions of society (i.e., in contrast with informal peaceful relations or inner peace). The argument is that there are often peaceful relations between people or peoples, or at least the desire for such, but that explicit or implicit institutional policies and practices obstruct the realization of a truly peaceful and just society.

---

development that we can find meaning and purpose in our lives; connect our past, present, and future; and understand death in terms of life and existence, rather than destruction and annihilation.

These are fundamental existential, spiritual issues at the core of a civilization of peace: based on verified truths; free from prejudice, superstition and dogma; in harmony with science and religion; promoting unity in the context of diversity; a source of beauty and creativity; a medium for the refinement of human character; and an enforcer of fundamental human rights and responsibilities within the framework of universal moral and ethical principles.

Based on our discussions in Unit 2 on Worldview and Unit 3 on Human Nature, we already recognize that human progress towards a more advanced stage of development—whether political, economic, social, moral or ethical—requires a corresponding transformation in worldview. Worldview transformation constitutes the catalyst of all human change and is a fundamental aspect of human development. This transformation can be a difficult, even painful, process as it demands the reformulation of our fundamental assumptions about ourselves, our purpose in life, the mode of our relationships, and the manner in which we construct and administer our society and its institutions.

As we reexamine the foundations of our worldviews and enter the process of change, it is common to experience two types of feelings: feelings of questioning, taking apart or letting go of old perspectives and behavior, and feelings of discovering, creating, or exercising new perspectives and capacities. In the turbulent affairs of humanity at this time, we see these same twin processes of breaking down and creating anew taking place in domains of governance, politics, academia, business, economy, public awareness, religion, and human relationships at all levels. For our purpose, we will call these

two trends "the processes of disintegration and integration."[8] What are these processes? What are their dynamics? Where do they lead us?

Definitions

Disintegration refers to the process of losing integrity, cohesion, unity; of becoming reduced to components, fragments, or particles.

Integration refers to the process of making into a whole by bringing all parts together; of unifying or joining with something else; unity.

A Closer Examination of the Twin Processes of Disintegration and Integration

A survey of human history demonstrates unequivocally that the 20th century was a particularly significant period of change for humanity. Only as we come to understand the implications of what happened during this recent period will we be able to meet the unique challenges that lie ahead.

Disintegration

When we examine the events of the 20th century, we clearly see the processes of disintegration and integration operating in the affairs of humankind. On the one hand, this century was characterized by unprecedented ruin wreaked upon the human race through successive wars and systematic violence against whole populations. Previously unthinkable weapons of mass annihilation were

---

8. We have adopted the concept of "integration and disintegration" from Shoghi Effendi, *The Advent of Divine Justice*, (originally published 1939), 4th ed., Wilmette, Illinois: Bahá'í Publishing Trust, 1984.

not only invented but also used with malicious intent. An estimated 60 million people were killed or permanently disabled in the First World War alone. The moral damage that the violence of such wars has done to our basic conceptions of human nature cannot be overestimated. Furthermore, the basic institutions of social order, including family, culture, value systems, and commonly accepted methods of decision-making, have rapidly disintegrated. Concomitantly, recognized standards of dignity in both public and private life have been abandoned. Entire nations have been bankrupted by corrupt governmental and economic leaders, and the environmental life of the planet has been bargained away for profits with little consideration to the global and irreversible harm that environmental destruction will bring.

An investigation into the causes of these catastrophic events reveals a common factor, namely, the surrender of the human mind and conscience to ideologies centered on power, identity, and dominance that have weakened moral, ethical, and spiritual foundations, both at individual and community levels, and played havoc with issues of responsibility and peaceful decision-making. The most destructive ideologies of the 20th century, including racism,[9] nationalism,[10] Nazism,[11] communism,[12] and, paradoxically, both religious fanaticism[13] and aggressive secularism,[14] have each attempted to justify the sacrifice of human life and relationships for the preservation of their ideologies.[15] Needless

to say, the grievous destruction caused by these ideologies has caused tragic obstructions to the process of building international peace.

One of the less criticized but equally compelling ideologies of the century has been that of materialism: both in terms of the superordination of economic gains over the values of justice, truthfulness, trustworthiness, and peace,[16] and the philosophical rejection of any reality or meaning beyond the material.[17] In simplified terms, materialism, especially in its most exploitive form as extreme "consumerism," exalts personal comfort over collective well-being, contributes to excessive individualism and the atomization of society, and, most seriously, causes the rupture of the moral fabric of the community.

The general deterioration of ethical and moral consciousness, if carefully examined, constitutes the "root cause" of our apparently unrelated problems of pollution, poverty, ethnic violence, public apathy, increase of crime, etc. Until there is a global change in moral consciousness and behavior within the parameters of a unity-based worldview, there can be no recovery from the damage which these destructive trends are causing.

Integration

When we familiarize ourselves with the terribly destructive character of the last century, it is easy to lose hope in the future of humanity. But we should also look at the unprecedented advances

9. See: <http://encyclopedia.thefreedictionary.com/racism.>

10. See: <http://www.worldhistory.com/wiki/n/nationalism.htm>.

11. See: <http://www.bartleby.com/65/na/NatlSoci.html>.

12. See: <http://www.bartleby.com/65/co/communism.html>.

13. See Eric Hoffer, *The True Believer: Thoughts on the Nature of Mass Movements.* Perennial Classics, 2002.

14. <http://www.worldhistory.com/wiki/s/secularism.htm>.

15. Find out more through the following Internet links: The Encyclopedia of World History, "Changing Global Patterns" <http://www.bartleby.com/67/2636.html>. "Lec-

tures on 20th Century Europe" <http://www.historyguide.org/europe/europe.html>. "The Legacy Project: Tragedies of the 20th Century" <http://www.legacy-project.org/about/index.html>. "Public Broadcasting Service (PBS) People's Century: 1900–1999" <http://www.pbs.org/wgbh/peoplescentury/> "TIME's 100 Most Important People of the Century" <http://www.time.com/time/time100/index.html>.

16. See: <http://www.bartleby.com/62/85/M0958500.html>.

17. See: <http://www.bartleby.com/65/ma/materialsm.html>.

that humanity has managed to achieve in recent times. Indeed, the 20th century has brought achievements that past generations could scarcely have imagined.[18]

To begin with, the history of humanity's disunity is also that of its unity. In its march toward maturity, humanity has achieved many remarkable acts of unity, such as the successive creation of families, clans, tribes, states, and nations. And now, as we begin the 21st century, it is clear that the process of unity is accelerating. Through scientific discovery, ethical and spiritual reflection, and experience dealing collectively with change and crises, humanity has undergone intensified growth in consciousness and in its ability to create greater unities in all areas of human life. To mention just a few examples:

- Transportation systems have reduced distances and brought people face-to-face from all parts of the world;

- Information technologies have obliterated national boundaries that previously prevented global communication, information-sharing, and trade;

- Significant advances towards universal basic education have been made;

- Women have emerged in most regions as partners with men in the spheres of public activity and governance;

- Constitutional governments have been established in many countries around the world, championing the rule of law, respect for the rights of all members of the human race, and promotion of social justice;

- The economic and financial integration of the world economy is increasingly visible;

- Nations are increasingly harmonizing their political agendas and practices to promote and protect human and environmental welfare;

- The concept of human rights and its paramount importance has been formally and universally declared and given a place of highest significance on the agenda of humanity, at all levels;

- The United Nations, European Union, and the more recent African Union have contributed to unprecedented international political unity and coordinated efforts to address global concerns;

- The World Health Organization and other multinational agencies[19] have coordinated global efforts to deal with the HIV/AIDS and SARS epidemics, as well as other global health hazards.

Unity of thought in world undertakings, a concept that could not even be conceived of at the start of the 20th century, is apparent today in vast programs of social and economic development, humanitarian aid, and concern for protection of the environment of the planet and its oceans.[20] Consider the vision declared by the 1000 international civil society organizations participating at the UN Millennium Summit preparatory conference in New York: "...we are one human family, in all our diversity, living on one common homeland and sharing a just, sustainable and peaceful world, guided by universal principles

---

18. Follow Internet links to find out more: "Greatest Engineering Achievements of the 20th Century" <http://www.greatachievements.org/>. "Public Broadcasting Service (PBS) People's Century: 1900–1999" <http://www.pbs.org/wgbh/peoplescentury/>. "TIME's 100 Most Important People of the Century" <http://www.time.com/time/time100/index.html>. The Encyclopedia of World History, "Changing Global Patterns" <http://www.bartleby.com/67/2636.html>.

19. See also UNAIDS <http://www.unaids.org/en/default.asp>.

20. Including: 1990 World Summit for Children; 1992 Earth Summit; 1995 World Summit for Social Development; 1997 World Food Summit; 2002 World Summit on Sustainable Development; and 2003 World Summit on the Information Society.

of democracy...."[21] And at the Millennium Summit itself, held in September 2000, the 149 member states of the United Nations declared in one accord the following:

> We solemnly reaffirm, on this historic occasion, that the United Nations is the indispensable common house of the entire human family, through which we will seek to realize our universal aspirations for peace, cooperation and development. We therefore pledge our unstinting support for these common objectives, and our determination to achieve them.[22]

Nothing so dramatically illustrates the difference between the world of 1900 and that of 2000 than this statement.

A Shift in Collective Worldview

The importance and long-ranging impact of these advances should not be underestimated. They are the first evidences of a process that is revolutionizing the character of our planet. Each and every one of these advances is contributing directly to a shift in the collective worldview of humanity, which will eventually enable it to

establish world peace.

As governments, institutions, families, and individuals struggle to expand their worldviews to embrace the reality of the oneness of humanity, tensions and conflicts between old and new ways of viewing ourselves and organizing our societies are clearly increasing. This transition—however tasking—is an inevitable and purposeful process that is gradually leading the majority of humankind towards a willing acceptance of the new and potential-laden phase of global peace.

Two primary challenges are currently before us:

1. **To envision** the characteristics of a new social order appropriate to the collective adulthood of humanity;
2. **To develop new skills** that can help us bring our daily practices into harmony with this vision.

Characteristics of a Peaceful Civilization

A culture of peace is the outcome of collective human maturity. This new social order will necessarily be characterized by a fresh understanding of certain principles, standards, and processes on which the creation of peace depends. Let's take a moment to review the principles and prerequisites of peace.

In order for **PEACE** to exist, its prerequisites must exist:

- **UNITY** is the fundamental prerequisite for peace. For a peaceful society to exist, individuals, groups, and institutions need to know how to create unity in the midst of their diversity. A global society is characterized by an infinite diversity of races, cultures, religions, industries, opinions, perspectives, and modes of interaction. Peace cannot exist if this

---

21. Millennium Forum, "We the Peoples Millennium Forum Declaration and Agenda for Action: Strengthening the United Nations for the Twenty-First Century," *United Nations Reform Measures and Proposals: The Millennium Assembly of the United Nations,* Forty-Fifth Session, Agenda Item 49(b), 8 August 2000. <http://www.un.org/millennium/declaration.htm>.
22. United Nations General Assembly, *United Nations Millennium Declaration* (Document no. A/55/L.2), 8 September 2000, section 32. <http://www.un.org/millenniumgoals>.

---

diversity becomes a basis for conflict and contention. Unity in the context of diversity enables humanity to benefit from the unique insights, talents, and skills that the diverse human family offers. However, unity, itself, has a prerequisite;

- **JUSTICE** is the fundamental prerequisite for unity. It is impossible to create a truly united and diverse society in the absence of justice. Humanity has suffered many wars, conflicts, and other injustices throughout history. This heritage has left many wounds that still need to be healed. Furthermore, many legal systems, cultural traditions, economic practices, and social norms permit fresh injustices to occur. A peace-inspiring society must examine these issues and make the necessary changes that the establishment of justice will require. However, justice also has a prerequisite;

- **EQUALITY** of rights and opportunities for all men and women, races, cultures, religions, and nations is the fundamental pre-requisite for justice. Until we value the humanness, dignity, and rights of all people equally, we will not establish the necessary measures for ensuring justice in our societies, nor be capable of appreciating when injustices have occurred. And equality also has a prerequisite;

- **MATURITY** is the fundamental prerequisite for equality. Maturity implies an ability to regard and treat others as our equals; a willingness to sacrifice selfish interests for the common good; and a dedication to truth, however challenging; to truthfulness, however self-incriminating; to unity, however demanding; and to service to others, however taxing. A high level of maturity among individuals and the social collective is needed before equality can be fully put into practice. Maturity necessitates leaving behind the immature thoughts, feelings, and behavior of childhood and adolescence. The sooner humanity discards its conflict-based worldviews and adopts a worldview based on the principle of the oneness of humanity, the sooner a culture of peace can emerge.

In reality, the issues of maturity, equality, justice, unity, and peace are entirely interrelated. Thus, by focusing on and developing any one of these qualities, we necessarily influence and develop all of them, as depicted in Figure 2 below.

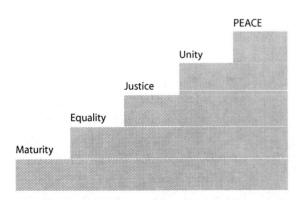

Figure 1: Prerequisites of peace

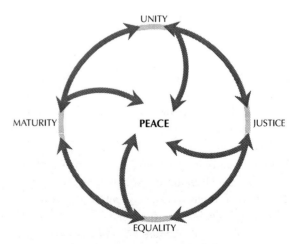

Figure 2: Prerequisites of peace

Effecting Positive Change

The task of creating fundamental change in our world, although difficult, is simultaneously inevitable, manageable, and highly rewarding. To creatively engage in a process of positive change, a clear "vision of the end at the beginning" is needed. We need to know both the dynamics of the process of change and its ultimate outcome. Such knowledge not only helps us to be less afraid and anxious about change but also actually enables us to become more effective decision-makers and helps us to avoid reactionary approaches to crises inherent in the dynamics of change.

When we are confused and afraid—as many people in today's world are—it is easy to make the mistake of believing it is better to "fight the negative"—i.e., to protest, criticize, oppose, and sabotage that which we feel is wrong—than to "strengthen the positive"—i.e., to build, promote faith in, sacrifice for, and encourage a nobler standard. The distinction between these two courses of action may appear subtle, but it is extremely important: While fighting the negative may give the impression that conditions are improving, it is in fact *only* through strategically strengthening the positive that real changes come into being.

We can adopt this approach in all intrapersonal, interpersonal, and intergroup aspects of life, while steadily moving towards that stage of maturation that is required for establishing a civilization of peace. As we exercise our powers of knowledge and will within the parameters of love, consideration, and unity in diversity, it naturally affects the way we interact with those around us, beginning with our families and extending outwards to our friends, classmates, and other members of our community. It is a creative process that starts with the individual and extends to the society, and is adopted by the society, which in turn, influences the individual.

Building a Civilization of Peace

The process of building a civilization of peace is an all-inclusive task. It requires a fundamental transformation in our attitudes and modes of behavior as individuals, groups, parents/guardians, teachers, leaders, media communicators, scientists, and artists—whoever we are and whatever we do. Here, we will review a few examples of how different segments of society can contribute to the task of building a civilization of peace. We encourage teachers and students to identify many other groups in their respective societies that can effectively contribute to this noble undertaking.

The Individual: Creating Peace Within

Individuals can make important contributions to peace by adopting a peace-based worldview and by practicing the principles of peace in all aspects of life. At the personal level we need to develop inner peace. In our relationships we best contribute to the cause of peace by relating to others in true spirit of equality, fairness, and efforts to show love, consideration, and kindness. These are qualities of a **mature and peaceful personal life** in action. In doing so, we promote not only the **idea** of peace but also the **practice** of peace by being peacemakers in our attitudes, personal choices, and behaviors towards others.

The Group: Establishing Unity and Peace

Groups can contribute to peace by using a unity-based consultative approach to decision-making and problem-solving. We will talk more in depth about consultation in Unit 8. Briefly, peace-oriented consultation revolves around the all-important issue of unity. We resolve conflicts by creating unity, and we create peace through creating unity. Unity-building is the central quality of a peaceful group. A note of caution here: Unity is beneficial only when it is universal, when it is free from prejudice and bias in favor of one group and against another. Unity is beneficial only when it has the highest regard for diversity and is free from authoritarian practices of domination, uniformity, and demand for conformity. Unity is beneficial only when the principle of equality is present with respect to equality of women with men, and equality of members of different races, religions, and ethnic groups. Consultative decisions are made in a spirit of real truth-seeking and justice—without the power-struggles that destroy so many group initiatives. Unity is the focus and becomes both the *means* and the *result* towards which the process is aimed. Practicing these ethics of peace is the basis of all structural peace.

Parents and Teachers: Training Future Peacemakers

Teachers and parents/guardians play a most significant role in creating peace by educating the next generation and helping them to search for and adopt worldviews that are peace-oriented. The most valuable gift from both parents/guardians and teachers to their children and students is the gift of love. Parents/guardians not only must love their children *unconditionally* but also must *teach their children how to love unconditionally*. To love with kindness, compassion, and care for all people is the hallmark of a truly peaceful and civilized person. Teachers give us the gift of "love for knowledge" so that we are able to *think critically*, to *search for truth,* to *free ourselves from prejudices and become universal thinking.* The twin gifts of *unconditional love,* given to us by our parents/guardians, and *the love of knowledge* taught to us by our teachers are the most precious resources we can possess. They help us to become lovers of humanity and of truth and justice, and to become effective promoters of unity and peace.

Community Leaders: Learning the Principles of Leadership for Peace

Youth—the leaders of tomorrow—must learn the art and science of *leadership for peace.* This means learning how, in all matters, to search for truth, respect diversity, create unity, and make decisions that foster peace. Leadership for peace also means learning to resist power's seductiveness and to use the power of leadership for good rather than against others or for personal gain. The most devastating interpersonal and intergroup events in human history have their genesis in the abuse of power and authority on the part of selfish, cowardly, and violent leaders. Today's youth need to learn how to put power and authority at the service of peace. Community leaders can set the example by discussing, adopting, and implementing policies that promote a just, unifying society. Then as the young people mature and become active members of the community and as some of them assume the mantle of leadership, they can set themselves the goal of creating a society distinguished by true equality, justice, unity, and peace, realized within the framework of a peace-based democracy.

The Media: Promoting Public Awareness of Peace

Many think that the role of the media is to report dysfunction in society. Too often, as well, the media is misused by those in power to manipulate public opinion. As we evolve to a mature society characterized by creativity, growth, and unity-in-diversity, we will expect our media representatives to reconsider their role in contributing to society: to choose thoughtful analysis over slander and libel; to observe situations less from conflict-perspectives and more from peace-perspectives; to promote unity in diversity, and to provide a forum for exchanging ideas on how to better the conditions of society through promotion of equality, justice, unity, and peace. Ultimately, the role of the media is to provide a forum for sharing knowledge, perspectives, experiences, and hopes—all for the betterment of the society and the good of the people.

Summary

In this unit, we have learned that:

Humanity is in the Midst of a Collective Transition

- Today, humanity is in the midst of a transition from a divided world to a unified world.

This Transition is Characterized by both Integration and Disintegration

- As governments, institutions, families, and individuals struggle to expand their worldviews in order to embrace the reality of human oneness, tensions and conflicts between old and new ways of viewing ourselves and organizing our societies are clearly increasing.

However Difficult, this Process is Inevitable and Purposeful

- This transition—however difficult—is an inevitable and purposeful process, and is gradually leading humankind towards a willing acceptance of the new and potential-laden phase of global peace.

Everyone has a Role to Play in the Advance Toward Peace

- Every sector of society, indeed every individual, can play a creative and constructive role in humanity's transition to a civilization of peace: the more conscious and systematic we are in creating unity, celebrating diversity, and preventing violence and war, the smoother this transition will be.

Key Questions for the Classroom

The following questions can be used to review and explore further the concepts of Unit 6 with your students:

1. What does "transition" mean?

2. What is a civilization?

3. What would be the characteristics of a civilization of peace?

4. What are some indicators that humanity is transitioning to a civilization of peace?

5. In the context of global change, what is meant by the phrase "processes of disintegration and integration"?

6. How can we deal with the problematic process of "globalization" that exhibits both positive and negative dimensions at this time in history?

7. There are a lot of really terrible things happening in the world every day. What evidence do we have that humanity is *not* doomed to destroy itself?

8. Politics, business, and the media are each very powerful sectors of society that tend to thrive on competition and conflict. If you were a politician, businessperson, or media personality, what might you do to bring a greater emphasis on unity, justice, and peace into your sector, and how might such a shift in focus affect the way this sector functions?

9. What are the prerequisites of peace?

10. What can the schools do to move their communities, nations, even the whole world closer to peace? How about the media? Government? Families? You?

Personal Reflection

Reflection is a very powerful learning tool. It helps us to make sense of the things we are studying and the experiences we are going through. The more we reflect on ourselves, our relationships, and the world around us, the better prepared we are to discern, prioritize, and act upon issues of importance.

Becoming a peacemaker is a very important and challenging task. By reflecting on the principles of peace, we are better equipped to make decisions about our own development that will help us to confidently undertake the goal of peace building.

As you go through each of the EFP Curriculum units, try to set aside some time for the process of reflection.

The following questions are provided to help you begin this process.

Questions for Personal Reflection

1. Reflections on Self

- The world is moving and changing—am I?
- Do I welcome change or back away from it?
- How do I feel about the condition of the world today?

Focus Questions

Knowing that the world is in a state of both disintegration and integration, where do you see yourself being involved? What vision do you have of yourself in the future:
- Will you stay on the sidelines? Why?
- Will you devote yourself to preventing the process of disintegration? How?
- Will you actively promote the process of integration? How?

2. Reflections on Family/Group

- Does my family support my desire to become an active promoter of peace with all people? How?
- Do I support the growth of my family members, friends, and colleagues to become active promoters of peace with all people? How?

Focus Questions

Envision the type of relationship you would like to have with your siblings, parents/guardians, teachers, or colleagues. What could you change in your thoughts and behavior in order to become an agent of change from conflict to peace?

3. Reflections on Society

- How do the leaders of my society feel about change towards a civilization of peace?
- Are they resistant, indifferent, or open to this process?
- How can I draw their attention to the need for greater unity and peace in our society?

Focus Question

The transition to peace involves letting go of conflict-based ideas and practices on the one hand, and strengthening unifying ideas and practices on the other hand.

- With this in mind, what would you advise your leaders to do in order to move your society closer to a lasting and all-inclusive peace?

4. Reflections on the World at large

- What can I say to reassure people who are pessimistic about world conditions?
- What can I do to effectively support the global movement towards peace?

Focus Questions

Take a moment to envision a more peaceful world in this century:

- What responsibilities and protections would exist between the different regions of the world then?
- What would individual states have to give up in order to gain greater peace, stability, and justice worldwide?

Classroom Tools

As a teacher in the Education for Peace Program, it is now your task to introduce discussion of humanity's transition towards peace to your class and to assist your students to explore the significance of this transition in their own lives and in the world at large.

The more our students understand the processes of disintegration and integration happening in the world around them, the more confident they will be to contribute to the process of integration and establishment of a culture of peace. Your role as their teacher and mentor in this process is tremendously important.

To help you get started, a number of tools are included in this section that you may find useful. These tools are only guides, and you are encouraged to develop your own ideas about how to best explore these topics with your students.

In addition to the examples here, please also refer to the Educational Methodology Unit, where you will find practical guidelines on how to make your classroom a creative, effective learning environment, as well as other great ideas from fellow teachers who are integrating Education for Peace into their various subject areas.

As you work with the Education for Peace concepts, you will surely develop new ideas for lessons, activities, and assessment approaches. We encourage you to pass along your thoughts, ideas, or resource links to Education for Peace so they can be added to our EFP Resource Bank for other teachers to use. Please send us an email at info@efpinternational.org, or mail your ideas to our address:

International Education for Peace Institute (Canada)
101, 1001 W. Broadway, Suite 900
Vancouver, BC V6H 4E4
Canada

We look forward to hearing from you!

Activity Ideas for Secondary Schools

Art/Drama

Use your creativity and imagination to design a poster, painting, collage, sculpture, drama, or dance that portrays the concepts of "disintegration" and "integration" at work.

Language/ Computer Science

How has the historical development of communication technologies enabled the process of global integration? Create models that show how different uses of communication technology have fostered integration processes at different levels of society.

Biology

In response to increasing environmental crises, many societies have developed eco-friendly technologies or ways of life to help protect the environment while meeting the challenges of population and settlement. Research some of these different eco-friendly strategies and then design an environmentally friendly city, town, or village based on the available resources in your area. Remember to include aspects of what you've learned from environmental protection programs in different parts of the world.

Home Economics

Design and create a unity-in-diversity meal that infuses the most popular flavors from 2 or 3 different parts of the world. Hold a feast with friends to celebrate these delicacies. **OR:** Design and create an outfit that integrates different textiles, patterns, or styles from 2 or 3 different parts of the world. Hold a fashion show to showcase these integrative designs.

Activity Ideas for Primary Schools

Art

Consider Picasso and the Cubist movement; have students look at and discuss paintings demonstrating how Picasso has taken the human face apart and placed it back together to create something new (process of disintegration and integration). Students can create their own Cubist-style images through creating a face out of clay, then taking the parts of the face and rearranging them in a new place. Or, students can cut out different facial features from magazines and create a face. Then they can take the same features and arrange them differently on the face so that they demonstrate the Cubist style of art. Older students can try their own Cubist-style painting or drawing.

Social Studies

Each individual has the opportunity to create positive change in the different areas of their lives. Have students suggest 3–5 different domains where they can use unity to make change in their lives and the lives of others (e.g., home, school, after-school sports). Divide the class into groups, each discussing a different domain and what they can actually do to create unity in these areas. Have students present their conclusions to the rest of the class, with the results displayed on a chart to be left in the classroom.

Unit 6, Sample Lesson 1: TRANSITION TO A CIVILIZATION OF PEACE

Focus: Characteristics of a Civilization of Peace

Context

Humanity is in the midst of a dramatic transition from its history of division, conflict, injustice, and war, to a new, global civilization characterized by unity-in-diversity, equality, justice, and peace. The process is slow and requires that we gain new understanding into the nature of civilization, in general, and the features of a civilization of peace, in particular.

Points for Understanding

- A civilization is a group of people living and working cooperatively together for the purpose of creating an organized society distinguished by common ideals and cultural and technological advancements.
- Today, humanity is in the midst of a transition from a civilization of conflict to a civilization of peace.
- This process of transition is characterized by both divisive and unifying forces which are reshaping the institutions, relationships and aims of humanity.

Key Questions

1. What is a civilization?
2. What would be the characteristics of a civilization of peace?
3. Do we currently have some features of a peaceful civilization?

Learning Process

(Adapted from
<http://school.discovery.com/lessonplans/pdf/towardcivilization/towardcivilization.pdf>)

1. Ask students what they think a *civilization* is. Write down their responses on a large sheet of paper. Help students arrive at the following conclusions:
   - A civilization is a group of people living and working cooperatively together for the purpose of creating an organized society distinguished by common ideals and cultural and technological advancements;
   - People living in civilizations have an ultimate and high-minded purpose towards which they work together cooperatively;
   - People living in civilizations communicate with each other and devise technological

and cultural advances that both demonstrate and assist them to achieve their ultimate purpose.

2. Form the class into small groups of two or three students. Give each group the option of researching either the Neanderthal civilization or that of ancient Egypt. As students research their topics, have them address these questions:
    *   What were the common ideals and ultimate purpose shared by the members of that civilization?
    *   What types of conflict resolution did members of that civilization use? What were their cultural achievements? Did they advance over time? How?
    *   In what manner did the members of that civilization relate with their neighboring societies?
    *   Did their technology, modes of communication, and culture assist them to achieve peace?
    *   How would you summarize the character of that civilization?

3. Give students class time to complete their research and prepare their presentations. Then, have each group select a representative to report its findings for class discussion.

4. As a second stage in the learning process, have students (in their groups) reflect on an imaginary civilization of peace and answer in detail the same questions listed under step 2. Have each group share their responses with the class and discuss. As sharing takes place, record each group's unique responses on a common board or paper.

5. For homework, give each student a copy of the accumulated list and have them assess which features of a "civilization of peace" can be seen in their society today.

Unit 6, Sample Lesson 2: TRANSITION TO A CIVILIZATION OF PEACE

Focus: The Dynamics of Social Transition

Context

Humanity is in the midst of a transition from a civilization of conflict to a civilization of peace. Both divisive and unifying processes are increasing and changing the nature of our social structures and relationships. The more we understand about these processes, the better able we are to influence consciously the ultimate direction of our collective transition.

Points for Understanding

- As humanity faces the challenges of a global age, tensions and conflicts between old and new ways of viewing ourselves and organizing our societies are clearly increasing;
- This transition—however difficult—is an inevitable and purposeful process, gradually leading the majority of humankind towards a willing acceptance of a peace-oriented worldview;
- The adoption of a peace-oriented worldview is necessary for humanity to realize the great potentials that this new era of global civilization has made possible;
- With the adoption of a peace-oriented worldview, a new spirit will animate the institutions of society. Families, schools, government, businesses, and media will gradually develop new aims and practices, and the character of society will change.

Key Questions

1. Why is the world today so turbulent?
2. It seems as if all the good that various people and organizations do is swept away by the conflict and violence of closed-minded and aggressive people. Will our efforts to contribute to peace make a difference?

Learning Process

1. Begin the class by introducing the terms "integration" and "disintegration." Write these terms on the board and have students discuss what they think these terms mean. Invite them to give examples from other subject areas such as biology, ecology, social science, and chemistry on the processes of integration and disintegration. Add their contributions to the board. Summarize and define the terms.

2. Introduce students to the idea that processes of integration and disintegration can also

be seen in macro sociopolitical processes worldwide. Give students a few minutes to individually think about and write down any and all examples that come to mind. Create a two-column table on the board with these terms as the headings. Invite students to share their examples; list their examples underneath the two headings.

3. Ask students why they think these twin processes are taking place. What is their **purpose**? Is there a purpose? Refer to the process of integration and disintegration in the environment, e.g., in the life stages of a flowering plant, from germination to seed-bearing.

4. Bridge the discussion to the processes of human development (see Unit 5 on the Developmental Model of Human Civilization). Review the characteristics required for human maturity and evaluate the sociopolitical examples against these characteristics. Help students to see that integration and disintegration are part of humanity's transition to maturity and the standards of peace.

5. Sometimes a positive advancement, like globalization, also bears negative dynamics that appear to be contributing more to disintegration than integration. Discuss this case with students, or have them analyze its dynamics as a homework assignment. How will the adoption of a peace-oriented worldview change the character of globalization?

Activities and Assignments

Teachers can choose from among the following sample assignments, or create their own:

1. **Group Work**: Read the "Open Letter to all Heads of Nations and Leaders of Government" on pages 84–85 in *Peace Moves*. Divide into groups and compose similar letters for leaders of religion, heads of business, the media, parents, and teachers. Send the letters and/or submit them to your local newspaper for printing.

2. **Performance:** Using one of the quotations at the end of this unit as your inspiration, create a dance, drama, or rap on the theme of rebuilding society through community involvement.

3. **Journal:** "Peace depends on unity; unity on justice; justice on equality; equality on maturity." Illustrate and/or analyze this formula with reference to your school, your society, your family, and/or the world.

4. **Action for Peace:** Read the attached award speech by Nelson Mandela. Create a community-building initiative in your school or local neighborhood with the help of your teachers, parents/guardians, and/or friends. Invite people from the community to get involved. After activity(ies) take place, hold an awards celebration to recognize the positive contributions that people have made. Invite your local television or newspaper to cover the event!

Additional Resources

Letters from *Peace Moves* to leaders of government, science, and religion, and to parents/
guardians.

Lesson Reading: Mandela speech.

Unit 6, Sample Lesson 3: TRANSITION TO A CIVILIZATION OF PEACE

Focus: What Can I Do for Peace?

Context

Each individual, group, and segment of society has a role to play in the creation of a civilization of peace.

Points for Understanding

- Peace requires that we examine our worldviews, and if necessary, reformulate assumptions we make about ourselves, our purpose in life, and the modes of our relationships;
- The more peace-oriented our worldview, the greater capacities and responsibilities we have to create unity, to celebrate diversity, to decrease conflict, and to prevent violence and war;
- Each individual, group, and segment of society has a role to play in the creation of a civilization of peace.

Key Questions

1. What can I do to move humanity closer to peace? How about my school? Government? Family? The media?
2. Do I need to change *myself* in order to better contribute to peace in my school, family, and community?

Learning Process

1. Following lesson 1 or 2, ask students about how they view their role in creating a civilization of peace. Students may have anxieties, aspirations, or doubts in addition to concrete ideas. Facilitate an open consultation among the class members and try to encourage students themselves to respond constructively and creatively to each other.

2. Expand the discussion by forming students into groups that represent different segments of the population, such as politicians, business people, parents/guardians, teachers, journalists, healthcare professionals, and youth. Have each group consult together and create a job description for their respective sector in which the overriding mandate is to advance a peace-oriented society. These job descriptions should include clear

statements of roles, responsibilities, and potential projects in which to be involved. A sample template is included with this unit.

3. Create a "career board" in a prominent place in your classroom or school and post each of the job descriptions for students and teachers to read as they pass by.

Activities and Assignments

Teachers can use the following sample assignment, or create their own:

1. **Action for Peace:** What role do you see yourself playing as a peace builder in your family? Among your friends? In your community? Choose three personal peace-building goals and write them down. Create a plan for achieving these goals by setting tasks for yourself that you could work on once a day, once a week, and once a month. Write these down as well. Re-read your goals regularly, and keep a log of your progress! Record observations and ideas when you feel your plan would benefit from adjustments.

Additional Resources

Letters from *Peace Moves* to leaders of government (pp. 84–85), science (pp.86–87), and religion (pp.88–89), to parents/guardians (p.90), and to fellow youth of the world (p.192).

Unit 6, Sample Lesson 1 – Activity Reading

Choose one of the following quotations and discuss:

"The different peoples of the world are just beginning to find each other. Whatever is best in any part is now being brought out into the light for the good of the whole. Whatever national geniuses have discovered is now being made the common possession of all nations....Great educational centers, like central suns, shine over all the earth. Multiply present conditions a hundred fold and then compute, if possible, what the world mind will be when it has come to its own inheritance."
—Raymond Landon Bridgman, Author, journalist
World Organization, pp. 114–15 (1905)

"The problems of all of humanity can only be solved by all of humanity."
—Friedrich Dürrenmatt (1921–1990), Swiss dramatist, novelist, essayist
The Physicists, 21 Points to The Physicists (1962) Trans. by Gerhard P. Knapp (1995)

"All the members of the human family, whether peoples or governments, cities or villages, have become increasingly interdependent. For none is self-sufficiency any longer possible, inasmuch as political ties unite all peoples and nations, and the bonds of trade and industry, of agriculture and education, are being strengthened every day. Hence the unity of all mankind can in this day be achieved."
—Shoghi Effendi (1897–1957), Historian, global administrator
The Promised Day is Come, p. 120 (1941)

"The historic ascent of humanity, taken as a whole, may be summarized as a succession of victories of consciousness over blind forces—in nature, in society, in man himself."
—Leon Trotsky (1879–1940), Russian revolutionary
"Conclusions," vol. 3, *The History of the Russian Revolution* (1933)

"Humanity should question itself, once more, about the absurd and always unfair phenomenon of war, on whose stage of death and pain only remains standing the negotiating table that could and should have prevented it."
—Pope John Paul II on arriving in Buenos Aires near end of conflict between
Argentina and Great Britain over the Falkland Islands, 11 June 1982

"Abolishing war was the common wish of Confucius and his disciples. At the Park of the Nung, Confucius asked his disciples, Zilu, Zigong and Yan Yuan, to debate on a peaceful world. Zilu proposed a war to end all wars, while Zigong proposed diplomacy to end the calamities of the world. Confucius sided with Yan Yuan's peace plan when Yan said that he wished to have an enlightened king or a sage ruler and assist and help him to educate the people. He would cause the city walls to have no need to be repaired; the ditches and moats to have no foe to cross over them, and the swords and spears to be beaten into plowshares; horses and cattle to be released on the plains and

in the moors; homes and families would not have thought of separation and bereavement; and in a thousand years there would be no misfortune of warfare and fighting."

—Confucius, Chinese philosopher

Source: <http://www.wam.umd.edu/~tkang/peace.html>

Unit 6, Sample Lesson 1 – Activity Reading

*Speech by President Mandela at the award ceremony for the
President's Award for Community Initiative*

Cape Town, 5 February 1998

Master of Ceremonies, Minister Valli Moosa, Honored guests:

As the President of South Africa it is my privilege to attend many functions as a representative of our people. All these functions are important, but today's ceremony has a special meaning, and it is a great pleasure and honor to share it with you.

Sometimes along the road to a better life, when we are faced with difficulties, when we stumble and fall, it is all too easy to despair and give up.

But when one hears of how our communities are joining hands to create a better life for themselves and those around them, then we regain the strength to meet whatever difficulties there may be.

Fundamental to the success of all our efforts at reconstruction and development is community action and participation. As we face the challenge of meeting our people's basic needs with limited resources, those who roll up their sleeves and take the initiative to uplift their conditions in the spirit of *masakhane*,[23] and in partnership with others, set an example for all of us to follow.

That was why the government decided to set up the President's Award for Community Initiative. It allows us, as a nation, to honor communities that act in this way and together celebrate what they have done.

The enthusiasm and determination with which South Africans are rebuilding their country is there for all to see in the number and the quality of projects nominated for these awards. All around this country, out of the headlines, people are joining hands in partnerships which spur development.

If they are to succeed they must, as those represented here have done, achieve much from few resources; find the path to sustainable creation of jobs and self-sufficiency; develop new skills; and involve their communities.

None of our plans can succeed without such efforts. Government on its own cannot provide what is needed, nor should it try to do so.

The function of government and parliament is to serve the people, by ensuring the conditions under which communities and every sector of society can work together with government to achieve the goals we have set ourselves as a nation. It is therefore only right that representatives of communities which are rising to these challenges should be present at the opening of the parliamentary year tomorrow.

---

23. A Xhosa word for "standing together."

On this occasion we should thank all those involved—communities, organizers, adjudicators and others—as the pioneers who have worked to make this first year of the Award such a success. You have set a standard that will challenge others to follow in your footsteps in future years.

In conclusion, to the communities you represent, and indeed to all the fifty communities and more who were runners-up, we say: Congratulations!

May the injection of resources which the prizes bring, help you build on the foundation you have laid. May your example reinforce the spirit of *masakhane* in our land. May it strengthen the partnership of government and communities!

Together we have made a good start. Let us work together to build the country of our dreams!

Issued by: Office of the President

Unit 6, Sample Lessons 1 & 3 – Activity Reading

An Open Letter to All Heads of Nations and Leaders of Government
(From *Peace Moves,* copyright 2004, EFP-International)

We are writing to invite you to become our leaders in peace. Today, the world of humanity is in great danger. Conflict and distrust are everywhere. New wars, ever bigger, ever more destructive, are constantly breaking out. The horrifying spectacle of a worldwide economic crisis, irreversible environmental destruction, ever escalating religious, ethnic, and ideological conflicts, ever more barbaric terrorism, even an accidental or premeditated nuclear conflict, or a combination of these events is ever present in our lives.

This cannot continue. This is a madness that must be stopped. You have the power to stop it. We are asking that through your leadership you help us to trust rather than suspect. Lead us to justice rather than injustice. Give us courage to wage peace rather than war and to use our knowledge for the betterment of human society. Provide us with the leadership to eradicate poverty, to overcome disease, to create a pollution-free, violence-free, and poverty-free world community. Above all, through your leadership, help us to unite. Humanity needs to leave its childhood and adolescent ages behind. This is the era of maturity, cooperation, justice, oneness, beauty, creativity, joy, and peace. It is within your powers to help humanity to achieve this.

There is no longer any honor in being powerful, in being strong, in being clever, if this power, strength, or know-how is used to divide people, to cause destruction, to bring about grief. No longer can the peoples of the world and their leaders pride themselves in their exclusive love of their nations or their own specific groups. Such a love should be combined with love for all humanity. The era of nation building is over. This is the age of universal perspectives. We can survive as distinct nations only if the world as a whole survives. The eras of competition, power struggles, survival of the fittest, and the law of the jungle are past. We are now in the age of cooperation, mutual assistance, survival of all, and dominance of the universal laws of love, unity, and justice. No longer will authoritarian and dictatorial systems of government be viable, no longer can the corrupted self-interest of those in power go unnoticed and unchallenged. This is the age of the flowering of the civilization of peace, the era of creativity, universality, and individual and collective responsibility.

We invite you as our leaders to lead us in the spirit of this new era and to help humanity usher in the long-awaited age of peace. We invite you to arrange for all the heads of the world's governments to come together to acknowledge the oneness of humanity and to inaugurate the era of unity in diversity, multilateral disarmament, and peace. We are eagerly awaiting your positive response, and we pledge our wholehearted support as you lead us in this endeavor.

Yours in peace,
[Signed,]
Name, Age, Gender, Country, Date, Email

Unit 6, Sample Lessons 1 & 3 – Activity Reading

An Open Letter to the Scientists of the World
(From *Peace Moves,* copyright 2004, EFP-International)

The greatest gift to humanity is the gift of knowledge, the capacity to understand, to discover, and to create. You, the scientists, are among the most important teachers of each generation. You help us to learn. You show us logical ways of looking at and understanding the world. You bring us new discoveries. You contribute immeasurably to our understanding of our selves, each other, and the world. However, you also give us the instruments of war. You have created the nuclear bomb, life-endangering chemicals, and many other instruments of destruction. This we say, not to blame, but to acknowledge that science has been used both in a constructive and destructive manner, and that the abuse of science is the responsibility of scientists and politicians and all others who take advantage of scientific discoveries for destructive objectives.

Humanity is now on the threshold of enormously critical scientific advances in such diverse areas as genetics, physics, the environment, space exploration, medicine, and pharmaceuticals. Now is the time for the convergence of the scientific and the spiritual. Scientific discoveries must be accompanied by the application of universal moral and ethical principles. It is neither realistic nor acceptable for scientists, in the name of objectivity and academic freedom, to absolve themselves of the moral and spiritual implications of the misapplication of their discoveries. The human species is one. Scientists, artists, politicians, and ordinary citizens are all members of the single body of humanity. The welfare of one is the welfare of all. There is no separation between people. We are totally interrelated, and therefore no segment of human society can exclude itself from the affairs of humanity and function in the so-called objective manner as an aloof, non-participant observer of the unfolding human drama of our times.

The head and the heart must reunite, the material and spiritual must converge, the personal and the universal must be synergized, so that in this state of unity we will be able to use our collective knowledge and insight in the service of humanity and for the advancement of an ever-advancing civilization. The time has come for the age-old mutual antagonism, suspicion, and disregard between science and religion to end. Science without religion is a dangerous tool in the hands of a desperate and lost humanity; while religion without benefit of the scientific method is in danger of becoming nothing but mere superstition and dogma. The doors must be opened between these two mighty sources of human enlightenment and advancement, and they must be allowed to harmonize and become integrated.

You are among the most respected and valued citizens of the world. Your ideas have immense power, which can be either used or abused. The ultimate responsibility to prevent the abuse of science rests with you and other leaders of society together. Scientific discoveries are, after all, your creations and deserve your careful attention so that they are not abused. We are your students, and we seek your guidance to establish peace. We are conveying to you what we have learned from you. We call upon you to educate us for peace.

Yours in peace,
[Signed,]
Name, Age, Gender, Country, Date, Email

Unit 6, Sample Lessons 1 & 3 – Activity Reading

An Open Letter to Leaders of Religion
(From *Peace Moves,* copyright 2004, EFP-International)

God, the Most Merciful, the Most Just, the Most Wise has created humanity to know, to love, and to serve. The purpose of existence is to create a spiritual civilization, to unite the peoples of the world, and to make it possible for love and justice to engulf the entire human race. These, we believe, are the essence of all religions and potentialities inherent in human reality.

This is our understanding of the purpose of our creation and of religion. God's religion must be the cause of humanity's unity, of love among people, of justice for all people, of our detachment from the evils of materialism, and of our attachment to a life of enlightened service to humanity. This is what we understand to be the true meaning of religion.

However, we look with dismay at what many leaders and followers of religion have done and continue to do in the name of religion. There is no way that war, murder, prejudice, segregation, hatred, cruelty, and ignorance can be justified in the name of God and religion. If a religion actively or passively sanctions such behavior, then it is better to be without it.

As leaders of religion, you are among the most influential and powerful leaders of humanity. You are in a position to guide people to do either good or evil. Now both good and evil are being encouraged and sanctioned by many religious leaders and organizations. We feel the "good" many religions do, in no way justifies, nullifies, or decreases the seriousness of the "evil" that is permitted in the name of religion. We are puzzled by the division created by religious leaders among their co-religionists, as well as between themselves and the leaders of other religious traditions. When we study various religions, we see that the basis of all the major religions is the same: the belief that God is the Merciful and Just Creator; that people should follow certain universal and ethical laws; that supreme among these laws are those related to love, unity, and equality; that the precious gift of life is to be honored and respected; and that the human spirit ought to be allowed to share its beneficial effects with others in this life and in its ongoing journey into eternity.

We see religion and science as the two main sources of human inspiration and enlightenment, and we see no contradiction between a pure religion and a true science. We see no justification for any antagonism toward each other. As humanity grows, both scientific and spiritual insights must also grow; therefore, we see life on this planet as an exciting panorama of growth and progression in all aspects of material civilization, scientific development, and spiritual progression.

It is in the context of these understandings that we are writing to ask you, for the sake of God, to put aside your differences and help us to bring about a new stage in the unity of humanity, a unity that will cover all aspects of life, make the advent of universal peace inevitable, and establish the Kingdom of God on earth.

Yours in peace,
[Signed,]
Name, Age, Gender, Country, Date, Email

Unit 6, Sample Lessons 1 & 3 – Activity Reading

An Open Letter to Parents/Guardians
(From *Peace Moves,* copyright 2004, EFP-International)

We love you, appreciate your sacrifices for us, and are most grateful that you brought us into this world, nurtured us to the best of your ability, and educated us in the ways you knew best. Thank you. Now we have begun to look at the world not through the eyes of children, who after all see the world, not through the eyes of their parents and teachers, but rather through the eyes of a young generation poised to assume its adult responsibilities.

As we look at this world, we behold its confusion, disorganization, pain, sorrow, bewilderment, and hopelessness. But these pale in the face of the true problems of humanity. We are aware of your discomfort regarding the condition of the world today. This is your legacy for us, and we see that you have the same ambivalent feelings about it as we do. It is a mixture of opportunities and threats, successes and failures, joys and sorrows, good and bad. We wish to make the condition of this world better for ourselves and our children. For this we need your help. We need your encouragement, love, and patience. We need your listening ears and receptive hearts, so that you can hear and understand what we are saying.

You may well ask what exactly are we saying. We are saying that we need new ways of thinking about life, about creating a new type of family, new ways of rearing children, new concepts of success and failure. No longer can success be measured according to the amount of money that a person earns, a position that an individual holds, powers that he/she may have, and influence that can be had on others. Rather, in our view, a successful person is one who is universally minded and who uses the wealth and position of this life for the betterment of the world of humanity, for cleaning and safeguarding our environment, for feeding the hungry, for caring for the sick, for the education of children, for defending the defenseless, and for making this life beautiful and high minded.

We are asking you, our parents, to support this vision so that we will grow to be hopeful, purposeful, and peaceful. Educate us for peace and help this present generation raise the banner of peace. Please.

Love,
Name

Unit 6, Sample Lessons 1 & 3 – Activity Reading

To the Youth of the World (with copies to parents/guardians and teachers)
(From *Peace Moves,* copyright 2004, EFP-International)

We feel that the present generation can make this world a better world, a peaceful world. We must not despair. We must act with wisdom and courage. Our ultimate aim is to bring about unity and peace. And we will accomplish this not through the use of force, not through military action, not through violence and anarchy, not through a disregard for law and order, not through abuse of science and religion, not through war, and not through deception.

We will achieve peace by peaceful means. We will fill this world with acts of love, togetherness, encouragement, cooperation, mercy, justice, creativity, beauty, and the celebration of the human spirit. We will also invite our leaders to participate in this process and to lead us in this undertaking. So, to attract the attention of our leaders, we are going to ask our parents/guardians and teachers to help us.

In every neighborhood, village, city, and country, let us, with the help and advice of others, contact the civic and government leaders of our communities; the judiciary; the academic, scientific, and religious leaders; professional and artistic groups; political and law enforcement agencies; leaders of business and commerce; governmental and non-governmental organizations.

Let the purpose of these contacts be to talk about peace with all the segments of our society; to give them a letter on peace similar to what has been summarized here; to engage them in a dialogue on peace; and to secure their support and participation in our peace action. We have no doubt that we will succeed. Let us aim for the establishment of political peace during the first two decades of the 21st century. May we soon witness the fulfillment of the fact that the earth is one country and humankind its citizens.

Together,
[Signed,]
Name, Age, Gender, Country, Date, Email

Extended Exploration

Related Readings

Danesh, H.B. (2006). *Fever in the World of the Mind: Unique Dimensions of Human Conflict and Violence.* Vancouver: EFP-International Publications.

————. (2004). *Peace Moves.* Sarajevo: EFP-International Publications.

Horowitz, S., and A. Schnabel. (2004). *Human Rights and Societies in Transition: Causes, Consequences and Responses.* Tokyo: United Nations University Press.

Miller, Riel. (2001). "Long-run Prospects: Policy Changes for a World in Transition." Organization for Economic Cooperation and Development. Available online: <http://www.oecd.org/document/30/0,2340,en_2649_34209_1903198_119696_1_1_1,00.html>.

O'Murchu, Diarmuid. (2000). *Our World in Transition: Making Sense of a Changing World.* New York: Crossroad Publishing Company.

United Nations General Assembly. (2000). *United Nations Millennium Declaration.* A/RES/55/2. Available online: <http://www.un.org/millennium/declaration/ares552e.pdf>.

Educational Web Links

Kreis, Steven. (2002). *The History Guide.* "Lectures on 20th Century History." <http://www.historyguide.org/europe/europe.html>.

"What is Civilization?" <http://www.historyguide.org/ancient/lecture1b.html>.

Discovery School. "Toward Civilization." Lesson Plan. <http://school.discovery.com/lessonplans/pdf/towardcivilization/towardcivilization.pdf>.

The World in Transition Series: By Continent (essays, videotapes and lesson plans). <http://www.southerncenter.org/world_in_transition.html>. Southern Center for International Studies.

United Nations Millennium Development Goals. <http://www.un.org/millenniumgoals/>.

United Nations Development Program. Human Development Reports. <http://hdr.undp.org/reports/default.cfm>.

General Online Resources

The Columbia Encyclopedia Online. <http://www.bartleby.com/65>.

The Encyclopedia of World History. <http://www.bartleby.com/67/>.

The Columbia World of Quotations. <http://www.bartleby.com/quotations>.

The Merriam-Webster Online Dictionary. <http://www.merriam-webster.com>.

The Stanford Encyclopedia of Philosophy. <http://plato.stanford.edu>.

Wikipedia: The Free Encyclopedia. <http://www.wikipedia.org>.

Public Broadcasting Service (PBS) TeacherSource – for K-12 lesson samples and resources for all subjects. <http://www.pbs.org/teachersource/>.

Art History Timeline: The Metropolitan Museum of Art. <http://www.metmuseum.org/toah/splash.htm>.

Unit 7

Power, Authority, and Leadership for Peace

This unit examines the historical uses and abuses of power and authority. As well, the unit attempts to identify modes of leadership that are conducive to equality, justice, freedom, unity, and peace.

Context

The misuse of authority and the greedy pursuit of power are often cited as two of the main causes of poor leadership, conflict, and injustice in our world. Historically, power and authority have been used in hierarchical, authoritarian ways in which a leader or a very small group of individuals make decisions for whole populations without their input and with the expectation of strict obedience from them. In recent centuries, various democratic approaches to power and authority have emerged in which elected leaders and representatives lead their societies, for better or for worse, usually on the basis of majority mandate and opinion.

Both approaches to governance and decision-making are seen throughout our world today. Each of these modes of leadership is open to abuse. Neither system is entirely free of injustice, inequality, or violence. However, democratic modes of government, particularly the non-adversarial democracies, are much more conducive to cooperation and peace than any other form of government designed by humanity, thus far. It is in this context that the principles of leadership for peace are reviewed in this unit.

In this unit we will review concepts of "power," "authority," and "leadership" within the framework of the concepts presented in the previous units.

Learning Process

In this unit, participants should be assisted to:

1. Explain how notions of power, authority, and leadership have evolved over the past few centuries from dictatorial to competitive and gradually to more consultative forms;

2. Analyze the characteristics of authoritarian, competitive, and unity-oriented modes of decision-making within families, institutions, and societies;

3. Reflect on their own capacities for leadership; develop awareness of their own leadership potential; and develop essential leadership characteristics;

4. Practice the "leadership for peace" approach in their communities.

Points for Understanding

Teachers can guide their students to understand and remember these main points:

- Power and authority have been misused throughout history. One main reason for this misuse has been the prevalence of conflict-based worldviews.

- Predominant uses of power are not conducive to peace: neither the force-based use of power by authoritarian societies, nor the competition-based use of power in libertarian societies can foster peace.

- An integrative, unity-oriented approach to power and leadership is the prerequisite for peace-oriented and peace-creating types of leadership.

- Leadership for peace can be exercised by everyone, in all aspects of life.

- Through service, humility, unity-in-diversity, and consultative decision-making, peace-oriented leaders seek to promote the oneness and nobility of humanity and to safeguard equality and justice.

Key Vocabulary

Anarchy: a state of lawlessness or disorder due to the absence or denial of an established authority.

Authoritarian: relating to or favoring blind submission to authority; relating to, or favoring a concentration of power in a leader or an elite.

Authoritative: having or proceeding from authority; showing evident/legitimate authority.

Authority: a person, group, or institution having the right and power to command, decide, rule, or judge; an accepted source of expert knowledge, proven example, or universally applicable principle.

Consultation: a process of investigation, discussion, decision-making, and/or problem-solving that seeks the views, insights, and experiences of others and that determines to find just solutions or answers while maintaining and promoting unity among all involved.

Dictatorial: oppressive to or arrogantly overbearing toward others.[1]

Dictator: one holding complete autocratic control; one ruling absolutely and often oppressively.

Integrative leadership: the process of assisting and directing groups and communities of people together to engage in activities conducive to the advancement of human nobility, the preservation of ethical standards of truth and trustworthiness, and the promotion of justice and unity in human affairs.

Integrate: to form, coordinate, or blend into a functioning or unified whole; to unite with something else; incorporate into a larger unit;[2] *integral:* essential to completeness.[3]

Legitimacy: the fact or quality of being "lawful," in accordance with recognized standards or codes.

Libertarian: an advocate of the doctrine of unfettered freedom; a person who upholds the principles of absolute and unrestricted liberty, especially of thought and action.[4]

Power: the ability to use one's capacities for knowledge, love, and will to comprehend, unify, and create.

Universality: the quality of being universal in principle, applicability, and/or scope.

Validity: the quality of being based on sound ethical and rational foundations.

---

1. *Merriam-Webster Online Dictionary.*
2. *Merriam-Webster Online Dictionary.*
3. *Merriam-Webster Online Dictionary.*
4. *Merriam-Webster Online Dictionary.*

What Is Leadership?

The notion of leadership is continually evolving. In today's businesses, political institutions, and community organizations, many different definitions and styles of leadership are employed.

It is generally agreed that the capacity for leadership is not **inborn** but rather is **cultivated** through education and practice. Each of us can learn and apply the principles and skills of leadership in our relationships, communities, and places of work.

Leadership can be studied from a variety of perspectives, including:

- The goals of leadership;
- The personality traits and attributes of good leaders;
- The ethics, values, and beliefs of good leaders;
- The "styles" of leadership;
- The events or crises that give rise to leadership opportunities;
- The acquired knowledge, skills, and techniques of leadership;
- The culture, practices, and history of the people who are to be led.

This unit will primarily examine the principles and qualities of **Leadership for Peace**. Extended resource links on leadership are provided at the end of the unit.

Definitions of Leadership

Ideas about leadership are continually evolving, and so are its definitions. Take a moment to compare and contrast the following definitions:

"Leadership is a process of getting things done through people."
—Ann Marie Harmony, 2002

"Leadership is the ability to help others meet their goals."
—Debra J. Jordan, 1996

"Leadership means to inspire and develop people (self, other individuals, team, organization) as you mobilize them towards goals."
—The Wharton School of the University of Pennsylvania

"Leadership is a shared process of engagement that enables leaders and followers to raise one another to higher levels of motivation and morality."
—Adapted from James MacGregor Burns, *Leadership*, 1982

"Leadership means:
1. Establishing direction—developing a vision of the future, and the strategies to create it;
2. Aligning people—communicating direction in words and deeds to everyone whose cooperation is needed to create the vision;
3. Motivating and inspiring—energizing people to overcome barriers to change by satisfying basic, but often unfulfilled, human needs."
—John P. Kotter, *Leading Change*, 1996

Not all of the preceding definitions of leadership provide a sufficient measure of true leadership. If leadership is simply the process of "getting things done through people," then Hitler and Gandhi would be accounted on equal planes. But this is not the case. If leadership were simply about "helping others meet their goals," then helping terrorists to bomb a public building and helping village women to pull their families out of poverty would be accounted equal. But they are not. In this unit we will study the nature and characteristics of True or Integrative Leadership, which is based on overriding principles of truth, unity, and justice. These principles make up the main values of Education for Peace and are presented in different context in all units of this Resource Book. Here is a more comprehensive definition.

Definition

Integrative leadership is the process of assisting and directing groups and communities of people to engage together in activities conducive to the advancement of human nobility, the preservation of ethical standards of truth and trustworthiness, and the promotion of justice and unity in human affairs.

The Need for a New Type of Leadership

Sadly, too often we see leadership reigns abused and the powers of human creativity distorted. History is filled with examples of the manipulation of leadership by corrupt individuals with misguided and even destructive objectives.

The misery and suffering of the world's peoples under the pressures of conflict and injustice necessitate that a new generation of leaders arise and take the bold steps necessary to lay the foundations of a just and peaceful global civilization.

Humanity is searching for enlightened, selfless, effective, and peace-oriented leaders: Could you be one of them?

Elements of Effective and Progressive Leadership

Modes of leadership can vary considerably depending upon what **authority** the leader has, whether that authority is **legitimate,** and for what purpose the leader uses his or her **power.**

Effective leadership is also dependent upon having a **vision** that is positive and universal enough to inspire others to share and participate wholeheartedly in its achievement.

Through consultative decision-making pro-cesses, effective leaders engage their constituents

and/or team members in collectively developing **strategic plans** to systematically achieve **goals**; taking the **initiative** to get the process started; and continuously **evaluating** the group's progress.

A leader recognizes the importance of **training, encouraging, and supporting** the team so that each person's capacities and talents are fully utilized and can continuously develop.

Above all, a leader understands that unity—always in the context of diversity of ideas, approaches, and objectives—is the most powerful vehicle for accomplishing great tasks, and aligns decision-making and problem-solving to the standards of **truth, justice,** and **unity**.

And since leadership, at its core, is about "taking people to places where they would not have gone alone," it necessitates **moral courage** to uphold and strive towards the guiding vision of righteousness and inclusiveness, even when others doubt and reject it.

Power, Authority, and Legitimacy

Among the elements of effective leadership, three elements are frequently misunderstood and misused. These elements are **power, authority, and legitimacy.**

In today's complex and troubled world, many of the conflicts that we face are due either to disagreements over the nature, validity, and legitimacy of authority or to the injurious consequences of the corruption and abuse of authority by those in power.

The result has been a general discrediting of authority that, in turn, has served to undermine universal values necessary for the healthy development and protection of human life, while strengthening the grip of ambitious individuals over the affairs of humankind.

Integrative leadership—one of the fundamental prerequisites of a peaceful civilization—depends on an appropriate understanding of authority, legitimacy, and power. Let us examine these three issues in more detail.

What Is Power?

Power has traditionally been equated with the ability to "force" or "control" others. But there are many other forms and uses of power.

Consider for a moment how we might refer to "a powerful piece of music or poetry," "a powerful machine," "a powerful sports team," "a powerful idea or argument," "a powerful state," or "a powerful leader or person."

From these examples we can see that the word *power* has many different meanings. In various instances, it might refer to:

- The ability to inspire or influence;
- A source or means of supplying energy;
- Physical might or skillful athletic ability;
- Intellectual, moral, or spiritual efficacy;
- Legal or official authority;
- The possession of control, authority, or influence over others.

What type(s) of power would a "leader for peace" need? What types of power are "constructive rather than destructive"?

Power and Worldview

While discussing the nature of power, two important issues need to be considered:

1. **Power is a Tool**
   Power is merely a tool that can be used in appropriate or inappropriate ways towards positive or negative ends. Power in itself is neither good nor bad.
2. **Power is Developmental in Nature**
   Human power is expressed in several different ways: physical, psychological, moral, legal, social, economic, or political.

Each type of power ultimately finds its source in human consciousness and worldview. The first element of human power is expressed in the act of decision-making followed by action. Though it may take less than a moment, we consider our thoughts, feelings, and intentions before doing anything. As such, power is subject to the dynamics and development of human consciousness and its expression in the form of our worldview.

> In other words, the nature and use of power changes as human consciousness and worldview evolve. The more universal and integrated a person's worldview, the more he or she will use the powers available for the creation of unity, justice, progress, and peace.

A Definition of Power

> **Definition**
>
> *Power refers to the ability to use one's capacities for knowledge, love, and will to act, to create, to produce an effect, or to influence.*

If any of these capacities are underdeveloped, ignored, or used in ways that are contrary to universal ethical principles of truth, unity, justice, or service to others, then the person's powers will be either diminished or will lead to negative effects.

The peaceful use of power depends on the adoption of a peace-oriented worldview. Within that worldview, one's capacities for knowledge, love, and will gradually mature in a healthy and holistic manner, to be used for the promotion of fellowship, prosperity, and justice for all humankind.

> Leaders for peace use their powers of knowledge, love, and will to discern the truth, to unite diversities, to foster collective well-being, and to motivate others to do likewise.

Power and Authority

Authority is the right to "author" or "cause" something. Authority may come from a variety of sources. Anyone who claims the right to exercise power, essentially claims to possess authority of some kind. Consider the statements in Table 1. What kind of authority do they claim?

What Is Authority?

Dictionary definitions of "authority" can be summarized as follows:

Definition

Authority refers to the moral right to decide, rule, or judge.

The possession of authority by an individual or group bestows upon them the **authorization** (permission) to exercise power, and renders their pronouncements and decisions **authoritative** (conclusive and correct).

In theory, the purpose of authority is to provide an ethical framework for the principled exercise of power and the creation of order. Too often, however, authority has been abused to serve selfish, partisan, or unethical purposes.

Where Does Authority Come From?

Authority may be granted in varying degrees from a variety of sources:

* **Sources of authority** range from universal to particular. **Universal** principles of an ethical, spiritual, or scientific nature apply to all human beings and exercise authority over all aspects of human life. **Particular** legal, cultural, or institutional frameworks bestow limited authority over specific groups for specific and restricted activities.

* **Legitimate forms of authority,** of whatever type, are based on moral principles that provide the essential *authoritative framework* for effective leadership. Through this framework, right is distinguished from wrong, truth from falsehood, reality from unreality, the constructive from the destructive, and the

Proverb	Type of Claim
"Power comes out of the barrel of a gun."	Physical or military authority
"Power is vested by God/the Holy Scriptures."	Divine or religious authority
"Power is inherited."	Traditional authority
"Power comes from the people."	Democratic authority
"Knowledge is power."	Rational/scientific authority
"Power comes from within."	Personal or experiential authority
"Power is the fruit of unity, justice, and peace."	Moral/spiritual authority

Table 1: Proverbs and claims to authority

moral from the immoral. Through this authoritative framework the appropriate use of power is defined.

Authority may be granted in varying degrees from a variety of sources as outlined in Table 2.

What Is Legitimacy?

Definition

Legitimacy refers to the fact or quality of being "lawful," in accordance with recognized standards or codes.

In essence, legitimacy refers to whether the source of authority is broadly recognized and approved of as authoritative and whether those who are subject to it consent to its rule.

A "legitimate authority" or "legitimate use of power" is one that is considered lawful, just,

acceptable, reasonable, and right. Respected leaders act ethically and model responsible behavior. As such, legitimacy is inseparably linked to the moral and ethical values of a society. Leaders must represent **both moral and legal** authority in order to be considered legitimate.

When Is Authority Not Legitimate?

Conflicts often arise when a source of authority is not universally recognized by all of the individuals or groups that are supposedly subject to its rule. When a source of authority is not accepted, it is viewed as *illegitimate*—meaning that the leader is perceived as *ruling without the right to rule*. **The more limited a source of authority is, the less likely it is that people will view it as legitimate.** The main reason for this is that limited authority renders the leader correspondingly less effective in terms of the scope of its mandate and the size of its constituency. Ultimately, the most authoritative and legitimate leadership is that which is based on the fact and universal application of the oneness

Type of Authority	Basis of Authority
Divine/Religious Authority	Authority of and derived from God, sacred texts, religious principles, and ordinances
Expert Authority	Authority based on expertise or competence in a particular area
Legal/Rational Authority	Authority based on objective, rationalized procedures such as authority of the state, law, and public offices
Moral Authority	Authority based on the practice of moral integrity
Personal/Experiential Authority	Authority based on personal experience
Popular Authority	Authority based on the will of the people as expressed through majority opinion
Scientific Authority	Authority based on empirical scientific investigation
Traditional Authority	Inherited or customary authority, such as monarchy

Table 2: Types and Bases of Authority

of humanity and the principles of truth, unity, and justice.

Legitimacy is most frequently lost when the moral foundation of leadership is perceived as corrupted, weakened, or defective. When this happens, the governing institution's objectives and modes of operation are called into question, their justification is doubted or rejected, there is a loss of confidence in their efficacy, and fewer and fewer people abide by its regulations.

What Makes Authority Legitimate?

Effective leadership and the legitimization of authority are both dependent on the *universality* and *validity* of the authoritative framework within which leaders function.

Condition #1: Universality

Definition

Universality refers to the degree to which an authoritative framework is universal in its principles, scope, and application.

The more universal an authoritative framework is, the more widely it will be accepted and the more conducive it will be to a harmony of purpose and function between those with authority and the rest of the population.

In contrast, when an authoritative framework is limited in its scope, the likelihood of its being accepted by the majority is low. History demonstrates that even when a large number of individuals submit to a limited authority, it typically takes place under conditions of threat, oppression, and force.

Condition #2: Validity

Definition

Validity refers to the degree to which an authoritative framework is based on sound ethical and rational foundations.

The authoritative frameworks that have been most influential in human history have encompassed enduring and verifiable principles, including:

- The understanding that life in general, and human life in particular, is sacred;
- That equality, justice, and freedom from oppression are prerequisites for the creation of truly civilized societies;
- That truth, truthfulness, and trustworthiness are essential for establishing a solid foundation for human relationships at all levels;
- That love, mutual acceptance, unity in diversity, and peace are and have been among the most universally sought after conditions by all peoples throughout history; and
- That creativity, meaning, and transcendence are inherent aspects of human nature and indispensable for living a truly civilized life.

These principles are universal and spiritual in nature, are verifiable and defensible in rational and scientific terms, and affect all aspects of human life: the material, psychological, and sociopolitical.

Authority and its Crisis in the 20th Century

The 20th century witnessed some of the most turbulent crises of authority in recorded history. The legitimacy of religious and monarchical institutions rapidly crumbled following the rise of scientific rationalism, constitutional democracy, and the revelation of countless episodes of moral hypocrisy within the institutions themselves.

These developments could be attributed to the abrupt transition of humanity from its earlier stages of its collective development to a new phase similar in ferocity to the adolescent period in individual development. At the core of these crises was transfer of both power and authority from religious and government leaders, respectively, to the scientific community and the general public.

In the midst of this rapid change, new (and not necessarily more benign) frameworks of authority were established. Notable among these frameworks of authority were ideological movements such as fascism, communism, and materialist capitalism. In today's world, some of the most influential sources of authority include the media, popular opinion, and the scientific community.

Three Modes of Leadership

We will now explore three different modes of leadership[5] and their respective approaches to authority and power:

1. **Control-Oriented Leadership**
   Varieties of this mode are also referred to as "authoritarian," "autocratic," or "directive" leadership;
2. **Liberty-Oriented Leadership**
   Varieties of this mode are also referred to as "libertarian," "laissez-faire," or "delegative" leadership;
3. **Unity-Oriented Leadership**
   Varieties of this mode are also referred to as "integrative," "participative," or "collaborative" leadership.

"Control-Oriented" Leadership

(Also known as "Authoritarian," "Autocratic," or "Directive" Leadership)

Emerging from the **survival-based worldview**, "control-oriented" leadership has been the most common form of leadership among families, institutions, and governments throughout history.[6]

Definition

Survival-Based Worldview: *associated with early phases in human development and emerging also in conditions of insecurity (such as poverty, injustice, anarchy, intense competition, physical threat, and war) where the concern for basic survival becomes paramount. Fear for survival leads to a preoccupation with security and power. This worldview is most often expressed in hierarchical power structures, and often leads to a proclivity to use force and violence to achieve desired objectives.*

---

5. It should be noted that in the academic and professional literature on leadership there is a lack of consensus on the different approaches to or styles of leadership. Consequently, many different and not necessarily compatible classification systems of leadership types exist. An attempt has been made here to cluster classification terminologies in similar, though not entirely identical, leadership types.

6. For elaboration of the control-oriented mode, see Theodor Adorno et al., *The Authoritarian Personality* (New York: Harper, 1950); Erich Fromm, *Escape from Freedom* (New York: Owl Books, 1994); Rollo May, *Power and Innocence: A Search for the Source of Violence* (New York: Delta Books, 1972); and Gordon W. Allport, *The Person in Psychology: Selected Essays* (Boston: Beacon Press, 1968).

In this mode, one individual or a few individuals assume complete authority and power. The control-oriented leader makes decisions on behalf of others with little or no input on their part, and issues commands which s/he expects the subordinates to obey. Also known as "authoritarian" leadership, the main motivation behind this approach is the desire to establish order within the group, and to maintain the leader's own power over the collective. The decisions of control-oriented leaders are usually enforced through coercion or threat of punishment.

Under control-oriented leadership, the subordinate members of the group either conform, or withdraw, or engage in subversive activities.

In the control-oriented leadership mode:

- Power is used to force others to conform to the leader's wishes.

- The goal of control-oriented leadership is to secure the superiority, safety, and pleasure of the leader.

Table 3 summarizes the main characteristics of control-oriented leadership.

An Assessment of "Control-Oriented" Leadership

The control-oriented, autocratic approach to decision-making seems easy because the leader makes decisions alone and may be able to create a temporary appearance of order. However, this form of decision-making is neither easy nor sustainable. This is so because such an approach contravenes human dignity and suppresses the fundamental survival and developmental needs of those affected by the leader's command. Under a controlling authority figure, people become either resentful and subversive, or defeated and

apathetic. The former group constitutes the nucleus for a future opposition to the seat of power, while the latter group becomes a burden on the society and weakens it in the process.

Control-oriented leadership is also limited in its creative abilities because it inhibits individual freedom and suppresses group diversity, and in doing so, fails to benefit from the talents, strengths, and perspectives of its peoples. A control orientation fundamentally denies the principles of equality and justice, both of which are essential aspects of enlightened and progressive leadership. Power is always susceptible to abuse, and, as such, the authoritarian use of power almost always leads to considerable injustice, conflict, and ultimately violence.

"Liberty-Oriented" Leadership

(Also known as "Libertarian," "Laissez-Faire," or "Delegative" Leadership)

Emerging from the **identity-based worldview**, "liberty-oriented" (libertarian) leadership is based on the view that "unfettered freedom," "self-determination," and "the pursuit of personal interests" are the supreme social values around which all other values ought to be organized.

Definition

Identity-Based Worldview: associated with the adolescent and early adulthood phases in human development and emerging also in "open" societies where freedom, the rejection of authority, and the quest for identity become paramount. Associated with the sudden increase of ideas, passions, attitudes, and physical and mental capabilities which that lead to competition for recognition and supremacy. This worldview is most often expressed in adversarial and competitive power structures, and often leading to excessive individualism and the division of society into discordant factions.

Characteristics of Control-Oriented Leadership

1. Power Fixation

Control-oriented leaders function within the survival-worldview. In this worldview, the world is perceived as a dangerous place, full of threats to the leader's security and position. Control-oriented leaders believe that if one has more power to control others and the surrounding environment, then one will be safer. However, power merely creates an **illusion** of safety. In reality, power creates vulnerability; for the more powerful one becomes, the more vulnerable one feels to attack, and so even more power is sought. Thus a vicious cycle is created: No matter how much power one has, it is never enough.

2. Survival-Based Worldview

A control-oriented leader usually holds a dichotomous worldview in which the world is divided into opposing groups. For example: men vs. women, us vs. them, good people vs. bad, friends vs. enemies. In doing so, the control-oriented person erects boundaries between him/herself and others. Paradoxically, in a society under control-oriented leadership, separations based on race, religion, ethnicity, language, gender, class, and political orientation are subjected to the forces of conformity and denial of the uniqueness of both individuals and communities of people.

3. Intellectual and Emotional Rigidity

Control-oriented leaders are not open to new ideas because of the change they might bring and the challenge such ideas might present to the leader's own power. New ideas are threatening. Furthermore, control-oriented individuals are not open to the range of human emotions such as love, fear, sorrow, and compassion, because they are perceived as showing weakness. Such individuals are, in fact, only comfortable with one emotion—anger—because anger gives the illusion of power and strength. Control-oriented individuals, institutions, and societies tend to be self-righteous (because they consider themselves as possessing absolute truth) and cruel (because the expression of love and compassion is discouraged).

4. Hierarchical Relationships

The control-oriented leader demands obedience from those who are accounted as holding a lower rank and is obedient to those who are his/her superiors. A militaristic mindset is adopted in which the process of "following orders" justifies all actions and absolves one from personal responsibility.

5. Force-Based Conflict Resolution

Control-oriented approaches to conflict resolution range from imposed adjudication and arbitration processes on the one hand, to the use of violent force and warfare on the other with a full range of threats and intimidation.

Table 3: Characteristics of Control-Oriented Leadership

Liberty-oriented leadership flourished in the 18th and 19th centuries when humanity—then in the midst of the adolescent phase of its collective development—rejected transcendent and traditional sources of authority in favor of the philosophy of individual liberty, expressed through such values as the right to personal freedom, limited government, and an openly competitive free-market economy.

The liberty-oriented mode views competition as a fact of nature and a necessary competency of the individual. It de-emphasizes responsibility to the collective, and whatever cooperation does exist is based on the idea of competitive advantage. Such allegiances are oriented towards maximizing profit and easily break down if greater advantage is found elsewhere. Whether in business, politics, or personal relationships, the modus operandi is defined by power-struggle and the survival of the fittest.

In the liberty-oriented leadership mode:

- Power is used to compete with and gain advantage over others.

- The goal of liberty-oriented leadership is to win.

Table 4 summarizes the main characteristics of liberty-oriented leadership.

Reflections on Control-Oriented and Liberty-Oriented Leadership

Neither the control-oriented nor the liberty-oriented approach to leadership can foster peace because both these approaches revolve around the issue of power—power as a force to control others and power as the means of competition. Neither force nor competition is conducive to peace. They both create conflict in human relationships at all levels.

Unfortunately, in the world today we can see that every society is characterized by the control-oriented and/or liberty-based modes of functioning. The shift from dictatorship to democracy has been good, but the process of human social development has to continue its upward progress towards ever more refined, progressive, unity-based, and peace-oriented types of leadership.

We now will examine the concept of unity-oriented integrative leadership and its approach to issues of power, decision-making, and freedom as well as its impact on fostering peace.

"Unity-Oriented" Leadership

(Also known as "Integrative," "Collaborative," or "Participative" Leadership)

Emerging from the **unity-based worldview,** "unity-oriented" (integrative) leadership develops, elicits, and harmonizes the diverse capabilities, insights, and talents of the collective in order to achieve the well-being of the whole community.

Defintion

Unity-Based Worldview: associated with the phase of maturity in human development. Grounded in the recognition of humanity's essential oneness and inherent nobility, this worldview enables the creation of unity-oriented relationships while respecting and celebrating humanity's rich diversity.

Both "unity" and "integrity" mean "wholeness"—a state of bringing together (unifying, integrating) all components. A society guided by leaders with integrity according to the principle of unity-in-diversity is a society in which all of the components are brought together and aligned with universal ethical principles, a society in which the rights and responsibilities of each component member are considered, harmonized, and implemented.

Characteristics of Liberty-Oriented Leadership

1. Pleasaure Fixation

Liberty-oriented leaders function within the framework of the identity-based worldview, which places emphasis on the importance of individual freedom, supremacy, and pleasure. Whether pleasure takes the form of material wealth, the satisfaction of physical appetites, the gaining of popularity and recognition, or other forms of self-gratification, the freedom to pursue pleasure is considered a basic right of every individual. Leadership in this mode often uses incentives and rewards to stimulate competition.

2. Identity-Based Worldview

In the liberty-oriented framework, everything revolves around the separate identity of the individual, and every person looks after his/her personal, self-centered interest. The individual is viewed as the most important unit of society, and the rights of the individual take precedence over those of the collective. **Individualism** is the inevitable outcome of the identity-based worldview.

3. Relativity of Ideas and Emotions

The liberty-oriented, "libertarian," or "laissez-faire" approach to leadership allows individuals and groups to operate in the context of freedom and competition, which usually results in a chaotic and/or relativistic approach to ideas, emotions, values, and responsibilities. In a liberty-oriented approach to leadership, everything is permissible, indeed, is a right. The poorly disciplined environment of liberty-based leadership creates a paradoxical situation in which the forces of freedom and chaos neutralize their respective benefits.

4. Anarchic Relationships

The relativistic approach to intellectual and moral values in the liberty-oriented mode leads to a condition of anarchy in human relationships mainly because there are no common/universal standards for the education and regulation of human behavior.

5. Competition-Based Conflict Resolution

Liberty-oriented leaders tend to adopt fundamentally competitive and adversarial approaches to the resolution of conflicts according to the concept of the "survival of the fittest" and the right of individuals to "win," usually at the expense of others.

Table 4: Characteristics of Liberty-Oriented Leadership

In a united and mature society, power and pleasure will give way to the dynamics and rigors of individual growth and transformation. The worldview recognizes the fundamental oneness of humanity, while at the same time celebrates the uniqueness and individuality of each person. The hallmark of intellectual and emotional maturity is creativity—the ability to bring seemingly opposite entities together to create a new, usually higher order of life and living. This is a true expression of freedom. Consultation, cooperation, and assumption of responsibility for one's activities would then characterize human relationships. Creation of unity in diversity will become the main objective of both leaders and their peoples.

Unity-oriented leadership does not allow power to remain only in the hands of a few people or in the hands of competing groups. Rather, all members of the community are assisted to develop and apply their individual powers of knowledge, love, and will to the service of the whole.

A society built on the foundations of integrative leadership transforms the industries of war into industries of peace and dedicates humanity's financial resources towards the growth and well-being of the community.

In the unity-oriented leadership mode:

- Power is used to create harmony, cooperation, and unity in the context of diversity both within and among communities and groups.

- The goal of leadership is to create a civilization of peace.

Table 5 summarizes the main characteristics of unity-oriented leadership.

Summary of the Three Modes of Power

Table 6 summarizes the main characteristics of each mode of leadership discussed in this unit.

A Summary of the Three Modes of Power

In the **control-oriented** mode, power is used to force others to conform to one's wishes. Through domination, control, and violence, the control-oriented leader seeks to maintain order, security, and the superiority of his/her own position.

In the **liberty-oriented** mode, power is used to compete and gain advantage over others. Liberty-oriented leadership exalts the principles of individualism and competition, makes cooperation conditional on personal advantage, and aims to win at all costs. Through competition, conflict, and even sabotage, the libertarian seeks to win, to gain the most, and to gratify appetites for pleasure to the extent possible.

In the **unity-oriented** mode, power is used to foster cooperation, transformation, and peace in the context of diversity. Through service, humility, unity-in-diversity, and consultative decision-making, the integrative leader seeks to promote the oneness, nobility, equality, justice, freedom, and peace of all humanity.

In Focus: Leadership for Peace

Now that we have reviewed the general characteristics of control-oriented, liberty-oriented, and unity-oriented leadership, let's take a focused look at the principles and priorities of Leadership for Peace.

Characteristics of Unity-Oriented Leadership

1. Growth/Transformation Orientation

The main aim of "unity-oriented"/"integrative" leadership is to foster the comprehensive and wholesome development of all the members of the society by creating opportunities for them to actualize their highest potential and transform their communities into models of a peaceful, prosperous, just, and free civilization. Growth and transformation become the overarching goals in service to which all the powers of society are channeled.

2. Interactive Worldview

The unity-oriented mode of leadership recognizes that diversity is a valuable resource in all creative endeavors. As such, integrative leaders encourage and facilitate efforts to develop, elicit, and harmonize all the diverse capabilities, insights, and talents of all citizens for the sake of fostering unity, creativity, and prosperity of the entire community.

3. Emotional and Intellectual Creativity

True creativity is the product of disciplined freedom. Neither discipline nor freedom alone can produce true creativity, for freedom without discipline leads to chaos and destruction; and discipline without freedom leads to inhibition, stagnation, and frustration. Integrative leaders recognize the value of fostering disciplined freedom at all levels of society; in doing so, the members of society have both the opportunities and framework necessary for true creativity and fruitfulness.

4. Consultative Relationships

"Unity-oriented" leadership rests on consultative decision-making. The word *consultation* as it is used here refers to a process of decision-making (in the spirit of unity and in the context of truth) for reaching just conclusions with due consideration for the best interests of all affected, both directly or indirectly, by the decision. Consultative process is neither based on power, nor on individual preferences, but, rather, on known facts and truths of the issue at hand.

5. Unity-Based Conflict Resolution

The main characteristic of unity-based conflict resolution is its ability to resolve present conflicts, to prevent their reappearance, and to do so without creating new conflicts in the process. Conflict-Free Conflict Resolution (CFCR) as one model of unity-based conflict resolution is the subject of the next unit, Unit 8.

Table 5: Characteristics of Unity-Oriented Leadership

Leadership for Peace is guided by an integrative, transcendent, universal, and valid authoritative framework, and aims at empowering all involved—both leaders and the populace—to use their unique and rich human powers for the betterment of their individual and collective lives.

Leadership for Peace is unity-oriented and aims at the creation of justice, peace, prosperity, and happiness of the peoples and nations. In essence, "leadership for peace is the process of leading people to the source of all good." Leaders for Peace, serving their communities with humility, have no ambition except to revive the world, to ennoble its life, and to regenerate its peoples. They are concerned for the welfare of both their people and the entire human race.

Can Anyone Be A "Leader for Peace"?

Leadership isn't just about heading a large organization, business, or government. Leadership is a quality that anyone can demonstrate—even in simple ways—throughout all aspects of life.

Being a leader for peace means "taking the lead" in your own life to understand the importance of unity, truth, service, and justice, and to bring these principles into being through action.

What distinguishes leaders for peace is their vision of the possibility of universal human well-being and justice, and their courage to faithfully and responsibly live by the ethical standards of that vision even when others do not. Even if they are not aware of it, leaders for peace inspire others by their sincerity, humility, and conviction, and they plant the seeds of transformation in the hearts and minds of those whom they meet.

What Characteristics Distinguish A "Leader For Peace"?

Leadership for Peace is not an easy role to fulfill. It both depends upon and calls forth the highest aspects of human character. A leader for peace is characterized by:

- Dedication to Truth
- Sincerity in Word and Deed
- Honesty and Courtesy
- Trustworthiness and Accountability
- Humility and Kindness
- Uprightness and Moderation of Conduct
- Service and Self-Sacrifice
- Wisdom and Justice in Decision-Making

	Control-Oriented	Liberty-Oriented	Unity-Oriented
Source of Authority	Ideology/Force	Public/Personal Opinion	Universal Spiritual/Scientific Principles
Role of Government	To control the people	Authority based on expertise or competence in a particular area	To create justice and unity
Goal of Decision-Making	To maintain power and control	To gain competitive advantage	To foster unity and growth
Mode of Decision-Making	Dictatorial	Competitive	Consultative

Table 6: Modes of Leadership

A leader for peace is someone whose capacities for knowledge, love, and will are awakened, are aligned with ethical principles, are harmonized and brought into focus through conscious reflection, and are exerted for the sake of creating things of worth in service to universal well-being. Such a leader produces positive effects in the world and influences many people.

What is on the Agenda of Leadership for Peace?

With the well-being of humanity as the primary goal of leadership, a leader for peace will consider it necessary to work vigilantly on the following issues:

- Promoting Consciousness of the Oneness of Humanity
- Prevention of Conflict and Promotion of Peace
- Advancement of the Equality of Women and Men
- Application of the Standard of Justice to all Affairs
- Protection of Human Rights
- Provision of Universal Access to Education
- Promotion of Work and Prosperity for the Generality of the Population
- Promotion of Sustainable Agriculture and Environmental Responsibility

A "Leader for Peace" Is...

A Visionary
One who holds a vision of human unity, equality, justice, and prosperity.

An Inspirer
One who engages others in that vision.

A Role-Model
One who demonstrates in his/her character the qualities of integrity, universality, and perseverance.

A Listener
One who actively and sincerely seeks the views, experiences, and skills of others in the process of decision-making.

A Communicator
One who communicates clearly, regularly, and positively with the entire team.

A Learner
One who is dedicated to continued personal growth and is willing to learn from others.

A Teacher
One who coaches and encourages others to develop their capacities and talents.

An Empowerer
One who encourages others to achieve personal and collective goals.

A Unifier
One who, above all, exemplifies through words and deeds, the spirit and principles of unity in diversity.

Principles of Good Leadership	
Honesty	The best leaders are truthful, even when that truthfulness is difficult.
Openness	Good leaders need to be eager to exchange views and discuss issues. They need to encourage others to present different points of view and be responsive to other people asking questions. Good leaders also need to be as free as possible from all forms of prejudice.
Accountability	Leaders need to take responsibility for their actions and be ready to explain those actions. Good leaders are always answerable to the members of their community.
Transparency	Leaders should set up their decision-making processes in such a way that other people can see what decisions are made and how they are made.
Responsibility	Good leaders fulfill their duties in a timely manner and are fully accountable for their actions.
Sensitivity	Leaders need to understand their community and the members of that community. They need to be aware of the difficult and touchy subjects relating to their community. Leaders also need to be empathetic and be able to put themselves in the place of others. They need to be able to think with their hearts and their mind, with compassion and reason.
Connection to the Community	A good leader needs to be deeply involved in the workings of his/her community. Only through being involved in the community can a leader truly address the needs of the community through his/her actions.
Knowledge	To be effective, leaders require information that is pertinent to the needs of their community. They are obligated to seek answers to questions related to the welfare of the communities they lead. However, since no individual has within themselves such extensive knowledge, one of the essential skills of leadership is to obtain knowledge through consultation with the informed and expert councils that the leader creates for this purpose.
Wisdom	Leaders need to go beyond knowledge as such, to the good judgment to choose those actions and decisions that are appropriate in a given situation. This sagacity comes about with extensive experience, deep reflection, and an open mind and heart.

Table 7: Principles of Good Leadership
Adapted from: Young Leaders Online <http://www.onlineleaders.info/leadership/character.html>

Summary

In this unit, we have learned that:

Power and Authority Have Been Misused Throughout History
- The reason for this misuse has been the prevalence of conflict-based worldviews.

Predominant Uses of Power are not Conducive to Peace
- Neither the force-based use of power by authoritarian societies, nor the competition-based use of power in libertarian societies can foster peace.

An Integrative, Unity-Oriented Approach to Power and Leadership is Needed
- To meet the challenges of the 21st century, a new form of leadership is needed: one that genuinely strives to discern the truth, to unite diversities, to foster collective well-being, to raise the standard of justice, and to motivate others to do likewise.

Leadership for Peace can be Demonstrated by Everyone, in all Aspects of Life
- Through service, humility, unity-in-diversity, and consultative decision-making, leaders for peace seek to promote the oneness and nobility of humanity, and to safeguard equality and justice.

Key Questions for the Classroom

The following questions can be used to review and explore further the concepts of Unit 7 on Power, Authority, and Leadership for Peace with your students:

1. What is power?

2. What forms does power take? Who holds it? How is it gained, used, and justified?

3. Are all types of power conducive to peace?

4. What is authority?

5. Are all authorities "leaders"? Do all "leaders" have authority? What, if any, is the difference between "an authority" and "a leader"?

6. What is a "leader"? What criteria define "good leadership"?

7. When are power and authority unacceptable/illegitimate?

8. On what does legitimacy depend? (List 5 criteria.)

9. What distinguishes a "leader for peace" from other types of leaders?

10. From what source does a "leader for peace" derive his or her authority and legitimacy?

11. How can I be a "leader for peace"?

12. What role does government play in control-oriented societies? In liberty-oriented societies? In an integrative, unity-oriented society?

13. Where does authority come from in a control-oriented society? In a liberty-oriented society? In an integrative, unity-oriented society?

14. Towards what goal does an authoritarian/a libertarian/a unifier use his/her power?

15. How are conflicts resolved in a control-oriented society? In a liberty-oriented society? In an integrative, unity-oriented society?

16. What are the benefits and challenges of including more people in decision-making and problem-solving processes?

17. What positive dimensions of authoritarian and libertarian societies are preserved when we move to a peace-oriented society?

Personal Reflection

Reflection is a very powerful learning tool. It helps us to make sense of the things we are studying and the experiences we are going through. The more we reflect on ourselves, our relationships, and the world around us, the better prepared we are to discern, prioritize, and act upon issues of importance.

Becoming a peacemaker is a very important and challenging task. By reflecting on the principles of peace, we are better equipped to make decisions about our own development that will help us to confidently undertake the goal of peace building.

As we go through each of the EFP Curriculum units, try to set aside some time for the process of reflection.

Questions for Personal Reflection

Self

Take a moment to ask yourself the following questions:
- Can I be a "leader for peace"?
- What peace-leadership qualities do I have?
- What peace-leadership qualities do I need to develop more?

Focus Question

Consider the following statement:

> "Leaders for peace use their powers of knowledge, love, and will to discern the truth, to unite diversities, to foster collective well-being, and to motivate others to do likewise."

How does being a "leader for peace" challenge my current modes of thinking, behaving and relating to others?

Family, Workplace, and Friendships

Reflect on your experiences in your family, workplace, and friendships:
- What forms of leadership can I observe in my family, school, and/or workplace?
- How are decisions made, and who makes them?
- What understanding of power is needed within the group for collective, consultative leadership to be effective?

Focus Questions

Unity-oriented decision-making requires consulting with others to seek their views, to benefit from their experience, and to meet their needs as well as one's own.

• What are the benefits and challenges of involving more people in the decision-making/problem-solving process?
• How can the challenges of consultative decision-making be overcome?

Society

Now consider the society in which you live:

• What forms of leadership exist in my society?
• How is leadership perceived by the general public? Is it viewed as something positive, negative, effective, ineffective, legitimate, illegitimate, etc?
• Is my society ready for "leadership for peace"? Discuss.

Focus Questions

Think of an authority in your community or wider society that you view as both *legitimate* and *effective*.

• What type of authority are they? (e.g., family, civil, political, or religious)
• From where do they derive their legitimacy?
• What do you think makes them effective in their leadership role?
• Would you consider them to be a "leader for peace"? Why?

World at Large

Finally, take a moment to consider the world as a whole:

• Are there any leaders in today's world that I would consider "leaders for peace"?
• What stands in the way of world leaders becoming "leaders for peace"?
• What might today's leaders have to sacrifice in order to become "leaders for peace"?

Focus Questions

Consider the following two statements:

"Global movement towards leadership for peace is a gradual but likely process."

"The main obstacle to leadership for peace is worldview."

How accurate are these statements in your view? How? Why?

Classroom Tools

As a teacher in the Education for Peace Program, it is now your task to include the discussion of "leadership for peace" in your class and to assist your students' exploration.

The more your students understand the qualities, principles, priorities, and procedures of leadership for peace, the more able they will be as the leaders of the future.

Your role as their teacher and mentor in this process is tremendously important.

To help you get started, a number of tools are included in this section that you may find useful. These tools are only guides, and you are encouraged to develop your own ideas about how to best explore these topics with your students.

In addition to the examples here, please also refer to the Educational Methodology Unit where you will find practical guidelines on how to make your classroom a creative and effective learning environment, as well as other great ideas from fellow teachers who are integrating Education for Peace into their various subject areas.

As you work with the Education for Peace concepts, you will surely develop new ideas for lessons, activities, and assessment approaches. We encourage you to pass along your thoughts, ideas, or resource links to Education for Peace so they can be added to our EFP Resource Bank for other teachers to use. Please send us an email at <info@efpinternational.org>, or mail your ideas to our address:

International Education for Peace Institute (Canada)
101, 1001 W. Broadway, Suite 900
Vancouver, BC V6H 4E4
Canada

We look forward to hearing from you!

Activity Ideas for Secondary Schools

Social Studies
Take Me To Your Leader: Imagine that you are living in a future society that is diverse and united, peaceful and dynamic, prosperous and just. Who are the leaders of this society? Write a creative piece that describes the leaders of this advanced society by using the following questions as your guide: What are the qualities of these leaders? How do they make decisions? When and with whom do they consult? By what process are they selected as leaders? What are their leadership priorities?

History
With the help of your teacher, the Internet, and your local librarian, try to identify and conduct some biographical research on 6–10 historical leaders for peace. Be sure to identify an equal number of women and men. Next, write a letter to your school principal and Minister of Education stating that you want your school's history textbooks to be rewritten with a focus on the heroic efforts and accomplishments of such leaders who advanced the cause of peace and noble civilization. Present your findings, letter, and any response you receive to your class. You may also consider contacting your local newsletter to share your project with the community at large.

Drama
Create a 3-part dramatic skit that contrasts the characteristics and outcomes of the 3 modes of leadership identified in this unit: control-oriented (authoritarian), liberty-oriented (libertarian), unity-oriented (integrative) leadership. Present your skit to your class, and then invite your classmates to share and discuss their observations.

Literature/
Creative Writing
Write a poem that portrays your vision of a true "leader for peace."
Or:
Create a recipe for "cooking up" a true "leader for peace."

Art
Create a collage of images and text from magazines, newspapers, or other print materials that represents your understanding of what it means to be a "leader for peace."
Or:
Use a camera to photograph "leaders for peace" in your own community. Remember: a leader for peace does not have to be a prominent person or in public office. You may find leaders for peace in your own school, local club or religious community, sports team, radio or television station, hospital, or your own family. Make a booklet or collage of your images, and write or describe why you consider them to be "leaders for peace."

Activities for Primary Schools

Classroom Environment	At the beginning of the year, challenge your students to become a class full of "Leaders for Peace." Together, create a chart of what it means to be a "Leader for Peace" to be displayed in the classroom for all to see and reflect upon throughout the year.
Language Arts	In bi-weekly journals, have students write about activities they engaged in that were conducive of a "Leader for Peace" or what they could have done to be a better "Leader for Peace."
Drama	Read a story about someone who does not make good choices or is always getting into trouble, and stop the story before the main character alters their choices and behavior. Have the students create a play that demonstrates how the principles of Leadership for Peace could be applied in this story and how the outcomes could be different.

Unit 7, Sample Lesson 1: LEADERSHIP FOR PEACE

Focus: Power

Context

Power is one of the most misused of human tools. It is responsible for the creation of humanity's great civilizations, scientific accomplishments, and sociopolitical advances, but also for humanity's bloody history of wars, as well as on-going social injustices, corruption, and conflicts. To create a civilization of peace, a transformation in our understanding and use of power is needed. This lesson familiarizes students with various concepts of power and trains them to evaluate the outcomes of its use. Defining power that is conducive to peace constitutes the concluding activity of the lesson.

Points for Understanding

- There are many types of power, each of which can be used properly, or misused and abused.
- In its broadest sense, power is the ability to act, to produce an effect, or to exert effort or influence of some kind.
- Uses of power that may be argued as "just" or "fair" may not, in fact, be conducive to unity and peace.
- In the context of peace, power is the ability to create and maintain unity in the midst of diversity (e.g., peoples, opinions, or needs), and to foster the growth and development of others.

Key Questions

1. What is power? Are all uses of power conducive to peace?
2. How can the peaceful use of power be defined?

Learning Process

1. Ask students the following questions: How many definitions of *power* can you think of? What is *power*? Brainstorm together and write suggestions on the board. To stimulate ideas about the meaning of the word *power*, consider notions of a "powerful piece of music, drama or poetry," a "powerful machine," a "powerful idea or argument," a "powerful fertilizer," a "powerful medicine," and finally, a "powerful leader or person."

Guide students to think broadly about power and to arrive at answers such as the following:

    a. Ability to act, produce an effect, or exert effort or influence;

    b. A source or means of supplying energy;

    c. Possession of control, authority, or influence over others;

    d. Physical might or the ability to wield force;

    e. Legal or official authority;

    f. Mental, moral, or spiritual efficacy.

2. Ask students whether they think all uses of power are right, just, or fair. Return to the examples of power above and discuss how they can be used in a healthy and balanced manner to create greater understanding, progress, prosperity, efficiency, unity, and health; or can be misused and abused to cause confusion, injury, corruption, and injustice.

3. Form the class into groups and have each group identify three uses of power (great or small) that they all agree are just and fair. Once they have completed this task, ask them to evaluate whether the examples they generated are conducive to greater unity and peace. Discuss which of the examples students would keep or discard from their list of "good uses of power," and why.

4. For homework, ask students to complete the following sentence: "In the context of peace, power is the ability to…." At the next class, ask students to share their definitions and discuss. Make connections that lead to the general idea that "In the context of peace, power is the ability to create and maintain unity in the midst of diversity, and to foster the growth and development of others." Generate examples of this type of power in action in different sectors of society.

Activities and Assignments

Teachers can choose from among the following sample assignments, or create their own:

1. **Journal:** Write a 2–3 page journal entry around the following questions: What powers do I have? In what ways do I use them that are good? In what ways do I use them that are not good? Which power(s) would I like to develop more and why?

2. **Drama:** Select one of the human powers (i.e., knowledge, love, will) and create a sketch or mime that demonstrates how it can be used either to foster the well-being of others, or to undermine it.

3. **Self-Assessment Questionnaire:** Give each student a copy of the "Am I A Leader for Peace?" self-assessment questionnaire. Provide an opportunity for students to complete the questionnaire, either in class or as homework. The questionnaire is designed for

private reflection and should not be collected or graded. However, after questionnaires are completed, teachers may invite students to volunteer any personal reflections that emerged during the process.

4. **Design a Community Improvement Project:** Present students with the challenge of designing a community improvement project. Form the class into working groups of 4–5 people and provide them with a period of 10–15 minutes to brainstorm and select a focus for their project. Examples of projects include: initiating a "positive media campaign" that calls upon media agencies to highlight positive actions in the local community; initiating a "youth city council" that regularly consults with local authorities on issues affecting the community and youth in particular; or forming a "peace dance troupe" that brings together diverse local youth to talk about the opportunities and prerequisites for peace, unity, and justice, and then creates and performs dance presentations on those themes for local schools, authorities, and the general public. Once students have identified the theme of their project, have them use the "Taking the Lead" planning framework to flesh out the details of their project plan.

5. **Class Discussion:** Divide the class into small groups. Have each group select one of the quotations included at the end of this unit. Discuss for 15 minutes in light of the concepts introduced in Unit 7 on Leadership for Peace. Re-convene and share conclusions.

6. **Written Assignment:** Read "Hickory by Choice" and analyze the leadership and decision-making processes that made rebuilding their community a success. Imagine how the story might have been different if the city authorities simply made all of the zoning and building decisions without consulting local residents. Create a 2x2 table (2-columns by 2-rows), with headings "Pros" and "Cons" across the top, and "Authoritarian" and "Consultative" along the side, to compare and contrast the use of a top-down authoritarian approach to decision-making versus a whole-community consultative approach, as described in the story.

Additional Resources

Activity Readings 1 and 2, "Am I A Leader for Peace?" Self-Assessment Questionnaire

Unit 7, Sample Lesson 1 – Activity Reading

Choose one of the following quotations and discuss:

"Dictators free themselves, but they enslave the people."
—Charlie Chaplin (1889–1977), British comic actor, filmmaker,
The Great Dictator (1940)

"Leadership consists not in degrees of technique but in traits of character; it requires moral rather than athletic or intellectual effort, and it imposes on both leader and follower alike the burdens of self-restraint."
—Lewis H. Lapham (b. 1935), U.S. essayist, editor.,
Money and Class in America, ch. 10 (1988)

"Today, the task befitting great rulers is to establish universal peace, for in this lies the freedom of all peoples."
—'Abdu'l-Bahá Abbas (1844–1921), Persian philosopher, humanitarian,
The Secret of Divine Civilization, p. 71

"What causes adolescents to rebel is not the assertion of authority but the arbitrary use of power, with little explanation of the rules and no involvement in decision-making. . . . Involving the adolescent in decisions doesn't mean that you are giving up your authority. It means acknowledging that the teenager is growing up and has the right to participate in decisions that affect his or her life."
—Laurence Steinberg (20th century), U.S. professor of psychology,
and Ann Levine (20th century), U.S. author and writer.
You and Your Adolescent, ch. 1 (1990)

"I have three precious things which I hold fast and prize. The first is gentleness; the second is frugality; the third is humility, which keeps me from putting myself before others. Be gentle and you can be bold; be frugal and you can be liberal; avoid putting yourself before others and you can become a leader among men."
—Lao-Tzu
<http://www.motivational-inspirationalcorner.com/getquote.html?startrow=31&categoryid=24>

Unit 7, Sample Lesson 2 – Activity Reading

Hickory by Choice: Public Participation Paves the Way for Progress

After several heated disputes between city officials and citizens over zoning and transportation issues, the city of Hickory [North Carolina, USA] decided to review their ordinances. A 25-member task force consisting of residents of the city and surrounding communities was selected by city council in 1998 to produce a citizen-derived growth plan called "Hickory by Choice." Members ranged from environmental activists to wealthy developers, but all called Hickory home. After familiarizing themselves with the region's current methods of growth and development, the committee, not city council, selected an outside consultant.

In what was probably one of the key elements to the success of Hickory by Choice, public meetings were held with the help of the consultant. Residents were shown a series of examples of various types of street and neighborhood design. Through this process, called a visual preference study, residents were able to point out exactly which elements they liked and disliked in each picture and explain why. As it turned out, most people from apartment developers to open space activists tended to like the same things—tree-lined streets, sidewalks set back from the road, and landscaped medians.

The citizen-led committee spent the next year developing a list of over 100 very specific statements that summarized the desires of residents on topics from street design to neighborhood development. More pictures were drawn that combined these and they were once again shared with the public. Afterwards, the committee released its report and held a second round of community-wide meetings. This time, participation was even better as more people came to voice their support and concerns over different aspects of the report.

The Hickory by Choice draft plan was left open for public comment for almost three years. This long comment period gave citizens and committee members time to recognize and resolve conflicts before the plan ever reached city council, and helped to ensure that the plan was approved.

Hickory has already begun to implement some parts of the plan, such as converting its downtown one-way streets into two-way streets. Traffic flow in the central business district was never heavy enough to warrant one-way streets, so this change has made it much easier to navigate downtown. Much of the implementation remains to be done, but the public involvement in the Hickory by Choice project has bolstered its success thus far.

See: <http://www.ci.hickory.nc.us/publicdocs/masterplans/Woolpertfinal/Default.htm>

Am I A Leader For Peace?

Leadership for Peace Self-Assessment Test

This self-survey is an exercise **just for you**. It will provide you with feedback on your readiness to become a leader for peace. Rate yourself on a scale of 1 to 5, with 5 being a definite YES and 1 being a definite NO. Be honest about your answers as this survey is intended only for your own self-assessment.

Circle the number that you feel most closely represents your feelings about the statement:

		NO				YES
a.	I am committed to helping improve world conditions.	1	2	3	4	5
b.	I can envision global peace, justice, and prosperity.	1	2	3	4	5
c.	I believe that world peace is really possible.	1	2	3	4	5
d.	I know with certainty that humanity is one.	1	2	3	4	5
e.	I am inspired by the courageous and sacrificial efforts of other peacemakers.	1	2	3	4	5
f.	I wish to inspire others with a vision of world peace.	1	2	3	4	5
g.	I am willing to work hard and to sacrifice so that the goals of peace can be accomplished.	1	2	3	4	5
h.	I feel it is my duty and my honor to do my best in every situation.	1	2	3	4	5
i.	I strive to continuously develop my intellectual, emotional, and spiritual capacities.	1	2	3	4	5
j.	I recognize that everyone, including me, is developing and needs opportunities and encouragement to grow.	1	2	3	4	5
k.	I enjoy learning from others and sharing my learning with them.	1	2	3	4	5
l.	I am always interested in learning new ideas and techniques.	1	2	3	4	5
m.	Creating peace is about action, and I have lots of ideas on how to create peace in my community/workplace.	1	2	3	4	5
n.	I enjoy collecting and analyzing information.	1	2	3	4	5

		NO				YES
o.	I enjoy setting goals and planning how to systematically achieve them.	1	2	3	4	5
p.	I feel comfortable sharing work and responsibilities with others.	1	2	3	4	5
q.	I feel accountable to the team for my areas of responsibility.	1	2	3	4	5
r.	I am eager to work with others on the goal of peace.	1	2	3	4	5
s.	I consider team diversity to be a strength and look for ways to draw on the insights and creativity that it offers.	1	2	3	4	5
t.	I strive to create an atmosphere of unity among the team members.	1	2	3	4	5
u.	I respect other people's views and feel comfortable asking others for feedback and advice.	1	2	3	4	5
v.	I praise people's strengths rather than criticize their weaknesses.	1	2	3	4	5
w.	I believe it is better to solve problems as a team than alone.	1	2	3	4	5
x.	When someone presents an idea that is better than my own, I gladly accept it.	1	2	3	4	5
y.	In the process of decision-making, it is better to be wrong and united, than right and disunited.	1	2	3	4	5
z.	Even if my efforts aren't rewarded with immediate results, I will keep trying.	1	2	3	4	5

Calculate My Score

My "Leadership for Peace Self-Assessment" score: _____

How To Interpret Your Score

A score of 78 or higher indicates that you have a desire to become a "leader for peace," and have many of the qualities and skills necessary to fulfill the role.

A score of 36 to 77 indicates that you may want to become a "leader for peace," but feel that you still need to develop certain capacities before taking on the role.

A score of 35 or less indicates that you are facing certain life challenges that can only be resolved when you adopt a unity-based worldview.

For feedback on specific aspects of your perceived "leadership for peace" readiness, you can calculate your subtotals here:

Category	Items	My Score	My Percentage
Vision	a–d	_____ of 20	_____ %
Determination	e–h	_____ of 20	_____ %
Growth	i–l	_____ of 20	_____ %
Goal-Setting	m–o	_____ of 15	_____ %
Teamwork	p–v	_____ of 35	_____ %
Consultation	w–y	_____ of 15	_____ %
Perseverance	z	_____ of 5	_____ %

You can also use these assessment questions to help you to determine what skills and abilities you can continue to improve (strengths) and what skills and abilities you need to develop (opportunities for growth).

Take a moment to reflect on and answer the following questions:

What are my strengths as a peacemaker?

How might I further develop my capacities with respect to Leadership for Peace?

TAKING THE LEAD

Planning Questions for Peacemakers

What is your vision of change/development in your community? What is your "culture of peace" project idea?

What barriers or obstacles will you need to overcome to achieve that vision?

What values will guide the development of your strategy?

Who else would you like to involve in this project? How will you foster cooperation and collaboration?

What will the members of your team need in order to feel capable and empowered to achieve their tasks?

What kind of support does your project need? How will you get it?

How will you keep your supporters engaged as your project unfolds?

How will you measure success? What will be your milestone achievements? How will you celebrate them?

How will you recognize and reward the contributions of your team members and other helpers?

How will you inform others of your group's progress and accomplishments? Who should know about what you're doing?

Extended Exploration

Publications

Adorno, Theodor et al. (1950). *The Authoritarian Personality.* New York: Harper.

Allport, Gordon W. (1968). *The Person in Psychology: Selected Essays.* Boston: Beacon Press.

Burns, James M. (1982). *Leadership.* New York: Harper & Row.

Danesh, H.B. (1979). "The Violence-Free Family: A Gift for Our Children." *Bahá'í Studies,* vol. 6.

Danesh, H.B., and R.P. Danesh (2005). "Comprehensive Leadership Development Program: A Training Manual." Unpublished.

Fromm, Erich. (1994). *Escape from Freedom.* Originally published 1941. New York: Owl Books.

Gregg, Richard B. (1984). *The Power of Nonviolence.* 3rd ed. New York: Greenleaf Books.

Kouzes, James M., and Barry Z. Posner. (2003). *Leadership Challenge.* 3rd ed. San Francisco: Jossey-Bass.

Kotter, John P. (1996). *Leading Change.* Boston: Harvard Business School Press.

May, Rollo. (1972). *Power and Innocence: A Search for the Source of Violence.* New York: Delta Books.

Web Links

"Leadership Development Curriculum (K–12) with 60+ activity ideas for the classroom." <http://www.pen.k12.va.us/VDOE/Instruction/leadership/index.html>.

"History of Leadership Research." <http://www.sedl.org/change/leadership/history.html#traits>.

"Leadership Characteristics that Facilitate School Change." <http://www.sedl.org/change/leadership/welcome.html>.

"The Art and Science of Leadership." <http://www.nwlink.com/~donclark/leader/leader.html>.

"Young Leaders Online." < http://www.freewebs.com/youngleadersonline/index.htm>.

"Public Broadcasting Service TeacherSource – for K–12 lesson samples and resources for all subjects." < http://www.pbs.org/teachersource>.

"A Force More Powerful: A Century of Non-violent Conflict." <http://www.aforcemorepowerful.org/>.

General Online Resources

Art History Timeline: The Metropolitan Museum of Art. <http://www.metmuseum.org/toah/splash.htm>.

The Columbia Encyclopedia Online. <www.bartleby.com/65>.

The Columbia World of Quotations. <www.bartleby.com/quotations>.
The Merriam-Webster Online Dictionary. <www.merriam-webster.com>.
The Stanford Encyclopedia of Philosophy. <http://plato.stanford.edu>.
Wikipedia: The Free Encyclopedia. <http://www.wikipedia.org>.

Media

The Great Dictator. (1940). Film by Charlie Chaplin.

Unit 8

Conflict-Free Conflict Resolution

This unit examines a nonadversarial, peace-oriented consultative process of decision-making called Conflict-Free Conflict Resolution (CFCR). CFCR moves beyond traditional methods of conflict resolution by fixing unity as its goal. In the seven-stage process of CFCR, unity is first cultivated through the recognition of a common purpose among participants. The approach also relies on several key principles, including openness to the ideas of others and the practice of detachment from one's own ideas. CFCR is based on a developmental perspective on individual and collective behavior and worldview, including a developmental understanding of conflict. By reviewing the range of developmental responses to conflict prior to engaging in resolution techniques, CFCR helps individuals reflect upon and perhaps alter the worldview in which they approach the conflict they are facing.

Context[*]

Most conflict resolution approaches frequently result in the creation of new conflicts. This new conflict occurs because these approaches are built upon the foundations of conflict and its possible prevention, rather than upon creating and safeguarding unity. The purpose of this unit is to provide participants with a new understanding and the tools to facilitate peace-oriented decision-making processes that result in a unified perspective on the issues they face. Conflict-Free Conflict Resolution synthesizes the principles of a peace-oriented worldview into a mature process of communication and decision-making for developing solutions within, between, and among groups.

Learning Objectives

In this unit, participants should be assisted to:

1. Understand how different levels of maturity are characterized by different modes of communication and how a mature, consultative approach to communication (namely, CFCR) is most conducive to harmonious and just relations.
2. Reflect on their own actions and behavior, and identify the methods of communication they tend to use at school, at home, and with friends.
3. Introduce more unity-building strategies in their interpersonal relationships and work through familiarization with and gradual practice of the principles,

---

[*] Conflict-Free Conflict Resolution is a unity-based theory and method of conflict resolution developed by Roshan Danesh and H.B. Danesh. Several theoretical articles describing CFCR have been published in various academic journals. This unit is partially based on these publications, which are identified in the reference section.

processes, and skills of Conflict-Free Conflict Resolution (CFCR).

4. Use their understanding of decision-making approaches to assess current community and world affairs, and establish alternative means for collectively resolving these issues.

Points for Understanding

Teachers can guide their students to understand and remember these main points:

- Conflict is the result of disunity.
- Conflicts are influenced by context, particulars, and worldviews.
- Decision-making and problem-solving approaches reflect the respective worldviews of the participants.
- The four main types of communication related to decision-making are:
  a. Playful communication is unrestricted, fantastical, and useful during the brainstorming phase of decision-making;
  b. Task-oriented communication focuses on the practical limitations of resources, time, and available opportunities, and is useful during the preplanning phase of decision-making;
  c. Comparative communication focuses on evaluating the relative benefits of various ideas and is useful in determining which course of action will be most appropriate;
  d. Integrative communication is the consummation of the various other forms of communication in the consultative process. Integrative communication must be characterized by truthfulness, patience, humility, inclusiveness, perseverance, and

---

detachment. An integrative approach to consultation makes it possible to create a forum for constructive and unity-creating decision-making.

- A consultative approach to decision-making and problem-solving considers unity, truth, and justice as the main priorities of the decision-making process.

- A consultative approach requires the shift from conflict-oriented language to conflict-free (i.e., unity-based) language and thinking.

- Such an approach assists individuals and groups to recognize opportunities for growth as they increasingly identify points of unity.

- In consultation the positive development of the group is facilitated, and a unifying outcome of the decision-making process is fostered.

Key Vocabulary

Adversarial: a condition or thing that is contending, opposing, resisting; involving antagonistic elements or perspectives.

Arbitration: the settling of disputes between two or more parties by an agreed-upon judicial third party, whose decision the contending parties are obliged to accept.

Compromise: settlement of differences by arbitration or by consent reached by mutual concessions; something intermediate between two different things.

Conflict: contention, discord, or direct clash resulting from disunity.

Consultation: a process of investigation, discussion, decision-making and/or problem-solving that assists the participants to use their unique views, insights, and experiences to search for truth, to create unity, and to make decisions together that are characterized by justice in the context of compassion.

Intractable: difficult to manage or govern; difficult to alleviate, remedy, or cure.

Maturation: (in human life) a conscious, willful process of progressing through stages of development until one's capacities of knowledge, love, and will attain their fullest expression, refinement, and harmonization.

Mediation: the settling of disputes between two or more parties by a neutral third party, who controls the discussion process and recommends a resolution strategy that may or may not be adopted by the contending parties.

Negotiation: the settling of disputes through a process of bargaining. Advocacy approaches aim to get as much for one side as possible (a "win-lose" scenario), whereas "principled" approaches aim at "mutual gain" or "win-win" scenarios.

Nonadversarial: a mode of interacting, decision-making and/or problem-solving that neither presumes opposition between participants, nor advocates on behalf of opposing positions or camps of thought. A nonadversarial approach promotes inclusive participation and strives to achieve unity-building solutions.

Tractable: easily managed or controlled; governable; easily handled or worked.

Transformative Mediation: a form of mediation aimed at achieving a settlement in the context of the "empowerment" and "mutual recognition" (though not necessarily the agreement) of the parties involved. Like traditional mediation, the structure of transformative mediation involves two or more "disputants" or "parties," and a "mediator" who helps participants to establish "ground rules" and facilitates the mediation process.

Worldview: a mental framework through which individuals and groups view the nature of reality, the nature and purpose of human life, and the laws governing human relationships.

What is Conflict?

"Conflict" has been defined in a variety of ways, most commonly as the perception of incompatible goals or as competition for scarce resources. Some conventional definitions include:

"Social conflict is a struggle between opponents over values and claims to scarce status, power and resources."

—Coser, 1956

"A conflict exists whenever incompatible activities occur...one party is interfering, disrupting, obstructing, or in some other way making another party's actions less effective."

—Deutsch, 1973

"Conflict is the interaction of interdependent people who perceive incompatible goals and interference from each other in achieving those goals."

—Folger, Poole, and Stutman, 1994

Underlying all conflicts, whether large or small, is the condition of disunity. As we discussed in Unit 1, the condition of unity is fundamental to all life, health, growth, and creativity. When this condition of unity is weakened or absent, conflict, decay, and destruction result. We therefore define "conflict" as "the absence of unity."

Conflicts are generally shaped by three factors:

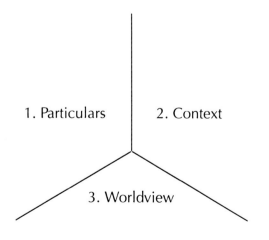

1. Particulars 2. Context

3. Worldview

Consider the following scenario:

Scenario: Road Rage

Mr. X is driving down the street in the busy downtown area of a large city. Mr. X sees free parking spot, pulls in front of it, and begins to parallel park. At the same time Mr. Y intentionally pulls into the spot from behind and blocks X from parking. The cars bump each other. X and Y get out of their cars and begin screaming and shouting at each other. There is even some pushing and shoving.

What is cause of this conflict?
Suppose you also knew the following information about the situation:

The city Mr. X and Mr. Y are driving in has recently been the site of serious tension between two racial groups. Mr. X is from one of the racial groups, and Mr. Y is from another.

Would your answer to the question: "What is the cause of this conflict" change?
Suppose you also had the following information:

Mr. Y believes that the racial tensions in the city are primarily caused by people of other races. Mr. Y feels he is in a state of competition with those from different races than his. He feels he is in competition with them and wants to succeed as much as possible.

Would your answer change again?
To fully understand the causes of this conflict scenario, we would have to understand the **context** of the conflict, the **particulars** of the conflict, and the **worldviews** of the participants in the conflict.

Particulars represent those facts on the surface of the conflict that we can observe: A dispute over a sum of money; an emotional struggle within a family; a fight in a schoolyard; a miscommunication; or a military confrontation.

Underneath this surface is the **context** in which a conflict arises. Conflicts appear within and in some respects are manifestations of the social, historical, and cultural contexts in which they occur. The same actions and choices that give rise to conflict in one context may not give rise to conflict in another. To understand conflict and resolve it, one has to understand and address the context in which a conflict occurs. For example, if one lives in a society where there is a lot of tension between different races, then interpersonal conflicts between individuals—particularly those of different races—may arise or be shaped by the larger racial tension within society.

Conflicts are also rooted in our **worldviews**. The way in which human beings view the world and their place in it contributes to their choice either to enter or not enter into a conflict and influences how they behave when in a state of conflict. For example, if we view the world as a place full of threats and danger, we are likely to respond to conflicts in ways that are forceful and give us the sense of control over the situation. [Revisit Unit 2 on Worldview and review the three main categories of worldview.]

This understanding of conflict suggests a number of important things, including the following:

- Conflicts—whether large or small, involving nations, groups, or just a few individuals—are influenced by particulars, context, and worldview.
- Individual choices to engage in conflict, the types of conflict they choose, and how they behave while in conflict will be shaped by their worldview, the current contexts they are operating within, as well as the particular circumstances of the incident of conflict.
- Our worldviews are often shaped by and shared with the groups of which we are a part. As such, the conflicts we get involved in may reflect patterns shaped by the worldview that most influences and represents the group(s) to which we belong.

Responses to Conflict

One of the main challenges of creating a culture of peace is to know how to peacefully resolve disagreements, disputes, and conflict when they arise. There are many approaches to problem-solving and conflict resolution that are familiar to us:

- **Force:** Some people respond to conflict by forcing their will on others;
- **Power-Struggle:** Some fight until winners and losers are identified;
- **Denial:** Some ignore the problem;
- **Passive Aggression:** Some pretend to agree on a solution and then attempt to undermine the decision that was made;
- **Avoidance:** Some people become afraid and run from the issue;
- **Negotiation:** Some try to negotiate a settlement that is beneficial to themselves and perhaps to the other party as well;
- **Compromise:** Some try to understand the different sides of the issue and arrive at a middle-way settlement solution.

As we learned in Unit 5, human life goes through specific developmental phases. Our self-knowledge, skills, relationships with others, and approaches to decision-making are all affected by the phases of maturation that we pass through and the worldviews we hold.

Likewise, as human individuals go through different stages of development, they perceive conflicts differently; behave distinctly when in a state of conflict; and attempt to resolve conflicts in varying manners. In other words, individuals involved in or attempting to resolve a conflict, behave differently based upon the developmental stage at which they currently are.

Having an understanding of human developmental stages

a. offers **insight into the behavior of people** in a dispute;

b. helps us to recognize that **conflict resolution processes themselves have developmental traits** and are classifiable according to developmental criteria;

c. enables therefore us to **evaluate whether the conflict resolution processes that participants are using are appropriate or inappropriate** to maintain or advance their developmental stage. To illustrate, few would argue that it is more developmentally mature to respond to a conflict with physical aggression than to try and resolve it through non-violent discussion;

d. provides those who intervene in the situation with a **framework for analyzing and perhaps pre-empting conflict-inducing behaviors** among the parties that might derail success.

Developmental Modes of Communication

Consider the primary methods of communication we employ as we develop. As young children, we are mainly playful with each other, with our friends and family members. Growing into older children, we learn better how to express our ideas and engage in communicating and collaboration with others to perform specific tasks. Entering adolescence, we gradually develop a concept of ourselves that we attempt to strengthen and clarify through what we say and do. At this stage, how we are perceived contributes greatly to our sense of identity. It therefore becomes important to us not only to express ourselves but also to position our ideas in relation to the ideas of others. Comparing and contrasting our ideas with those of others help us to clarify exactly what we believe and thus to express more faithfully who we are.

As we mature further, our sense of identity is stronger, and we are more comfortable with ourselves in the context of our relationships. On the one hand, we recognize that our ideas, thoughts, and actions shape the type of person we are, and we want to communicate these to others so that they know and understand our point of view. On the other hand, we also have confidence that when certain issues or the ideas that we express are perceived differently by others, we can gain new perspectives, can learn new things, and grow from the perspective and contribution of others to our thinking. As a result, we become less attached to our own specific ideas and become more interested in the process of communicating effectively and creatively within a group.

These four types of communication—playful, industrious, competitive, and integrative—correspond roughly to the respective developmental stages of infancy and early childhood; childhood; adolescence; and adulthood. We can use what we learned in Unit 5 on the Developmental Model of Human Life to look at how these modes of communication might map onto groups of individuals or societies. At any given time, these four types of communication can be found among the adult population of any given society. The most predominant mode of communication in that society can indicate its level of collective growth. For example, a society in its phase of collective adolescence would tend to communicate in a highly competitive and individualistic manner. It should be noted that it is healthy for different types of communication to be practiced among individuals at different times. In fact, all four types of communication have a legitimate place in the consultative process.

Playful communication is based on fantasies, hopes, and aspirations of those who are communicating. It allows the participants in an interaction to project themselves into the future, to use the power of their imagination, and to dream of conditions in which ideal communication could take place and problems could be solved as though by magic. This type of communication, also called "brainstorming," is very helpful, especially during the beginning stages of the consultative process of CFCR. It forms the basis for more complex and specific discussion later on. It is useful then to include in a consultative process a period in which participants are able to express their hopes, aspirations, and fantasies without fear of being judged as unrealistic, superficial, utopian, or silly.

Industrious or task-oriented communication is the second level of communication and corresponds with late childhood. This can be observed among individuals who are engaged in concrete and specific tasks such as building a home, creating a new company, or rebuilding a society following a disaster or revolution. Participants in these processes are willing to work hard, and their main form of communication is about the practical realization of a common enterprise. Participants know more about each other's skills and capacities than about the

subtleties of one another's thoughts and feelings. This type of communication is particularly useful in the course of consultation when members are engaged in fact-finding and research on the issues before them. In this case, the various expertise and knowledge of each person is valued highly.

The third type of communication is characterized by comparison and competitive discourse. **Comparative communication** takes place in the context of an interface of the wills of participants. All humans have unique thoughts and feelings that they wish to communicate to others. The ways in which these thoughts and feelings are communicated determine the nature of the communication. Thus, when several willful individuals begin to share their considered views with force and authority, a situation of comparison and competition is created within the consultative process. Ideas are compared and weighed against other ideas and evaluated in light of the facts of the situation and also the perspectives of all members of the group. Inevitably, some ideas will be rejected, others will require modification, and still others will be received with enthusiasm and applauded. These conditions create an environment where individuals are focused on who they are—as represented by their ideas—and on how they wish to be perceived.

Naturally, we all want to have the best ideas and to be perceived as being very intelligent, capable, and insightful by others. Therefore, it should not be surprising that a certain degree of comparison, competition, and clash of ideas takes place through the course of solving problems and dealing with issues. However, because CFCR helps participants to elevate their skills of communication and discourse to the higher level of adult operation, the same types of communication that in other modes of decision-making and conflict resolution would become obstacles to the process instead are transformed by CFCR into vehicles through which the process is both enriched and facilitated.

The fourth type of communication is most integrative and creative, corresponding with yet a higher degree of maturity akin to what we observe in our more mature stages of personal development. We refer to this type of communication as **integrative communication.** Maturity calls for both **self-assurance and selflessness**. In a mature stage, information and knowledge are used with insight and wisdom. The capacities of patience, perseverance, and contemplation are considerable. Humility, genuine respect, and regard for others are ever present, as is the willingness to consider the views of others with the same degree of attention and care as one's own views. Mature communication—by virtue of its truthfulness, inclusiveness, and universality—is both unifying and edifying in its effects. This is obviously the acme of human communications and cannot easily be mastered by everyone who engages in the CFCR approach. Nor may mature communication necessarily be displayed by the same person under every circumstance. Conflict-Free Conflict Resolution calls for maturity and therefore enhances the maturity of those engaged in its process. Thus, CFCR is a creative and integrative process, which can effectively resolve existing conflicts and in the process prevent the appearance of new conflicts by exercising the mature capacities of its participants.

Conflict-Free Conflict Resolution (CFCR)

Conflict-Free Conflict Resolution is a special method of **decision-making** based on principles of **consultation**. The main objective of this method of conflict resolution is to **search for truth** in order to **reach a just agreement** in a **condition of unity**. In CFCR, unity is the standard by which the process of decision-making and its ultimate outcome is measured.

Any decision made in a state of disunity is neither a satisfactory nor sufficient decision. Therefore,

many times it becomes necessary to postpone a decision until unity can be achieved. Alternatively, if a decision must be made by majority vote because an impasse would be even more harmful to the participants, then immediately all involved are called upon to test the efficacy of that decision by supporting and implementing it **as though it were a unanimous decision.**

This method of conflict resolution aims to transcend distinctions of majority and minority. The entire group is engaged in seeking the best possible solution to the issue before them, while assiduously safeguarding the integrity and unity of the group and protecting the individual rights of each and every one of its member. The objective is to reach unanimity if at all possible, and if not, the decision is either postponed, or in cases of emergency the choice of the majority is accepted wholeheartedly by all, including those who voted against it. To achieve unity, people involved in CFCR consultative processes must always refer to the criteria of truth and justice so that the human rights of every person affected by the decision are safeguarded. In our consultation, we can create conditions of unity and justice if, on the one hand, we are frank and open, and respectful, trusting, and trustworthy, on the other hand.

One very important aspect of consultation is that once an idea is expressed, it immediately becomes the property of the consulting group and no longer belongs to the individual who initially expressed the idea. Now this is really important. Many times people say something that they are later embarrassed about or realize was not as well developed as it might have been. However, we can become trapped into defending our old ideas if we are stuck at the adolescent level of competitiveness and feel we must stand up for our own views even after we ourselves have rejected them. Protection of our identity becomes confused with defending old ideas instead of moving freely into new, more appropriate ideas. In the CFCR method of consultation, one shares an idea with frankness and to the best of one's ability; then one respectfully listens to other people, and if someone else comes up with a better idea, one is immediately free to accept it since the objective of consultation is finding the best solution.

Another subtle process in CFCR occurs when the idea one presents appears to be the best, but the majority, for whatever reason, is not ready to accept it. At that point in the process, it is better to go with the majority decision for the sake of the group's unity. For, together, the group will test the efficacy of the majority's idea in application, to see what the results are. If the results are favorable, then the decision has been well and good; if the results are not as effective as desired or needed, then the group becomes willing to look for alternatives and may now be receptive to reconsidering the idea that was presented earlier. This is the reason that in this form of unity-oriented consultation, it is better to be wrong and united, than right and disunited.

Obviously, this kind of consultation is difficult. Above all, our motives have to be pure. We cannot contribute to the process creatively if we carry beneath the surface some ulterior motives or hidden agendas. It also helps very much if we can adopt the attitude of humility that is needed to listen to others in an open and receptive way. In this way, we achieve a maturity that frees us to learn from others, to express ourselves effectively, and to accept the best ideas whether they come from ourselves or from someone else.

This is the starting point from which we work to build a stronger sense of unity. **The starting point for resolving conflicts or averting potential conflicts is to find currently existing points of unity.** In order to create a meaningful and lasting sense of unity among a group, there needs to be an appreciation for any unity, however slight, that currently exists. This process may begin as simply as having individuals sit together and ask, "Is there anything we agree about?" This is a simple, but potentially difficult exercise. Often when people are in conflict or on the verge of being so, they are feeling fear, anxiety, or anger as they feel their perspective is being threatened. We need to rise above this, to support our group as it begins the process of creating a "culture of unity."

This approach can be taken in managing a classroom over the course of a school year. The year could start with a discussion about the fact that if we are united as a class group, we will learn together much better. Therefore, we will begin by trying to lower the levels of fear, to raise the levels of safety, and to initiate the process of becoming friendly, by introducing ourselves to one another and learning about each other. And when there is a problem or difficulty, we will agree to resolve it together. Rather than trying to solve things in isolation, the strategy would be to discuss it with the entire group and, as a group, trying to find points of unity. Then the collective level of tension lessens. The entire classroom becomes a place for the resolution of conflict—the creation of more unity. Emphasis should be on creating unity, rather than on getting rid of something.

Note that more emphasis is placed on building unity than on reaching compromise. It is true that compromise is better than conflict. Creating unity, though, is very much better than compromise. We should not content ourselves with going only half way. We should strive to go the entire way—to truly find the best solution for all parties in most respects. Compromise can be seen as the establishment of a balance of power; hence, compromise doesn't get beyond the basic power base and specific interests held by the parties involved. If the power base were to change, the compromise agreement is undermined. Compromise is always short-lived.[1]

---

1. One of the most systematized forms of consultation is practiced by the Bahá'í community. Many of the concepts of consultation used in CFCR are drawn from the Bahá'í method of consultation. For more information, see *Consultation: A Compilation* (multiple authors), rev. ed., London: Bahá'í Publishing Trust, 1990.

Main Principles and Challenges of CFCR

The main principles of CFCR can be summarized as follows:

1. The main prerequisite for CFCR is unity in the context of diversity.
2. The main objective of CFCR is to make just and compassionate decisions.
3. The main principles of CFCR are truth-seeking and truthfulness.
4. The main tools of CFCR are frankness and openness in the context of mutual respect and mutual trust.
5. The main personal challenges in CFCR are objectivity (detachment) and freedom from prejudice (purity of motive).
6. In CFCR it is better to be wrong and united than right and disunited.

Unity

As stated earlier, the unity paradigm is the framework in which CFCR operates. Normally, participants in a consultative process do not come together having already developed a unified view of the issues before them. They may have many diverse perspectives, some of which are totally at odds with one another. The aim of CFCR is to achieve and maintain unity of thought, sentiments, and approach among the participants. To achieve this objective, participants need to share a unity of purpose with each other. In effect, the main prerequisite of CFCR is the harmonious agreement among the members of the consultative process that they wish to make the best decisions for all involved, while maintaining and ideally increasing their unity.

Truth

Truth, in the context of CFCR, refers to finding the best possible understanding of the issue at hand. As such, we are dealing with **relative truth** and not **absolute truth**. Consequently, the consultative group will not always find the total, fully accurate truth about the issue before them so as to make the right decision and occasionally needs to reconsider its decisions in the light of new facts and information. Two important yardsticks that the participants in the consultative process can use to measure the degree of "truth" of their decisions are unity and justice. To the degree that a decision increases the **unity** of all involved and reaches **just** outcomes, to the same degree that decision is in accord with the principles of **truth**. Unity and justice are interdependent. Therefore, it follows that those engaged in the consultative process should be always searching for just solutions, which would safeguard the rights of both the individual and the group, and would promote ever higher levels of unity. This is only possible when a decision not only **is** just but also **perceived to be just.**

Frankness and Openness

Nothing destroys the effectiveness of the consultative process more than lack of candor and openness do. Hidden agendas are totally contrary to the spirit of CFCR, as are backroom politicking and intrigue. CFCR calls for integrity of character and courage of conviction. It also calls for full trust in and respect for our fellow human beings. When these qualities are all present, then there will be no fear of frankness in CFCR. When we, as members of a decision-making/conflict-resolution group, participate free from prejudice and with purity of motive, then we are able to open our hearts and minds to express what needs to be said without fear of being rejected and without intentionally hurting others. In the same spirit, we will be able to listen to others and receive their input with due care and without feeling hurt or angry if our views are rejected or misunderstood.

However, under all circumstances we need to follow the principles of compassion, care, humility, and moderation in expressing our views. Justice requires that we practice what we expect of others. Frankness is a very challenging and difficult art. It could easily deteriorate into verbal abuse and injury. It is easily prone to exaggeration and, not infrequently, is perceived to be an act of hostility and arrogance. Due to these facts, it is essential that frankness be moderated by the characteristics of mature communication described earlier. Also, the consultative body must put in place the necessary guidelines, reminders, and procedures that will continuously encourage the frank and open expression of views, while protecting against deleterious statements in the guise of frankness. The duty for ensuring a united, frank, and loving CFCR is, at once, the responsibility of each individual separately and of the consulting group as a whole.

Objectivity

All ideas, once expressed in the course of CFCR, become the property of the consulting group and not of the individual who initially expressed the idea. This concept has profoundly freeing properties. It helps us to maintain our objectivity and not to be unreasonably attached to our ideas. Very often in decision-making and conflict-resolution groups, we observe individuals who either pitifully defend a half-formed or ill-conceived idea they have expressed, or else are viciously attacked by others for the shortcomings of their views. Under these circumstances a battleground of perspectives is created, and opportunities for making the best decisions are lost. CFCR brings a totally unexpected dimension to the decision-making process. In CFCR, the decision-making group—i.e., all individuals involved in the issue/conflict before them—assumes possession of all ideas expressed by its members thus freeing all members to examine and re-examine, agree and disagree, and revise and confirm their views freely without any need for self-defense or attack. In the consultative

process, it is not at all unusual for members to disagree with their own original views and choose a new approach emerging from the group discourse. This freedom is a very precious aspect of the consultative process, however to achieve it, the members must make a conscious effort to develop the qualities of objectivity, detachment, humility, and trust, which are among the main principles of CFCR.

Unity

Here, we are brought full circle back to the all-important issue of unity.

Earlier it was stated that **truth is one** and **unity is oneness.** While "truth" is one by definition, our access to truth is always relative, depending on our unique circumstances, knowledge, and understanding. However, in the context of a unified search for truth, our relative and divergent access to "truth" becomes "one" as we gradually begin to have a greater appreciation and insight into all aspects of the issue before us. To the degree that personal and subjective perspectives are shared and are made a component of "common understanding," to that same degree a unified formulation of the group's "collective truth" emerges and facilitates the decision-making process.

Without unity, mistrust and suspicion are introduced into human relationships, and consequently all possibilities for finding the truth about anything are lost. Due to this fact, unity—as an expression of mutual acceptance, respect, and trust—assumes the primary position in the consultative process. Without unity, we lose our access to truth: thus in CFCR, it is better to be wrong and united than right and disunited. As long as we maintain and nurture our unity, our opportunities for finding the truth and making the best decisions are open to us. However, as soon as we become disunited, we lose all those opportunities to access the truth and to make creative, just decisions.

The Seven Steps of CFCR in Action

The practice of CFCR is best achieved by following seven specific, interrelated steps.

Step 1 – Unity of Purpose

Unity of purpose must exist among those engaged in Conflict-Free Conflict Resolution. This unity is required both in respect to the principles and to the purpose of CFCR. As CFCR progresses, other areas of agreement will develop, and eventually a decision, ideally unanimous or otherwise by vote of majority, will be made. Often, the first point of unity in highly charged conflicts is the very fact of the willingness of those involved to try CFCR to deal with issues before them.

Step 2 – Personal Preparation

Because of the challenging nature of CFCR, all individuals involved in the consultative process will greatly benefit by constantly reminding themselves, both before and during CFCR, that decision-making and problem-solving are not merely technical and peripheral activities. In fact, these activities are reflections of some of the most important aspects of ourselves as human beings, including our worldviews, personal and social priorities, ethical principles and spiritual orientation. The participants need to recall that in CFCR they succeed only when they approach their task with objectivity, freedom from prejudice, active search for truth, cooperation, humility, and constant attention to the all-important principles of unity, truth, and justice. In this process of personal preparation, various individuals employ different strategies ranging from physical activity and relaxation pursuits to self-reflection, prayer, and meditation, or often a combination of these and other approaches.

In addition to these attitudinal preparations, all individuals involved in CFCR also have the duty to familiarize themselves with the facts of the issues before them and to inform themselves of the principles involved. The issue of principles refers to those scientific and ethical issues that need to be considered if the decision made by the group is to be reasonable, factual, ethical, and just. These are among the main prerequisites for reaching a unifying decision.

Step 3 – Group Preparation

A period of time is set aside at the beginning and at different intervals in the course of CFCR, as the need arises, for group preparation. The purpose of this preparation is to create an internal and interpersonal condition conducive to mutual respect, trust, cooperation, encouragement, and humble fellowship. The participants will remind themselves that they are engaged in CFCR in order to find, together, the best answers to the questions and problems before them. They will recall that their objective is to make just decisions while maintaining and increasing the level of their unity. They also need to remember that the consultative process is not conducive to power-struggle, domination, or control. The objective is not merely a compromise or even a win/win result, but, rather, to make a just decision based on the most complete information available, while making utmost effort to maintain the unity of those involved. The manner in which the preparation period is arranged varies according to the characteristics and orientation of the group and its members as well as the magnitude of the challenge before them. Sometimes the group needs only a brief and simple period of preparation, and at other times it takes a much longer and complex process, including professional expert counsel and detailed background research. Furthermore, before the process of consultation and discourse begins, it is important to create an atmosphere conducive to a calm, thoughtful, and pleasant deliberative process. Both the beauty and comfort of the venue should reflect the peace-based orientation of CFCR.

In addition to these preparations, the consultative group also needs to identify the main scientific and ethical principles applicable to issues before them. The group needs to ensure that all members agree on both the significance and applicability of these principles to the case at hand. Through this careful approach, the CFCR process is facilitated, and confusion and misunderstanding are avoided. Furthermore, identification of principles makes it much easier for those involved to remain objective and free from their preconceived notions, which are often poorly or even erroneously formulated. The scientific principles refer to expert views—medical, legal, technical, etc.—which are necessary to clarify the parameters of the issues before the decision-making body. Ethical principles are more complex and difficult to determine. However, as a rule, the ethical principles (in their very nature, applicability, and effect) are universal, truth-based, unifying, and just. They are essential for protection of human rights and identification of individual and group responsibilities, both of which matters are equally relevant to proper resolution of human conflicts, disputes, and disagreements. The very process of attention to these matters and their presence in the consultative process help both the group and its members not only to make better decisions but also to further develop both as individuals and groups.

Step 4 – Discourse

All individuals engaged in the CFCR consultative process are strongly encouraged to freely share their ideas, thoughts, sentiments, hopes, and despairs with frankness, moderation, and care. They are urged to consider with total respect, attentiveness, and sensitivity the input of each person who contributes to the consultative process. If someone chooses to be silent, the group respects this decision; however, through encouraging words and attitude, all involved would make efforts to facilitate expression of views by everyone. In this respect, more vocal and

forceful individuals have a special responsibility to be particularly sensitive to the hesitation that many people may have under these circumstances, particularly when the participants come from many different backgrounds and socioeconomic/educational strata of society. Also, men, in general, and assertive men, in particular, must assume major responsibility for facilitating the expression of views by women.

By not allowing themselves to have ulterior motives, neither will the participants in the consultation introduce to the consultative process their own private and hidden agendas, nor will the consultative body allow any of its members to do so. The sole objective must be to deal with the issue(s) with objectivity, frankness, knowledge, and detachment. In the CFCR process, personal preferences and prejudices should not be allowed to take precedence over the fundamental objectives of the consultative process: to search for truth in a condition of unity in order to make just decisions.

Although to assist the process, the consultative group is encouraged to elect or appoint, (depending on the nature and permanence of the group) a chairperson(s) and a recording secretary(s), nevertheless, it should be remembered that these individuals have no special privileges or station in the group. The duty of the chairperson is to serve the group and facilitate the process of CFCR. Under no circumstances should this person be seen as the leader, nor be allowed to assume such a position. Likewise, the responsibility of the recording secretary is to faithfully and accurately record the decisions of the consultative group and convey them, in the same manner, to those who must receive the results of the deliberations.

Note: Decision-making groups with an ongoing mandate often adopt the procedure of rotating both the chair and the recording secretary at each meeting. This practice has several benefits. It removes entirely the attribution of special rank to any member of the consulting group. It raises the sensitivity of the group members toward these functions and makes the group more cooperative with both the secretary and the chair. It also gives all members of the group the opportunity to improve their own level of skills for handling these difficult roles.

Objectives of the Consultative Group

The objectives of the consultative group are:

- To find solutions that are based on truth;
- To find solutions that are just and compassionate;
- To find solutions that maintain, and preferably increase, the unity of the group.

Consultation should begin and end with unity. Any consultation that ends with disunity has not been successful.

Step 5 – Decision-Making

In CFCR, it is preferable to try to reach a unanimous decision. This is essential when CFCR is used for resolution of conflicts. However, when CFCR is used as a conflict-free and peaceful approach to decision-making, then, although unanimity is preferable, a majority vote is acted upon with the full support of the group. In this manner, the CFCR consulting group make the majority decision a unanimous one. It is important to note that a decision is not a composite of opinions, thoughts, and feelings expressed by different members. Rather, a true decision is a new creation emerging from the unencumbered interchange of thoughts, feelings, and wills in a unified atmosphere of CFCR. As such, the final decision is greater than the sum of all the views expressed. Such a creative outcome requires that individuals involved in the consultative process be prepared to sacrifice their individual preferences in their unified search for the best solution to the issue before them.

It is reasonable that, from time to time, each of the various members of the consulting group will feel some degree of unease with the direction of the consensus. Nonetheless, in order to prevent descending into minority/majority tensions, the unifying framework of CFCR requires that all participants make full efforts to move forward by actively supporting and implementing the decision they have reached, even if some of the individual members do not find it completely satisfying. In a condition of unity, all decisions can be implemented, evaluated, and revised as necessary. In a condition of disunity, the group is powerless to act constructively.

Note: If, however, a pattern appears in which some members of the decision-making group are *always* satisfied with the decisions, and others are *always* dissatisfied, then the group must put itself on notice that its implementation of unity-oriented consultation is significantly flawed, and a thoughtful review by them of the main principles of CFCR is needed.

Step 6 – Implementation

The consultative process is not complete without the implementation of the decisions reached in a united and harmonious manner.

No decision, however lofty and honorable, is of value unless it is put into action and bears its fruits of justice and unity. To achieve these ends, all involved in CFCR must participate also, either directly or indirectly, in its implementation and offer unconditional support to those who have been given the task of carrying out the decision. If, in the course of implementing a decision, it becomes evident that a new course of action is needed, the consultative group must be willing and available to reconsider the matter. The objective here is not to have winners and losers, rather the main purpose is to reach a just and unifying decision that best serves the interests and welfare of all involved.

Step 7 – Evaluation

CFCR is scientific in its method. By following certain established protocols and guidelines, and by preserving as its main objective the search for truth, CFCR becomes an excellent vehicle for finding the best answer to the issue at hand. It requires of its participants a considerable degree of objectivity, detachment, and ethical conduct; and demands that the conclusions reached be free from personal and political or ideological preferences, but instead be based on facts and scientific and ethical principles. Finally, the results of the implementation of the decisions reached through CFCR must be subject to thorough evaluation. This evaluation is necessary, so that we can learn from experience and gradually add to our knowledge of the dynamics of decision-making and conflict-resolution.

Universal Ethical Principles of CFCR

CFCR is a mode of group decision-making in which neither power nor authority is abused. In a CFCR consultative group no one member has more power than another—all members are equal. Authority is anchored to the guiding principles of the consultative process and, when appropriate, to specific roles assigned to individuals within the consulting group.

Several key ethical principles should be understood and observed by all of the members of CFCR consulting group. These all-important principles are:

- **Unity:** A CFCR consultative group must start from a focus on unity. For instance, if you want to consult on how to create peace awareness in the schools, creating peace will be the specific focal point of unity for that specific consultation.
- **Humility:** Humility is accepting the notion that the decisions which emerge from the group consultation are superior to the views of the individual group members. Thus humility contributes to the unity and unity leads to even greater ideas.
- **Frankness:** This is the practice of honesty in the expression of one's ideas. People have to be free to express themselves openly and frankly. In a process of CFCR consultation, the group must make it possible for all individuals to share their ideas and opinions without censure or threat of reprisal.
- **Equality:** In CFCR, every person's ideas are equally valuable to the consultative process. Therefore, even as we wish to share our ideas openly, we must be prepared to give equal value and consideration to the ideas of others.
- **Moderation:** Since freedom of expression can create much passion and make people very excited or eager to share, the principle of moderation must be applied. Moderation is a sign of maturity, while extremism is the sign of both childhood and adolescence.
- **Patience:** There has to be a willingness on the part of the individual to go through the consultative process with patience. Without this commitment, the group consultation will suffer setbacks.

Summary

In this unit, we have learned that:

Conflict is the Result of Disunity

- Whether large or small, the underlying cause of conflict is disunity of some kind. Conflicts are also influenced by context, particulars, and worldviews.

Our Response to Conflict is Developmental

- Modes of conflict resolution and decision-making may be classified according to developmental characteristics of infancy and early childhood [Survival (S)-mode], late childhood [Authoritarian (A)-mode], adolescence [Power-struggle (P)-mode], and adulthood [Consultative (C)-mode].

Peaceful Conflict Resolution Focuses on Unity

- The consultative approach to conflict resolution is most conducive to a culture of peace because it takes a nonadversarial approach to the search for truth and aims for decisions that are both unifying and just.

"Conflict-Free Conflict Resolution" (CFCR) Involves 7 Steps

1. Unity of Purpose
2. Personal Preparation
3. Group Preparation
4. Consultative Process
5. Decision-Making
6. Implementation
7. Evaluation

Key Questions for the Classroom

The following questions can be used to review and explore further the concepts of Unit 8 with your students:

1. How do I communicate: with my friends? At home? With my teachers? At work?

2. How can I improve the way I communicate with those around me?

3. Why is "unity of purpose" so important to the process of CFCR? What other principles are keys to the success of CFCR consultative decision-making?

4. How do we know if a decision resulting from consultation is good?

5. How is freedom increased by the quality of objectivity during the CFCR consultative process?

6. How does objectivity help the consultative group to find the truth?

7. Why is it important for all participants to be united on the final decision even if they are not sure it is the best decision?

8. What can each participant do to ensure that the CFCR participants have the fullest access to the truth during their deliberations?

9. What can each participant do to increase the sense of unity among the CFCR group members both during and following the process of their deliberations?

Personal Reflection

Reflection is a very powerful learning tool. It helps us to make sense of the things we are studying and the experiences we are going through. The more we reflect on ourselves, our relationships, and the world around us, the better prepared we are to discern, prioritize, and act upon issues of importance.

Becoming a peacemaker is a very important and challenging task. By reflecting on the principles of peace, we are better equipped to make decisions about our own development that will help us to confidently undertake the goal of peace building.

As we go through each of the EFP Curriculum units, try to set aside some time for the process of reflection.

The following questions are provided to help you begin this process.

Questions for Personal Reflection

1. Reflections on Self

    1.   How do I make decisions?
    2.   Do I consider the views of others?
    3.   What are my prejudices?

Focus Questions

Personal preparation is so important to peaceful conflict resolution. It gives one a time to reflect, establish inner harmony, and enter into the process of consultation with patience and detachment.

    a.   How can I prepare myself before entering a CFCR process?
    b.   Why is this step vital to the process?

2. Reflections on Family/Group

    1.   During group decision-making, what role do I play?
    2.   What is my primary communication mode? Playful? Task-oriented? Competitive? Integrative?
    3.   Which aspects of CFCR might be most challenging for me at home and at school? Why?

Focus Questions

When a problem or conflict arises in your family, in what conflict-resolution mode is it dealt with?

a. Is this the same way you approach problems at school or with friends?

b. What prevents you from using a unity-based approach to conflict resolution in your relationships?

c. How might this be overcome?

3. Reflections on Society

1. What kinds of conflict are affecting my society the most?
2. How is my society dealing with these conflicts?
3. Could I start a community-level consultation to address these issues?

Focus Task

Now that you have knowledge of Conflict-Free Conflict Resolution, you can use it to draw your community together in a collective effort to resolve the problems it faces.

As preparation for sharing CFCR with others, try to recount its main principles and steps in your own words.

4. Reflections on the World at Large

1. In which conflict-resolution mode do you feel the world most functions? Think of examples.
2. What influences global conflicts more: context, particulars, or worldviews?

Focus Questions

Think of a major conflict happening in today's world:

a. What is the social, historical, and/or cultural *context* of this conflict?

b. What are the *particulars* surrounding the conflict?

c. What *worldview(s)* do the people in the conflict hold?

d. What *point of unity* exists between them upon which a process of CFCR could be initiated?

Classroom Tools

As a teacher in the Education for Peace Program, it is now your task to introduce the discussion and practice of Conflict-Free Conflict Resolution in your class so that your students can learn how to resolve conflicts peacefully and so that your school can develop a culture of peace.

Resolving conflicts peacefully is a challenging process—one that demands a considerable degree of patience, detachment, humility, openness, and confidence that a just and unifying solution to each difficulty can ultimately be found. Students have the capacity to develop these attitudes and embody them in their behaviors if given opportunities to discuss and practice them. Your role as their teacher and mentor in this process is tremendously important.

To help you get started, a number of tools are included in this section that you may find useful. These tools are only guides, and you are encouraged to develop your own ideas about how to best explore these topics with your students.

In addition to the examples here, please also refer to the Educational Methodology Unit where you will find practical guidelines on how to make your classroom a creative and effective learning environment, as well as other great ideas from fellow teachers who are integrating Education for Peace into their various subject areas.

As you work with the Education for Peace concepts, you will surely develop new ideas for lessons, activities, and assessment approaches. We encourage you to pass along your thoughts, ideas, or resource links to Education for Peace so they can be added to our EFP Resource Bank for other teachers to use. Please send us an email at <info@efpinternational.org>, or mail your ideas to our address:

International Education for Peace Institute (Canada)
101, 1001 W. Broadway, Suite 900
Vancouver, BC V6H 4E4
Canada

We look forward to hearing from you!

Activity Ideas for Primary Schools

Drama

Humility, frankness, equality, moderation, truth, and patience are all required principles for consulting within the framework of CFCR. Divide the class into six small groups and ask each group to create a play in which one of the six principles is portrayed. Ask the students to perform their play and ask the others in the class to guess which principle was presented.

Science

Truth is multidimensional, and at a given time each person understands only some dimensions of truth so that when we do not try to find out the other aspects of truth it can lead to the wrong conclusion and conflict. In a study of the five senses, break the class into five small groups and assign them to use only one of their senses. Ask the students to deduce what "secret objects" are at different stations in the room only using the one sense that they have been assigned. Have students record their deductions. Bring the class together and discuss each group's findings. Are there any discrepancies? Ask the students to pose reasons as to why there might be discrepancies. Read the story *Seven Blind Mice* by Ed Young or *The Blind Men and the Elephant* <http://members.aol.com/Wildlifer/blindmen.htm>. Revisit the earlier conversation.

Older students can discuss what other notions of truth exist and how the search for truth involves investigating all truth.

Unit 8, Lesson 1: CONFLICT-FREE CONFLICT RESOLUTION

Focus: The Four Modes of Communication

Context

Learning to recognize the four modes of communication in ourselves and others is necessary for understanding the process of CFCR and being able to engage in conflict-free decision-making and conflict resolution.

Points for Understanding

There are four main types of communication: playful, task-oriented, comparative, and creative.

- **Playful** communication is unrestricted, fantastical, and useful during the brainstorming phase of decision-making.
- **Task-oriented** communication focuses on the practical limitations of resources, time, and opportunities, and is useful during the preplanning phase of decision-making.
- **Comparative/ or "competitive"** communication focuses on evaluating the relative benefits of certain ideas in comparison with others and is useful determining which course of action will be most appropriate.
- **Integrative** communication takes place in the context of truthfulness, patience, humility, inclusiveness, perseverance, and objectivity. This type of communication is ideal for the integration of the other forms of communication into the constructive and unity-creating process of CFCR.

Key Questions

1. What are the characteristics of the four modes of communication: playful, task-oriented, competitive, and creative?
2. What would happen if people functioned only in the playful mode? Task-oriented mode? Competitive mode?
3. How does the integrative mode of communication tie all the others modes together?
4. What are the main challenges of the integrative mode of communication?
5. What can we do if the process of consultation gets stuck?

Learning Process

1. Select four volunteers from among the students, and give them each one role from the "Modes of Communication Role-Play" document (see pages 260–61).

2. While they are preparing themselves individually for the role play, briefly introduce the other students to the idea that different modes of communication exist and that being aware of them can both decrease communication conflicts and increase creative output in life.

3. Have the volunteers act out the role play in front of the class. Each role is designed to emphasize one of the four types of communication in a problem-solving exercise. Because the characters are unaware of each other's modes, they may find it difficult to arrive at a solution. Have the class observe the role play and try to identify what communication modes the role players are using.

4. Following the role play, ask the class to share their observations and try to create a classification of communication modes based on what they observed.

5. Next review the four modes of communication: playful, task-oriented, competitive, generative. Under the four headings, write the characteristics of each in four columns on the board.

6. Discuss with students the limitations of using only one of the first three modes, and then describe how, in an organized CFCR decision-making process, each form of communication has its valuable role.

7. If time allows, re-do the role play but have the players go through the four communication modes together in sequence, with the aim of arriving at a unified and constructive solution.

Activities and Assignments

1. **Journal:** What patterns of communication can you observe in your family, among your friends, in your classroom, or in other groups you are associated with? How might discussion in playful or competitive modes be moved to an integrative mode of communication?

2. **Reflection and Planning Assignment:** Give students a hypothetical problem to resolve (see "Sample Problems for Resolution" for ideas). As homework, provide students with the "Communication Worksheet," which provides a writing space for each of the four modes of thinking and communication. Have students work through the problem in each of the four modes sequentially. In a follow-up class, ask them to discuss the challenges and benefits they experienced while exercising their thoughts in these four modes.

Additional Resources

Role-Play: Modes of Communication
Sample Problems for Resolution
Communication Worksheet

Unit 8, Lesson 2: CONFLICT-FREE CONFLICT RESOLUTION

Focus: Understanding the Factors in a Conflict

Context

Conflicts are generally influenced by three factors: the context of the conflict, the particulars of the conflict situation, and the worldviews of the participants in the conflict. Our ability to recognize and evaluate these factors better equips us both to address and to prevent conflicts in an appropriate manner.

Points for Understanding

Conflicts, large or small, are influenced by context, particulars, and worldview.
- "**Particulars**" represent those immediate factors that we can observe on the surface of the conflict situation.
- "**Context**" refers to the social, historical, and cultural environments in which conflicts appear. Actions that give rise to conflict in one context may not do so in another context.
- "**Worldviews**" contribute to a person's choice to either enter or not enter into a conflict and influence how they behave when in a state of conflict.

Key Questions

1. Which factors that influence a conflict are obvious and which less obvious?
2. How can we address not only the particulars of a conflicted situation but also the context surrounding it and the worldviews underlying it, in order to intervene effectively and resolve it?

Learning Process

1. Review with students the Road Rage scenario that appears at the beginning of this Unit and initiate a discussion regarding particulars, context, and worldview which contributed to that conflict scenario.

2. Form the class into three groups. Using the "Role Play: Particulars, Context, Worldview" document (see pages 266–68), provide each group with one of the scenario descriptions. Each scenario emphasizes a different factor of the same conflict.

3. Each group should discuss the conflict scenario (10 minutes) and then prepare a

dramatization of the conflict (20 minutes). The dramatization should be between 1–2 minutes long. It is very important that the dramatization try to convey the "cause of the conflict" as it is described in the scenario. The dramatization should also convey all of the information provided in the scenario.

4. Have each group take a turn performing their dramatization in front of the class.

5. Ask students to describe what they noticed and how they felt as each of the role plays revealed different factors.

Activities and Assignments

1. Written assignment: Give students a conflict scenario to research and ask them to identify in a 1–2 page assignment what the particulars, context, and worldview(s) surrounding and contributing to the conflict are.

Additional Resources

Role Play: Context, Particulars, Worldview

Unit 8, Lesson 3: CONFLICT-FREE CONFLICT RESOLUTION

Focus: Principles of Conflict-Free Conflict Resolution

Context

Being able to facilitate a CFCR process is key to promoting communication among individuals and groups of individuals towards a unified resolution.

Points for Understanding

- Participants should be able to employ basic principles of CFCR in their own discussions, demonstrating an understanding of the importance of a unified end result.

Key Questions

1. Why is unity of purpose important? What will we have if we do not have unity of purpose?
2. What is the purpose of consultation?
3. How do we know if a decision resulting from consultation is good?
4. Why are frankness and openness important in the process of consultation?
5. What can each participant do to assist in creating an atmosphere of frankness and openness?

Learning Process

1. Initiate brainstorming on the conditions that are needed for a unity and justice-oriented decision-making process.
2. Building on the brainstorm session, review with students the main principles and features of CFCR. See Activity Reading 5 (pages 271–72).
3. Have students read aloud and discuss the CFCR handout.
4. Discuss the 7 steps of CFCR and why each one of the steps is needed to have a fruitful consultation.
5. Follow-up with a CFCR practice session, using a conflict scenario selected by the students.

Activities and Assignments

1. Following a review of the principles of CFCR, divide the class into small groups of 4–5 students and assign them a problem or issue requiring resolution (see "Sample Problems for Resolution" on pages 262–63). Groups will be given 45 minutes to consult on the matter following the 7 steps of consultation. Each group is required to arrive at a minimum of one point of unity on the issue, if not a complete plan of resolution, within the 45-minute duration. Following their consultations, each group will report through a representative on what they accomplished and what the dynamics of their process were.

2. **Assignment** (1 page): Describe the importance of the concepts of openness and detachment/objectivity in the CFCR process. Consider the following questions in crafting your essay: What is meant by being open to another's ideas? What is meant by being able to present your ideas while not being attached to them? How can individuals be detached from their ideas without compromising their values?

3. **Journal:** What do you feel is the greatest challenge of the seven stages of CFCR?

Unit 8 – Activity Reading 1

Role Play: Modes of Communication

Select four volunteers from the class and give each of them one of the following role descriptions. Each role emphasizes one of the four communication modes: playful, task-oriented, competitive, and integrative. Have the students act out the role play for 3–5 minutes in front of the class. Allow enough time for the role players to convey their assigned perspective clearly. Follow-up the role play with a class discussion around such questions as:

- What modes of communication could you observe?
- What were the challenges in this discussion?
- What moments worked best in terms of achieving an inclusive, unifying, and creative solution?

Scenario – Planning a Peace Event

The following four characters are a part of a group of students who have volunteered to plan a Peace Event in their school that will be open to the public. The aim of the event is for students to present artistic peace performances to the community at large, with the hope of increasing respect for diversity, warming people to the notion of interethnic harmony, and bringing some healing to the wounds of past intergroup conflicts. To prepare for the event, these four students must consult together and create a strategy that reflects a unified and practical plan.

Role 1 – Playful Communication Mode

Your character sees this event as an incredible opportunity to do something hugely dramatic that will singularly impact society in a way that will change the course of history! In your view, the bigger the event, the better! If the goal is to influence public opinion, large numbers of people have to be reached, and they have to be impressed with what they see. You think there should be a major lightshow on the stage, and a live satellite connection to schools in other countries. There should be event posters and banners on every street corner across the region. You also want all the major news agencies, like CNN and BBC, along with all the national and local media stations to cover the event. No matter what others in the planning group say about budget and time constraints, you think it can be bigger, brighter, and more dramatic. You're not concerned with the details, and you don't like to get stuck on limitations. You come up with an infinite number of new ideas at every turn in the discussion.

Role 2 – Task-Oriented Communication Mode

Your character wants to get down to the details. You're not interested in brainstorming for hours on ideas that are impossible given the budget and timeline available for planning the event. There is only $500 available for any and all Peace Event expenses, and you want to be very practical about how much every invitation and paper cup will cost. You are less concerned about the impact of the event than you are on getting it done within budget and time constraints, and with the least pressure possible. You feel that a lot of people have great ideas, but they are not realistic about the amount of work it will require. Before the conversation gets carried away on another fantasy, you want very clear numbers and plans laid out, with roles and responsibilities of each person clearly defined.

Role 3 – Competitive Communication Mode

Your character has participated in Peace Events before, and so you know something about how they work. Okay, some of the others have also participated in Peace Events, but after being chairperson of the student council for two years, you have more experience organizing activities at school and you feel confident that for this event to be successful, it is best if you to take a leadership role in this process. In your eyes, this planning team has a lot of good ideas, but on certain key issues you are quite sure that you have the best and most effective idea. When others resist your suggestions or come up with a different approach, you get annoyed because you feel that they have not really been listening; if they had, they would have appreciated the full advantages of your suggestion. Therefore, you try to explain a second or even a third time, because you're really sure that everyone will come on board once they "get it." You frequently cut people off mid-sentence when something comes to your mind that you want to say.

Role 4 – Integrative Communication Mode

Your character is full of anticipation about the process itself that this group will be using to work together on the project. You have participated in a Peace Event before and have certain ideas of your own on how this one might be held, but you appreciate the diversity of experience in this particular group, and you're really interested to hear what the others have thought of because something even more creative can be prepared when different ideas, talents, and points of view are brought together. Therefore, you respect each person's turn when brainstorming and discussing, and encourage people who haven't said anything to share their views on the subject. You are positive in your outlook towards the group and express appreciation for each person's suggestions. You are also aware of the practical limitations of the financial, time, and human resources available for this event, so you listen for and reflect on what could be both interesting and feasible ideas. You expand the circle of unity by making creative suggestions about forming a team of additional volunteers and getting families and local businesses to provide donations of materials, food, and other needed articles for the event. Whatever the group decides to do, even if it doesn't correspond exactly to what you had personally envisioned, you will wholeheartedly support.

Unit 8 – Activity Reading 2

Sample Problems for Resolution

The following scenarios can be used for two types of activities. Refer to the instructions below for guidance.

Communication Worksheet: Instructions

Using the Communication Worksheet, ask students to arrive at a solution for one of the scenarios below by working through each of the four modes of communication sequentially. In a follow-up class, ask them to discuss the challenges and benefits they experienced while exercising their thoughts in these four modes.

Group Consultation Practice: Instructions

Following a review of the seven steps of consultation, break into groups of 4–6 students and choose one of the following scenarios to consult upon. You will have 40 minutes to consult: strive to arrive at a minimum of three concrete suggestions that the group feels unified to act upon. Record your ideas to share with the class. If time allows, discuss with your class the process you went through and identify what challenges and benefits this process of consultation had.

Scenario 1

Recently, one of the teachers of your class has been acting very harshly. Some of you have been misbehaving during the lessons—talking when the teacher isn't looking, making jokes, passing notes to each other, etc.—but nothing that would warrant such strong reactions from him. His apparent negativity towards the class has become so intense that students requesting study help from him have been abruptly turned down, and the general feeling among students is that he is being too hard even on those who have never done anything wrong. He used to be a warmer, more approachable teacher—even somewhat popular—but in the last few weeks this has changed. The meaner he becomes, the less students like him and the less cooperative they are in class. Some students suspect he may have problems in his personal life that are affecting his mood. What might be done to improve the situation in class?

Scenario 2

Forest Park is located approximately half-way between two high schools: School A and School B. During lunch breaks and in the afternoon, students from both schools like to gather there and use the park's one basketball court for impromptu games. Recently, angry scuffles between a few of the popular boys from each school over who can use the court have prompted increased rivalry between the schools. Larger numbers of students have begun gathering in the park to watch the hostilities, provocative slurs against each side have been graffitied on the park benches, and hostile verbal exchanges have become a daily occurrence. People expect a major fight to break out between the two schools soon. Several teachers have become aware of the situation, but so far, no one knows what exactly should be done. How might the interschool hostilities be defused? Is there a way to bring the schools closer together?

Unit 8 – Communication Worksheet

Briefly describe the conflict:

What resolution would you bring to this conflict if you were thinking and communicating in the following modes:

PLAYFUL MODE
If anything were possible and there were no limitations, ideas for resolving this situation could include:

TASK-ORIENTED MODE
Are there any limitations that might affect the selected outcome which ought to be noted:

COMPARATIVE MODE

Not all proposed resolutions are as attractive or appropriate for this situation as some others. Describe which idea(s) are perhaps more beneficial and why. Are there any remaining doubts or questions that need to be considered?

INTEGRATIVE MODE

Considering all of the above, the resolution(s) most conducive to the creation of unity in this situation is/are:

Unit 8 – Activity Reading 3

Role Play: Particulars, Context, Worldview

1. Divide into three groups.

2. Each group will be given a conflict scenario. The scenarios each emphasize different factors of the same conflict.

3. Each group should discuss the conflict scenario (10 minutes) and then prepare a dramatization of the conflict (20 minutes). The dramatization should be between 1 and 2 minutes long. *It is very important that the dramatization try to convey the "cause of the conflict" as it is described in the scenario. The dramatization should also convey all of the information provided in the scenario.*

4. Perform the dramatizations for the other groups.

   The dramatizations should provide an opportunity for students to explore the dimensions of conflict and to understand how worldview and context shape these situations.

   Scenario #1 focuses on particulars. The dramatization by this group should emphasize the lack of communication, rumors, and issues of pride and honor that are involved.

   Scenario #2 focuses on context. The dramatization by this group should emphasize the context of ethnic division and tension within which conflicts between members of the different groups occur.

   Scenario #3 focuses on worldview. The dramatization by this group should emphasize the worldviews held by the various characters.

5. Ask students to describe what they noticed and how they felt as each of the role-plays revealed different factors.

Scenario #1

Michelle and Keisha are two high-school students in the same school. They have known each other for four years and consider themselves friends. They have not had problems with each other in the past. While they are both in the same grade (9th), they are in different classes so they don't see each other much during school except during dance practice after school. Michelle has been seeing a boy named Anthony, and she considers him her boyfriend.

At dance practice a conflict broke out between Michelle and Keisha. Amber, a friend of Michelle's, heard a rumor that Anthony was seen with his arm around Keisha the day before.

Amber told Michelle the rumor. Michelle is not sure if the rumor is true. Michelle came to dance practice and started screaming at Keisha, and challenging her to a fight. Keisha didn't know why Michelle was so angry, but being screamed at made her furious. Keisha said she would fight Michelle after school on the playground and then left the dance practice.

Scenario #2

Michelle and Keisha are two high-school students in the same school. They have known each other for four years and consider themselves friends. They have not had problems with each other in the past. While they are both in the same grade (9th), they are in different classes so they don't see each other much during school except when during dance practice after school. Michelle has been seeing a boy named Anthony, and she considers him her boyfriend.

At dance practice a conflict broke out between Michelle and Keisha. Amber, a friend of Michelle's, heard a rumor that Anthony was seen with his arm around Keisha the day before. Amber told Michelle the rumor. Michelle is not sure if the rumor is true. Michelle came to dance practice and started screaming at Keisha, and challenging her to a fight. Keisha didn't know why Michelle was so angry, but being screamed at made her furious. Keisha said she would fight Michelle after school on the playground and then left the dance practice.

There has been a lot of tension within the school. The school is predominantly populated by students from two different ethnic groups. There have been a number of violent incidents between members from the different groups. A lot of students don't like it when a student from one ethnic group dates a student from the other one. Anthony and Keisha are from the same ethnic group. Michelle is from a different group, and that is why her successful relationship with Anthony has provoked jealousy, hostility, and mischief from the rumor-mongers.

Scenario #3

Michelle and Keisha are two high-school students in the same school. They have known each other for four years and consider themselves friends. They have not had problems with each other in the past. While they are both in the same grade (9th), they are in different classes so they don't see each other much during school except during dance practice after school. Michelle has been seeing a boy named Anthony, and she considers him her boyfriend.

At dance practice a conflict broke out between Michelle and Keisha. Amber, a friend of Michelle's, heard a rumor that Anthony was seen with his arm around Keisha the day before. Amber told Michelle the rumor. Michelle is not sure if the rumor is true. Michelle came to dance practice and started screaming at Keisha, and challenging her to a fight. Keisha didn't know why Michelle was so angry, but being screamed at made her furious. Keisha said she would fight Michelle after school on the playground and then left the dance practice.

Michelle is used to being the center of attention at school and is considered one of the "cool" kids. She tends to get her way and is very sensitive to how she is perceived by other students. She wants to be seen as in charge and control. This is why she confronted Keisha so publicly and aggressively. She did not expect Keisha to be aggressive back. Michelle is nervous.

Keisha comes from a lower social class than Michelle, and even though she is part of the ethnic majority has always felt she had to fight for everything in life. She does not seek out conflicts, but when challenged, she tries to win. If Michelle wants to fight, Keisha will do what it takes to win. If Michelle were willing to back down, then Keisha would not pursue the matter.

Unit 8 – Activity Reading 4

The following real conflict scenarios may be used by students to explore the particulars, context, and worldview(s) that contribute to manifest conflicts.

Scenario 1: Genocide in Rwanda

In the 1990s a horrendous genocide took place in Rwanda.

Rwanda is populated mostly by members of the Hutu and Tutsi tribes. There is a history of violent animosity between the two groups. Independence was achieved in 1962, but violence between the two groups continued. In the early 1990s, the civil war between the two groups appeared to be ending, through the formation of a multiparty constitution and the signing of a power-sharing agreement. After the Hutu president's plane was shot down, the Hutus began a massacre of Tutsis. In 100 days, approximately 800,000 Tutsis and moderate Hutus were killed.

During the massacres, massive numbers of refugees fled to Zaire. The war also spread into Zaire. International governmental agencies, including the United Nations, did not act swiftly to prevent or mitigate the genocide, even though they were fully informed that it was taking place.

The violence has largely stopped, but many issues remain, including facilitating the return of refugees, reconciliation, trauma relief and healing, as well as meting out justice for the genocide. An International Criminal Tribunal for Rwanda has also been established.

The Rwandan Genocide is one of the most horrific episodes in recent history. It illustrates the brutality that human beings are capable of committing. It also highlights the weaknesses and failings of current systems of international order.

There is a wide range of information on the Rwandan Genocide available online. Some good starting points for finding additional information include:

*   A background report on the genocide produced by the U.S. Public Broadcasting Service (PBS) show "Frontline" at: <http://www.pbs.org/wgbh/pages/frontline/shows/evil/>
*   The official website of the International War Crimes Tribunal for Rwanda at: <http://www.ictr.org/>
*   A Human Rights Watch report on the genocide at: <http://www.hrw.org/reports/1999/rwanda/>

Scenario 2: A School in Crisis

In a school in the Canadian Arctic there are many incidents of bullying, suicide, and low-level harassment. There is also a high drop-out rate—only 50% of students graduate. The majority of students are Inuit. The minority students are "southerners," the term used to refer to all non-Inuit students. The school always seems to be in a state of crisis—dealing with the effects of a suicide, a violent incident, or the challenges of motivating and engaging students. There is tension within the community about the state of the school. Many Inuit parents express the view that the school is biased in favor of the non-Inuit minority. They stress, for example, the fact that instruction in the school is in English as opposed to Inuktitut, the language of the Inuit.

When there is an incident of bullying or harassment in the school, little tends to be done. Those participating might be separated; there may also be suspensions or other forms of discipline. There is a group of students who have formed a nonviolence group and who want to promote nonviolence and harmony. However, they have little support from the school administration and are really like a "club" that gets together and does activities together.

In trying to improve conditions in this school, many ideas are being explored including:

a. A zero-tolerance policy for students who commit more than one act of violence;
b. The use of cameras in the school to monitor student behavior;
c. The teaching of intervention techniques like mediation to students and faculty to resolve disputes between students.

To find more information, visit these sites:

- Inuit Tapiriit Kanatami : <http://www.itk.ca/english/inuit_canada/history/contact.htm>
- Brief Inuit History: <http://www.yomee.com/Religions/Other/Inuit.htm>

Scenario 3: Your Experience

Pick a conflict with which you are familiar in your life. Analyze it based on its particulars, context, and worldview.

Unit 8 – Activity Reading 5
The Main Features of Consultation

The main objective of consultation is to make a just and compassionate decision

The decision making will lead to action to resolve the problem at hand in a way that is just and compassionate. The worth of a decision can be measured by the degree to which it increases the sense of unity and promotes justice among all involved. If the decision made is not perceived as just, then the unity of the group will be compromised.

The main prerequisite for consultation is unity

Unity should characterize both the process of consultation and the result of consultation. When participants come together to consult in a spirit of unity, this does not mean that all of their thoughts and feelings are the same. Coming together in a spirit of unity means coming together with unity of purpose. Through the consultation process—characterized by unity of purpose—unity of thought, feeling, and approach can be found and maintained.

The main resource of consultation is the truth

In the context of consultation, "finding the truth" leads to finding the best possible solution to the issue at hand. If an important element of truth is not considered in the consultation, then the unity of the group will be compromised. Sometimes, when new information or facts are learned, a previous decision will need to be reconsidered by the consulting group in order to find a better solution that will promote justice and create higher levels of unity.

The main tools of consultation are frankness and openness

To find the truth, consultation requires that all participants openly share their thoughts, feelings, and ideas. This is possible when the atmosphere is characterized by respect for one another, encouragement, and when each individual participates with purity of motive. At the same time, every speaker should remember to measure what they want to say within the principles of love, care, humility, and moderation, in order to avoid causing hurt or injury.

The main personal challenge of consultation is objectivity

When we share ideas in the process of consultation, these ideas become the property of the group and not the individual. All ideas can be considered freely. In this context, the group is free to accept, modify, or discard ideas without attaching negative feelings to any of the participants in the consultative group. When ideas belong to the group and not to the individual, no one needs to feel self-defensive or undervalued. The ability to detach oneself from ideas shared in consultation is increased when individuals develop the qualities of both humility and self-acceptance.

In the process of consultation, it is better to be wrong and united, than right and disunited

Without unity, mistrust and suspicion enter human relationships. When this happens, all possibilities of finding the truth and arriving at unifying, just decisions are lost. Unity is therefore the most important condition for both the process and the result of consultation. When a decision is made in consultation, all participants should be united in supporting and carrying through this decision. Even if a decision made by the group is wrong, a united consultative group will have greater capacity to re-examine the issue in the light of truth, than will a disunited and nonconsultative group.

Extended Exploration

Publications

Consultation: A Compilation. (1990). Rev. ed. London: Bahá'í Publishing Trust.

Coser, L.A. (1956). *The Function of Social Conflict.* New York: The Free Press.

Danesh, H.B., and R. Danesh. (2004). "Conflict-Free Conflict Resolution Process and Methodology." *Peace and Conflict Studies* 11.2: 55–84.

———. (2002a). "Has Conflict Resolution Grown Up? Toward a New Model of Decision Making and Conflict Resolution." *International Journal of Peace Studies* 7.1: 59–76.

———. (2002b). "A Consultative Conflict Resolution Model: Beyond Alternative Dispute Resolution." *International Journal of Peace Studies* 7.2:17–33.

Deutsch, M. (1973). *The Resolution of Conflict.* New Haven: Yale University Press.

Folger, J. P., M. S. Poole, and R. K. Stutman. (1993). *Working through Conflict.* 2nd ed. New York: Harper Collins.

General Online Resources

The Columbia Encyclopedia Online. <http://www.bartleby.com/65>.

The Columbia World of Quotations. <http://www.bartleby.com/quotations>.

The Merriam-Webster Online Dictionary. <http://www.merriam-webster.com>.

Wikipedia: The Free Encyclopedia. <http://www.wikipedia.org>.

Unit 9

CREATING A CULTURE OF HEALING

This unit examines the concept of a "Culture of Healing." It defines the key processes of individual and community healing, analyzes popular approaches to recovery from post-conflict and traumatic disorders, and presents the characteristics of a Culture of Healing as fostered within the Education for Peace Program.

Context

In a previous unit we discussed the dynamics and effects of violence on individuals and sought answers to the question of how to prevent violence at the interpersonal and intergroup levels. In this unit, we will review the impact of violence on individuals and communities of people and consider two questions: "Can *entire populations* recover from the effects of violence? And if so, how?"

Appreciation of the psychological, social, and economic impacts of violence on successive generations has increased in recent decades as the world has witnessed accelerating waves of violence among competing religious, ethnic, tribal, and political groups.

With nations suffering the devastating effects of past and present violence each day, it becomes evident that a systematic approach to the healing of entire populations is critically needed if significant advances towards global justice, peace, and well-being are to be achieved.

This unit outlines the "Culture of Healing,"[1]a new approach to the challenge of collective recovery from violence. A Culture of Healing is one that helps entire populations of individuals— adults and children, victims and aggressors, government leaders and citizens, rich and poor alike— overcome the effects of severe psychosocial trauma from violence, war, and other atrocities. This approach is based on a unique perspective regarding the nature of healing and the process of recovery, both founded on the paradigm of unity.

Learning Objectives

In this unit, participants should be assisted to:

1. Understand the concept of Culture of

---

1. This unit draws heavily from a paper (now under review for publication in a refereed peace studies journal) on the theme of Culture of Healing as well as on other published work authored by H.B. Danesh.

Healing and why it is important to the creation of a culture of peace;

2. Contrast the Culture of Healing with current mainstream approaches to post-trauma recovery;

3. Reflect upon what a Culture of Healing offers to you personally and how such a culture could assist your community;

4. Broadly identify the strategies, institutions and community-level processes necessary for initiating and supporting a Culture of Healing.

Points for Understanding

Teachers should help their students to understand and remember these main points:

- Health is a state of wholeness, equilibrium, balance, and harmony—in brief, organic unity;

- In a Culture of Healing, psychological healing and social recovery from the destructive impact of violence and war on individuals and communities takes place within the tripartite processes of knowledge-acquisition, relationship-formation, and behavior-transformation;

- At the core of this process is the essential transformation from conflict-based to unity-based ideas, relationships, and practices—in brief, our worldviews;

- In the Culture of Healing, the process of recovery is guided by the principles of unity in diversity and the fundamental nobility of humanity that engender conditions conducive to the healing of individuals and communities—trust, hope, cooperation, understanding, and forgiveness among the previously warring populations;

- A Culture of Healing is characterized by mutual acceptance, sustained encouragement, and transformative growth, which

Key Vocabulary

Aggressor: the person who initiated a harmful action or crime.

Counseling: assisting individuals to deal with personal and interpersonal conflicts by providing direction or advice as to a decision or course of action.

Culture of Healing: a unifying culture in which all members of the community—adults and children, victims and aggressors, leaders and citizens, rich and poor alike—are assisted and participate in healing from the effects of psychosocial and moral traumas of conflict, violence, and war.

Healing: the process of creating unity in all aspects of human individual and community life—physical, emotional, social, and spiritual.

Health: a state of wholeness, equilibrium, balance, and harmony—in brief, organic unity.

Perpetrator: a person or a group who causes and/or commits a violence act.

Psychotherapy: treatment of psychological disorders using psychiatric or psychological methods such as the reliving of traumatic experiences through remembering, introspection, behavior modification, and other such techniques.

PTSD or Post-Traumatic Stress Disorder: a psychiatric disorder that can occur following the experience or witnessing of life-threatening events such as military combat, natural disasters, terrorist incidents, serious accidents, or violent personal assaults like rape and abuse. Symptoms include nightmares and flashbacks, insomnia, estrangement, depression, and memory loss. The disorder is also associated with impairment of the person's ability to function in social and family life, including problems like occupational instability, marital problems and divorces, family discord, and difficulties in parenting.

Rehabilitation: the process of helping a person debilitated, either psychologically and/or physically, by disease or injury to regain the highest level of function, independence, and quality of life of which he or she is capable.

Truth and Reconciliation Commission (TRC): a commission tasked with discovering and revealing past wrongdoing by a government and other holders of power, in the hope of restoring conditions of justice, understanding, and forgiveness among the conflicted populations. TRC reports can provide proof against historical revisionism of state terrorism and other crimes and human rights abuses.

Victim: a person or a group acted upon and usually adversely affected by a force or agent.

Violence: any act—physical, psychological, verbal, or structural—that intentionally or accidentally results in harm to oneself, another living being, the environment, or one's own or another's property. Violence is always destructive and represents the final act in a series of conflicted developments within the individual, group or institution that commits it.

are some of the main expressions of the human capacity to form authentic and harmonious relationships.

What is Violence?

In an earlier unit we discussed the nature and dynamics of violence and its impact on individuals. Briefly, we defined violence as follows:

Definition

Violence is any act—physical, psychological, verbal, or structural—that intentionally or accidentally results in harm to oneself, another living being, the environment, or one's own or another's property. Violence is always destructive and represents the final act in a series of conflicted developments within the mind of the individual, group, or institution that commits it.

We explored the roots of violence and concluded that human beings are not biologically or genetically condemned to violence. Rather, violence is a process that begins in the mind and employs human biological and psychological powers in a harmful and destructive manner. Violence is strongly influenced by our worldviews, which are shaped by our education, life experiences, and basic needs. As such, violence can be prevented. Nonetheless, violence—both individual and collective—is widespread in today's world, and its devastating effects are felt throughout every society on the planet.

How Does Violence Affect the Victims and Perpetrators of Violence?

Violence has a range of negative impact on the victims, the perpetrators, the environment, the economy and the social welfare of society.

Violence negatively affects individuals and groups of people at physical, psychological, relational, moral, and spiritual levels. While both the victims and perpetrators of violence suffer from all these conditions, the degree of severity and long-term effects differ in each group. Generally speaking, the victims of violence suffer mostly with respect to physical (bodily injury, illness, death) and psychological (sadness, anger, fear, guilt, and discontent) aspects of their life. Both victims and perpetrators also suffer great disruption in the interpersonal, social, and economic spheres of their lives. Both groups experience interpersonal difficulties, including marital conflict, family breakdown, and mutual mistrust; and social problems such as violence, crime, racism, and extensive drug and alcohol abuse. Other psychosocial challenges such as gender inequality, extreme poverty, prejudice, and disregard for universal human rights and responsibilities also fall within the scope of large-scale psychosocial ill-health. However, the perpetrators of violence seem to suffer particularly devastating consequences with regard to the moral, ethical, and spiritual aspects of their lives.

While the victims of violence tend to respond rather well to attempts to help them to recover from the negative impact of violence on them, the situation for the perpetrators is usually more negative in the long term. The perpetrators of violence usually deal with the negative consequences of their own actions in three distinct ways:

- Self-destruction through carelessness, neglect, alcohol and substance abuse, self-loathing, and other personal and interpersonal destructive habits and actions;
- Self-delusion based on the notion that they have committed no wrong and, in the words of Dewey, "do not have enough conscience to want to do healing

work" (2004, p. 94). These individuals often commit more atrocities;

- Atonement for their own misdeeds through good deeds, repentance, acceptance of punishment, prayer, and begging for forgiveness.

The Need for Healing

Clearly, when violence occurs, life cannot return to normal, for either the victim or perpetrator, without a process of healing taking place.

But what does the process of healing involve? Consider the biological processes that take place when a tissue wound to the body occurs:

> When living tissue is wounded, a set of events takes place in a predictable fashion to repair the damage. These events overlap in time and must be artificially categorized into separate steps, called the inflammatory, proliferative, and maturation phases.
>
> In the first phase, bacteria and debris are engulfed, destroyed and removed, and factors are released that cause the migration and division of cells involved in the second phase.
>
> The second phase is characterized by the growth of new blood vessels from pre-existing vessels; the formation of basic structures for the creation and support of new tissue growth, differentiation, and regulated intercellular communication; the formation of protective cells over the wound to cover it and regulate the tissue's interaction with the outer environment; and the contraction of the wound

through the work of special cells which grip on the wound edges and contract—drawing the sides of the wound together—until the reconstitution process is complete, at which point unneeded cells stop functioning and are discarded.

> And finally in the third phase, the body restores an organized elasticity to the former wound site and near-original strength and functionality returns. [2]

A Definition of Healing

Certain parallels between biological and psychosocial processes of healing can be drawn.

We find, for example, that "healing" or the creation of "health"—whether biological or psychosocial—is synonymous with the creation of "unity": the establishment of a dynamic equilibrium within ourselves and our interactions with the world.

Definitions

Health is a state of wholeness, equilibrium, balance, and harmony—in brief, organic unity.

Healing is the process of creating unity in all aspects of human individual and community life—physical, emotional, social, and spiritual.

The World Health Organization (WHO) states that "health is a state of complete physical,

---

2. Source: "Wound Healing," Wikipedia: <http://en.wikipedia.org/wiki/Wound_healing_phases>. See also Thomas Romo, III, et al., "Wound Healing, Skin" <eMedicine: http://www.emedicine.com/ent/topic13.htm>.

mental and social well-being and not merely the absence of disease or infirmity" (WHO, 1946).

Psychological Health in Focus

Individual psychological health depends on three fundamental processes:

1. Knowledge-acquisition;
2. Relationship-formation; and
3. Behavior transformation.

Knowledge-acquisition refers to the process of ever better understanding of self, others, and the world (nature, ideas, beauty, God) in the context of truth and trust—the two most important conditions for authentic and scientific understanding.

Relationship-formation, in addition to truth and trust, requires love, without which it is impossible to form healthy relationships. Environments conducive to such relationships are characterized by love of self, others, and the world.

Behavior-transformation comes into effect within the framework of such healthy relationships and newly acquired knowledge and insight, and our attitudes and approaches towards self, others, and the world begin to alter (H.B. Danesh, 2006).

Psychological Health and Worldview

These three processes of psychological health are expressions of the main powers of the human psyche: the powers of *knowledge* (i.e., the power to search for, recognize, understand and communicate *truth*), of *love* (i.e., the power to create *unity* by giving to, receiving from, and including others universally), and of *will* (i.e., the power to make decisions that are *just* and to willingly be of *service* to others) that we have discussed in earlier units.[3]

When an individual engages constructively in the three processes of knowledge-acquisition, relationship-formation, and behavior-transformation, s/he gradually develops a more universal and inclusive identity—a process identified in previous units as the formation of a *"unity-based worldview."*[4]

Healing Individuals

Today, the process of healing individuals is most commonly based on the practice of psychotherapy. Modern psychotherapeutic practices, drawing their concepts and approaches from the psychoanalytic, behavioral, cognitive, and other schools, focus fundamentally on one or more of the three powers of the psyche: knowledge, love, and will.

In the therapeutic context, the tasks of acquiring ever deeper self-knowledge, of establishing more authentic and mature relationships, and of acting in more creative and constructive ways are usually pursued through the *recounting of one's life history and experiences*—its successes and failures, joys and sorrows, hopes and despairs, misfortunes and misjudgments, challenges and opportunities—in the hope of re-evaluating their significance and gaining new understandings or "insights"; combined with *learning to receive and give love to self and others in a healthy manner.*

Psychological healing is a highly personal process and, in the words of prominent

---

3. See in particular *EFP Curriculum Manual*, Unit 3: "The Concept of Human Nature."

4. The Unity-Based Worldview is associated with the phase of maturity in human development. Grounded in the recognition of humanity's essential oneness and inherent nobility, this worldview enables the creation of unity-oriented relationships while respecting and celebrating humanity's rich diversity. For more on the concept of worldview, see *EFP Curriculum Manual*, Unit 2: "The Concept of Worldview."

psychoanalyst Hans Loewald, "is in essence a cure through love."[5]

Healing Communities

When many individuals in a given society suffer from the impact of violent and destructive episodes of war, famine, natural disasters, and disease, we witness the emergence of *large-scale psychosocial ill health.*

Symptoms of large-scale psychosocial ill health include feelings of sadness, anger, fear, guilt, and discontent; interpersonal difficulties including marital conflict, family breakdown, and mutual mistrust; and social problems such as violence, crime, racism, and extensive drug and alcohol abuse.

Other psychosocial challenges such as gender inequality, extreme poverty, intergroup prejudice, and disregard for universal human rights and responsibilities also fall within the scope of large-scale psychosocial ill health.

Community-level healing needs are similar in many respects to individual healing needs. After all, as individuals we become who we are within the context of our relationships; and it is in the context of our relationships that we create healthy or unhealthy communities.

The community is essentially an aggregate of relationships; a grouping of people within a framework of unity based on certain shared beliefs, assumptions, and knowledge; agreed ways of expressing concern, care, compassion, and love; and accepted codes of conduct and interpersonal relations.

Conflict and violence damage these relationships and threaten the social life of the community. Violence and war also have destructive impact on the economy, the environment, the family, and other institutions of society.

When communities are in need of healing from conflict and violence, the processes of *knowledge-acquisition, relationship-formation,* and *behavior-transformation* are critically necessary, but are accompanied by certain unique challenges in part because of the scale of the endeavor. Thus, a unique approach to community healing—tailored to the complex needs and constraints of large populations—is needed.

Current Approaches to Healing and the Challenge of Large Populations

Today, three main approaches are used to assist communities to recover from violence-related psychosocial trauma and ill-health:

1. Curative or Therapeutic Approach
2. Advice-Giving or Counseling Approach
3. Rehabilitative or Restorative Justice Approach

Each approach has merits, but none is fully adequate to respond to the conceptual, practical, and economic challenges of healing large populations.

1. The Curative or Therapeutic Approach

The curative or therapeutic approach refers to the efforts of members of the medical and health professions who have been entrusted by society with the mandate of decreasing the suffering and healing the diseases of the individual, and when required and possible, of large afflicted groups. Among the most widely used therapeutic approaches are those used for a condition broadly referred to as Post-Traumatic Stress Disorder (PTSD). The therapeutic approach—practiced by psychiatrists, psychologists, and a few other trained health professionals—is person-centered;

---

5. Hans Loewald, 1960, "On the Therapeutic Action of Psychoanalysis," *International Journal of Psychoanalysis* 1(Jan.–Feb.): 16–33.

focused on individuals, small groups, and possibly their families, and only rarely on issues of societal health and well-being.

The psychotherapeutic approaches used to treat PTSD basically revolve around the process of reliving the traumatic experience by remembering, imagining, role playing, and other such techniques in the safe and relatively relaxed environment of a therapeutic office.

This approach is particularly suited for individuals and small groups. It needs to be administered by highly trained and qualified practitioners and is quite costly. As such, the PTSD form of therapy cannot realistically be considered for helping large populations of people affected by such traumatic experiences as war, ethnic cleansing, torture, mass rape, and other crimes against humanity that are and have been practiced widely around the globe. Furthermore, the psychotherapeutic approach primarily deals with one side of the violence equation, usually the victim. PTSD is neither focused on, nor practical for helping all the participants in a violent conflict to overcome its calamitous effects.

Furthermore, psychiatric practice is increasingly now focused on biochemical treatments rather than on psychological exploration, as was advocated by its creators at the start of the 20th century. As such, the therapeutic approach has become very limited in both the scope of its healing objectives and the extent of its benefits to large populations.

2. The Advice-Giving or Counseling Approach

The advice-giving or counseling approach is an ancient practice that in many societies is assumed by the elders, persons of esteemed repute, those in positions of authority, and by friends, usually in an informal context, though increasingly on a formal basis as well. The primary function of these individuals is to give advice and to suggest modes of behavior and lines of action according to their own experience, knowledge, and worldview, which are based on the cultural norms and traditions. These forms of advice-giving and counseling, although usually not based on scientific foundations, have provided adequate benefit on a mass basis and can be integrated into programs of psychosocial recovery.

Since the middle of 20th century, advice-giving has flourished, particularly in the West, in the form of the counseling profession. This profession is still evolving, however, and not all individuals who practice it have the necessary training and experience to deal appropriately with the profound and lasting impacts of trauma. When counseling lacks the scientific rigor of the therapeutic approaches and the authority of traditional advice-giving, its benefits are limited and can sometimes do more harm than good.

3. Rehabilitative or Restorative Justice Approach

The rehabilitative or restorative justice approach aims to rehabilitate populations through formalized practices that assist individuals and communities to overcome post-violence disorders so that they can resume normal functioning and thus live a healthier, individual and relational life.

The *Truth and Reconciliation Commissions (TRCs)* are included in this category and represent one of the main models of systematic whole-population recovery to date. The goal of the TRC approach is to address the particular wounds sustained by the victims of violence and its perpetrators in a context of truth-sharing and forgiveness. The philosophy is that national unity can be restored when victims, witnesses, and even perpetrators of violence are given a chance to publicly tell their stories without fear of prosecution. Past atrocities are discussed openly, and the perpetuators of violence are given an opportunity to confess their deeds, ask for forgiveness, and undertake reconciliatory actions.

A Closer Examination of Truth and Reconciliation Commissions

Since 1973, variations of the Truth and Reconciliation Commission have been formed in more than 20 countries. These commissions have been sponsored by a wide range of organizations and have had a mixed record of success. The reasons for these results are varied, but important clues can be found when we examine the conceptual foundations of the Truth and Reconciliation approach—truth, justice, and reconciliation.

First, it is necessary to acknowledge that issues of truth, justice, and reconciliation have both subjective and objective qualities, and as such they are open to misperceptions and varied interpretations. Thus, the task of finding *truth* about violence committed by one party against another, of identifying a path of *justice* satisfactory to both the perpetrators of violence and their victims, and of achieving *reconciliation* between them has proven to be fraught with many challenges.

Truth

Truth is often withheld for fear of punishment, for reasons of an individual's personal sense of shame, and for the possibility of being shunned by the loved ones and members of one's own community. Furthermore, confusion and misunderstanding—both common under conditions of threat—play havoc with the aim of obtaining authentic truth. Reports and analyses of TRCs clearly point to the difficulty of getting to the *truth of what happened* among those who were involved in the violent incidents. In the absence of such agreement, it is almost impossible to deliver justice and to achieve true reconciliation. The main challenge here is to create a safe environment for both victims and perpetrators of violence to share the truth about the atrocities they have respectively experienced and committed.

Justice

Justice is also a subject that arouses intense emotions and profound concerns on the part of those who are directly or indirectly involved in violence. The main question is how to enact justice in a community devastated by violence. There are many valid questions about and objections to the manner in which TRCs approach the issue of justice. Some feel that the principles of reward and punishment are not adequately addressed by the TRC approach. Others feel that even when a certain degree of reward to the victims or punishment for the aggressors is meted out, it is usually insufficient. Justice is essential for the creation and maintenance of harmony and peace in the society. Therefore, the search for fairer approaches to the issue of justice is ongoing.

Reconciliation

Reconciliation is possible when all individuals affected by violence—victims, perpetrators, and bystanders—feel that truth has been uncovered and that justice has been meted out. Considering the challenges that the TRCs usually face with respect to issues of truth and justice, it is not surprising that true reconciliation in these communities is not easily or readily accomplished, if at all. True reconciliation requires a definitive transformation from conflict-based worldviews to those that are based on the fact of the oneness of humanity in the context of unity in diversity. The dynamics of such a transformation were discussed in Unit 2 of this Manual. You will find a review of that unit helpful in understanding this complex issue.

Creating a Culture of Healing

The Education for Peace experience offers a model for collective recovery from the impact of violence. This model, which we have designated as a "Culture of Healing," incorporates the positive aspects of other models within the orienting framework of the law of unity.

A "Culture of Healing" has two objectives:

1. To help entire populations of individuals—adults and children, victims and perpetrators, leaders and citizens, rich and poor—overcome the after-effects of severe psychosocial trauma from violence, war, and such atrocities; and

2. To create the necessary social institutions and modes of governance that are conducive to the prevention of future episodes of violence and the eventual establishment of a culture of peace. (Danesh, 2007b)

Foundations of a Culture of Healing

In the EFP concept of a Culture of Healing, both the nature of healing and the process of recovery are viewed from the unique perspective of unity. Disunity is recognized as a condition that not only creates violence but also thwarts all efforts at recovery from the injurious consequences of violence. In a review of the literature about the requirements for collective recovery from the impact of violence and war, and, based on our observations in the course of six years of implementation of the EFP Program in more than 100 schools across Bosnia-Herzegovina, an effective Culture of Healing must be able to adequately meet the following fundamental needs:

1. *Human Survival Needs*, including creation of environments free of violence or war;

availability of food, shelter, clothing, health care, and basic comfort; and offering opportunities to the community members to be free and relatively self-sufficient in attending to these needs;

2. *Human Association Needs*, including the presence of standards of truth and truthfulness, equity and justice, and compassion; and forgiveness in and among all conflicted parties, including the victims, perpetrators, and by-standers; and

3. *Human Superordinate (Spiritual) Needs*, the need to understand the genesis of their conflicts and to learn how to transcend them.

These fundamental needs can only be met in the context of unity, where safety is assured, diversity is respected, truth-seeking is the norm, justice is the standard, and compassion and forgiveness are practiced. Only within such a true and comprehensive state of unity can these requisites for recovery from the destructive impact of violence be adequately met.

From the above it is clear that in a Culture of Healing both individual/group rehabilitation and legislative/judicial/executive reform are required. In other words, in order to achieve true recovery from the impact of violence and war, we simultaneously need to meet the survival needs of all citizens, create a state of harmony and cooperation among individuals and groups, put into motion effective processes for enforcing justice—all in the context of truth, universality, and transparency.

This daunting task is only possible within the safe and progressive framework of unity in diversity in the context of a peace-based worldview. In the absence of unity, security is absent, truth is hidden, justice is conflicted, compassion is missing, forgiveness is lacking, and the threat of new violence is ever present.

What Does Creating A Culture of Healing Entail?

Creating a "Culture of Healing" consists of constructing environments characterized by:

1. Truth-seeking, truthfulness, trustworthiness (knowledge-acquisition component);
2. Mutual and unconditional acceptance, respect, and care for all parties involved in the context of unity in diversity (relationship-formation component); and
3. Collaboration, forgiveness, and service to one another in interpersonal relationships, and enforcement of the principles of justice and rule of law in societal practices (behavior-transformation component).

As a "Culture of Healing" starts to take root, we begin to see what Luc Huyse identifies as the three stages of reconciliation and more:

1. Replacing fear by non-violent coexistence;
2. Creating conditions in which fear no longer rules and confidence and trust are being built; and
3. Moving of the involved community towards "empathy." (Huyse, 2003, p. 19)

He, furthermore, states that "all steps in the process [of reconciliation] entail the reconciling of not only individuals, but also groups and communities as a whole" (Huyse, 2003, p. 22).[6]

Outcomes and Indicators of a Culture of Healing

How Do We Know When a Culture of Healing Is Emerging?

A Culture of Healing begins to be established when:

- *Mutual trust* between the victims and perpetrators and across the lines of conflict is increasingly present;
- Feelings of *hope* about the ability to recover from the impact of violence and *optimism* regarding the capacity to prevent and peacefully resolve future conflicts increase; and
- Gradual but definite steps are made to meet the *basic human needs and rights* of all members of the community.

The Step-by-Step Process of a Culture of Healing

Based on the lessons learned from six years of Education for Peace among thousands of students, educators, and parents/guardians in Bosnia and Herzegovina, the following requisites for creating a Culture of Healing are identified:

1. **Accept that Healing is a Prerequisite of Peace**
   Community leaders and citizens need to recognize that the process of creating a Culture of Peace is inseparable from the process of creating a Culture of Healing.

2. **Foster Worldview Transformation through Community Education**
   In order to create both a Culture of Peace and a Culture of Healing, all participants need to acquire an understanding and appreciation of the role of worldview in human individual and group conduct and to learn the dynamics of transformation from conflict-based to unity-based worldviews.

---

6. Luc Huyse, *Reconciliation after Violent Conflict: A Handbook,* ed. David Bloomfield, Teresa Barnes, and Luc Huyse, International Institute for Democracy and Electoral Assistance, 2003.

3. **Nurture Mutual Trust through Demonstration of the Principle of the Oneness of Humanity**

The foundation of both a Culture of Peace and a Culture of Healing is *mutual trust*. The task of creating trust among individuals and groups with the history of conflict, violence, and war is extremely difficult and is only possible in the context of the realization and acceptance of the principle of the *oneness of humanity*—that there is only one humanity and that the noblest expression of human oneness is in the context of unity in diversity.

4. **Create Opportunities for Forming New, Positive Relationships**

Human psychological processes impel us to give love and receive love under practically all conditions. Whenever and wherever an environment of trust and goodwill, however small, is created, the willingness and readiness of the participants to establish more positive relationships are significantly increased. Thus a creative upward cycle begins to emerge. The unity-based worldview engenders mutual trust—trust in the fact that we are one human race and that our fundamental needs are the same. This realization, in turn, makes new positive relationship possible and further broadens our understanding and appreciation of our fundamental oneness. These processes are aspects of the *relationship-formation* component of healing.

5. **Harness New Hope, Optimism, and Motivation to Rebuild Social Institutions**

New positive and authentic relationships engender a considerable degree of *hope, optimism, and motivation;* and the process of effective transformation of modes of behavior and conduct, in both the personal and social domains of life, is facilitated and accelerated to a remarkable level. Soon, a much greater degree of cooperation among these hitherto strangers becomes evident. They begin to see that their hopes and aspirations for themselves and their children are the same, that their sorrows and joys are parallel, and that their moral and ethical principles are analogous. This discovery of sameness in the context of their profound past estrangement, combined with their recent focus on the concepts of oneness of humanity and unity in diversity, gives them courage and confidence to follow their deepest quest—to make peace. We begin to see a remarkable *behavior-transformation*—from conflict and violence, to unity and peace.

The Integrative Nature of a Culture of Peace, a Culture of Healing, and the Process of Healing in the EFP Curriculum

Main Elements of the EFP Curriculum

1. Worldview Analysis and Transformation
   - Survival-Based Worldview (violence-prone)
   - Identity-Based Worldview (conflict-prone)
   - Unity-Based Worldview (peace-creating)

2. Relationship Analysis and Transformation
   - World is Dangerous (power-based relationship)
   - World is a Jungle (competition-based relationship)
   - World is One (unity in diversity)

3. Behavior Analysis and Transformation
   - From dichotomous to integrative thinking
   - From self-focus to all-focus interests and concerns
   - From indifference and conflict to empathy and unity

Main Elements of a Culture of Peace

1. Unity-Based Worldview
   - Unity is the supreme law of existence
   - Unity is the main prerequisite for peace
   - Unity and diversity are inseparable

2. Consciousness of Oneness of Humanity
   - Humanity is one
   - Human oneness is expressed in diversity
   - Human diversity is its source of beauty and richness

3. Peaceful Resolution of Conflicts
   - Conflict is absence of unity
   - Conflict resolution is the process of unity-creation
   - Peace is the outcome of unity, justice, and equality

Main Elements of a Culture of Healing

1. Mutual Trust
   - Trust in the fundamental nobility of human nature
   - Trust in the power of unity
   - Trust in the reality of goodness

2. Satisfaction of Basic Human Needs and Rights
   - Survival needs/rights(security, food, shelter, etc.)
   - Association needs/rights (justice, freedom, equality, etc.)
   - Spiritual needs/rights (purpose, meaning, etc.)

3. Hope, Optimism, and Resolve
   - Hope to overcome the negative impact of violence
   - Optimism to transcend the past justly and peacefully
   - Resolve to prevent future violence and war

Main Elements of the Process of Healing

1. Knowledge Acquisition
   - Truth Seeking
   - Truthfulness
   - Trustworthiness

2. Relationship Formation
   - Unity in Diversity
   - Mutual trust
   - Mutual acceptance and care

3. Behavior Transformation
   - Collaboration, forgiveness, and service at individual level
   - Justice and rule of law at societal level
   - Involving all members of the community in the task of creating a culture of peace

Figure 1: The Integrative Nature of a Culture of Peace and a Culture of Healing in the EFP Curriculum (Danesh, 2007b)

Key Questions for the Classroom

1. What is healing?

2. How would you describe the opposite of healing?

3. Can people heal from the effects of extreme violence?

4. Are the victims of violence more prone to becoming violent themselves?

5. Do such historical acts of violence as colonialism and slavery sow the seeds of future violence, involving future generations, as history seems to indicate?

6. Is the current violent state of the world due to its violent past?

7. Is there a relationship between violence and its frequent companions—poverty, disease, and corruption?

8. What conditions foster individual healing?

9. What conditions foster societal healing?

10. How do we know that healing from violence has taken place?

11. What are the characteristics of a healthy community?

Activity Ideas for Secondary Schools

Physical Education/ Biology	Research the biological processes associated with healing from a wound such as a cut or a broken bone. How does the body respond to the wound? What does the body do to heal it? And what parallels may be drawn with the healing of social wounds?
Dance/Drama	Animate, using creative movement, the process of healing. You can choose either physical healing (representing the tissues, cells, blood, antibodies, etc. of the body) or psychosocial healing (representing the thoughts, feelings, interactions, and relationships of the people or groups involved) or moral/ethical healing by demonstrating the process of transformation of an individual or group from conflict and violence to unity and peace.
Language/ Philosophy	Research the origins (etymology) of the term "healing" in several languages and, from that information, try to construct a cross-cultural philosophy of what healing involves and/or necessitates.
Religion	What perspectives on healing can be found in different religious traditions? Use the Internet to search the key words "religion and healing," "religion and unity," and "religion and peace" and see what you find. Try to gather perspectives from at least three different religious traditions and present your findings to your class using scriptural quotations, analogies/metaphors, and/or visual imagery.

Activity Ideas for Primary Schools

Classroom Management/ Language Arts	At the beginning of the year, discuss the three areas of knowledge-acquisition, relationship-formation, and behavior-transformation in relation to the role each student can play in the creation and functioning of a healthy classroom and school environment. Students can create a book consisting of three segments for each of the above three areas. Students are asked to write what they have achieved in each of the areas throughout the course of the year. Periodically, meet with each student to discuss his/her progress.
Social Studies	During the course of study of your country's history, discuss the impact of war and/or violence on different populations and persons in the society. Hold a discussion about what could have been done after the violent period to assist with the healing of the people. In small groups or as a large group, create plays, music, and other artistic modalities about how this group of people could have been healed after the violent event.
Science	In exploring the body, ask students to describe what has happened to them when they have been hurt or ill. Write the responses on a chart. Then ask the students to describe their feelings when they have been emotionally hurt (when a friend or family member has hurt their feelings), also writing them on a chart. Compare and contrast the similarities and differences in the ways of being hurt. A similar process can be repeated in discussing healing, with students describing the various conditions that need to be in place for healing from the physical and emotional hurts to take place.

In all of the above three activity ideas and those that you yourself would create, bring to the attention of the students the central role of *unity* in the process of healing, prevention of violence, and peaceful resolution of conflicts.

Personal Reflection

Reflection is a very powerful learning tool. It helps us to make sense of the things we are studying and the experiences we are going through. The more we reflect on ourselves, our relationships, and the world around us, the better prepared we are to discern, prioritize, and act upon issues of importance.

Becoming a peacemaker is a very important and challenging task. By reflecting on the principles of peace, we are better equipped to make decisions about our own development that will help us to confidently undertake the goal of peace building.

As we go through each of the EFP Curriculum units, try to set aside some time for the process of reflection.

The following questions are provided to help you begin this process.

Questions for Personal Reflection

Self

1. Am I in need of psychological healing from a traumatic experience(s)?
2. Can I transcend this traumatic experience and in the process create unity within myself and between myself and those whom I have been, and possibly still am, in conflict?
3. Can I accept from and care for those who are different from me?
4. Can I trust in the reality of "goodness" despite witnessing the widespread presence of "evil"?

Focus Question

Describe the nature and dynamics of "Inner Unity" and its impact on the personal healing process.

   a. What steps towards healing can you map out for yourself, based on the three processes of (1) knowledge-acquisition, (2) relationship-formation, and (3) behavior-transformation?

Family/Group

1. What are my current concerns regarding past violence in my family?
2. What can I do in my relationships to help to create a less-conflicted family?
3. Which of the following aspects of the healing—knowledge-acquisition, relationship-formation, and behavior-transformation—can I and my family develop to help foster healing both individually and as a family?

Focus Question

Describe the nature and dynamics of "Family Unity" and its impact on the personal healing process.

    a.   What steps can you map out for helping a family to recover from the impact of violence, based on the three processes of (1) knowledge-acquisition, (2) relationship-formation, and (3) behavior-transformation?

Society

    1.   How can a society recover from the impact of past and present violence and war?

    2.   How is the past history of violence in my society sowing seeds of present and possibly future violence?

    3.   How might I, along with other members of my society, strengthen the foundations of justice and rule-of-law in the institutions of our society?

Focus Question

Consider a recent violent conflict that has taken place in your own or another society:

    a.   What steps towards healing can you map out for the individuals and groups involved in this conflict, based on the three processes of (1) knowledge-acquisition, (2) relationship-formation, and (3) behavior-transformation?

World at Large

    1.   How is the current violent state of the world due to its violent past?

    2.   What is the relationship between violence, poverty, and disease?

    3.   To what extent and in what manner have large-scale social healing processes been effective in dealing with issues of violence in various countries throughout the world?

    4.   If we are to create peaceful communities and nations, what role does my country could play in the creation of conditions necessary for the development of a healthy global community?

Focus Question

The fact that the excessive gap between the rich and the poor is one major symptom of a violent world, what steps you and your friends and community can take to significantly help to remedy this situation?

Unit 9, Sample Lesson 1: Creating a Culture of Healing

Focus: The role of Knowledge-Acquisition, Relationship-Formation, and Behavior-Transformation in a Culture of Healing

Context

In a Culture of Healing, psychological healing and social recovery from the destructive impact of violence and war on individuals and communities take place within the processes of knowledge-acquisition, relationship-formation, and behavior-transformation.

Points for Understanding

Individual psychological health depends on three fundamental processes:

1. Knowledge-acquisition;
2. Relationship-formation; and
3. Behavior-transformation.

Knowledge-acquisition refers to the process of ever better understanding of self, others, and the world (nature, ideas, beauty, God) in the context of truth and trust—the two most important conditions for authentic and scientific understanding.

Relationship-formation, in addition to truth and trust, requires love, without which it is impossible to form healthy relationships. Environments conducive to such relationships are characterized by love of self, others, and the world.

Behavior-transformation comes into effect within the framework of such healthy relationships and newly acquired knowledge and insight, and our attitudes and approaches towards self, others, and the world begin to alter (H.B. Danesh, 2006).

When an individual engages constructively in the three processes of knowledge-acquisition, relationship-formation and behavior-transformation, s/he gradually develops a more universal and inclusive identity—a process identified in previous units as the formation of a "unity-based worldview."

Key Questions

1. What are the characteristics of a unity-based worldview?
2. How does the formation of a unity-based worldview help in the process of healing from the traumas of violence at a community level?
3. How can individuals actively construct the processes of knowledge-acquisition, relationship-formation, and behavior-transformation in order to cultivate peaceful and healthy relationships?

Learning Process

1. Write the following question on the board: "What kinds of wounds can conflict and violence inflict on individuals and groups?" Brainstorm with students on wounds of various types: physical, emotional, psychological, moral/spiritual, etc. Write key words on the board.

2. Invite students to begin a thought-experiment in which they have been given the task to determine a process of recovery and healing for an individual who has suffered the negative impacts of violence.

3. Write the following question on the board: "What are the characteristics of a healthy individual?"

4. Ask students to provide some suggestions—write ideas on the board. Encourage students to think of not only physical health, but especially psychological, emotional and moral/ethical/spiritual health.

5. Placing emphasis on the dimension of psychological health, ask students to share ideas in small groups on how individuals can nurture their own health. Ask them to classify their suggestions according to the three processes of knowledge-acquisition, relationship-formation, and behavior-transformation, and share with the class.

6. Ask students to consider whether these processes/strategies need to be pursued sequentially or simultaneously.

7. Affirm the contributions of the students while providing a review of the processes of knowledge-acquisition, relationship-formation, and behavior-transformation as treated in this unit.

Activities and Assignments

Teachers can choose from among the following sample assignments, or create their own:

1. **Journal**: In what ways have you been affected by violence—as a victim, a perpetrator, and/or bystander? How has this affected you? What are some things you can do to help yourself (and perhaps others) heal from the negative impact of violence?

2. **Design a Community Healing Project:** Discuss how violence has affected people in your community. Are there certain people who have been the victims? Are there identifiable perpetrators? Are the lines between victim and perpetrator blurred? Drawing on the idea of healing as a tripartite process of knowledge-acquisition, relationship-formation, and behavior-transformation, design a project and/or activity idea that could engage a large number of people from your community to help in the process of healing from the violence. Create an outline and action plan for implementing this project.

Additional Resources

Unit 2: Worldview, Review of Unity-based Worldview

Unit 9, Activity Reading 1

"Words of kindness are more healing to a drooping heart than balm or honey."
—Sarah Fielding (1710–1768), British novelist
The Adventures of David Simple, volume 5, bk. 7, ch. 10 (1754)

"America's present need is not heroics but healing; not nostrums but normalcy; not revolution but restoration."
—Warren Gamaliel Harding (1865–1923), U.S. president (1921–1923)
speech, June 1920, Boston

"From of the most High cometh healing."
—Ecclesiastes 38:2 (Old Testament)

"Rash words are like sword thrusts, but the tongue of the wise brings healing."
—Proverbs 12:18 (Hebrew Bible)

"America needed recovery, not revenge. The hate had to be drained and the healing begun."
—Gerald R. Ford (1913–2006), U.S. president (1974–1977)
A Time to Heal, p. 161

"Let him Who was love's teacher teach you too love's cure; Let the same hand that wounded bring the balm. Healing and poisonous herbs the same soil bears, And rose and nettle oft grow side by side."
—Ovid (Publius Ovidius Naso), (43 BC–AD 17–18), Roman poet
Remedia Amoris, ll. 43–46

"Most people live, whether physically, intellectually or morally, in a very restricted circle of their potential being. They make use of a very small portion of their possible consciousness, and of their soul's resources in general, much like a man who, out of his whole bodily organism, should get into a habit of using and moving only his little finger. Great emergencies and crises show us how much greater our vital resources are than we had supposed."
—William James (1842–1910), American psychologist and philosopher
<http://seekers.100megs6.com/healing_quotes.htm>

"O Allah, the Lord of the people! Remove the trouble and heal the patient, for You are the Healer. No healing is of any avail but Yours; healing that will leave behind no ailment."
—Prophet Muhammed
Hadith, Bukhari, vol. 7

"The Prophets of God should be regarded as physicians whose task is to foster the well-being of the world and its peoples, that, through the spirit of oneness, they may heal the sickness of a divided humanity."

—Bahá'u'lláh (1817–1892), Persian nobleman, prophet
Gleanings from the Writings of Bahá'u'lláh, p. 79

"All the religions of the world, while they may differ in other respects, unitedly proclaim that nothing lives in this world but Truth."

—Mohandas Gandhi (1869–1948), lawyer, non-violent activist,
former leader of Indian national Congress
<http://headlines.agapepress.org/archive/6/272006jj.asp>

"Though force can protect in emergency, only justice, fairness, consideration and cooperation can finally lead men to the dawn of eternal peace."
—Dwight D. Eisenhower (1890–1969), U.S. Army general and president (1953–1961)
<http://www.bellaonline.com/articles/art43663.asp>

Extended Exploration

Publications

Danesh, H.B. (2007a). "Education for Peace: The Pedagogy of Civilization." *Sustained Peace Education for Social Cohesion in International Conflict and Post-Conflict Societies* (working title). Editors: Zvi Beckerman and Claire McGlynn. Forthcoming.

———. (2007b). "A Culture of Healing." Chapter in a collection of papers. Jerusalem: Hebrew University of Jerusalem. Forthcoming.

———. (2006). "Towards an Integrative Theory of Peace Education." *Journal of Peace Education* 3.1 (March): 55–78.

———. (2002). "Breaking the Cycle of Violence: Education for Peace." *African Civil Society Organization and Development: Re-Evaluation for the 21st Century.* United Nations, New York, September 2002.

———. (1997). *The Psychology of Spirituality: From Divided Self to Integrated Self.* 2d ed. Hong Kong: Juxta Publishing.

———. (1995). *The Violence-Free Family: The Building Block of a Peaceful Civilization.* Ottawa: Bahá'í Studies Publication.

———. (1979). "The Violence-Free Society: A Gift for Our Children." *Bahá'í Studies* 6. Ottawa: Bahá'í Studies Publications.

Dewey, Larry. (2004). *War and Redemption: Treatment and Recovery in Combat-related Posttraumatic Stress Disorder.* Burlington, VT: Ashgate.

Hamber, B., and R. Wilson. (1999). "Symbolic Closure through Memory, Reparation and Revenge in Post-conflict Societies." Paper presented at the Traumatic Stress in South Africa Conference. Parktonian Hotel, Johannesburg, South Africa, 27–29 January 1999.

Hamber, B. (2003). "Healings." In *Reconciliation after Violent Conflict: A Handbook.* Stockholm, Sweden: International Institute for Democracy and Electoral Assistance.

———. (1995). "Dealing with the Past and the Psychology of Reconciliation: A Psychological Perspective of the Truth and Reconciliation Commission." The Centre for the Study of Violence & Reconciliation: Johannesburg, South Africa. Occasional Paper.

Huyse, Luc. (2003). Chapter 2: "The Process of Reconciliation." In *Reconciliation after Violent Conflict: A Handbook.* Ed. David Bloomfield, Teresa Barnes, and Luc Huyse, Stockholm: International Institute for Democracy and Electoral Assistance.

Loewald, Hans. (1960). "On the Therapeutic Action of Psychoanalysis." *International Journal of Psychoanalysis* 1(Jan.–Feb.): 16–33.

Reconciliation after Violent Conflict: A Handbook, Stockholm, Sweden: International Institute for Democracy and Electoral Assistance. Available online: <http://www.idea.int/publications/reconciliation/index.cfm>.

World Health Organization. *Constitution of the World Health Organization.* Geneva: World Health Organization, 1946. <http://www.searo.who.int/aboutsearo/const.htm>.

Web Links

Romo, Thomas, III, et al. "Wound Healing, Skin." <eMedicine: http://www.emedicine.com/ent/topic13.htm >.

"Wound Healing." <http://en.wikipedia.org/wiki/Wound_healing_phases>.

General Online Resources

The Columbia Encyclopedia Online. <http://www.bartleby.com/65>.

The Columbia World of Quotations. <http://www.bartleby.com/quotations>.

The Merriam-Webster Online Dictionary. <http://www.merriam-webster.com>.

Wikipedia: The Free Encyclopedia. <http://www.wikipedia.org>.

Unit 10

EDUCATIONAL METHODOLOGY GUIDE

This unit presents a variety of tools, guides, and printable templates that have been compiled to aid educators like you to integrate the Education for Peace concepts into your classroom in creative, engaging, and effective ways.

In this unit you will find:

- An introduction to the educational philosophy of the EFP Program;
- An overview of the teaching for understanding approach;
- A step-by-step guide to understanding-oriented lesson design;
- A framework for facilitating reflective processes in the classroom;
- A practical toolkit of teaching tips, activity ideas, and classroom management strategies;
- A guide to assessing your students' creative projects;
- Links to other great online resources for teachers.

A Message to the Youth

You are among the brightest and most idealistic members of today's global community. You represent world's future leaders, thinkers, and citizens. Before you lies both the opportunity and responsibility to lead the development of a civilization of peace in your respective countries and throughout the world. We sincerely hope that your primary concern will be to become peacemakers. Peace has always been the object of humanity's quest. However, as you all know, this quest has never been totally fulfilled.

Humanity has not been able to create a civilization of peace because it must first establish the main prerequisite for peace, which is **unity**. A world that is disunited and intolerant of its inherent diversity cannot be peaceful.

However, you will not be able to create unity until you first establish the main prerequisite for unity: **justice**. A world in which there is so much injustice cannot be united.

However, you will not be able to create justice unless you first establish its prerequisite: **equality**. A just world must be based on the equality of all its peoples in the context of the equality of women and men. Not until these two halves of humanity have equal rights and opportunities will justice be possible.

However, you will not be able to relate on an equal basis with each other unless you first achieve the prerequisite for equality: **maturity**. Such a maturity must characterize your psychological, social, political, moral, and spiritual development.

However, attainment of maturity is only possible when you have a **new worldview** and mindset based on the consciousness of humanity's fundamental **oneness** and **nobility**. It is through the impact of this new consciousness and worldview that you learn to become less self-centered. Your vision becomes world-embracing. Your thoughts become focused on the welfare of all humanity. Your conduct toward others becomes marked by humility. Your love becomes unconditional and all-embracing. It is then that your primary objective in life becomes to serve the peace and well-being of all humanity.

In order to achieve a lasting and progressive peace, you must simultaneously concentrate your thoughts, emotions, and willpower on the issues of the oneness of humanity, equality, justice, unity, and peace.

The world needs new courageous, righteous generations of peacemaker, and we hope you will arise as the first of these new generations.

—H.B. Danesh, Director, EFP-International
(Adapted from *Peace Moves*)

A Message to the Teachers

As you begin to familiarize yourself with the Education for Peace Program, you will no doubt recognize that we are engaging in an historic process together: the process of systematically raising up a generation of young people to create a culture of peace.

Humanity has always longed for peace but has never have been able to accomplish it. As we look at our world today, we see that it is burdened with conflict, misunderstanding, violence, and war. Something has to be done....Some group of people has to decide to create a culture of peace. Somewhere in the world, people with courage and vision must arise and organize their society in ways that are different from the others to become examples for the rest of the world.

Why should we make peace our primary focus and concern? Because the world has become dangerously afflicted with conflict and war. Humanity has suffered too much, is becoming seriously enfeebled with its persistent conflicts, and longs for positive change. And now that time is ripe for humanity to create peace throughout the world for the vision, conditions and means necessary for the establishment of peace are at hand. Indeed, every effort towards peace in this age has a greater impact than in every other epoch in human history.

In July 2000, when the first EFP pilot program began in Bosnia and Herzegovina (BiH), we were not sure that the process of building a culture of peace would be successful in a devastated country emerging from a most calamitous civil war. The conflict and violence had left deep and damaging wounds in the souls of the people and all aspects of life in that country. Then something remarkable began to happen: teachers, students, parents, and guardians from all segments of BiH society demonstrated a profound understanding and love for peace. After only 6 months, government officials in all parts of the country called for the introduction of the EFP Program in every school in BiH. So, the EFP staff and with BiH educators together developed a strategy for the introduction of EFP in all BiH schools. As of June 2006, the program has been introduced in a total of 112 schools, and plans have been approved and initiated for the inclusion of the EFP Program in the curriculum of all BiH schools (approximately 2,200) with more than 1.2 million students. The process has been neither perfect nor easy. But the majority of people involved have welcomed EFP enthusiastically, winning continuous successes through their efforts and revitalizing the spirit of optimism and hope in BiH, which is beginning to reverberate with the chords of peace again. We are now in a strong position to offer this highly successful program to teachers and educators all over the world.

Teachers are the most important catalysts in this process because it is ultimately education that shapes our students' worldviews, nurtures their capacities of mind and heart, helps them to envision a peaceful future, and determines their role in realizing it. We recognize and honor your determination to create a different future for your children and students than you yourself had to endure. Through your noble endeavors you will be setting the direction for the destiny of your respective communities and contributing to the well-being of the present generation and of generations to come. We wish you complete success and peace.

—H.B. Danesh, Director, EFP-International

Section 1

PHILOSOPHY OF
EDUCATION FOR PEACE

Education for a Civilization of Peace

The EFP educational philosophy maintains that human beings are subject to the processes of biological, emotional, intellectual, ethical, and spiritual development. Each is created with the inherent potential to develop his or her uniquely human capacities to know, to love, and to choose. Education for Peace upholds that, when properly educated and trained, a human being will use his or her capacities, talents, and energies in service to the creation of peace, justice, and prosperity for all humanity.

Rather than studying peace as a separate subject, Education for Peace proposes that peace should constitute the very framework within which *all* subjects of primary and secondary education are studied. Peace results from the holistic application of a "peace-based worldview" to all aspects of life, identity, relationships, learning, professional pursuits, societal organization, and leadership.

The principles of a peace worldview include:

- Recognition that humanity is one;
- Recognition that the oneness of humanity is expressed in diversity;
- Recognition that the fundamental challenge before humanity is to maintain its oneness while celebrating and fostering its diversity, and
- Recognition that this task cannot be accomplished through violence, but rather through open, creative, peaceful, just, and unifying processes of decision-making and problem-solving.

At the heart of the EFP process is the integration of these principles of peace into the daily lessons of every subject and every classroom. In such areas as literature, history, sociology, music, and even sports, the connections between the subject matter and the issue of peace may seem more explicit than in other subjects such as math, computer science, or physics. The universal character of these principles of peace, however, makes them relevant to every aspect of human learning and activity. In each subject area it is possible to (1) discern truths about the characteristics and prerequisites of peace, and (2) apply the perspective of a peace-oriented worldview to the direction, development, and application of that field of knowledge.

Worldview, Civilization, and Peace

(Excerpted from "An Integrative Theory of Peace" by H. B. Danesh, ©2004)

The formation of worldview and its ongoing development and revision is a lifelong process. Early on, through our life experiences and education, we begin to form our views on reality, human nature, the purpose of our life, and the nature of our relationships.

Worldview construction is an inherent aspect of the development of human consciousness and is therefore an inevitable and essential aspect of development of human individuals and societies alike. Every individual and every society has a worldview shaped by religious beliefs, philosophical concepts, political ideologies, and particular life experiences and environmental characteristics. In all societies, the main vehicle for both transfer and formation of worldview is education, both formal and informal.

Deliberately or inadvertently, however, most children around the world are educated within the framework of conflict-based worldviews. When we critically review the worldviews that shape and inform our current pedagogical philosophies and practices, it becomes evident that our approach to education revolves around the issue of conflict. This is equally true about education at home, in school, within the community, through the example of ethnic and national heroes and leaders, and through mass information and entertainment media.

When conflicts deteriorate into destructive and violent behaviors, the outcome is injury, suffering, waste, misery, and loss. Societies that have been affected by considerable conflict and/or violence bear the burden of these outcomes and, if not addressed in a healthy and healing manner, pass them on to future generations. Too frequently, unhealed wounds from past violence become the seeds and justification for future violent behaviors.

If we are to curb the reproduction of cultures of conflict and violence, then the conflict-based worldviews that inform most of our educational endeavors must be replaced with peace-based worldviews.

The Education for Peace Program views the purpose of education to be the cultivation of a world-encompassing civilization of peace. Towards this objective, the EFP Program considers the following four overarching, interrelated educational goals as priorities:

1. Development of a unity-based worldview;
2. Creation of a culture of peace;
3. Creation of a culture of healing;
4. Use of peace education as the framework for all educational activities.

The first objective necessitates that the members of a school community be systematically assisted to reflect on their own worldviews and gradually try to develop a peace-based worldview.

The second objective necessitates that a sense of trust be systematically cultivated within and among school communities—a process that is assisted by providing opportunities for shared peace-oriented activities through regularly held Peace Events.

Based on the mutual trust, hope, and optimism cultivated during intra- and inter-school peace events, the EFP Program approaches its third objective, namely, the creation of a culture of healing within and among the participating schools—a process in which communities gradually, but effectively, recover from the damages of war and protracted conflict that affect them, their families, and community life.

The fourth objective has far-reaching implications because it calls for a fundamental shift in our philosophy of education. It entails students in every classroom and subject being guided to examine the impact of a unity-based worldview on that subject. For example, how would history books be different if they were written from the perspective of a unity-based worldview rather than from the point of view of conflict, as they are written now? How would geography or biology or literature, or religious studies textbooks change? How would our approach to economics, political science, and sociology change when approached from the perspective of peace? When approached in this way, students and teachers alike become painfully aware of the bias with which they normally study various arts and science—a bias that always favors conflict. By establishing peace as the framework for all education, communities learn how to successfully prevent new conflicts and to resolve those that do arise in a peaceful manner, without resorting to violence.

A comprehensive program of peace education requires attention to the welfare of the family and modes of parenting; to the content of school curricula and pedagogical methodologies; and to community relationships, economic conditions, sociopolitical policies, and leadership practices. In essence, true education is a humanizing process with its ultimate aim to create a civilization of peace.

Educating for Peace and Healing

(Excerpted from "An Integrative Theory of Peace" by H. B. Danesh, ©2004)

Creating A Culture of Peace

One of the main objectives of the Education for Peace Program is to help members of the participating school communities create a culture of peace in and among their schools. The first and the most crucial step towards achievement of this goal is to create an atmosphere of trust among all participants. EFP approaches this task through three fundamental strategies: (1) It engages all participants in a deep and sustained reflection on their personal and group worldviews, and their role in either creating disunity and conflict or peace. (2) It engages students in every classroom and subject matter to examine the impact of application of the unity-based worldview on each subject. (3) It infuses a sense of trust into the school community and helps the participants in their efforts to create a culture of peace within and among their respective school communities by creating opportunities for shared peace-oriented activities. This is done through the institution of "peace events" at local, regional, and state-wide levels. These peace events take place at least twice every academic year and involve all students, teachers, school staff, parents/guardians, and the larger community. In the course of these events, students in every classroom, under the guidance of their teachers, make a number of presentations, usually using the medium of arts (music, dance, drama, film, paintings, poetry, etc.). The purpose of these presentations is to share with the school community and community at large the impact of a unity-based worldview on every aspect of human life. The themes often chosen are issues of family relationships, gender equality, unity in diversity, interethnic and interreligious harmony, the environment, and various approaches to governance, such as authoritarianism vs. democracy. In a very real sense, during these events, students become teachers of their parents and other adults in the audience. And because students from all grades (1–12) participate in this process and because students in every classroom are engaged, the whole community of people becomes actively involved in these peace events.

A representative number of students, teachers, and parents/guardians from each EFP school then travel to another city for participation in the regional and national peace events. Hundreds of individuals (students, teachers, parents/guardians, leaders, the media) from all parts of the country participate in this celebration of peace and share the profound hunger and desire of the students and many of their teachers and parents/guardians to re-establish normal and healthy relationships with their fellow citizens, to share in the joys and sorrows of life, and gradually to begin to heal the wounds of conflict, violence, and war through the healing remedy of peace.

Creating A Culture of Healing

Another of the main objectives of the Education for Peace Program is the creation of a culture of healing within and among the participating communities. During the first year of the implementation of the EFP Program in war-torn Bosnia and Herzegovina, while we were focused on the task of creating a culture of peace through worldview transformation, an enlightening and unexpected experience pointed to a second fundamental issue—creating a *culture of healing*—that must also be the main objective of successful peace education.

Several important issues emerged with respect to the process of healing the psychosocial and moral/spiritual wounds and trauma sustained as a result of severe conflict, violence, and war. First and foremost is the issue of *mutual trust*. A high degree of mutual trust needs to be established among the participants themselves and between the participants and the EFP training team. The second prerequisite for a culture of healing is the presence of the necessary conditions to satisfy the tripartite *human needs* for security, identity, and meaning. The third requisite for the process of healing is the presence of conditions of *hope and optimism*—hope for a better future and optimism for the ability to overcome future conflicts without recourse to violence.

These conditions—mutual trust, meeting fundamental human needs, and hope and optimism—are among the most important prerequisites for creating a culture of healing. These three conditions are also the essential components of the state of *unity* required for the process of physical, psychological, social, and spiritual healing. The World Health Organization (WHO) defines health as a positive state of physical, emotional, and social well-being. This definition covers physical, emotional, and social aspects of health, however, it does not include the moral-ethical-spiritual dimension, which is also an important aspect of both individual and community health. Within the context of the culture of healing, this latter dimension of health is particularly important. The idea of inclusion of spiritual health into the concept of culture of healing is particularly relevant to the issue of peace education, because, peace, like health, is at once a state of physical, emotional, social, and spiritual wholeness and unity. The moral dimension of peace is particularly relevant to the issue of culture of healing. Such issues as justice, equality, and concern for others are moral issues with significant social, political, and economic expressions; and all are extremely important in alleviating some of the wounds of conflict and violence.

Section 2

Teaching for Understanding

Teaching for Understanding

> To begin with the end in mind means to start with a clear understanding of your
> destination. It means to know where you're going so that you better understand where
> you are now so that the steps you take are always in the right direction.
> —Stephen R. Covey, *The Seven Habits of Highly Effective People*

The process of teaching can have many different goals: it can aim to transfer information and skills, to shape attitudes and perspectives, and to foster deep understanding of abstract concepts. Any complex unit of study will involve many targets simultaneously: knowledge, skills, attitudes, habits of mind, and understanding. Above all, teaching must create in the hearts of students a deep love of learning and in their minds an unceasing quest to search for truth.

Unfortunately, due to testing performance pressures, many schools focus only on teaching certain facts or skill sets. Students leave the class with knowledge of these facts, but very often do not know how to apply this knowledge, neither understanding its significance in the world at large, nor recognizing its relationship to other areas of knowledge.

For peace education to have a transformative effect on the lives of students, they must not only **know** at an intellectual level what peace is and what peace requires but also **understand deeply, personally, and practically** that authentic approaches to peace require a searching examination of our perceptions of reality, of human nature, of ourselves, of the purpose of our lives, and of the purpose of society. With this understanding firmly in place, they must also acquire the skills to apply their learning in the real world.

An "understanding-oriented"[1] approach to teaching makes complex ideas more accessible to students by involving them in active questioning, trying theories out, and rethinking what they thought they knew. It gives students a deeper understanding of the broader concepts or "big ideas" underlying specific lessons, helps them recognize larger connective patterns among various subjects, and applies their understanding in real-life activities. Through guided inquiry, abstract ideas become more accessible, connected, meaningful, and useful.

Such an approach is particularly useful for integrating the concepts of Education for Peace into standard curriculum topics, since the universal principles of peace transcend and connect all subjects, and since the goal of Education for Peace is to learn how to put peace into action.

---

1. The "understanding-oriented" approach described here is based on the "Backwards Design" method developed by Grant Wiggins and Jay McTighe. See *Understanding by Design,* Alexandria, Virginia: Association for Supervision and Curriculum Development, 1998.

Six Facets of Understanding[2]

How can you tell if a student has understood something? The most common way to demonstrate understanding is by explanation. If you can explain something, you probably understand it fairly well. But there are other ways of demonstrating understanding, and students frequently differ in which "style of understanding" they feel most comfortable with. If allowed, students can often demonstrate understanding better through assessment methods that tap into other understanding styles. The book *Understanding by Design* asserts that there are six facets of understanding (see Table 1).

Facets of Understanding	Associated Key Questions
Facet 1: Explanation Ability to offer explanations or theories that provide knowledgeable and defendable accounts of events, actions, and ideas.	• Why is that so? • What explains such events? • How can that be proven? • To what is this connected? • How does it work?
Facet 2: Interpretation Ability to decipher narratives, metaphors, images, and artistic renderings that contain meaning.	• What does it mean? • Why does it matter? • What does it illustrate or illuminate in human experience? • How does it relate to me?
Facet 3: Application Ability to use knowledge effectively in new situations and different contexts.	• How and where can we use this knowledge, skill, or process? • How should my thinking and action be modified to meet the demands of this particular situation?
Facet 4: Perspective Ability to see critical and insightful points of view.	• From whose point of view? • From which vantage point? • What is assumed that needs to be made explicit? • Is there adequate evidence? • What are its limits?
Facet 5: Empathy Ability to get "inside" another person's feelings, to adopt another perspective or worldview.	• How does it seem from their perspective? • What do they see that I don't? • What do I need to experience if I am to understand? • What was the artist or agent feeling, seeing, and trying to make me feel and see?
Facet 6: Self-Knowledge Ability to recognize one's ignorance and how one's patterns of thought and action inform as well as prejudice understanding.	• How does who I am shape my views? • What are the limits of my understanding? • What are my "blind spots"? • What am I prone to misunderstand because of prejudice, habit, or style?

Table 1: Six Facets of Understanding
(Excerpted from *Understanding By Design,* Grant Wiggins and Jay McTighe, ©1998)

---

2. Copyright: Association for Supervision and Curriculum Development, 1998. Used with permission. The Association for Supervision and Curriculum Development is a worldwide community of educators advocating sound policies and sharing best practices to achieve the success of each learner. To learn more, visit ASCD at <www.ascd.org>.

Performance Verbs[3]

(Based on the "Six Facets of Understanding")

When planning authentic assessment and learning activities, the style of understanding you are aiming the activity at is related to what it is you are asking the students to do; therefore, the verb is an indicator of the understanding style you are prompting students to exercise. Table 2 depicts verbs that seem to be best suited for each of the various styles of understanding.

Explain	Interpret	Apply	Perspective	Empathy	Self-knowledge
Demonstrate	Create analogy	Adapt	Analyze	Assume role of	Be aware of
Derive	Critique	Build	Argue	Be like	Realize
Describe	Document	Create	Compare	Be open to	Recognize
Design	Evaluate	Decide	Contrast	Imagine	Reflect
Exhibit	Illustrate	Invent	Criticize	Consider	Self-assess
Justify	Make sense of	Produce	Infer	Relate	Predict
Translate	Solve	Role-play	Prove	Tell a story	Test
Show		Use			

Table 2: Performance Verbs based on the Six Facets of Understanding

This list is by no means exhaustive, but rather gives examples of how the action determines the style of understanding that the teacher is aiming for. All units should use a few styles since students naturally vary in their preferred styles and should be allowed to approach material from a few styles.

---

3. Source: Grant Wiggins and Jay McTighe, *Understanding By Design*, Alexandria, Virginia: Association for Supervision and Curriculum Development, 1998.

Bloom's Taxonomy of Learning

As a point of comparison with the "Six Facets of Understanding" model, Benjamin Bloom's taxonomy[4] classifies cognitive learning into six categories of intellectual skills, arranged by increasingly challenging levels of abstraction (See Table 3).

Knowledge	Comprehension	Application	Analysis	Synthesis	Evaluation
Arrange	Classify	Apply	Analyze	Organize	Appraise
Define	Convert	Sequence	Appraise	Assemble	Argue
Duplicate	Discuss	Demonstrate	Observe	Integrate	Assess
Label	Explain	Dramatize	Compare	Compose	Verify
List	Interpret	Employ	Contrast	Design	Attach value to
Memorize	Identify	Illustrate	Criticize	Create	Defend
Name	Indicate	Carry out	Detect	Develop	Estimate
Order	Locate	Operate	Discover	Summarize	Judge
Recognize	Extrapolate	Repair	Explore	Formulate	Predict
Relate	Restate	Perform	Break down	Theorize	Rank
Recall	Abstract	Solve	Question	Generalize	Support
Reproduce	Translate	Use	Test	Conclude	Evaluate

Table 3: Bloom's Taxonomy of Learning

Bloom does not include affective learning in his taxonomy. Affective learning is demonstrated by behaviors indicating attitudes of awareness, interest, attention, concern, and responsibility, the ability to listen and respond in interactions with others, and the ability to demonstrate those attitudinal characteristics or values that are appropriate to the situation and the field of study. This domain relates to emotions, attitudes, appreciations, and values, such as enjoying, conserving, respecting, and supporting. Verbs applicable to the affective domain include accepts, attempts, challenges, defends, joins, judges, praises, questions, shares, supports, and volunteers.

---

4. Adapted from: B.S. Bloom, ed., *Taxonomy of Educational Objectives: The Classification of Educational Goals,* Handbook I, *Cognitive Domain,* New York: Longman, 1956.

Designing Learning Goals / Standards

(Adapted from Grant Wiggins and Jay McTighe, *Understanding By Design,* ©1998)

One of the first steps involved in designing an "understanding-oriented" unit is to identify the learning goals for the unit and/or lesson based on what enduring understandings you would like your students to gain. Clear learning goal statements are central to designing coherent learning activities.

To craft effective learning goal statements, it can be helpful to distinguish three degrees of specificity and clarity (See Table 4).

Topical statements are the least specific. They merely define the topic to be addressed without specifying what is to be understood or how:

"Students will understand poverty."

General understandings are a bit more specific. They identify what needs to be understood in an overall sense, but provide little help into the specific insights to be gained or the methods and assessments best used to gain and display such understanding:

"Students will understand the causes and effects of poverty."

Specific understandings not only summarize the particular understandings sought but also suggest the kinds of work needed to achieve and show such an understanding:

"Students will demonstrate through social and statistical analysis and role-plays their understanding of poverty as a global crisis in which millions of people chronically lack the resources, capabilities, opportunities, security, or power necessary to support basic well-being and dignity."

Table 4: Three degrees of specificity and clarity

Teacher-designers will often need to amplify or sharpen the framing of the content standards into useful matters of understanding.

As you develop your EFP-integrated lesson plans, it can be useful to identify in your learning goal statements both the general and specific understandings you wish students to gain.

A worksheet for developing understanding-oriented goal statements is provided on the next page.

Designing Learning Goals/Standards: Worksheet (Example)

Lesson/Unit Topic: Civil War

Students will understand:

Topic	General Themes	Specific Themes & Processes
• Poverty	• Causes of poverty • Effects of poverty	• Definition: lack of means for basic well-being and dignity • Expanded notion of "means": resources, capabilities, opportunities, security, power, etc. • Global dimensions: millions affected around the world

Projects, Performances, Assessment Measures

Students will demonstrate their understanding through:

• Statistical and social analyses
• Role-plays

Statement of Learning Goal/Standard

Now re-state the overall learning goal by integrating all of the elements identified above:

Students will demonstrate through social and statistical analysis and role-plays their understanding of poverty as a global crisis in which millions of people chronically lack the resources, capabilities, opportunities, security or power necessary to support basic well-being and dignity.

Designing Learning Goals/Standards: Worksheet[5]

Lesson/Unit Topic:	

Students will understand:

Topic	General Themes	Specific Themes & Processes
•	• •	• • • •

Projects, Performances, Assessment Measures

Students will demonstrate their understanding through:

Statement of Learning Goal/Standard

Now re-state the overall learning goal by integrating all of the elements identified above:

---

5. Adapted from *Understanding By Design*, Grant Wiggins and Jay McTighe, ©1998.

Essential Questions: The Doorways To Understanding[6]

(Excerpted from Grant Wiggins and Jay McTighe, *Understanding By Design*, ©1998)

A key component in the design and delivery of good "understanding-oriented" lessons is the posing of "essential questions."

Questions render a unit design more coherent and engage students more directly in the learning process. Without using questions to focus instruction and pursue overarching ideas, teaching can easily fall into superficial and purposeless coverage, leaving students to feel confronted with a set of disconnected activities. In such a classroom environment, minimal understanding of important ideas takes place. **Important ideas must be questioned and verified if they are to be understood.**

What types of questions might guide our teaching and engage students in uncovering the important ideas at the heart of each subject? Not just any question will do. Consider the following questions and notice how they differ from those typically posed during daily lessons and in textbooks:

- Is there enough to go around (e.g., food, clothes, water)?
- Is history a history of progress?
- Does art reflect culture or shape it?
- Are mathematical ideas inventions or discoveries?
- Must a story have a beginning, middle, and end?
- When is a law unjust?
- Is gravity a fact or a theory?
- What do we fear?
- Who owns what and why?
- Is biology destiny?

These types of questions cannot be answered satisfactorily in a sentence—and that's the point. To get at matters of deep and enduring understanding, we need to use provocative and multilayered questions that reveal the richness and complexities of a subject. We refer to such questions as "essential" because they point to the key inquiries and the core ideas of a discipline. Note that there may not be "right" or "wrong" answers to essential questions. Their purpose is not to measure student understanding but to guide students to probe and understand further.

We find it helpful to distinguish between two types of curriculum-framing questions: *essential* questions and *unit* or *topical* questions. Unit questions are more subject- and topic-specific, and therefore better suited for framing particular content and inquiry, leading to the often more subtle essential questions.

Good essential questions have the following criteria in common:

- Open-ended questions that resist a simple or single right answer;

---

6. Copyright: Association for Supervision and Curriculum Development, 1998. Used with permission. The Association for Supervision and Curriculum Development is a worldwide community of educators advocating sound policies and sharing best practices to achieve the success of each learner. To learn more, visit ASCD at <www.ascd.org>.

- Deliberately thought-provoking, counterintuitive, and/or controversial;
- Require students to draw upon content knowledge and personal experience;
- Can be revisited throughout the unit to engage students in evolving dialogue and debate;
- Lead to other essential questions posed by students.

Such questions are not just posed once orally by teachers. They are posted on blackboards, are used as the headings of student pages in notebooks, and are printed in unit handouts. They frame and structure the lessons and give rise to appropriate research, note taking, and final performance.

A worksheet for developing essential questions for your unit or lesson is provided on the following page.

Essential Questions: Worksheet (Example)

Graphic organizers can help you develop essential questions for your unit or lesson. Look at the following examples for ideas. Blank organizers are provided on the next page.

Unit/Lesson Topic: Ecosystems		
Enduring Understandings	**Essential Questions**	**Topical Questions**
Unity is life; life is unity.	What makes life possible? What holds life together?	What is the organizing principle of ecosystems? At how many levels of an ecosystem can the condition of unity be found?
Unity is the purposeful integration of diverse entities in a state of harmony and cooperation.	What is unity?	What do ecosystems teach us about the principle of "unity-in-diversity"?
Unity results in the creation of new, evolving entities usually of a higher nature.	How can we know if unity is present in a given situation?	What happens when the unity of an ecosystem is damaged?

Enduring Understanding: Unity is life; life is unity	
Facets of Understanding	**Essential Questions**
Explanation	What makes life possible? What force maintains life?
Interpretation	What can the relationship between unity and life be likened to?
Application	If unity is essential to life, what skills ought schools teach young people to become unifiers?
Perspective	Are all types of unity beneficial? Does the statement "unity is life" need further qualification?
Empathy	It's hard to be unified with some people. What positive characteristics do they and I share? How do I appear from their perspective?
Self-Knowledge	What habits or prejudices do I have that possibly prevent me from being more of a unifier? What positive steps could I take to become a unifier?

Essential Questions: Worksheet

Here are two graphic organizers that can help you create the essential questions for your unit or lesson.

Unit/Lesson Topic:		
Enduring Understandings	**Essential Questions**	**Topical Questions**

Enduring Understanding:	
Facets of Understanding	**Essential Questions**
Explanation	
Interpretation	
Application	
Perspective	
Empathy	
Self-Knowledge	

How Students Learn Best

(Source: John L. Brown, *Making the Most of Understanding by Design*, ©2004)[7]

Research into the best practices in education indicates that:

- Students learn actively, not passively.
- Students learn best when they actively construct meaning through experience-based learning activities.
- A student's culture, experiences, and previous knowledge (i.e., cognitive schema) shape all new learning.
- Learning depends on three dominant brain functions: (1) an innate search for meaning and purpose when learning; (2) an ongoing connection between emotion and cognition; and (3) an innate predisposition to find patterns in the learning environment, beginning with wholes rather than parts.
- Students' application and transfer of learning to new situations and contexts does not occur automatically. Teachers must help students to scaffold knowledge and skills; they plan for transfer by helping the learner move from modeling to guided practice to independent application.
- Knowing or being able to do something does not guarantee that the learner understands it.
- Students benefit from a curriculum that cues them into big ideas, enduring understandings, and essential questions.

---

7. Copyright 2004. The Association for Supervision and Curriculum Development. All rights reserved. <http://www.ascd.org/portal/site/ascd/template.chapter/menuitem.ccf6e1bf6046da7cdeb3ffdb62108a0c /?chapterMgmtId=fe73177a55f9ff00VgnVCM1000003d01a8c0RCRD>. Accessed 05-01-2005. Used with permission. The Association for Supervision and Curriculum Development is a worldwide community of educators advocating sound policies and sharing best practices to achieve the success of each learner. To learn more, visit ASCD at <www.ascd.org>.

Varying Teaching Styles

While designing lesson plans and activities, it is useful to remember that the teaching process can be structured in a variety of ways. There are four basic types of teaching styles:

- **Teacher-centered:** The teacher provides and controls the flow of content that the student is to receive and assimilate. Uses didactic methods, lectures, teacher-prepared notes, and exercises.
- **Teacher-assisted:** The instructor demonstrates and models what is expected (viz. skills and processes) and then acts as a coach or guide to assist students to apply the knowledge. Uses class discussion and interactive exercises.
- **Student-assisted:** The teacher designs activities, social interactions, or problem-solving situations that allow students to practice applying course content. Responsibility is placed on the students to take initiative and help each other to achieve results for the various tasks. Often involves small group work and research processes.
- **Student-centered:** The instructor delegates and places much of the control and responsibility for learning on the students. Students may be required to design and implement complex tasks that require student initiative and often group work to complete, with the teacher functioning solely in a consultative role. Often involves seminar formats, group initiated projects, and group presentations.

Each teaching style has certain advantages and limitations. Given that students vary in terms of their preferred learning styles, it is beneficial if teachers can vary their use of these different teaching styles into the course of given unit or lesson, thereby increasing the opportunities for all students to learn effectively.

Some teachers find that the following time allocations for various teaching styles within a given lesson period work very well:

- Teacher-centered (10 mins.)
- Teacher-assisted (10 mins.)
- Student-assisted (20 mins.)
- Student-centered (20 mins.)

Indicators of Teaching for Understanding[8]

(Excerpted from "Indicators of Teaching for Understanding" by Jay McTighe and Eliot Seif)

What are the characteristics of an "understanding-oriented" classroom?

A good "understanding-oriented" study unit:

- Reflects a coherent design—big ideas and essential questions clearly guide the design of assessments and teaching/learning activities.
- Makes clear distinctions between big ideas, essential questions, and the knowledge and skills necessary for learning the ideas and answering the questions.
- Uses multiple forms of assessment to let students demonstrate their understanding in various ways.
- Incorporates the six facets of understanding into instruction and assessment—students are provided opportunities to explain, interpret, apply, shift perspective, empathize, and self-assess.
- Assesses understanding through authentic performance tasks calling for students to demonstrate their understanding and apply knowledge and skills.
- Establishes clear performance criteria for teacher-, peer-, and self-evaluations of student products and presentations.
- Creates opportunities for students to revisit and rethink important ideas to deepen their understanding.
- Incorporates a variety of resources. The textbook is only one resource among many.
- Extends learning beyond the classroom.

The teacher:

- Informs students of the big ideas and essential questions, performance requirements, and evaluation criteria at the beginning of the unit or course.
- Captures and holds students' interest through creative teaching strategies to help them explore big ideas and essential questions.
- Facilitates students' active construction of meaning (rather than simply telling them what to know).
- Promotes opportunities for students to "unpack their thinking"—to explain, interpret, apply, shift perspective, empathize, or self-assess (incorporates the six facets of understanding).
- Uses questioning, probing, and feedback to stimulate student reflection and rethinking.
- Teaches basic knowledge and skills in the context of big ideas and explores essential questions.
- Uses information from ongoing assessments as to check for students' understanding and to adjust instruction.
- Looks beyond the textbook and uses a variety of interdisciplinary and real-world resources to promote understanding.

---

8. Copyright Jay McTighe and Eliot Seif. Used with permission. Source: <http://www.ubdexchange.org/resources/news-articles/article4.html>. (Accessed 05-01-2005.)

The learners:

- Can describe the goals (big ideas and essential questions) and performance requirements of the unit or course.
- Can explain what they are doing and why (i.e., how today's work relates to the larger unit or course goals).
- Are captivated at the beginning and remain engaged throughout the unit or course.
- Can describe the criteria by which their work will be evaluated.
- Are engaged in activities that help them to learn the big ideas and answer the essential questions.
- Are engaged in activities that promote explanation, interpretation, application, perspective taking, empathy, and self-assessment (the six facets of understanding).
- Demonstrate that they are learning the background knowledge and skills that support the big ideas and essential questions.
- Have opportunities to reflect and generate relevant questions.
- Are involved in self- or peer-assessment based on established criteria and performance standards.
- Use the criteria or rubrics to guide and revise their work.
- Set relevant goals for further development based on assessment feedback.
- Carry their learning beyond the classroom into other subject areas and real-world experiences.

In the classroom environment:

- The big ideas and essential questions are central to the work of the students, the classroom activity, and the norms and culture of the classroom.
- Big ideas, essential questions, and criteria or scoring rubrics are posted.
- Students are expected and encourage to arrive at an understanding of the big ideas and to answer the essential questions.
- Samples or models of student work are made visible.
- The environment is challenging but nonthreatening, and students receive ample encouragement to learn and develop personally. All students and their ideas are treated with dignity and respect.

Section 3

Creating "Understanding-Oriented" Lessons

Lesson Planning

Lesson plans are part of a well-structured and systematic curriculum. They function as aids for teachers to transfer knowledge to, examine attitudes with, and develop skills among students through developmentally appropriate learning processes. Lesson plans reflect the educational philosophy of the educator and when well designed are self-explanatory and enhance the professional capability of the teachers using them.

There are many schools of thought regarding the best approach to lesson design. The approach adopted in the EFP Program is based on the "Backward Design" method.[9] This approach is widely viewed as a "best practice" in modern pedagogy and harmonizes well with the educational objectives of Education for Peace. The model is referred to as a "backward design" method because it begins by examining the desired outcomes of the learning process, and builds activities backwards to achieve those outcomes. In the EFP-World Program, this method has been adapted to suit the particular needs of EFP and is referred to as the "Understanding-Oriented" approach to lesson design.

In the "understanding-oriented" approach, teachers place priority on the enduring understandings they wish students to gain. By focusing on understanding broader principles and concepts, students develop the ability to contextualize information and data, and to connect learning in one area with relevant issues in other fields.

Teachers like you who recognize the importance of rearing the young generation to be capable and committed peace-builders can apply an "understanding-oriented" approach to help students explore the principles of peace within and across subject areas, and to apply these principles to challenges both within and beyond the classroom.

To help you get started, a number of templates are provided on the following pages.

---

9 Grant Wiggins and Jay McTighe, *Understanding by Design*, Alexandria, Virginia: Association for Supervision and Curriculum Development, 1998.

How the Understanding-Oriented Approach Works

The understanding-oriented approach[10] to lesson design and teaching begins by identifying the enduring understandings students should gain and works backwards from there.

Standard Lesson Topic

What topic/curriculum standards does the unit address?

Step I	(A) Identifying the Desired Results/Enduring Understandings What are the big ideas and EFP principles underlying and/or associated with this unit?
Step II	(B) Identifying the Essential Questions/Activities What essential questions/activities will guide this unit and focus the teaching/learning process? What questions connect this subject with other overarching themes and ideas?
Step III	(C) Identifying the Knowledge and Skills to be Acquired What key knowledge and skills will students acquire as a result of this unit?

Most approaches to lesson plan design start with Step C move to B, and if there is any time get to A. The "understanding-oriented" approach aims to do exactly the opposite: to prioritize authentic and lifelong understanding in students.

---

10. Based on the work of Grant Wiggins and Jay McTighe, *Understanding By Design,* Alexandria, Virginia: Association for Supervision and Curriculum Development, 1998. The Association for Supervision and Curriculum Development is a worldwide community of educators advocating sound policies and sharing best practices to achieve the success of each learner. To learn more, visit ASCD at <www.ascd.org>.

Introducing EFP into Standard Lessons

Bringing EFP into the classroom does not mean that the word *peace* has to be used at every opportunity. In fact, an entire lesson can be taught without referring specifically to "peace," while nonetheless still discussing principles that are relevant to peace and that illustrate the dynamics and prerequisites of peace.

The dimensions and dynamics of peace are universal. The process of infusing peace principles into every lesson is best achieved when teachers use an interdisciplinary approach to lesson design. Students will understand concepts more clearly if examples are given that help them to connect the big ideas to identifiable patterns in the subject-specific content and to life experience.

What curricular elements might be taught with an understanding orientation? Here are some examples:

- *Principles, laws, theories, or concepts* that students can verify, induce, or justify through inquiry and construction;
- *Counterintuitive, nuanced, subtle, or otherwise easily misunderstood ideas*, such as gravity, evolution, imaginary numbers, irony, texts, formulas, theories, and concepts;
- *The conceptual or strategic element of any skill* (e.g., persuasion in writing or "creating space" in soccer): the clarification of means and ends, and insight into strategy, leading to greater purposefulness and less mindless use of techniques. Such mindfulness can only come about by active reflection upon and analysis of performance (i.e., what works, what doesn't, and why).

It is true that not everything we ask students to learn must be thoroughly understood. The purpose of a course or unit of study, the age of the learners, and the time available all determine how much or how little teachers can expect students to understand. Nevertheless, every unit will have features or themes that can be developed from an understanding-oriented perspective.

"Understanding-Oriented" Lesson Design Worksheet

Grade/Topic:

Stage 1: Desired Results
Enduring Understandings
• What enduring understandings are desired? • What EFP concepts should students **understand**? • What are the "big ideas"?

Knowledge & Skills	Essential Questions
• What key knowledge and skills will the students acquire during this unit? • What **culture of peace skills** will students acquire?	• What essential questions will **guide** this unit and **focus** both teaching and learning? • What challenges to current thinking does a peace-oriented worldview raise?

Stage 2: Authentic Assessment
• Through what authentic assessment tasks will students demonstrate their understanding, knowledge, and skills? • What quizzes or tests would help them demonstrate discrete knowledge? • What sorts of sample work or behaviors will demonstrate the students' understanding, knowledge, and skills? • How will students reflect upon and self-evaluate their learning?

Stage 3: Learning Activities
How will the unit: • Help students know where the unit is going? • Engage the students' interest? • Help students explore the issues and key ideas? • Provide opportunities for students to rethink and revise their understandings? • Help student **apply** their understanding to issues in the contemporary world? • Allow students to evaluate their work and its implications? Learning activities can involve artistic/dramatic/creative projects, research, presentations and/or written assignments. You can include teacher-centered, teacher-assisted, student-assisted, and student-centered instructional approaches. Refer to the "Six Facets of Understanding" and the "Performance Verbs" for ideas. Try to include participatory, investigative, and/or consultative exercises!

Adapted from *Understanding By Design*, Grant Wiggins and Jay McTighe, Alexandria, Virginia: Association for Supervision and Curriculum Development, 1998. Used with permission.

"Understanding-Oriented" Lesson Design Worksheet

Grade/Topic:

Stage 1: Desired Results
Enduring Understandings

Knowledge & Skills	*Essential Questions*

Stage 2: Authentic Assessment

Stage 3: Learning Activities

Source: *Understanding By Design,* Grant Wiggins and Jay McTighe, Alexandria, Virginia: Association for Supervision and Curriculum Development, 1998. Used with permission.

Sample "Understanding-Oriented" Lesson

Grade/Topic:

Stage 1: Desired Results
Enduring Understandings
• Unity is Life, Life is Unity • The importance of Unity in Diversity for the preservation of healthy relationships • The importance of Gender Equality in family life and society

Knowledge & Skills	Essential Questions
• Critical analysis of Shakespeare's play: poetry, character development, superstition in Elizabethan times	• What can be obstacles to unity? • What does the preservation of unity require? • What does gender equality add to the experience of love? • How does inequality affect decision-making?

Stage 2: Authentic Assessment
• Rewrite the scene between Juliet and her father so that both characters have family unity as their goal. • Ask two students to memorize and present the scene as written by Shakespeare and the new scene written by the class. Present these scenes to a younger class and ask them what the basic underlying differences between the two scenes are.

Stage 3: Learning Activities

Teacher-Centered
- 15 min. lecture on an aspect of Elizabethan theatre.

Teacher-Assisted
- Informal quiz on previous day's work. Leads into class discussion.
- Play will be read orally with pauses for "translating" Shakespeare's meaning in the text.

Student-Assisted
- In small groups the students will answer written questions.
- In small groups students will memorize and perform a scene.

Student-Centered
- Students will write in a daily reflective journal about their thoughts on the play's themes. Students may read them aloud if they wish as a basis for class discussion.
- Students will write and present an independently prepared presentation linking the enduring understandings to the play or to the life and times of Elizabethans. Must be multimedia, contain a creative component, and contain an interactive component with the other class members.

Sample Lesson Copyright 2007 Barbara Rager.

Preplanning Questions for Teachers

As you set out to prepare an "understanding-oriented" lesson plan, take a moment to ask yourself the following questions:

- What are the bigger issues in this unit/lesson?

- What Education for Peace principles and themes correlate to the unit/lesson topic?

- What background experience, knowledge, or other factors (e.g., culture) do my students come with to the classroom?

- What resources are available (fieldtrips, guest speakers, etc.)?

- What methods of assessment are possible and/or required?

- What various points of view can be taken on the subject?

- What activities can involve students in designing, exploring, discovering, and evaluating key issues related to the topic?

- How can the students apply what they learn in an "action for peace" mode?

- What are the curriculum and teaching goals that should be met?

Key Education for Peace Themes

Bringing EFP into the classroom does not mean that the word *peace* has to be used at every opportunity. In fact, an entire lesson can be taught without referring specifically to "peace" in society while nonetheless still discussing principles that are relevant to peace and that illustrate the dynamics and prerequisites of peace.

The following represent some of the central themes of the Education for Peace Program that could be used to frame and explore topics in different subject areas. This list is certainly not exhaustive and could be augmented.

- Unity is Life, Life is Unity

- Unity in Diversity

- Oneness of Humanity

- Equality of Women and Men; Equality of All Peoples

- Concepts of Human Nature (evil/good, animal, machine, noble)

- Worldviews (Survival-based, Identity-based, Unity-based)

- Developmental Model of Human Life (Childhood, Adolescence, Maturity)

- Developmental Model of Human Societies (Formative, Assertive, Integrative)

- Developmental Capacities of Knowledge, Love, and Will

- Humanity's Transition to Maturity and Peace

- Social Transition and the Twin Processes of Integration and Disintegration

- Use and Abuse of Power and Authority

- Leadership for Peace

- Prerequisites of Peace: Unity, Justice, Equality, Universality, Maturity

- Modes of Communication (Playful, Industrious, Competitive, Integrative)

- Modes of Decision-Making (Self-Centered, Authoritarian, Power-Struggle, Consultative)

- Conflict-Free Conflict Resolution

- Life Challenges and Opportunities (healthy and unhealthy responses)

- Primary Violence Prevention: Creating Encouraging and Nonthreatening Environments in the Context of a Unity-Based Worldview

Subject Integration Ideas

The following are some ideas on ways to explore the principles and dynamics of peace in relation to various subject areas.

Subject	Possible Explorations
Art	• Unity in Diversity: expressed through visual composition—the science and aesthetics of visual harmony; • Human Development: Evolution of human ability to express knowledge of itself, the universe, and meaning; • Human Nature: Understanding the historical, social, and religious influences on evolving depictions of human nature in art; • Human Oneness: World art studies of the diverse representations of humanity's oneness; • Human Oneness: Expressed through artistic subject matter (love, beauty, perfection, spirituality, suffering, joy, humility, justice, etc.); • Worldview: Worldview studies in the subject matter of art across various periods in history.
Astronomy	• Human Nature: How views of human nature have been influenced by the evolving science of astronomy and perceptions of the purpose/organization of the universe (interaction of religion and science); • Universal Laws: Parallels between the law of gravity/the universal principles of attraction and unity—their properties and effects in the world and the universe.
Biology/ Environmental Studies	• Human Genome Project and the oneness of humanity; • Unity is Life, and Unity in Diversity: Expression of these principles in the structure of biological organisms, their characteristics, dynamics, and purposes; • Prerequisites of Peace: Understood through examination of the characteristics of healthy biological systems (equity, justice, unity, etc.); • Ecological unity in diversity.
Chemistry	• Chemistry in the service of human betterment—history and future possibilities; • Principles of unity and the nature of chemical compositions; • Unity in diversity and the chemical nature of the universe; • Justice and the principles of organic chemistry.

Subject	Possible Explorations
Geography	• Agriculture, trade, technology: Policy development within a peace-oriented framework; • World without Borders: Historical movement of the world towards physical, political, economic, and sociocultural integration; • Globalization and Peace: Issues in governance and economics; • Re-examination of historical population migration, its challenges and contributions to consciousness of the oneness of humanity.
History/ Philosophy	• History of humanity's development toward world unity; • History of thought and evolving concepts of peace and justice; • Exploration of humanity's collective cultural and spiritual heritage; • History of peaceful developments, collaborations, enterprises—at the local, national, and/or international levels.
Information Sciences	• Information revolution and the unification of humankind in the 20th century; • Information technology as a vehicle for human betterment or suffering; • Technological advancements and the elimination of barriers to global integration; • Justice and Peace: Whether policies and regulations on use of global information networks is needed to safeguard social/political/economic welfare, justice, and peace.
Literature	• Developmental model of humanity reflected in literature: themes, characters, genres, etc.; • Prerequisites of Peace: Characterization and critique of concepts of peace, justice, power, love, etc. in literature of different periods, discussed within the developmental model of humanity; • Worldviews: Literature's challenge to prevailing contemporary worldviews; • Equality of Women and Men: Female characters and authors—their stories, struggles, roles in society, and notions/realizations of equality with men.
Mathematics	• History of mathematical theories and the development of human consciousness; • Mathematics as a universal language; • The role of mathematics in the unification of humankind through scientific exchange, invention, and philosophy; • Contributions of women to the development of mathematical theory and achievements.

Subject	Possible Explorations
Music	• Unity in Diversity: Expressed through musical harmony—the science and aesthetics of musical harmony; • World Integration: Expressed through emerging "world music" and its characteristics; • Migration and "world music" throughout the ages; • Science of harmony, its historical development and impact on the cultural and spiritual traditions of world communities; • Humanity's Transition: Evolution in musical composition and subject matter as a reflection of the integration and disintegration taking place in the world—reflections of transition; • Human Nature: Subject matter of music as an expression of human nobility: love, beauty, God, suffering, joy, sacrifice, aspiration, etc.
Physics	• Atomic (quantum) physics and the oneness of the universe; • Physics for Peace: Use of physics for human betterment—new applications, inventions, policies; • Harmony of Science and Religion: History of modern physics and the relationship between science and religion.
Religion	• Unity of Religions: Identifying and discussing principles, teachings, and aims that are common throughout all religions of the world; • Religion and Civilization: Contributions of religions to the positive development of human civilizations; • Science and religion as the two main sources of knowledge of humanity, and their harmonious interrelationship.
Social Studies	• Micro/macro-level worldview development—processes of worldview change in individuals and societies; • Dynamics of social change: Integration/disintegration, social issues moving from unconsciousness into consciousness, becoming the norm in consciousness, and remaining present in the subconscious. • The great diversity of human sociocultural systems (anthropology), and even greater commonality; • Development of local, national, and international legal systems that reflect and are conducive to the peace-oriented worldview.

Unit of Study:

Curriculum Themes/Goals	EFP Themes/Goals

Styles of Understanding:

Explanation	❑
Interpretation	❑
Application	❑
Perspective	❑
Empathy	❑
Self-knowledge	❑

Teaching Styles:

Teacher-centered	❑
Teacher-assisted	❑
Student-centered	❑
Student-assisted	❑

Evaluation methods:

Teacher (objective)

- Tests	❑
- Essays	❑
- Reports	❑
- Rubrics	❑
- Portfolios	❑

Teacher (subjective)

- Observation	❑
- Presentations	❑
- Rubrics	❑

Self-Evaluation

- Rubrics	❑
- Reflections	❑

Peer Evaluation

- Rubrics	❑

Learning Process (add more steps if necessary)

Lesson/Activity 1

Lesson/Activity 2

Lesson/Activity 3

Lesson/Activity 4

Lesson/Activity 5

Assessment Methods (describe in detail the assessment methods/themes you will use)

Formal (performance, essays, tests, "product")

Informal (small group, oral, self–assessment, "process")

Section 4

FACILITATING REFLECTION IN THE CLASSROOM

Reflection and Transformation

Reflection is a very powerful learning tool. It helps us to make sense of our experiences and the things we study. The more we reflect on ourselves; our relationships; various concepts, ideas, and truths; and the world around us, the better prepared we are to discern, prioritize, and act upon issues of importance.

Becoming a peace-builder is a very important and challenging task. Essentially, it requires a process of transformation in us as individuals, as professionals, as family members and as participants in the life of our communities. Transformation in the context of peace education refers to the transformation of our worldviews from a conflict-orientation to a peace-orientation—a process that must re-orient and change our perceptions, thoughts, feelings, attitudes, actions, and ways of relating to others.

As educators, one of the most important things we can do is to help the young generation to actively reflect on their respective worldview and its relationship with peace. By doing so, young people are better equipped to make decisions about their own development as peace-makers and to confidently participate in the process of building a civilization of peace.

The EFP Reflection Framework

The Education for Peace Curriculum Manual aims to structure the process of reflection around a series of simple and profound questions that direct the learners to think critically about their identity, purpose in life, assumptions about the world around them, and their role in creating a peaceful civilization.

The reflection framework rests on four questions related to the key elements of all worldviews. The four key reflection questions are:

1. What is reality?
2. What is human nature?
3. What is the main purpose of human life?
4. What are the laws governing human relationships?

These key questions are then applied to four levels of human experience:

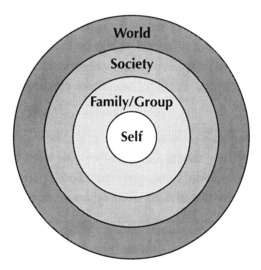

In each EFP-World unit, this basic framework for reflection is used to habituate students to think critically about both micro- and macro-level issues as well as about what impact the application of peace principles can have on various aspects of life and the world at large. The framework is not intended to be prescriptive; it is offered just as a starting point and can be expanded and modified in many ways to best suit the learning process of the class.

Remember: Deep personal reflection is a prerequisite for individual growth and transformation. To the extent that teachers actively and regularly foster opportunities for reflection in the classroom and to the degree that students are encouraged to approach the process of reflection with sincerity and an appropriate level of focus, to that same degree will their introspection yield the fruits of discovery, realization, and personal growth.

Suggestions for Reflective Activities

(Adapted from: *Using Structured Reflection to Enhance Learning from Service* <http://www.compact. org/disciplines/reflection/types.html> Accessed 05-01-2007)

A variety of activities can be used to facilitate student reflection. Reflection activities can be open-ended or prompted by particular questions or issues. When constructing reflection activities, it can be helpful to consider the following:

- Students with different learning styles may prefer different types of activities. Selecting a range of reflective activities will better meet the needs of different learners.
- Different types of reflection activities may be appropriate at different stages of the learning experience. Some are more preparatory, others are more review-oriented.
- Reflection activities can involve reading, writing, doing, and telling. Some examples of reflective activities are briefly described below.

Learning Logs/ Reflective Diaries	Ask students to record thoughts, observations, feelings, activities, and questions in a journal at regular intervals. Journals have many benefits: they can be used to enhance observational skills, explore feelings, analyze challenges or conflicts, assess personal progress, and refine communication skills.
Structured Journals	Structured journals provide prompts to guide the reflective process and connect personal experience to class work by directing student attention to important issues/questions. Some parts of the journal may focus on affective dimensions while others relate to problem-solving activities.
Group Reflection	Use a team journal and/or group discussions to promote interaction among students and to introduce them to diverse perspectives on an issue. Students can take turns sharing their experiences, reactions, and observations, and responding to one another's perspectives.
Integrative Papers	Students can be asked to write an integrative paper on a subject they are studying: in addition to the social, historical, or technical elements of the subject, students can include their reflections on how the topic affects them personally, how it influences or challenges their worldview, and how the topic might be viewed in light of or be affected by the application of peace principles.
Presentations	Students can be asked to prepare a presentation (oral, visual, or dramatic) on their experience and/or research and discuss it in terms of concepts/ theories discussed in class.

Interviews	Students can be interviewed on their experiences and reflections as a means of helping them to articulate and consolidate their learning. Interviews may be conducted by the teacher or by peers as a class activity.
Self-Evaluation	Students can be guided to collectively develop assessment measures (e.g., of the qualities of a peace-builder) and then conduct self-assessment according to these measures at various stages in their learning and development process.
Questionnaires/ Surveys	Questionnaires based on "closed" questions tend to produce limited student reflection, though carefully worded questionnaires that combine questions in past, present, and future tense can guide students to consider their development over time.

Reflection Question Matrix

Here are a few reflection questions that classrooms might use as a starting point for the process of reflection. Feel free to develop your own reflection questions or reflection matrix.

		Levels of Human Experience			
		Self	Family	Society	World
Elements of Worldview	**Reality** *Assumptions about the character of existence*	• What is my view and understanding of the nature of reality? • What/Who am I? • Where do my views on reality come from? • What happens to me after death?	• What qualities truly describe the reality of my family? • What are the qualities of an authentic family?	• What kind of society do I live in? • Are societies static, or do they change? • What is the basis of a stable society?	• What kind of world do we live in? • Is the world now as it has always been? • What will it be like in the future?
	Human Nature *Assumptions about human tendencies and potentials*	• What is my true nature? • What are some of my unique potentials? • What capacities do I have? • What are my values as a human being?	• What did I learn from my family about human nature? • What are the predominant values of my family?	• What is the dominant view on human nature in my society? • Do we consider human beings good, evil, neither, both? • Does society shape the individual or the individual shape society?	• What view(s) of human nature do the world's major leaders appear to hold? • Do all people have the same potential? • Is a lasting world peace possible?
	Purpose of Life *Assumptions about goals and motivations*	• What is the main purpose of my life? • Why do I do the things I do? • What am I willing to sacrifice for? • Has my purpose in life changed over time?	• What is the purpose of the family? • What is most important to my parents? • In our family, what are we willing to sacrifice for?	• What are the primary items on the agenda of my society? • What do people in my society want most? • Do I share my society's values? Why/why not?	• Does humanity have a collective purpose? • What values and aspirations are common to all cultures and peoples?
	Laws Governing Relationships *Assumptions about right principles of conduct and organization*	• Am I satisfied with the nature of my relationships? • What do I consider to be the most important force in human relationships? • How do I use love and power in my relationships?	• What roles and responsibilities ought a family to assume in order to foster the health and well-being of each of its members? • What holds a family together? • How is power defined and used in a healthy family?	• What is the correct relationship between the individual and society? • What holds a society together? • What responsibilities would the institutions and members of a just and peaceful society have towards each other?	• In a global civilization of peace, what obligations would states have to each other? • What would be the guiding principles of a sustainable civilization of peace?

Section 5

Creative Classroom Activities and Classroom Management Strategies

Creative Learning Activities

There are many great creative teaching and learning activities that you can use to enliven the learning process in your classroom. Here is a starter list of ideas that you can use, adapt, and/or add to:

- **Role playing** is a good way of enabling students to explore topics that may be new to them. It encourages them to empathize with characters in unfamiliar or difficult situations and can challenge them to use their problem-solving skills in ways they haven't tried before.

- **Drama** can allow students to choose the aspects of personality or situation they wish to explore. Students could be asked to write a dialogue between characters or historical figures. Scenes could then be read or performed.

- **Dance/Creative Movement** performances prepared by students can be an interesting alternative to dramatic presentations. If given adequate time to prepare, dances can be a great tool for storytelling and for exploring more emotive aspects of a subject.

- **Brainstorming** is a method for getting ideas out of people in order to discuss a topic. For example, the class can be asked to brainstorm any and all words that they associate with a particular concept. Write them on a large sheet of paper for all to see. The list of words then forms the basis for choosing the areas on which to work further.

- **Roundtables** are a version of brainstorming where a pad of paper is circulated for each team member to write his or her ideas while saying them aloud. In three minutes or less, teams can generate a wide range of ideas.

- **Guest Speakers/Field Trips:** Many organizations will provide guest speakers if invited. A guest speaker can be great for showing students the real-world application of what they are studying. If the possibilities exist, fieldtrips to a workplace, factory, museum, performance, or historical site can really pique students' curiosity. Almost every unit has a real-world application—pick one and look up an organization or individual that can come as a guest speaker to your classroom or arrange a site visit for you.

- **Photo-Essays/Collages:** Students can build a pictorial timeline or an exhibition project of some kind using photography or visual collage techniques. When accompanied by a presentation or written submission, visual projects can make great unit- or year-end assignments. They can be displayed in class, around the school, or at Peace Events.

- **Jigsaw Puzzles:** There are a number of ways to divide content into segments and assign different members of a class (individually or in teams) to learn one of the segments to then share with the others. When all the segments have been completed, students will be able to put the pieces of the jigsaw puzzle together. It's a great way for students to learn from each other.

- **Sharing Moment:** Teacher poses a question and before getting responses, gives students a minute to talk to someone nearby. The chance to interact and compare ideas allows for more complex thinking; it also lets students find that their ideas are worth sharing. In only a couple short minutes, this social energy can give a class a valuable boost.

- **Think-Pair-Share**: The instructor poses a question demanding analysis, evaluation, or synthesis. Approximately one minute is given to think through an appropriate response and write it down. Students share their response with a partner, and then teams share responses with entire class in discussion.

- **Flash Cards:** Each student in a team writes a review problem on a flash card. Teams reach consensus on answers and write them on the backs of the cards. Each group's stack of questions passes to another group, which attempts to answer them and checks to see if they agree with the sending group. If not, they write their answer as an alternative. Stacks of cards can be sent to a third and fourth group. Stacks of cards are finally returned to the senders, who may discuss the alternative answers.

- **Peer Teaching:** Students digest and define their own understanding of concepts by tutoring others. Peer teaching can be in the form of the "Question Pairs" where learners prepare for class by reading an assignment and generating questions focused on the major points or issues raised. At the next class meeting pairs are randomly assigned. Partners alternately ask questions of each other and provide corrective feedback as necessary.

- **Newspapers:** Using a selection of current newspapers, students can be asked to cut out all the features and stories relating to a particular theme. These could be used for a display; to initiate an investigation into the historical development of that theme; as the basis for views or journalistic styles. Students could also create newspapers with reports of their own, explorations of a theme from different perspectives (i.e., like different newspaper sections), as well as context- or period-specific advertisements and headlines.

- **Television News:** Students can be asked to monitor the news during a set period for accounts of a given theme and critique how the reports are presented.

- **Portfolios:** Students can be asked to select and organize evidence related to their specific learning goals and accomplishments in a portfolio. Portfolios can include drafts of documents, analysis of problems/issues, project activities/plans, creative work and collections, or an annotated bibliography. Ask students to organize their collection according to the learning objectives you agreed on together.

- **Story Telling:** This is one of the most potent learning activities. Share stories about yourself and those you know, and encourage students to do likewise. Make sure that stories depict the ever-present human struggle to understand, to love, to sacrifice, to serve, to deal with calamities, and to find meaning and purpose.

Remember: Good understanding-oriented activities draw upon key questions and a variety of understanding styles. Refer back to the *"Six Facets of Understanding"* and *"Performance Verbs"* for ideas. Also, well-designed learning activities connect the student to real life situations, and place equal emphasis on both the learning process as well as the learning product. Creative and diverse activities, including written work, portfolio collections, performances, and presentations challenge students to be multidimensional in their thinking and action.

Ideas for Teaching with Excellence

(Excerpted from *The Berkeley Compendium for Teaching with Excellence,* by Barbara Gross Davis, Lynn Wood, and Robert Wilson)[11]

Give Lectures That Are Easy to Outline

- Let students know what you're going to discuss and why;
- Write an outline on the blackboard before you begin;
- Give students a list of essential and/or topic questions;
- As the lecture develops, outline the main points on the blackboard.

Explain Clearly

- Focus your lesson on a few main points;
- Carefully define all concepts and terms;
- Use lots of concrete or memorable examples;
- Demonstrate (rather than describe) a concept or idea.

Discuss Points of View Other Than Your Own

- Assign readings that represent a variety of viewpoints;
- Present contrasting theories;
- Invite guest speakers with differing points-of-view;
- Draw upon the diverse backgrounds of your students.

Emphasize Conceptual Understanding

- Give students a conceptual framework;
- Stress the most enduring values or truths;
- Repeatedly touch back to the fundamentals or basics;
- Pose paradoxes for students to solve.

Summarize Major Points

- Begin and end the class with a summary statement;
- Call attention to the most important ideas;
- Use the blackboard for summarizing main points;
- Assign students responsibility for summarizing major points;
- Hand out a brief summary of the last class.

Encourage Class Discussion

- Integrate discussion into your lesson;
- Move around the room to promote discussion;
- Encourage students to ask questions and/or identify discussion questions in advance;

---

11. Copyright: University of California, Berkeley, 1983. Used with permission. <http://teaching.berkeley.edu/compendium/sectionsmenu.html> Accessed 05-01-2005.

- Give students enough time to think about and respond to questions;
- Respond to students questions, or ask other students to reply;
- Admit when you don't know the answer and encourage research to find the answer;
- Use an opinion questionnaire as a basis for discussion;
- Draw upon common experiences to encourage input;
- Prompt discussion through the use of key phrases;
- Allow heated debates to develop, but intercede if the discussion breaks down.

Invite Students to Share Their Knowledge and Experiences

- Call on students who might provide an interesting viewpoint;
- Introduce students to examples of good work done by their peers;
- Encourage students to apply their unique backgrounds/perspectives to their work;
- Encourage students to make presentations to the class.

Present Lessons in Interesting Ways

- Relate the course material as a story;
- Begin with an incident, example, or anecdote;
- Focus on particular students in different parts of the room during your lecture;
- Exaggerate everything about your presentation;
- Vary the pace and instructional activities of the course;
- Invite guest speakers to your class.

Give Interesting Assignments

- Set up student panels;
- Use classroom debates;
- Create opportunities for role playing;
- Ask students to give oral presentations;
- Use case studies and simulation techniques;
- Give thought-provoking assignments;
- Do assignments for "real world" clients;
- Give students field-experience assignments;
- Give assignments typical of certain professions;
- Assign independent research projects;
- Assign analysis of an essay or article;
- Give exercises for problem visualization and solution.

Keep Students Informed of Their Progress

- Return tests and assignments quickly;
- Discuss solutions or answers to tests and assignments;
- Return a "perfect" exam along with the corrected exam;
- Make extensive constructive comments on student work;
- Have students peer-edit each other's work;
- Have students keep a logbook of their progress.

Creating a Peaceful Classroom

> The purpose of education is to nurture the unique human capacities of knowledge, love, and will. Through education we learn to use our knowledge in pursuit of truth and enlightenment, our love to create unity and celebrate diversity, and our powers of will to serve humanity through justice and peace.
>
> —H.B. Danesh

Creating a culture of peace at school begins with creating a culture of peace in the classroom. When students experience the classroom as a caring, supportive place where there is a sense of belonging and everyone is valued and respected, they also tend to participate more fully in the process of learning.

A positive classroom climate is characterized by the spirit of unity in diversity, by pleasant physical surroundings, by high expectations and encouragement, by opportunities for growth and creativity, and by caring and respectful relationships among all the members of the classroom community.

Every classroom is characterized by diversity: diversity of thought, of talents and capabilities, of experiences, and of identity (based on racial, cultural, religious, or gender dimensions). It is beneficial, therefore, if lessons celebrate the presence and value of diversity, while also always affirming the all-important principles of inclusiveness and universality. In other words, the class should be assisted to create a culture of "unity-in-diversity."

Classroom management is not an easy task. It requires careful and thoughtful preparation, willingness to risk, and a commitment that embraces the unexpected challenges students can offer any teacher at any time. Difficulties in classroom dynamics can arise, and knowing how to deal with them in appropriate and peaceful ways can be challenging. There are many guides for teachers on the Internet: be sure to visit the **links** section for some starting points. In the meantime, here are a few quick tips on how to foster and maintain positive classroom dynamics.

Some Quick Tips

- **Enable students to get to know and trust each other and you as teacher**

  - Spend as much time as needed at the beginning of the term using exercises to help the students get to know one another and build a sense of trust in the classroom.

- **Communicate positive regard and high expectations for all children**

  - Approach each class with a positive attitude. If you feel this is a "bad class," your students will perceive your attitude and fulfill your expectations.

- **Promote cooperative, rather than competitive classroom strategies**

  - Use creative learning activities that rely on group cohesion, along with authentic assessment strategies to develop a cooperative and noncompetitive classroom atmosphere.

- **Affirm positive behaviors, encourage rather than discourage**

    - On a daily basis, praise each student for his/her effort, contribution, and/or attitude in the class.

    - On a daily basis before the class is finished, review the positive events that took place (e.g., "We had a lively discussion today and what really pleased me the most, beside the intelligent opinions that were expressed, was the way you all *listened* to each other. Your skills in this area are really improving every week.")

- **Foster reflective strategies for thinking about and discussing social interactions**

    - Incorporate a daily reflection activity into your teaching routine to accustom students to the practice of reflection.

    - From time to time, invite students read aloud some of their journal entries to encourage an atmosphere of sharing and group reflection.

- **When difficulties arise, discuss concerns and feelings openly as a group**

    - For example, if a student shows lack of interest in the subject, engage the student at their level (e.g., "I can see by your opinions, Mathias, that this poetry unit does not interest you. Let's close our books for a couple of minutes and see whether in small groups we can find any constructive reasons for studying poetry.")

    - If an argument or hostile act occurs between students and is disturbing the classroom dynamics, engage the whole class in discussing it (e.g., "Our classroom is a community; whatever affects one of us affects the whole community. We now have a conflict that is affecting the classroom. Let's close our books and turn our chairs into a circle, and try to address it. We will listen while Jana and Miro explain what is happening, and then I would like each person to share their thoughts or feelings on how it is affecting our community and what might be done about it.")

- **Guide students how to seek and obtain assistance when in difficulty**

    - Create a student-student and student-teacher mentoring system.

    - Role-play situations in which students turn to fellow students, parents/guardians, teachers, trusted adults, and professional counselors for different types of assistance.

    - Develop an "assistance backup plan" with students in case adequate help is not forthcoming from their primary contact person, and post it in the classroom.

- **Model peaceful leadership in the classroom**

    - Be open, warm, and encouraging;

    - Be courageous and clear about the students respecting your authority;

    - Be consistent and unrestrained in conveying respect for the students' integrity.

Modes of Classroom Management – A Comparison

Classroom management techniques, like most human activities, are affected in part by the worldview of the teacher. The following table identifies characteristics of different classroom management styles based on three worldview modes.

Classroom approach to:	Authoritarian Mode	Libertarian Mode	Integrative Mode
Authority	Teachers see it as their right to impose their authority, will, and power on students arbitrarily.	Students see it as their right to challenge the authority of the teacher.	Students respect the authority of the teacher, and the teacher respects the value and experiences of the students.
Discipline	Teachers believe that using their power to control and punish students is the most effective means of establishing/maintaining discipline in the classroom.	Teachers hesitate to discipline the students for fear of being accused of violating the rights of their students to explore degrees of self-discipline freely. Therefore, classroom discipline expectations are neither clearly set out, nor consistently applied.	Teachers view self-discipline as an essential skill for lifelong learning and growth, and as an ethical pre-requisite for healthy, creative, and just community life. Teachers discuss with students the kinds of discipline—inner and interpersonal, as well as institutional and collective—needed for supporting a healthy learning environment and encourage students to apply these principles consistently.
Obedience	Students either obey the teacher for fear of punishment, or become blind conformists in the expectation of approval and reward. Both groups, however, may seek opportunities to disobey the teacher covertly and when the occasion allows.	Students openly disobey the teacher as a means of building their own sense of power and individuality. An unspoken agreement between teacher and students allows anarchy to become the class norm.	Students have self-discipline, and the classroom has clear and just principles for all manners of activity and relationship. Neither blind obedience nor anarchic disobedience is present in such a classroom

Classroom approach to:	Authoritarian Mode	Libertarian Mode	Integrative Mode
Teacher-Student Relationship	*Teacher-student relationship is militaristic.* Teachers forcefully maintain their power-hold in the classroom, but may be hated and/or feared by students. Opportunities for fuller relationships and psychosocial development in the classroom are stunted.	*Teacher-student relationship is competitive.* An open, continuous competition and conflict between teacher and students takes place. Teachers feel disempowered and may resort to authoritarian measures that likewise prove ineffective and often worsen the classroom dynamics.	*Teacher-student relationship is harmonious and consultative.* Teachers' authority may occasionally be challenged but is maintained by establishing a sense of trust that everyone in the classroom is and ought to be respected within the parameters of a unity-based worldview.
Student Contributions	The value of students' contributions to the lesson is diminished. Conformity is expected, and student creativity is discouraged. A culture of passive learning is created.	Students' wishes are given prime value and take precedence over a structured approach to learning. As such, students who are confident to undertake self-directed learning do well, and others become lost and perform poorly.	Students' contributions to the lesson are highly valued; diversity of views and styles is appreciated; and a balance between open and structured activities is created for maximum learning efficacy.
Teaching Style	Teacher is rigid, dogmatic, controlling; and adheres inflexibly to prescribed content plans.	Teacher attempts a wide variety of teaching styles to capture the attention of students but struggles to maintain their focus because students lack discipline and purpose.	Teacher is flexible, creative, and consultative in her/his approach to prescribed content, varying lessons in a creative way to engage the interest of students and foster their love of learning.

Classroom approach to:	Authoritarian Mode	Libertarian Mode	Integrative Mode
Assessment	Assessment is standardized, rigid, and often perceived to be unjust.	Assessment is infrequent, inconsistent, and often perceived to be arbitrary.	Assessment is frequent, fair, and uses a variety of methods that reflect the purposes of the lessons and also the different learning styles of the students.
Outcomes	Disempowers students by diminishing their sense of individual worth and creative potential.	Allows students to tyrannize the teacher and each other by placing inordinate importance on individual prerogative.	Empowers both students and teacher by establishing a sense of mutual respect and by adhering to the principles of fairness and unity.
	Creates a win-lose situation in favor of the teacher.	Creates a win-lose situation in favor of the students.	Creates a win-win situation for both teachers and students.
	The general atmosphere is tense and oppressive. Students perceive the classroom as a threatening environment. The stakes of success or failure are very high.	The general atmosphere is either chaotic or pessimistic. Students do not have a sense of purpose and therefore make minimal efforts to learn. In turn, the rewards of learning are also minimal.	The general atmosphere in the classroom is peaceful, positive, creative, cooperative, and respectful of each individual's place.
	Produces more discipline conflicts because it attacks the basic integrity of the student.	Produces more discipline conflicts because it fails to cultivate within students inner discipline and a recognition and willing adherence to principles of dignity, moderation, and accountability.	Produces fewer discipline conflicts because it values the basic integrity of the students and maintains a sense of accountability to the community.

Classroom Management Case Study

After reviewing the "Modes of Classroom Management," consider the following scenario.

The class has begun, and the teacher has asked the students to write a 10-minute journal entry on four themes in literature: a human being's relationship to other human beings; a human being's relationship to him/herself; a human being's relationship to society; and a human being's relationship to nature. A student suddenly comes to the door, swings it open and slams it loudly as he or she enters the class 10 minutes late. The teacher calls the student's name to stop at her desk. Without looking at the teacher, the student storms to his/her desk. Consider the following possible responses:

1. The teacher becomes very angry and tells the student to report to the detention room after school.
2. The teacher is bothered by the student's apparent lack of respect but feels powerless to modify his/her behavior and/or expects increased misbehavior if the issue is opened up.
3. The teacher asks the student if he/she wants to discuss what is happening; and if the student refuses to do so, teacher involves the whole class in a consultative process on how to deal with the issue. However, if the student requests the matter be discussed in private, the teacher will decide on the time of this discussion depending on the nature and urgency of the issue at hand. After all, a classroom is a community of people, and whatever happens to one member of the community affects the whole community.

Which modes of classroom management did the responses represent (authoritarian, libertarian, or integrative)?

A teacher who has confidence in his/her role and who approaches the classroom within an integrative, unity-oriented, and consultative framework keeps an eye on the big picture. In the case described above, the big picture had several components: tardiness, defiance, and acting out anger. If permitted, such behaviors will render the classroom increasingly unruly. At the same time, the school year has just begun and the long-term relationship between the student and the teacher is important. It would be detrimental to the whole class if the mode of disciplining these misbehaviors sets up a power-struggle between the teacher and student that lasts the whole year. By appearing to give the student a break regarding his tardiness, the teacher focuses corrective remarks on the defiant and inappropriate entrance—behaviors that were within the student's arena of choice.

Students are more likely to maintain classroom discipline and to respect the authority of the teacher if they are given opportunities to discuss and give input into classroom expectations. This does not necessarily mean that the students decide a course of discipline for another student, or are given the right to ignore or override the disciplinary decisions of the teacher. Rather, discussion provides an opportunity for students to understand and reflect on what is expected of them, and may help the teacher and students together to set fewer but more meaningful standards for the class to follow. It is best if classroom principles describe appropriate behavior and lead into the big picture. An example would be:

THIS CLASSROOM IS GOVERNED BY THE PRINCIPLES OF TRUTH, JUSTICE, AND UNITY AS WELL AS RESPECT FOR SELF, OTHERS, AND PROPERTY.

Such a rule is then owned by the whole class, backed by the authority of the teacher, and not to be violated or compromised. If infringements of this rule happen, they can be consulted upon with the class as a whole. For example: During a class discussion, everyone starts talking at once; no one is listening to the others; and the noise level is rising. The teacher reacts by giving a sign for the class to be silent. Then she asks how they can continue if no one is listening. A short consultation between teacher and students follows, resulting in some suggestions made by the students such as:

THE STUDENTS MAY ELECT ONE CHAIRPERSON TO FACILITATE THE DISCUSSION. THE CHAIRPERSON WILL MAKE SURE THAT EACH PERSON WHO RAISES HIS/HER HAND GETS TO SPEAK IN ORDER. EACH PERSON WILL LISTEN UNTIL IT IS HIS/HER TURN.

A teacher who functioning in the authoritarian or libertarian mode would handle this situation quite differently. An authoritarian would insist on an abundance of rules, from the way a student should sit to where he should put his text book when not in use. These kinds of detailed rules serve only one purpose: to increase the teacher's apparent control over his/her students. Frequently, students will perceive such detailed control as unnecessary and unjust, and will attempt to subvert these rules when possible. The teacher is then constantly busy dealing with disturbances. Likewise, sending a student out into the hall or down to the Principal's office for small infractions reinforces a power-struggle dynamic and forfeits opportunities to model peaceful solutions in the classroom. It merely shifts responsibility for the problem to someone else, and at best provides only a temporary solution.

Section 6

Assessment

Authentic Assessment Tools

(Adapted from: "Education Place," Houghton Mifflin Company. Source: <http://www.eduplace.com/rdg/res/litass/> Accessed 04-08-2007. Used with permission.)

Assessments are important for gauging the learning progress of students and for reporting their achievements. In traditional school systems, assessment practices center primarily on examinations and tests. These tests commonly measure whether the student has committed to memory the prescribed information contained in the course unit and rarely attempt to measure the student's ability to discuss the subject intelligently, critically, or to apply their understanding to wider and diverse contexts.

For a program like Education for Peace, memorization of the "principles of peace" is not sufficient to effect a change in the attitudes and behaviors of young people. Another approach to learning and assessment activities needs to be taken.

"Authentic assessment" approaches aim at not only measuring students' knowledge but also guiding students to higher levels of understanding by engaging them in real and complex tasks. Authentic assessment methods correspond as closely as possible to real world experience. The instructor observes the student in the process of working on something real, provides feedback, monitors the student's use of the feedback, and adjusts instruction and evaluation accordingly. Authentic assessment takes this principle of evaluating real work into all areas of the curriculum. It is a formative type of assessment because it becomes an ongoing part of the whole teaching and learning process. Students themselves are involved in the assessment process through both peer- and self-assessment resemble actual situations in which those abilities are used.

The formats for performance assessments range from relatively short answers to long-term projects that require students to present or demonstrate their work. These performances often require students to engage in higher-order thinking and to integrate many skills. Consequently, some performance assessments are longer and more complex than more traditional assessments. Within a complete assessment system, however, there should be a balance of longer performance assessments and shorter ones.

Authentic assessment activities have value beyond the classroom because they pose a challenge to students to use what they have learned in meaningful ways. For assigning grades, well-designed assessment activities include a student self-evaluation component, along with clear standards for evaluation or judgment by the teacher.

Authentic assessment accomplishes each of the following goals:

- Requires students to develop responses rather than select from predetermined options;
- Elicits higher-order thinking in addition to basic skills;
- Directly evaluates holistic projects;
- Uses samples of student work (portfolios) collected over an extended time period;
- Stems from clear criteria made known to students;
- Allows for the possibility of multiple human judgments;
- Relates more closely to classroom learning;
- Teaches students to evaluate their own work.

Forms of Classroom Assessment

Classroom assessment processes have several benefits: students benefit from receiving feedback early and often; they also benefit from evaluating the quality of their own learning; and, by gauging the learning quality of students, teachers gain valuable feedback that can help them improve and tailor their methods of instruction.

Classroom assessment techniques incorporate a series of tools and practices designed to give teachers accurate information about the quality of student learning. Information does not have to be collected for grading purposes only. It can be used to facilitate dialogue between students and teacher on the quality of the learning process, and how to improve it.

There are different types of assessment.

Formal Assessment

Some formal assessments provide teachers with a systematic way to evaluate how well students are progressing in a particular instructional program. For example, after completing a 4–6 week theme, teachers will want to know how well students have learned the theme skills and concepts. They may give all the students a theme test in which students read, answer questions, and write about a similar theme concept. Teachers might use a skills test to examine specific skills or strategies taught in a theme. Two points of comparison are available: the student's growth over time and the student's performance as compared with his or her grade-level peers.

Informal Assessment

Other forms of authentic assessment are more informal, including special activities such as group or individual projects, experiments, oral presentations, demonstrations, or performances. Some informal assessments may be drawn from typical classroom activities such as assignments, journals, essays, reports, literature discussion groups, or reading logs. Other times, it will be difficult to show student progress using actual work, so teachers will need to keep notes or checklists to record their observations from student-teacher conferences or informal classroom interactions. Sometimes informal assessment is as simple as stopping during instruction to observe or to discuss with the students how learning is progressing.

Varying Assessment Methods

It is generally considered a good pedagogical practice to employ a range of assessment methods, since any one assessment format or process will disadvantage some students and the continual use of the same assessment method will repeatedly disadvantage the same students.

Classroom Assessment Questions

The three basic questions that a teacher should ask him/herself while conducting an assessment are:

1. What are the essential understandings and skills I am trying to teach?
2. How can I find out whether students are learning them?
3. How can I help students learn better?

Classroom Assessment Process

For the assessment process to yield positive results, each of the following steps need to be carried out:

1. Choose a learning goal to assess;
2. Choose an assessment technique;
3. Apply the technique;
4. Analyze the data;
5. Share the results with students;
6. Respond to the data by affirming students' accomplishments and engaging with students to improve the necessary areas of learning.

Student Self-Assessment

Involving students in the assessment and evaluation process is an essential part of balanced assessment. When students become partners in the learning process, they gain a better sense of themselves as readers, writers, thinkers, and actors.

To guide students in understanding the pro-cess of self-evaluation, it can be good to begin by having them complete a Self-Reflection/Self-Assessment sheet that you design. Self-assessment can take many forms, including:

- Discussion (whole-class or small-group);
- Reflection logs;
- Weekly self-evaluations;
- Self-assessment checklists and inventories;
- Teacher-student interviews;
- Self-assessment rubrics.

Students can compare their work over time, create evaluation criteria for a project, discuss their strategies for reading difficult texts, work with peers to evaluate and revise a piece of writing, and judge their reading preferences and habits by reviewing their reading journals.

These types of self-assessment share a common theme: they ask students to review their work to determine what they have learned and what areas of confusion still exist. Although each method differs slightly, all should include enough time for students to consider thoughtfully and evaluate their progress.

Once students have reflected on their learning, they are ready to set new goals for themselves. Keeping a class journal can help students reaffirm their goals and move towards accomplishing them. With practice, students who self-assess develop the habit of self-reflection. They learn the qualities of good work, how to judge their work against these qualities, how to step back from their work to assess their own efforts and feelings of accomplishment, and how to set personal goals. These are qualities of self-directed learners, not passive learners.

At first, you may need to guide their reflection with questions such as these:

- What did I learn today?
- What did I do well?
- What am I confused about?
- What do I need help with?
- What do I want to know more about?
- What am I going to work on next?

A key to this process is ensuring that students understand the criteria for good work before they begin an activity. The clearer the performance criteria are the better. Students can also be involved in setting criteria for good work. This involvement gives them more ownership over the activity and over their own performance.

Students' observations and reflections can also provide valuable feedback for refining your instructional plan. As your students answer questions about their learning and the strategies they use, think about their responses to find out what they are really learning and to see if they are learning what you are teaching them. Note: Gender and culture will affect the way in which students assess themselves.

Assessment Tools: Rubrics

(Source: "The Webquest Page." Educational Technology Department, San Diego State University <http://webquest.sdsu.edu/rubrics/weblessons.htm>. Accessed 04-08-2007. Used with permission.)

Regarding an assignment, has a student ever said to you, "But, I didn't know what you wanted!" or "Why did her paper get an A and mine a C?" Students must understand the goals we expect them to achieve in course assignments, and especially, the criteria we use to determine how well they have achieved those goals. Rubrics provide a readily accessible way of communicating and developing our goals with students and the criteria we use to discern how well students have reached them.

The Rubric is an authentic assessment tool that is particularly useful in assessing complex and subjective criteria.

Rubrics are scoring guides that assess multiple criteria of an assignment or project using a ranked scale of performance indicators. The purpose of a rubric is to make transparent to students what constitutes a "good" and "complete" piece of work and how close to the achievement of those criteria they are, in order for them to have a clear understanding of how they can improve their knowledge, skills and/or presentation style for improved future achievement. As students become familiar with rubrics, they can assist in the rubric design process. This involvement empowers the students, and as a result their learning becomes more focused and self-directed.

The advantages of using rubrics in assessment are that they:

- Allow assessment to be more objective and consistent;
- Focus the teacher to clarify his/her criteria in specific terms;
- Clearly show the student how their work will be evaluated and what is expected of them;
- Promote student awareness of about the criteria to use in assessing peer performance;
- Provide useful feedback regarding the effectiveness of the instruction;
- Provide benchmarks against which to measure and document progress.

Rubrics can be created in a variety of forms and levels of complexity. A good rubric exhibits the following qualities:

- Addresses all relevant content and performance objectives;
- Clearly defines performance standards and helps students achieve them by providing criteria with which they can evaluate their own work;
- Provides students with the opportunity to succeed at various levels;
- Is easy to understand and use;
- Is applicable to a variety of tasks;
- Yields consistent results, even when administered by different scorers.

Rubrics are an effective assessment tool in evaluating student performance in areas that are complex and vague. By involving students in the creation of the rubric, the students take more responsibility for their own learning, are empowered by being involved in the teaching/learning process, and have a clearer idea of what is expected in terms of specific performance. Teachers clarify their goals, expectations, and focus; and even find that their paperwork is reduced because students are a part of the process of assessment development.

How To Design Your Own Rubric

In groups or individually, follow the process steps below:

1. Using the Rubric Template on pages 369–370, select the desired student performance standards you would like to evaluate. Here are some suggestions to start, but feel free to devise your own:
   - Ideas in the essay are well organized;
   - Student shows leadership in working with small group;
   - Student demonstrates ability to work independently;
   - Evidence of the student's applying objectives of peace in group work;
   - Oral presentation showed evidence of understanding that one's personal attitude can influence the harmony of the group;
   - Project demonstrates the qualities of unity (or justice, or equality, or the creative challenge of conflict).

2. Working backwards along the scale from most complete to least complete, fill in the template with your criteria. Write specific descriptions of expected student performance for each level.

3. It is a good idea to share your completed rubric with another person/group for feedback. Sometimes it is necessary to clarify the performance criteria or demonstration descriptions for students to fully understand what is expected of them.

Teacher's Name: _____ School: _____

Assessment Rubric for Education for Peace Lesson Plans

Performance Criteria	4	3	2	1	Mark
1. Integrates EFP concepts with the overall subject matter	Overall integration is in-depth; EFP concepts are clear & relevant.	Overall integration is evident; EFP concepts do not directly illuminate the subject area.	Overall integration is weak; EFP concepts and their relevance to subject are not clear.	Overall integration is lacking; EFP concepts are not used to illuminate the subject.	
2. Applies a peace-oriented worldview to examine the subject	A peace-oriented perspective on the subject (content and/or application) is coherently and thoroughly explored.	A peace-oriented perspective on the subject (content and/or application) is evident but requires more development.	A peace-oriented perspective is not attempted.	The principles of a peace-oriented worldview are contradicted by other concepts in the lesson.	
3. Includes a variety of authentic assessment activities.	The authentic assessment activities are well developed and guide the overall teaching objectives of the lesson plan.	More than one authentic assessment activity is provided; quality is adequate or good.	Only one authentic assessment activity is provided; quality is adequate.	Assessment activities are unrelated to the teaching objectives or have not been provided at all.	
4. Assessment activities focus on students' understanding of EFP concepts.	Assessment activity clearly nurtures and demonstrates the students' understanding of EFP concepts.	Assessment activity assists students somewhat to demonstrate their understanding of EFP concepts.	Assessment activity focuses very little on EFP concepts.	Assessment activity bears no relation to EFP concepts.	

Performance Criteria	4	3	2	1	Mark
5. Addresses a diversity of learning styles that support full exploration of EFP concepts.	Teacher incorporates audio, visual, kinesthetic, musical, experiential, and media activities appropriate to the full exploration of EFP concepts.	Some diversity of learning styles is addressed; this diversity bears some appropriate relation to EFP concepts.	Class activities focus heavily on one style of learning; appropriateness to EFP concepts is not clear.	No consideration is given to diversity of learning styles or to their appropriateness to the EFP concepts.	
6. Encourages creative activities that apply the EFP concepts.	Teaching objectives require students to engage in creative activities that directly apply EFP concepts.	Encourages creative activities vaguely related to EFP concepts.	Classroom activity is limited in scope; activity does not focus on EFP concepts.	Little student initiative or creative activity is supported by unit; existing activities bear no relation to EFP concepts.	
Sub-Total	Of marks on rubric				/24
7. Student Self-Assessment	Include an appropriate percentage for self-assessment in the final mark				/6
Total					/30

Evaluator's comments:

Date: _____

Student: _____ Class: _____ Assignment: _____

Assessment Rubric

Performance Criteria	4	3	2	1	Mark
1.					
2.					
3.					
4.					

Performance Criteria	4	3	2	1	Mark
5.					
6.					
Sub-Total	Of marks on rubric				/24
7. Student Self-Assessment	Include an appropriate percentage for self-assessment in the final mark				/6
Total					/30

Evaluator's comments:

Date: _____

Student: _____ Class: _____ Teacher: _____

Sample Assessment Table on Affective Behavior

Performance Criteria	Consistently	Inconsistently	Rarely/ Not At All
1. Student related to others in the group with **respect**	3	2	1
2. Student showed interest in **diversity**	3	2	1
3. Student took personal **responsibility** to complete the project	3	2	1
4. Student **empowered** others	3	2	1
5. Student demonstrated **cooperation** rather than competition	3	2	1
6. Student sought **peaceful** resolutions to difficulties	3	2	1
7. Student expressed differences of opinion in a **positive** way	3	2	1
8. Student contributed to a sense of **camaraderie**	3	2	1
9. Student demonstrated a spirit of **service**	3	2	1
Sub-Totals			
Total			

Evaluator's comments:

Date: _____

Assessment Tools: Portfolios

(Source: F.L. Paulson, P.R. Paulson, and C.A. Meyer, "What Makes a Portfolio a Portfolio?" *Educational Leadership* (February 1991): 60–63.)

A portfolio is a purposeful collection of student work that exhibits the student's efforts, progress, and achievements in one or more areas of the curriculum. A portfolio comprises a *collection* of items rather than being a single piece of work.

Typically a portfolio includes only the best work, a product portfolio. The alternative is a process portfolio, which includes examples of different stages of the development and allows a much richer understanding of the process of change. A portfolio can be used as a framework for formative feedback, as it can promote discussion between student groups and their tutors. It can also be used as a means of cumulative assessment, as the final product demonstrates what students know or can do.

The collection must include the following:

- Student participation in selecting contents;
- Criteria for selection;
- Criteria for judging merits;
- Evidence of a student's self-reflection.

It should represent a collection of students' best work or best efforts, student-selected samples of work experiences related to outcomes being assessed, and documents according growth and development toward mastering identified outcomes.

Why Use a Portfolio?

(Source: Burke, Fogerty, *Mindful School: Portfolio Connection*, Palatine, IL: IRI/Skylight Publishing, 1994.)

In this new era of performance assessment related to the monitoring of student mastery of a core curriculum, portfolios can enhance the assessment process by revealing a range of skills and understandings on the part of students; support instructional goals; reflect change and growth over a period of time; encourage student, teacher, and parental reflection; and provide for continuity in education from one year to the next.

In order for thoughtful evaluation to take place, teachers must have multiple scoring strategies to evaluate student progress. Criteria for a finished portfolio might include several of the following:

- Thoughtfulness (including evidence of students' monitoring of their own comprehension, meta-cognitive reflection, and productive habits of mind);
- Growth and development in relationship to key curriculum standards and indicators;
- Understanding and application of key processes;
- Completeness, correctness, and appropriateness of products and processes presented in the portfolio;
- Diversity of entries (e.g., use of multiple formats to demonstrate achievement of designated performance standards).

It is especially important for teachers and students to work together to prioritize those criteria that will be used as a basis for assessing and evaluating student progress, both formatively (i.e., throughout an instructional time period) and summatively (i.e., as part of a culminating project, activity, or related assessment to determine the extent to which identified curricular expectancies, indicators, and standards have been achieved).

Rubrics, rules, and scoring keys can be designed for a variety of portfolio components. In addition, letter grades might also be assigned, where appropriate. Finally, some for of oral discussion or investigation should be included as part of the cumulative evaluation process. This component should involve the student, teacher, and if possible, a panel of reviewers in a thoughtful exploration of the portfolio components, students' decision-making and evaluation processes related to artifact selection, and other relevant issues.

Tips for Classroom-Based Assessment

(©1997 "Education Place," Houghton Mifflin Company. All Rights Reserved. Used with permission. <http://www.eduplace.com/rdg/res/litass/effec.html>. Accessed 04-08-2007)

- Focus assessment on the most important outcomes in the curriculum.
- Be clear about the goals of instruction and make them explicit to the students.
- Make self-assessment a dependable, integral part of your classroom. Begin with non-academic activities, such as judging how well the class is working in groups or discussing favorite artwork. Gradually habituate students to step back from their work or their behavior, to think reflectively and consider the qualities of good performance as objectively as possible.
- Help the class to develop criteria for a good report or project and then have them evaluate their work according to the criteria.
- Schedule portfolio visits with your students. These are times when you and your students can review accumulated portfolio work, steppng back to look at work over time. Sometimes these visits should be collaborative, sometimes independent. By spending time with several portfolios each week, you will be able to keep track of individual student progress and to make sure that no students are slipping through the cracks. Use portfolios to celebrate accomplishments as well as to identify needs.
- Use classroom assessments and portfolios to help with grading. You do not need to grade every piece of work or even the portfolio as a whole. Together, graded and ungraded artifacts provide strong evidence for your grading decisions.
- Begin classroom assessment slowly. It will take time for you and your students to develop a system for using and keeping track of classroom assessment. The time you spend with students organizing and reviewing portfolios or classroom work is time well spent. Through these activities students learn about qualities of good work.

Section 7

FURTHER RESOURCES

Useful Links

"Teaching for Understanding" (Online Professional Development Video - 1 hour).
   <http://www.learner.org/channel/workshops/socialstudies/session2/index.html>.

"Assessing Students' Learning" (Online Professional Development Video - 1 hour).
   <http://www.learner.org/resources/series176.html#>.

"Teaching for Understanding" by Prof. David Perkins.
   <http://www.21learn.org/arch/articles/perkins.html>.

"Teaching for Understanding: Putting Understanding Up Front."
   <http://learnweb.harvard.edu/alps/tfu/index.cfm>.

"Essential Questions by Theme."
   <http://www.greece.k12.ny.us/instruction/ela/6-12/Essential%20Questions/Index.htm>.

"Reflection Questions for Teachers."
   <http://learnweb.harvard.edu/alps/reflect/index.cfm>.

"Reflection Guides for Service-Learning."
   <http://www.uvm.edu/~dewey/reflection_manual/>.
   <http://www.compact.org/disciplines/reflection/>.

"Rationale for Using Authentic Assessment."
   <http://www.uwstout.edu/soe/profdev/assess.shtml>.

"Sample Rubric for Assessing Student Presentations."
   <http://www.ncsu.edu/midlink/rub.pres.html>

"Tools for Reading, Writing, and Thinking."
   <http://www.greece.k12.ny.us/instruction/ela/6-12/Tools/Index.htm>.

"General Resource on All Aspects of Teaching."
   <http://honolulu.hawaii.edu/intranet/committees/FacDevCom/guidebk/teachtip/teachtip.htm#techniques>.

"K-12 Activity Ideas By Topic/Theme."
   <http://www.eduplace.com/activity/>.

"The Educator's Reference Desk (2,000+ lesson plans and other resources)."
   <http://www.eduref.org/>.

"Classroom Management: Game-Plan for Success."
   <http://www.pgcps.pg.k12.md.us/~elc/gameplan.htm>.

"Creating Positive Classrooms and Managing Behavior."
   <http://www.teachernet.gov.uk/professionaldevelopment/nqt/behaviourmanagement>.

"Berkeley Compendium for Teaching with Excellence."
   <http://teaching.berkeley.edu/compendium/sectionsmenu.html>.

Bibliography

Adams, D., and S. Bosch. 1987. "The Myth that War is Intrinsic to Human Nature Discourages Action for Peace by Young People." In *Essays on Violence.* J. Martin Ramirez, Robert A. Hinde, and Jo Groebel, eds. Seville: University of Seville. 123–37. Available online: <http://www.culture-of-peace.info/myth/title-page.html>.

Adams, D., et al. 1989. *The Seville Statement on Violence.* Adopted by UNESCO at the 25th Session of the General Conference, 16 November 1989. Available online: <http://www.culture-of-peace.info/ssov/title-page.html>.

Adorno, T., et al. 1950. *The Authoritarian Personality.* New York: Harper.

Allport, G.W. 1968. *The Person in Psychology: Selected Essays.* Boston: Beacon Press.

Beswick, R. 1990. "Racism in America's Schools." ERIC Digest Series EA49 (ED 320196). Eugene, Oregon: ERIC Clearinghouse on Educational Management. Available online: <http://www.ed.gov/databases/ERIC_Digests?ed320196.html>.

Bindorffer, G. 1997. "Double Identity: Being German and Hungarian at the Same Time." *New Community: The Journal of the European Research Centre on Migration and Ethnic Relations* 23:3 (July): 399–412. Available online: <http://www.ercomer.org/nc/nc23-3.html>.

Bjola, C. 1999. "Deconstructing the Nation State: The Case of the European Integration Process." Central European University Department of International Relations and European Studies Ph.D. candidate working paper. Available online: <http://www.gesw.de/ethnicity/bjola.html>.

Bjorkqvist, K., and D.P. Fry. 1997. "Conclusions: Alternatives to Violence." In D.P. Fry and K. Bjorkqvist, eds. *Cultural Variation in Conflict Resolution: Alternatives to Violence.* Hillsdale, NJ: Lawrence Erlbaum Associates. 243–54.

Bloom, B.S., ed. 1956. *Taxonomy of Educational Objectives: The Classification of Educational Goals.* Handbook 1. *Cognitive Domain.* New York: Longman.

Bortoft, H. 1996. *The Wholeness of Nature: Goethe's Way toward a Science of Conscious Participation in Nature.* Herndon, VA: Lindisfarne Press.

Brewer, J. 2003. *Post-Violence as a Sociological Issue.* School of Sociology and Social Policy. Belfast: Queen's University. Available online: <http://regnet.anu.edu.au/program/pastevents/link_documents/papers/2003/Postviolenceasasociologicalissueversion2JohnBrewer.pdf>.

Bringa, T. 1993. "Nationality Categories, National Identification and Identity Formation in Multinational Bosnia." *The Anthropology of East Europe Review (Special Issue: War Among the Yugoslavs)* 11(1 & 2), Spring and Fall: 80–89.

Brown, J.L. 2004. *Making the Most of Understanding by Design.* Alexandria, VA: Association for Supervision and Curriculum Development.

Burke, K., R. Fogarty, and S. Belgrad. 1994. *The Mindful School: The Portfolio Connection.* Palatine, IL: IRI/Skylight Publishing.

Burns, J.M. 1982. *Leadership.* New York: Harper and Row.

Burton, J. 1997. *Violence Explained: The Sources of Conflict, Violence and Crime and Their Prevention.* Manchester: Manchester University Press.

Chae, M.A. 2002. "Gender and Ethnicity in Identity Formation." *New Jersey Journal of Professional Counseling* 56 (Winter 2001/2002): 24–30.

Clarke, S. 2001. "Talking Peace, Thinking Conflict: The Challenge of Worldview in Peace Education." Landegg International University. Unpublished.

Consultation: A Compilation. 1990. Rev. ed. London: Bahá'í Publishing Trust.

Crombie, A.C. 1995. *The History of Science from Augustine to Galileo.* New York: Dover.

Danesh, H.B. Forthcoming. "Education for Peace: The Pedagogy of Civilization." Chapter in *Sustained Peace Education for Social Cohesion in International Conflict and Post-Conflict Societies.* Zvi Beckerman and Claire McGlynn, eds. Scheduled for publication in 2007.

———. Forthcoming. "A Culture of Healing." Chapter in a collection of papers. Jerusalem: Hebrew University of Jerusalem.

———. 2006a. "Towards an Integrative Theory of Peace Education." *Journal of Peace Education* 3(1): 55–78.

———. 2006b. *Fever in the World of the Mind: Unique Dimensions of Human Conflict and Violence.* Volume 3. *Integrative Education for Peace Curriculum* Series. Vancouver: Education for Peace Publications.

———. 2004. *Peace Moves.* Sarajevo: EFP-International Publications.

———. 2002. "Breaking the Cycle of Violence: Education for Peace." *African Civil Society Organization and Development: Re-Evaluation for the 21st Century.* United Nations, New York, September 2002.

———. 1997. *The Psychology of Spirituality: From Divided Self to Integrated Self.* 2d ed. Hong Kong: Juxta Publishing.

———. 1995. *The Violence-Free Family: Building Block of a Peaceful Civilization.* Ottawa: Bahá'í Studies Publications.

———. 1986. *Unity: The Creative Foundation of Peace.* Toronto: Fitzhenry-Whiteside. Ottawa: Bahá'í Studies Publications.

———. 1980. "The Angry Group for Couples: A Model for Short-Term Group Psychotherapy." *The Psychiatric Journal of the University of Ottawa* 5:2: 118–24.

———. 1979. "The Violence-Free Family: A Gift for Our Children." *Bahá'í Studies.* Volume 6.

———. 1978b. "The Authoritarian Family and Its Adolescents." *Canadian Psychiatric Association Journal* 23(7): 479–85.

———. 1978a. "In Search of a Violence-Free Community." *Mental Health and Society* 5: 63–71.

———. 1977. "Anger and Fear." *American Journal of Psychiatry* 134:10 (October): 1109–12.

Danesh, H.B., and R. Danesh. 2005. "Comprehensive Leadership Development Program: A Training Manual." Unpublished.

———. 2004. "Conflict-Free Conflict Resolution Process and Methodology." *Peace and Conflict Studies* 11.2: 55–84.

———. 2002a. "A Consultative Conflict Resolution Model: Beyond Alternative Dispute Resolution." *International Journal of Peace Studies* 7.2:17–33.

———. 2002b. "Has Conflict Resolution Grown Up? Toward a New Model of Decision Making and Conflict Resolution." *International Journal of Peace Studies* 7(1): 59–76.

Davidson, R.J., K.M. Putnam, and C.L. Larson. 2000. "Dysfunction in the Neural Circuitry of Emotion Regulation—A Possible Prelude to Violence." *Science* 289 (2000): 591.

Dewey, L. 2004. *War and Redemption: Treatment and Recovery in Combat-related Posttraumatic Stress Disorder.* Burlington, VT: Ashgate.

Dollard, J., et al. 1980. *Frustration and Aggression.* Westport, CT: Greenwood Press.

Donaldson, M. 1979. *Children's Minds.* London: Fontana/Collins.

Dusek, I.B., and W.J. Meyer. 1980. "A Dialectic Analysis of Learning Theory: Contributions to Understanding Human Development." *Human Development* 23(1980): 382–88.

Erikson, E. H. 1968. *Identity: Youth and Crisis.* New York: Norton.

———. 1963. *Childhood and Society.* 2d ed. New York: W.W. Norton.

———. 1959. *Identity and the Life Cycle.* New York: International Universities Press.

Featherman, D.L., R.M. Lerner, and M. Perlmutter, eds. 1992. *Life-Span Development and Behavior.* Vol. 11. Hillsdale, NJ: Lawrence Erlbaum Associates.

Fukuyama, F. 1992. "By Way of an Introduction." *The End of History and the Last Man.* London: Penguin Publishers.

Fromm, E. 1994. *Escape from Freedom.* Originally published 1941. New York: Owl Books.

Gavious, A., and S. Mizrahi. 1999. "Two-Level Collective Action and Group Identity." *Journal of Theoretical Politics* Vol. 11. No. 4. 497–517. Available online: <http://www.sagepub.co.uk/journals/details/issue/sample/a009905.pdf>.

General Assembly. 2000. *United Nations Millennium Declaration.* A/RES/55/2. Available online: <http://www.un.org/millennium/declaration/ares552e.pdf>.

Gregg, R.B. 1984. *The Power of Nonviolence.* 3rd ed. New York: Greenleaf Books.

Gross-Davis, B., L. Wood, and R. Wilson. 1983. *The Berkeley Compendium for Teaching with Excellence.* Berkeley: University of California. Available online: <http://teaching.berkeley.edu/compendium/sectionsmenu.html>.

Guerra, N.G., L. Eron, L.R. Huesmann, P. Tolan, and R. Van Acker. 1997. "A Cognitive-Ecological Approach to the Prevention and Mitigation of Violence and Aggression in Inner-City Youth." In D. P. Fry and K. Bjorkqvist, eds. *Cultural Variation in Conflict Resolution: Alternatives to Violence.* Hillsdale, NJ: Lawrence Erlbaum Associates. 199–213.

Hägglund, S. 1999. "Peer Relationships and Children's Understanding of Peace and War: A Sociocultural Perspective." In Amiram Raviv, Louis Oppenheimer, and Daniel Bar-Tal, eds. *How Children Understand War and Peace.* San Francisco: Jossey-Bass. 190–207.

Hamber, B., and R. Wilson. 1999. "Symbolic Closure through Memory, Reparation and Revenge in Post-conflict Societies." Paper presented at the Traumatic Stress in South Africa Conference, Parktonian Hotel, Johannesburg, South Africa, 27–29 January 1999.

Hamber, B.E. 1995. "Dealing with the Past and the Psychology of Reconciliation: A Psychological Perspective of the Truth and Reconciliation Commission." The Centre for the Study of Violence and Reconciliation: Johannesburg, South Africa. Occasional Paper.

———. 2003. "Healing." In *Reconciliation after Violent Conflict: A Handbook.* Stockholm, Sweden: International Institute for Democracy and Electoral Assistance. Available online: <http://www.brandonhamber.com/publications/Chapter%20Healing.pdf>.

Hobbes, T. 1651. *Leviathan, or the Matter, Forme, and Power of a Common-Wealth, Ecclesiasticall and Civill.* London: Andrew Crooke.

Hogg, M., D. Terry, and K. White. 1995. "A Tale of Two Theories: A Critical Comparison of Identity Theory with Social Identity Theory." *Social Psychology Quarterly 58*: 255–69.

Horowitz, S., and A. Schnabel. 2004. *Human Rights and Societies in Transition: Causes, Consequences and Responses*. Tokyo: United Nations University Press.

Huyse, L. 2003. Chapter 2: The Process of Reconciliation. In *Reconciliation after Violent Conflict: A Handbook*. Ed. David Bloomfield, Teresa Barnes, and Luc Huyse. Stockholm: International Institute for Democracy and Electoral Assistance.

Kotter, John P. 1996. *Leading Change*. Boston: Harvard Business School Press.

Kouzes, J.M., and B.Z. Posner. 2003. *Leadership Challenge*. 3rd ed. San Francisco: Jossey-Bass.

Laszlo, E. 1996. *The Systems View of the World: A Holistic Vision for Our Time (Advances in Systems Theory, Complexity and the Human Sciences)*. Cresskill, NJ: Hampton Press.

Lewis, B. 1988. *The Political Language of Islam*. Chicago: University of Chicago Press.

Loewald, H. 1960. "On the Therapeutic Action of Psychoanalysis." *International Journal of Psychoanalysis* 1(Jan.–Feb.): 16–33.

Lorenz, Konrad. (1966). *On Aggression*. Originally published 1963. Reprint, London: Routledge.

Lustick, I.S. 2000. "Agent-Based Modeling of Collective Identity: Testing Constructivist Theory." *Journal of Artificial Societies and Social Simulations* 3 (January). Available online: <http://www.soc.surrey.ac.uk/JASSS/3/1/1.html>.

Lyles, M. A., A. Yancy, C. Grace, and J.H. Carter. 1985. "Racial Identity and Self-esteem: Problems Peculiar to Biracial Children." *Journal of the American Academy of Psychiatry* 24: 150–53.

Mahoney, Andrew S. 2001. "The Gifted Identity Formation Model: In Search of the Gifted Identity, From Abstract Concept to Workable Counseling Constructs." *Roeper Review* 20(3): 222–26. <http://www.counselingthegifted.com/articles/insearchofID.html>.

May, R. 1972. *Power and Innocence: A Search for the Source of Violence*. New York: Delta Books.

Miller, P.H. 2002. *Theories of Developmental Psychology*. 4th ed. New York: Worth.

Miller, R. 2001. "Long-run Prospects: Policy Changes for a World in Transition." Organization for Economic Cooperation and Development. Available online: <http://www.oecd.org/document/30/0,2340,en_2649_34209_1903198_119696_1_1_1,00.html>.

Mindell, Arnold. 1993. *The Leader as Martial Artist*. New York: HarperCollins.

Moscovici, S. 1993. Introductory address given at the First International Conference on Social Representations. Ravello, Italy, 1992. *Papers on Social Representations: Threads of Discussion* 2: 160–70.

Murray, M. *Moral Development and Moral Education: An Overview* (summarizing the main theories of Piaget, Kohlberg, Turiel, and Gilligan). Department of Studies in Moral Development and Education: University of Illinois. Available online: <http://tigger.uic.edu/~lnucci/MoralEd/overviewtext.html>.

Norberg-Hodge, Helena. (1992). *Ancient Futures: Learning from Ladakh*. Oxford: Oxford University Press.

O'Murchu, D. 2000. *Our World in Transition: Making Sense of a Changing World*. New York: Crossroad Publishing.

Oka, J.M. 1994. "Self-concept and Parental Values: Influences on the Ethnic Identity Development of Biracial Children." Thesis. San Jose State University.

Paulson, F.L., P.R. Paulson, and C.A. Meyer. 1991. "What Makes a Portfolio a Portfolio?" *Educational Leadership* (February 1991): 60–63.

Rothman, J. 1997. *Resolving Identity-Based Conflict in Nations, Organizations, and Communities.* San Francisco: Jossey-Bass.

Shoghi Effendi. 1984. *The Advent of Divine Justice.* Originally published 1939. 4th ed. Wilmette, Illinois: Bahá'í Publishing Trust.

Sørensen, A.B., F.E. Weinert, and L.R. Sherrod, eds. 1986. *Human Development and the Life Course: Multidisciplinary Perspectives.* Hillsdale, NJ: Lawrence Erlbaum Associates.

Steinberg, L.D. 1999. *Adolescence.* 5th ed. New York: McGraw-Hill.

Stevenson, L. 1974. *Seven Theories of Human Nature.* Oxford: Oxford University Press.

Suutarinen, Sakari. 1998. "Does the Content of Teaching National Identity Meet the Requirements of the Present Time in Finnish Schools?" University of Jyväskylä, Finland. Working paper. <http://www.jyu.fi/ktl/SaSuPape.htm>.

Thomae, H., and U. Lehr. 1986. "Stages, Crises, Conflicts and Life Span Development." *Human Development and the Life Course: Multidisciplinary Perspectives.* Ed. Social Science Research Council (U.S.) et al. Hillsdale, NJ: Lawrence Erlbaum Associates. 429–43.

Thornton, T., et al., eds. 1972. *Best Practices of Youth Violence Prevention: A Sourcebook for Community Action.* Georgia: Division of Violence Prevention, National Center for Injury Prevention and Control. Available online: <http://www.cdc.gov/ncipc/dvp/bestpractices.htm>.

Tillich, P. 1936. "The Two Roots of Political Thinking." In *The Interpretation of History.* Trans. Rasetzki and Talmey. New York: Charles Scribner's Sons.

Van Slyck, M.R., M. Stern, and S. Elbedour. 1999. "Adolescents' Beliefs about their Conflict Behaviour." In Amiram Raviv, Louis Oppenheimer, and Daniel Bar-Tal, eds. *How Children Understand War and Peace.* San Francisco: Jossey-Bass. 208–30.

Vorster, P.J., and C.M. Sutcliffe. 2001. "The Role of Teachers in the Identity Formation of Adolescents Restrained in their Becoming." *South African Journal of Education* 20(1): third article (online journal). <http://www.easa.ac.za/execsum/201.html#3> .

Waever, O. 1995. "Identity, Integration and Security." *Journal of International Affairs* 48(2): 389–432.

Wiggins, G., and J. McTighe. 1998. *Understanding By Design.* Alexandria, VA: Association for Supervision and Curriculum Development.

Wilson, J.Q. 1998. *Crime and Human Nature.* New York: Free Press.

World Health Organization. *Constitution of the World Health Organization.* Geneva: World Health Organization, 1946. <http://www.searo.who.int/aboutsearo/const.htm>.

Youniss, J., J.A. Mclehha, and M. Yates. 1999. "Religion, Community Service, and Identity in American Youth." *Journal of Adolescence* 22(2): 243–53.

Zanna, M.P., and J.K. Rempel. 1988. "Attitudes: A New Look at an Old Concept." In D. Bar-Tal and A.W. Kruglanski, eds. *The Social Psychology of Knowledge.* Cambridge: Cambridge University Press. 315–34.

About the Authors

Dr. H. B. Danesh is the founder and president of the International Education for Peace Institute and the former president of Landegg International University, Switzerland (1998–2003). He is a retired professor of conflict resolution and peace education at Landegg International University (1998–2003) and tenured associate professor of psychiatry at the University of Ottawa, Canada (1973–1983). Dr. Danesh has conducted research and published on issues of peace education, leadership studies, the causes and prevention of violence, Conflict-Free Conflict Resolution (CFCR), and the psychology of spirituality. He is the creator of the Education for Peace Program and co-creator of Leadership for Peace/Peaceful Governance with Dr. Roshan Danesh. In 2005 they worked with the UNDP/SACI project and developed the Malawi Comprehensive Executive Leadership Training Program as a part of this collaboration. Dr. Danesh resides in Vancouver, Canada, where he directs the international work of the EFP programs.

Sara Clarke-Habibi is a founding member and associate director of the International Education for Peace Institute, Switzerland. Ms. Clarke-Habibi was national coordinator of the Education for Peace pilot project in Bosnia-Herzegovina from June 2000 to January 2002 and continues to serve as an advisor to its program and policy activities. She is co-author of the *Education for Peace Curriculum Manual* and the 10-module multimedia *EFP-World e-Learning CD-ROM*. She completed her Master of Arts in Consultation and Conflict Resolution at Landegg International University, Switzerland, and her Bachelor of Arts in Cultural Anthropology and Ethics, Society and the Law at the University of Toronto. Ms. Clarke-Habibi currently resides in Switzerland, where she contributes to the on-going international development of Education for Peace programs and educational resources.

About the Contributors

Dr. Roshan P. Danesh is a lawyer, consultant, and scholar, who works, teaches, and publishes in the areas of conflict resolution, constitutional law, law and religion, and public law. Dr. Danesh was previously the chair of Department of Conflict Resolution at Landegg International University, Switzerland. He is the co-author of the Conflict-Free Conflict Resolution (CFCR) Program, Leadership for Peace Program, and creator of the Youth Peacebuilders Network (YPN) of the Education for Peace Program. He completed his doctoral studies at Harvard Law School, his law degree at the University of Victoria, and his undergraduate studies at McGill University. Dr. Danesh currently lives in Vancouver where he works with First Nations on nation-building, constitutional, legal, and dispute resolution issues. He is a consultant in Leadership for Peace/Peaceful Governance with international organizations, including the UNDP/SACI program (2005).

Dr. Elaine K. McCreary is an adult educator who currently works for the British Columbia Ministry of Advanced Education as government liaison for community colleges and province-wide curriculum sectors. She was a tenured associate professor at the University of Guelph, Canada (1984–1991) where she trained mid-career professionals from the disciplines of agriculture and health sciences in methods of conducting social research and delivering public-education programs in the field of international development. Later, Dr. McCreary coordinated a global research department and provided in-service professional development training in the Middle East, as well as directed a service-learning program for an international high-school in Canada. Her research and publications cover a range of subjects, including educational technology, adult learning theory, and processes of social development. She earned her BA in Andragogy (the study of delivering instructional material to adults) at Concordia University, Montreal; her MA in adult education; and her EdD at the University of British Columbia, on the subject of the Information Society.

Barbara Rager was born in Ottawa, Canada, and has spent her adult lifetime teaching. In China, Switzerland, the Czech Republic, Bosnia-Herzegovina, and Canada, she has worked with students from a diversity of cultural and ethnic origins. She has also trained teachers to bring the principles of peace into the lives of their students. Mrs. Rager earned her BA in English literature at Mt. Allison University, Canada and her BEd at the University of Toronto, Canada. A peace school that she and her husband launched in Switzerland in 1993 has expanded to the United States and the Congo. She enjoys the role of educational consultant and now, in retirement from the classroom, plans to devote more time to writing projects.

John Rager was born in Brooklyn, New York, and has been a teacher and administrator in Ottawa, Canada, for 30 years. He has taught in the Faculty of Education at the University of Ottawa and served as an educational consultant to the Psychology Department of the Children's Hospital of Eastern Ontario. Mr. Rager earned his BA in psychology at the University of Ottawa, his BEd at Queen's University, and his MEd with a major in counseling at the University of Ottawa, Canada. He and his wife, Barbara Rager, co-direct the Transformation for Peace Program in Europe and North America. He has written curriculum documents for the Ottawa public school system, as well as for the Education for Peace Project in Bosnia-Herzegovina. He is recently retired and plans to do more writing in the fields of education and childrearing.

The Education for Peace Integrative Curriculum Series

The *Education for Peace Integrative Curriculum Series* offers a unique model of peace education based on the view that peace and education are inseparable aspects of civilization. No civilization is truly progressive without education, and no education system is truly civilizing unless it is based on the universal principles of peace. The *Education for Peace Integrative Curriculum Series* (EFP Curriculum Series) is guided by three main concepts:

1. Unity, not conflict, is the main force in human relationships;
2. Worldview—our view of reality, human nature, the purpose of life and human relationships—is the main framework within which all human individual and group behavior takes shape; and
3. Peace is the main outcome of a unity-based worldview.

The EFP Curriculum Series is interdisciplinary in its approach and draws from various fields of study as they apply to the issue of peace at intrapersonal, interpersonal, intergroup, and international levels. The curriculum is based on current, cutting-edge research and literature on peace education, as well as insights drawn from the fields of psychology, political science, sociology, law, religious studies, history, conflict resolution, the arts, and other peace-related fields. Through ongoing research, seminars, workshops, field work, and consultation and collaboration with colleagues in various disciplines, the conceptual framework and methodological approach of the EFP Program have evolved to meet the needs and concerns of diverse sectors of society, in various cultural and regional contexts.

The EFP Curriculum Series is designed in a flexible format, allowing it to evolve and be modified in light of new research findings and insights gained from implementing it and other peace education programs in schools around the world. The Series currently comprises nine (9) volumes which have been prepared as interrelated but independent publications and are being made available both in print and electronic/multimedia formats. Together these works comprise one of the most comprehensive and integrative peace education curricula available anywhere.

For more information or to order volumes from the EFP Curriculum Series, please contact:

International Education for Peace Institute
Publications Office
101-1001 W. Broadway, Suite 900
Vancouver, B.C.
Canada V6H 4E4
Tel: +1-604-733-9424
Email: academic@efpinternational.org

The Education for Peace Integrative Curriculum Series

Volumes	Topics	Authors
Volume 1	**Education for Peace Curriculum Manual** (Electronic, print, and multimedia formats for both teachers, students in the higher grades, and others)	H. B. Danesh Sara Clarke-Habibi
Volume 2	**Peace Moves** (Electronic, print and multimedia formats primarily for students, to be studied in the earlier grades with the help of teachers and parents/guardians)	H. B. Danesh
Volume 3	**Fever in the World of the Mind: Unique Dimensions of Human Conflict and Violence** (Electronic and print formats. For teachers, parents/guardians, students in the higher grades, and others)	H. B. Danesh
Volume 4	**The Unity-Based Family** (Electronic and print formats. For teachers, parents/guardians, students in the higher grades, and others)	H. B. Danesh
Volume 5	**Conflict-Free Conflict Resolution** (Electronic and print formats. For teachers, students in the higher grades, conflict-resolution practitioners, and others.)	Roshan Danesh H. B. Danesh
Volume 6	**Leadership for Peace** (Electronic and print formats. For teachers, students in the higher grades, and leaders at all levels)	Roshan Danesh H. B. Danesh
Volume 7	**Youth Peacebuilders Network Manual** (Electronic and print formats. For teachers, students, and others.)	Roshan Danesh
Volume 8	**Education for Peace Reader Collection of Articles on EFP** (Electronic format only. For teachers, students in the higher grades, and others)	Multiple Authors
Volume 9	**The Mysterious Case of the IWs** (A storybook on how to deal with death and loss for children and their parents/guardians, teachers, and others. Electronic and print formats.)	H. B. Danesh

Lightning Source UK Ltd.
Milton Keynes UK
UKOW030652111011

180109UK00001B/26/A

9 780978 284510